Swan and Shadow
Yeats's Dialogue with History

Critical Studies in Irish Literature
Edward Engelberg, *General Editor*

Swan
and Shadow
Yeats's Dialogue with History

THOMAS R. WHITAKER

Critical Studies in Irish Literature
VOLUME 1

The Catholic University of America Press
Washington, D.C.

The paper used in this publication meets the minimum re-
quirements of American National Standards for Information
Science—Permanence of Paper for Printed Library Materials,
ANSI Z39.48-1984.

∞

Library of Congress Cataloging-in-Publication Data
Whitaker, Thomas R.
  Swan and shadow : Yeats's dialogue with history / by Thomas R.
Whitaker.
      p.   cm.—(Critical studies in Irish literature : v. 1)
  Reprint with new pref. Previously published: Chapel Hill :
University of North Carolina Press, 1964.
  Based on the author's thesis (Ph. D.)—Yale University.
    1. Yeats, W. B. (William Butler), 1865-1939—Knowledge—History.
2. Ireland in literature.   3. History in literature.   I. Title.
II. Series.
PR5908.H5W4   1989
821'.8—dc20   89-9861
ISBN 0-8132-0680-4 (alk. paper)

For my Father and Mother

CONTENTS

FOREWORD

Few countries of Ireland's size, beset with "troubles" for centuries, can claim as many major literary voices as Ireland, but this has been especially true of the Classic Modern Period, approximately the time between the waning decades of the nineteenth century and the greater part of the twentieth. Oscar Wilde, George Moore, Bernard Shaw, W. B. Yeats, James Joyce, Æ, Sean O'Casey, and Samuel Beckett—Anglo-Irish literature would be impoverished without them. Critical Studies in Irish Literature undertakes to publish some of the best books on such Irish writers and related literary movements that have, for one reason or another, gone out of print.

Our Editorial Advisory Board consists of experts and bibliographers on major and minor writers and various literary movements in Ireland. The criteria for selection are the excellence of the critical study and its continued usefulness for research and teaching. Older studies, if they meet that test, will be considered in addition to more recent titles.

It is our aim to keep alive the best critical work on Irish literature in the Classic Modern Period, for we believe that the richness, beauty, and importance of that literature need continued sustenance by its best interpreters. We will attempt, in each instance, to bring the republication up to date. Our procedure will, of course, vary. An author who is alive will be given the opportunity to add a new preface, update bibliographical material, and correct factual errors. If the author is no longer alive, a member of the Editorial Advisory Board will assume those responsibilities.

We are pleased to begin this enterprise with the publication of Thomas R. Whitaker's *Swan and Shadow: Yeats's Dialogue with His-*

tory, first published in 1964. In his *Anglo-Irish Literature: A Review of Research* (Modern Language Association, 1976), Richard J. Finneran called Whitaker's book "a major contribution to Yeats studies." That comment has stood the test of time. Whitaker's book remains the most thorough and revealing study of Yeats's dialectic "dialogue" with the past. In a series of chapters, divided into two sections—"History as Vision" and "History as Dramatic Experience"—Whitaker comes to terms with Yeats's "System" as articulated both in that vexing but indispensable volume, *A Vision* (and related prose), and in the poetry and plays themselves. Few books on Yeats succeed in doing true justice to both these aspects of Yeats's *oeuvre* in a single volume. In addition, Whitaker was among the first to recognize the impact on Yeats of such figures as Vico, Blake, Pater, and Nietzsche—names we now take for granted in any discussion of Yeats.

For the occasion of this republication, Whitaker provides a new preface in which he lists and discusses, amply and generously, the volumes succeeding *Swan and Shadow* that have taken up the theme he began. But such additions enrich; they do not in this case come near to replacing. And Yeats scholars, as well as those generally interested in the subject of how a major Modern Poet reified his relationship to History, will welcome this volume's new life. Though Yeats might protest, critics, too, create "Monuments of unageing intellect."

Edward Engelberg

PREFACE

THE FIRST VERSION of this book was written more than thirty-five years ago as a doctoral dissertation at Yale University. Its main arguments were formulated and most of its research was carried out under the gracious supervision of Cleanth Brooks. (So much for the frequent charge in recent years that to Brooks history was anathema!) Over the next decade, as I revised and expanded a manuscript that had failed to interest several editors, I received repeated encouragement from the late Richard Ellmann. Without Brooks and Ellmann there would have been no *Swan and Shadow,* though neither was responsible for its specific strategies and conclusions.

It is gratifying but also rather surprising to find that a book completed at that time, well before most of the editions, commentaries, transcriptions of manuscripts, concordances, and biographical and critical explorations that now constitute "Yeats studies" had come into being, can still provide useful interpretations of that poet's work. And I am delighted that David J. McGonagle, Director of The Catholic University of America Press, has responded affirmatively to Edward Engelberg's kind suggestion that *Swan and Shadow* be reprinted.

If I were to attempt such a book today, it would necessarily take a very different form. There would be, of course, a fair number of additions and corrections in matters of detail. Some arguments would need qualification, others expansion. And the entire study would have to respond to a detailed knowledge of Yeats's life and work that was simply not available in the 1950's. Indeed, the variety and complexity of the recent critical conversation about Yeats might even dissuade me from entertaining some of the rather bold hypotheses that shaped my early explorations. But that would be a pity: youthful enthusiasm and necessary ignorance have their advantages. My arguments sought to accommodate a dialogical understanding of human experience, an openness to unconscious and transcendental sources of thought and action, and a conviction that poetic form can be a very precise medium for the discovery and articulation of our responses to life. I still believe that those assumptions provide the most adequate grounding for the study of poetry—and for the study of what was surely one of the more capacious and subtle poetic minds in recent centuries.

As for additions and corrections in matters of detail, two rather small items may stand here as illustrative. Soon after the publication of *Swan and Shadow,* I discovered that Yeats's quotation in 1902 of the phrase "the house of the Poor, the lonely house, the accursed house of Cromwell," which I had related to "The Curse of Cromwell" but had been unable to trace to its source, rather clearly derives from George Borrow's story of an Irish encounter:

> An old woman, at least eighty, was seated on a stone, cowering over a few sticks burning feebly on what had once been a right noble and cheerful hearth; her side-glance was towards the door as I entered, for she had heard my footsteps. I stood still and her haggard glance rested upon my face. "Is this your house, Mother?" I demanded in the language which I thought she could best understand. "Yes, my own house, my own house; the house of the broken hearted . . . my own house, the beggar's house, the accursed house of Cromwell."

Along with much else, Yeats's memory of that passage in Borrow's *Lavengro* lies behind the elegiac and satirical rhetoric of his late poem. Also soon after publication of *Swan and Shadow,* Thomas McAlindon showed in detail that Yeats's celebration of Byzantium as an ideal historical moment, which I had understood to be a development of a pre-Raphaelite ideal, was in fact much more specifically indebted to William Morris's historical vision than I had suspected. ("The Idea of Byzantium in William Morris and W. B. Yeats," *Modern Philology,* 64 [1967]: 307–319.) Indeed, it is now clear that pre-Raphaelite thought was much more important to Yeats in a variety of ways than I had managed to suggest.

Nevertheless, there can be no question of revising a book that was written by a much earlier version of myself and under conditions very different from those that now obtain. *Swan and Shadow* must stand as the utterance of its own historical moment, and as part of a continuing conversation to which it may in some measure still contribute. Even an updated bibliography of relevant scholarship and criticism must seem inadequate; for what serious publication concerning Yeats has *not* had some bearing on his dialogue with history? Anyone who is unfamiliar with the current extent of Yeats studies might well begin by consulting the "Bibliographical Essay" that Edward Engelberg has added to the reprint of *The Vast Design: Patterns in W. B. Yeats's Aesthetic,* Second Edition, Expanded (Washington, D.C.: The Catholic University of America Press, 1988). Indeed, the first edition of Engelberg's book (Toronto: University of Toronto Press, 1964) would have been very useful to me had it appeared somewhat earlier, for his dialectical understanding of Yeats's imagination is close to my own, his emphasis on painting and sculpture complements my rather narrow focus on the verbal and conceptual, and his placing of Yeats's aesthetic within a broad European context seems to me exactly what must continually be attempted.

Despite the difficulty of updating the scholarly and critical context within which *Swan and Shadow* must be read, I must surely make a few gestures in that direction. Let me pass over the mass of articles on Yeats, many of them valuable indeed, and take note of some other books that have enriched or extended my view of Yeats's imagination and its intellectual backgrounds. There are, of course, such now-essential tools of research as the "Cornell Yeats," a projected multivolume edition of manuscripts, texts, and variants, with several volumes already in print; *Uncollected Prose by W. B. Yeats,* Vol. I edited by John P. Frayne and Vol. II by Frayne and Colton Johnson (London: Macmillan, 1970, 1975); *A Critical Edition of Yeats's "A Vision" (1925),* edited by George Mills Harper and Walter Kelly Hood (London: Macmillan, 1978); *The Collected Letters of W. B. Yeats,* the first volume of which (1865–1895) has now appeared under the editorship of John Kelly and Eric Domville (Oxford: Clarendon Press, 1986); *Letters to W. B. Yeats,* edited by Richard J. Finneran, George Mills Harper, and William M. Murphy (2 vols.; New York: Macmillan, 1978); and such valuable studies of Yeats's processes of composition as Jon Stallworthy's *Between the Lines: Yeats's Poetry in the Making* (Oxford: Clarendon

Press, 1963) and *Vision and Revision in Yeats's Last Poems* (Oxford: Clarendon Press, 1969); Curtis Bradford's *Yeats at Work* (Carbondale: Southern Illinois University Press, 1965); and David R. Clark's *Yeats at Songs and Choruses* (Amherst: University of Massachusetts Press, 1983). These works have provided many factual details that would affect the contour or shading of my arguments.

A great variety of biographical, historical, and critical works would also have to be taken into account. I have continued to learn about the nature of Yeats's poetic achievement from the quite different approaches of Thomas Parkinson in *W. B. Yeats: The Later Poetry* (Berkeley: University of California Press, 1964), Denis Donoghue in *William Butler Yeats* (New York: Viking, 1971), and Harold Bloom in *Yeats* (New York: Oxford University Press, 1970)—critics whose styles I admire even as I do those of Brooks and Ellmann. Though Bloom's judgments of specific poems and of the shape of Yeats's career have not persuaded me that my own were seriously in error, I would want to deal with his arguments. And though his conception of "influence" seems to me too narrowly based on a model of ego-assertion, antagonism, and anxiety, he has demonstrated more complex relations between Yeats's work and that of Blake and Shelley than I had discerned. More congenial to my own dialogical approach, no doubt, are Douglas Archibald's *Yeats* (Syracuse, N.Y.: Syracuse University Press, 1983), which focuses on "encounters" with family and friends, and with political and poetic traditions, and Patrick J. Keane's *Yeats's Interactions with Tradition* (Columbia: University of Missouri Press, 1987), a more densely argued and original book, which treats of such antecedents as Burke, Wordsworth, and Nietzsche, and also engages more broadly the Platonic and Christian traditions. And yet other books have brought various critical strategies interestingly to bear upon selected parts or aspects of Yeats's poetry: Allen Grossman's *Poetic Knowledge in the Early Yeats: A Study of "The Wind Among the Reeds"* (Charlottesville: University Press of Virginia, 1969); Steven Putzel's *Reconstructing Yeats: "The Secret Rose" and "The Wind Among the Reeds"* (Totowa, N.J.: Barnes & Noble, 1986); Bernard Levine's *The Dissolving Image: The Spiritual-Esthetic Development of W. B. Yeats* (Detroit: Wayne State University Press, 1970); Daniel Albright's *The Myth Against Myth: A Study of Yeats's Imagination in Old Age* (London:

Oxford University Press, 1972); and Hazard Adams's *Philosophy of the Literary Symbolic* (Tallahassee: University Presses of Florida, 1983).

Several of these books have complicated my sense of how Yeats was working within the Romantic tradition. So too have George Bornstein's *Yeats and Shelley* (Chicago: University of Chicago Press, 1970) and *Transformations of Romanticism in Yeats, Eliot, and Stevens* (Chicago: University of Chicago Press, 1976). Yet other books have complicated my sense of how Yeats was working within the Anglo-Irish tradition: Donald Torchiana's *W. B. Yeats and Georgian Ireland* (Evanston, Ill.: Northwestern University Press, 1966); Daniel Harris's *Yeats: Coole Park and Ballylee* (Baltimore: Johns Hopkins University Press, 1974); and Colin Meir's *The Ballads and Songs of W. B. Yeats: The Anglo-Irish Heritage in Subject and Style* (London: Macmillan, 1974). And Yeats's relations with a variety of other writers have been more deeply explored by Rupin W. Desai in *Yeats's Shakespeare* (Evanston, Ill.: Northwestern University Press, 1971), Otto Bohlmann in *Yeats and Nietzsche* (Totowa, N.J.: Barnes & Noble, 1982), and Marjorie Reeves and Warwick Gould in *Joachim of Fiore and the Myth of the Eternal Evangel in the Nineteenth Century* (Oxford and New York: Clarendon Press, 1987).

There is a serious risk, of course, in source studies and histories of ideas: they may construct complex patterns of historical relationships within which individual literary works have been reduced to oversimplified paraphrase or collections of fragments taken out of context. As I have indicated in an extended review of *Joachim of Fiore and the Myth of the Eternal Evangel* (forthcoming in the 1989 issue of *Yeats: An Annual of Critical and Textual Studies*), I greatly admire its learned tracing of Yeats's relations not only to Joachim of Fiore but also to Nietzsche, Walter Pater, Oscar Wilde, Lionel Johnson, and several strands of late-nineteenth-century aestheticism and several varieties of apocalyptic expectation. At the same time, that admiration is qualified by some serious reservations about the book's disintegrative and reductive readings of "The Tables of the Law," "Rosa Alchemica," and other portions of Yeats's work. I am much more in agreement with the procedures by which, for example, Daniel Harris and Patrick Keane manage to show how a remarkable complexity of thought and feeling becomes tempered and precariously harmonized within Yeats's individual works. A useful corrective to any approach to Yeats that places major emphasis upon words or concepts can be found in Elizabeth Bergmann Loiseaux's *Yeats and the Visual Arts* (New Brunswick and London: Rutgers University Press, 1986). Pursuing one of the lines of exploration charted by Engelberg in *The Vast Design*—and earlier, of course, by Giorgio Melchiori in *The Whole Mystery of Art: Pattern into Poetry in the Work of W. B. Yeats* (London: Routledge and Kegan Paul, 1960)—Loiseaux relates the poet's theory and practice to both painting and sculpture. Here there is, no doubt, a corresponding risk: Loiseaux can sometimes appear to assume that a poem or play is the virtual equivalent of a work of visual art. But her emphasis on that realm of the imagination where the two media seem interchangeable is certainly justified; and her discussions of "Dove or Swan," "Lapis Lazuli," and "The Statues" are useful supplements to my own.

Another area of exploration that bears upon the arguments of *Swan and Shadow* is the vast and never finally chartable terrain where, for Yeats at least, religion, philosophy, magic, and psychology somehow overlap or converge. George Mills Harper's patient tracing of Yeats's occult allegiances and his dialogues with the realm of "spirits," in *Yeats's Golden Dawn* (London: Macmillan, 1974) and *The Making of Yeats's "A Vision": A Study of the Automatic Script* (2 vols.; Carbondale: Southern Illinois University Press, 1987), would provide firmer ground for some of my speculations about such matters. Kathleen Raine's more passionately committed elucidations of the same terrain in *Yeats the Initiate* (Mountrath, Ireland: Dolmen Press, and London: George Allen & Unwin, 1986) would help to prevent me from lapsing into what Blake called "single vision and Newton's sleep." And my use of some Neo-Platonic and Jungian assumptions would now be considerably strengthened by James Olney's *The Rhizome and the Flower: The Perennial Philosophy, Yeats and Jung* (Berkeley: University of California Press, 1980). In their quite different ways, these books all stand as warnings to those scholars or critics who wish to understand "tradition" merely as a set of relations among literary texts. And I remain convinced that anyone who would understand Yeats's dialogue with history must try to move toward a point of view that in some way encompasses his own amazing capacity for intellectual syncretism and passionate irony.

Yeats's relations to his contemporaries, to which *Swan and Shadow* was able to give only cursory attention, have now been studied in considerable detail. Richard Ellmann again led the way in *Eminent Domain: Yeats Among Wilde, Joyce, Eliot, and Auden* (New York: Oxford University Press, 1967). Philip Marcus has usefully explored a more immediate context in *Yeats and the Beginning of the Irish Renaissance* (Ithaca: Cornell University Press, 1970). Elizabeth Cullingford has carefully gone into the vexed questions of politics in *Yeats, Ireland and Fascism* (New York: New York University Press, 1981). And James Longenbach has provided a detailed account of Yeats's relations with Ezra Pound in *Stone Cottage: Pound, Yeats, and Modernism* (New York: Oxford University Press, 1988). Yeats's artistic renderings of his own life, which I had drawn upon but not brought into satisfactory focus as individual works, have now been examined by Joseph Ronsley in *Yeats's Autobiographies: Life as Symbolic Pattern* (Cambridge, Mass.: Harvard University Press, 1968), Daniel O'Hara in *Tragic Knowledge: Yeats's Autobiography and Hermeneutics* (New York: Columbia University Press, 1981), and David G. Wright in *Yeats's Myth of Self: The Autobiographical Prose* (Totowa, N.J.: Barnes & Noble, 1987). Critical responses to the increasingly difficult problem of placing Yeats relative to "modernity" and "modernism" are surveyed by Edward Engelberg in the Conclusion to the reprint of *The Vast Design*. He argues persuasively against the recent tendency to separate Yeats from the truly modern—a tendency resulting from a recognition of his complex romantic allegiances and a desire to define the "modern" rather narrowly in terms of the avant-garde explorations against which Yeats often set himself. In the next quarter of a century, Engelberg suggests, Yeats "will likely be fully rehabilitated as a genuine Modern." It seems to me that Terence Diggory's *Yeats and American Poetry: The Tradition of the Self* (Princeton: Princeton University Press, 1983) already constitutes one interesting step in that direction.

Another area insufficiently explored in *Swan and Shadow* is Yeats's work in the theater. If I were to develop this project today, I would want to argue more strongly for the importance of Yeats's drama as a modernist revision of romantic impulses and aims. Just as I now find in "Coole Park and Ballylee, 1931" a revision of that stream evoked by Wordsworth in Book XIV of *The Prelude* (traced from "the blind cavern" to the "open day," lost sight of and then greeted "as it rose once more" to reflect "from its placid breast / The works of man and face of human life"), so I now find in the theatrical apocalypse of "Lapis Lazuli" ("Black out; Heaven blazing into the head") a revision of the Alpine apocalypse in Book VI of *The Prelude* ("when the light of sense / Goes out, but with a flash that has revealed / The invisible world"). And so I now suspect that the Old Man in *Purgatory* may be partly a response to Lord Herbert in Wordsworth's *The Borderers,* as I have suggested in "Reading the Unreadable, Acting the Unactable," *Studies in Romanticism,* 27 (1988): 355–367. Certainly Yeats's theater of masks, with its borrowings from the Japanese Nō and its reliance on Irish heroic material, maintains the romantic desire for a theater of the mind, advances importantly upon symbolist practice, and prepares for later developments in the work of Samuel Beckett and others. Yeats's vision of history gains within this medium a participatory complexity and force that many of his text-oriented critics have missed. In working out that aspect of his achievement, I would find useful those studies of his drama that have emphasized its potential for theatrical realization. They would include David R. Clark's *W. B. Yeats and the Theatre of Desolate Reality* (Dublin: Dolmen Press, 1965); John Rees Moore's *Masks of Love and Death: Yeats as Dramatist* (Ithaca: Cornell University Press, 1971); Leonard E. Nathan's *The Tragic Drama of William Butler Yeats: Figures in a Dance* (New York: Columbia University Press, 1974); Reg Skene's *The Cuchulain Plays of W. B. Yeats* (New York: Columbia University Press, 1974); Akhtar Gamber's *Yeats and the Noh* (New York: Weatherhill, 1974); George Mills Harper's *The Mingling of Heaven and Earth: Yeats's Theory of Theatre* (New York: Humanities Press, 1975); *Yeats and the Theatre,* eds. Robert O'Driscoll and Lorna Reynolds (London: Macmillan, 1975); James W. Flannery's *W. B. Yeats and the Idea of a Theatre: The Early Abbey Theatre in Theory and Practice* (New Haven: Yale University Press, 1976); Richard Taylor's *The Drama of W. B. Yeats: Irish Myth and Japanese Nō* (New Haven: Yale University Press, 1976); Barton R. Friedman's *Adventures in the Deeps of the Mind: The Cuchulain Cycle of W. B. Yeats* (Princeton: Princeton University Press, 1977); Karen Dorn's *Players and Painted Stage* (Totowa, N.J.: Barnes & Noble, 1984); and Maeve Good's *W. B. Yeats and the Creation of a*

Tragic Universe (Totowa, N.J.: Barnes & Noble, 1987). The details of Yeats's collaboration with Lady Gregory have also been further illuminated by her recently discovered autobiography, *Seventy Years, 1852–1922,* edited by Colin Smythe (New York: Macmillan, 1974).

Any rethinking today of Yeats's dialogue with history would have to take into account something like this array of studies, amplified further by the many articles that I have not attempted here to sort or summarize. If I were to undertake such a rethinking, I would want to develop yet more fully Yeats's relations to Romanticism and Modernism, to the visual arts and the theater, and explore in greater detail his use of the prosodic resources of poetry as a medium for complex responses to the past. I would also want to recognize more fully the ways in which his poems converse with each other through the architecture of the volume as has been urged by Hugh Kenner in *Gnomon* (New York: Ivan Obolensky, 1958), John Unterecker in *A Reader's Guide to William Butler Yeats* (New York: Noonday, 1959), and David Young in *Troubled Mirror: A Study of Yeats's "The Tower"* (Iowa City: University of Iowa Press, 1987). And finally, I would want to place the book's understanding of Yeatsian dialogue more precisely in its own historical context. Ideally, *Swan and Shadow* should claim less transparency as a glass through which to read Yeats: it should make more explicit its own historical moment, and the resources and limitations inherent in the confluence of previous voices that suggested its peculiar blend of close reading, intellectual biography, history of ideas, and the figurative and dialogical exploration of human destiny. Perhaps this Preface can be understood as a belated step in that direction.

Whatever the limitations of *Swan and Shadow,* I remain confident that its dialogical approach (development on the basis of my reading of Martin Buber and C. G. Jung but closely related to the more recently available work of Hans-Georg Gadamer and Mikhail Bakhtin) affords in principle a continuing opportunity for the enrichment and transformation of both poetic and historical understanding. At a T. S. Eliot Centenary conference, a scholar-critic who has helped us to read that poet in ways unimagined in the 1940's and 1950's suggested that Yeats is now critically "dead," that the "Yeats industry" is elaborating a tomb, and that he will revive only when we can learn how to read his work with fresh eyes and understand it differently. That judgment contains an uncomfortable measure of truth. But just as Yeats was not "dead" for Eliot or Beckett, or for Wallace Stevens, Robert Lowell, or Seamus Heaney as they explored their own thematic and stylistic responses to his formidable chorus of voices, so he need not remain "dead" for any reader who brings to his work a dialogical openness and alertness. "Much has man learnt . . . ," said Hölderlin, "Since we have been a conversation / And have been able to hear from one another." Yeats would have understood the definition of humankind embedded in that sentence, and surely each new reader of Yeats's work must come to recognize its profundity.

Thomas R. Whitaker

ACKNOWLEDGMENTS

I SHOULD LIKE to thank generally the many persons who have given me assistance and encouragement during the preparation of this book. I am especially grateful to Cleanth Brooks, who supervised the doctoral dissertation at Yale University from which this study has grown; to Richard Ellmann and John V. Kelleher, who read and criticized early drafts of the manuscript; and to Dorothy Barnes Whitaker, whose help over the years has taught me more about the book's central metaphor than she may readily believe.

Portions of the book have appeared previously, in somewhat different form: material from Chapters II and V in *PMLA*, from Chapter III in *The Sewanee Review*, from Chapter IV in *Modern Philology*, and from Chapter VII in *Edwardians and Late Victorians: English Institute Essays 1959*, edited by Richard Ellmann and published by Columbia University Press. I thank the editors and publishers of this material for their kind permission to use it here. Material from *The Collected Poems of W. B. Yeats*, copyright 1903, 1906, 1907, 1912, 1916, 1924, 1928, 1931, 1934, 1935, 1940, 1944, 1945, 1946, 1950, 1956 by The Macmillan Company, and copyright 1940 by Georgie Yeats, is used with the permission of the publisher. The Macmillan Company has also authorized my quotations from the other works of Yeats to which it holds copyright.

Oberlin, Ohio   T. R. W.
December 1963

I remember as a boy showing the poet some drawings I had made and wondering why he was interested most of all in a drawing of a man on a hill-top, a man amazed at his own shadow cast gigantically on a mountain mist . . .

—George Russell

The swan on still St. Mary's Lake
Float double, swan and shadow!
—Wordsworth, "Yarrow Unvisited"

I begin to see things double—doubled in history, world history, personal history. At this moment all the specialists are about to run together in our new Alexandria, thought is about to be unified as its own free act, and the shadow in Germany and elsewhere is an attempted unity by force. In my own life I never felt so acutely the presence of a spiritual virtue and that is accompanied by intensified desire. Perhaps there is a theme for poetry in this "double swan and shadow." You must feel plunged as I do into the madness of vision, into a sense of the relation between separated things that you cannot explain, and that deeply disturbs emotion. Perhaps it makes every poet's life poignant, certainly every poet who has "swallowed the formulas."

—Yeats to Dorothy Wellesley, 1937

Fundamentum artis est sol et eius umbra.
—Hermes Trismegistus, *Rosarium Philosophorum*

As thou hast begun so proceed, and this Dragon will turn to a Swan, but more white than the hovering virgin snow when it is not yet sullied with the earth. Henceforth I will allow thee to fortify thy fire till the Phoenix appears. It is a red bird of a most deep colour, with a shining, fiery hue. Feed this bird with the fire of his father and the ether of his mother . . . and he will move in his nest and rise like a star of the firmament. Do this and thou hast placed Nature *in horizonte aeternitatis.*

—Thomas Vaughan, *Lumen de Lumine*

To write poetry means to hold
A judgment day over oneself.
—Ibsen, *"Et Vers"*

Swan and Shadow
Yeats's Dialogue with History

I · INTRODUCTION: THE DIALOGUE

Every argument carries us backwards to some relig·
ious conception, and in the end the creative energy of
men depends upon their believing that they have,
within themselves, something immortal and imperish·
able, and that all else is but as an image in a looking·
glass.

—"First Principles"[1]

I call to the mysterious one who yet
Shall walk the wet sands by the edge of the stream
And look most like me, being indeed my double,
And prove of all imaginable things
The most unlike, being my anti-self,
And standing by these characters, disclose
All that I seek . . .

—"Ego Dominus Tuus"

---

i.

A GREAT POET who claims that he has lived and worked "in history,
the history of the mind,"[2] requires of us a kind of study which
Yeats has thus far received only casually or tangentially. We know, of
course, that T. S. Eliot has declared him one of those few poets "whose
history is the history of their own time, who are part of the consciousness of an age which cannot be understood without them."[3] We
know that his poems, plays, essays, and autobiographies form a rich

if fragmentary drama of contemporary life; that his prophecies of
coming violence, though seemingly occult in their basis, have a disturbing objectivity; and that both drama and prophecies gain breadth
by means of a symbolism that recalls his admonition to Sean O'Casey:
"the whole history of the world must be reduced to wall paper in
front of which the characters must pose and speak."[4] But we have not
yet given sustained attention to the various ways in which history was
central to Yeats's poetic development and to the meaning of his work.

In brief, I shall suggest that history was for Yeats a mysterious
interlocutor, sometimes a bright reflection of the poet's self, sometimes a shadowy force opposed to that self. He conversed with it as
with his double and anti-self. He could endow it with his own
imaginative life, seeing it "but as an image in a looking-glass"; but
he could also expect it to disclose all that he sought, all that seemed
contrary to his own conscious state, all that lurked in his own depths,
unmeasured and undeclared. This visionary and paradoxical dialogue
—both strikingly individual and highly traditional—was a central fact
underlying Yeats's complex and sustained growth. It led him beyond
a facile subjectivism toward an awareness of his own more comprehensive nature and toward a passionate self-judgment that was also
a judgment of the dominant qualities of his time. And it enabled
him to view history as a "necessity" which, when accepted and understood, might "take fire" in the head and become "freedom or virtue."[5]

A subjective dialogue of this kind is quite different, of course,
from what Martin Buber has called the pure dialogue of I and Thou,
in the "simplicity of fulness."[6] Indeed, at one of its two extreme
moments it seems a manifold monologue of mirrors—for Yeats shared
that narcissistic reverie of our modern imagination which is explicit
in Gide's *Le Traité du Narcisse* and Valéry's *Cantate du Narcisse*
and which enters such visions of history as Tate's "Ode to the Con-
federate Dead," Eliot's *The Waste Land,* Pound's *Cantos,* and Joyce's
Ulysses and *Finnegans Wake.* It is no accident that one of Yeats's
poetic touchstones was Mallarmé's *Hérodiade,* which he knew in
Symons' translation:

> I live in a monotonous land alone,
> And all about me lives but in my own
> Image, the idolatrous mirror of my pride,

> Mirroring this Hérodiade diamond-eyed,
> I am indeed alone, O charm and curse![7]

And he also knew, of course, Mallarmé's frozen and exiled swan:

> Il s'immobilise au songe froid de mépris
> Que vêt parmi l'exil inutile le Cygne.[8]

His knowledge of such lines was not merely literary: he knew the states of soul which Mallarmé evoked. That is one reason why the almost frozen surface of "The Indian to His Love" is so strangely disturbed:

> A parrot sways upon a tree,
> Raging at his own image in the enamelled sea.

In *Calvary,* during a more exultant moment in that narcissistic reverie, a musician cries, "What can a swan need but a swan?"[9] What can subjective man need but himself? But the play itself provides an ironic answer—an answer which assumes more personal form in "Meditations in Time of Civil War" when the speaker, a kind of exiled swan, meets his anti-types, a "brown lieutenant and his men":

> I count those feathered balls of soot
> The moor-hen guides upon the stream,
> To silence the envy in my thought;
> And turn toward my chamber, caught
> In the cold snows of a dream.

For Yeats too the swan-white dream becomes, of necessity, paralyzingly cold.

At first glance, the manifesto of "First Principles" might seem to celebrate that dream or "curse" as a "charm": does it not proclaim an exhilarating solipsism as the condition of creative power? Also at first glance, the invocation of "Ego Dominus Tuus" might seem to present a diametrically opposed view: does not the speaker hope to gain the same creative power through contact with all that now lies beyond him? Properly understood, however, these two statements are not contradictory but complementary. They do not oppose claustral monologue to pure dialogue; they set forth the two paradoxical moments in Yeats's subjective dialogue. On the one hand, the "some-

thing immortal and imperishable" which is reflected by the external
world is not the ego mirrored in a monotonous land (though the
ego is always capable of introducing such perversion into one's vision),
but the psyche in its wholeness reflected in a various and still mysterious world. Hence the early Yeats could say without irony, "We
perceive the world through countless little reflections of our own
image."[10] And the later Yeats could say, more succinctly, "all knowledge is biography."[11] On the other hand, the invoked anti-self is, even
in its very unlikeness to the conscious self or ego, a reflection of a
hidden or at least potential self. One's double or shadow, though it
is not merely a projection, constellates in projected form all that remains in darkness within the self, all that is denied or repressed by
the ego. The interrogation of that shadow may therefore lead the
poet toward an understanding, simultaneously, of two areas which
seem dangerously "other": one in the world beyond himself, one in
his own hidden nature. If the shadow appears in the guise of current
history, he may partly discover, in a single act of perception, the evils
of his time and his own secret complicity.

As I shall later point out, this ambiguous subjective dialogue has
been described in some psychological detail by C. G. Jung. Yeats
himself clearly knew it not only through his own immediate experience but also as described in cosmic terms by various gnostic systems,
some of which Jung has also investigated. As Yeats put the matter
in his late comment on "swan and shadow," he had "swallowed the
formulas"—and those gnostic and alchemical formulas helped him to
organize and extend his dialogue with history. According to theosophical metaphor, at the beginning of time (which is to say, at every
moment) the Spirit of God moves over the waters, creating by reflection a world. But that creation is also a fall. The imperfect world
is as much shadow as reflection; it is, in fact, the dark yet glittering
inversion of God—the Dragon, the Serpent himself.[12] Man, who is
made in God's image, is also a source of light; and in moments of
creative intensity he must see all else as but an image in a looking glass.
However, he must also recognize that he does not create all things
to his heart's desire, that history is his dark reflection, his adversary.
In other words, only in the unfallen or completely regenerated world
could a happy solipsism exist, with man deified and his world a self-

contemplation. There Narcissus might find his beautiful reflection unsullied; there the white dream would not be paralyzingly cold. Man would in fact be Brahma, sometimes called Kala-hansa or "Swan in the eternity."[13] Yet in a world fallen into division, that adversary, Dragon, Serpent, or shadow can itself be a gnostic means of redemption. Man darkly discerns in all that is "evil," all that is "other," his antithetical *daimon,* a hidden manifestation of God or of his deeper self. If he makes the heroic effort to open himself to the fullness of experience, he may be led by that anti-self toward an understanding of both microcosm and macrocosm.

What can a swan need but a swan? Its shadow. No mere biological accident makes Yeats's isolated moor hen guide "feathered balls of soot" upon the reflecting stream that symbolizes all temporal matrices. "Some shadow fell." The "swan drifts upon a darkening flood."[14] Recognizing both the inevitability and the teleological necessity of the shadow, Yeats moves from Hérodiade's monologue to a profound subjective dialogue with history, his co-walker and anti-self. In sum, that dialogue is a comprehensive and lifelong attempt to justify and transcend the fallen world, that "dim glass the demons hold."[15] The speaker of "Nineteen Hundred and Nineteen" is satisfied if the "troubled mirror" of the stream of time may show the swan an "image of its state." But that "state," however exalted, is always ambiguous. As the image glitters or glooms, it reflects Yeats's continual movement between man's condition as creator, imitating the primal act of God in a mirroring universe, and his condition as finite sufferer, enduring and yet transcending the serpentine cycles of history.

Such a visionary dialogue, flowering in great meditative poetry, is no abstract dialectic. Yeats sharply criticized those who "continually mistake a philosophical idea for a spiritual experience."[16] He believed that "All that we do with intensity has an origin in the hidden world, and is the symbol, the expression of its powers."[17] He was essentially in agreement with the ancient alchemical view of a *meditatio* as "an inner dialogue with someone unseen ... with God, when He is invoked, or with himself, or with his good angel."[18] Characteristically, Yeats did not commit himself irrevocably either to a reductive psychological interpretation of such dialogue or to a religious affirmation of its ontological basis. Nevertheless, Buber's description of lyric poetry as "the tremendous refusal of the soul to be satisfied with self-commerce" may still apply to Yeats's work—at least if we allow the "soul" to be the "conscious self" and accept the possibility of a more radical immanence than Buber's theology postulates. For Yeats's poetry is, as Buber says of all poetry, "the soul's announcement that even when it is alone with itself on the narrowest ridge it is thinking not of itself but of the Being which is not itself, and that this Being which is not itself is visiting it there, perplexing and blessing it."[19]

From that perplexing and blessing result Yeats's greatest weaknesses, discontinuity and lack of sustained vision, and his greatest strengths, continual growth and a passionate if momentary completeness. The dialogue saved him, by and large, from a sentimental and romantic self-deification; it saved him also from a religious countertemptation—a pessimistic self-abasement before his own shadow. It helped him to balance—and, at moments of artistic triumph, to fuse—the pride of creation and the humility of perception, the transcendental vision of the gnostic and the tragically illuminating experience of the scapegoat. At such moments of triumph might come that poetic transcendence of the fallen world toward which his work always tends: a tragic joy born not of escape from the human condition but of a fullness of self-knowledge and self-judgment. Then from "Plato's ghost"—the *daimon* who participates in all that Plato called a silent conversation of the soul with itself—there might come not the ironic taunt, "Lie down and die," or the repeated counterchallenge, *"What then?"* but the ecstatic cry, "Rejoice!"[20]

ii.

That dialogical process, which helps to explain the dominance of an elliptical counterpoint in Yeats's prose and poetry, will dictate the organization of this study. Just as Yeats believed that there "are always two types of poetry," that of "vision" and that of "self portraiture" or "dramatic expression,"[21] so he viewed history from two different perspectives. The first, that of creative vision, affords a God's-eye view of the panorama of history. Psychologically, it corresponds to the view adopted in "First Principles" (history is the landscape upon which the soul projects its image), and it is the perspective maintained by most system-builders. Kierkegaard, considering it part of the Hegelian heritage, attacked it as an intellectual delusion and a retreat from the ethical demands of life; for the system-builder, like the gnostic, is tempted to ignore his own involvement in the world of change and contingency and to find a self-deceptive haven in his nontemporal vision.[22] The second perspective is, in a sense, the *daimon's* retort to the potential or actual *hubris* in the first. It is the perspective of dramatic experience, of existential immersion in history, where the anti-self may be, as in "Ego Dominus Tuus," more disturbingly and dangerously confronted. A man so immersed may travel back in imagination through past events, but he is always aware that even his own imaginative act has its place in the historical drama. He does not soar loftily above the stream of time; he "walks the wet sands," or indeed time flows through him and around him. He has then a keen sense of history's concreteness, contingency, and dramatic conflict. Because he experiences man's freedom, he will not be tempted to reduce history to a neat deterministic pattern; however, he may find it difficult to perceive any pattern whatsoever.

Yeats, of course, did not hold to this existential perspective, nor did he step out of existence (as Kierkegaard claimed that Hegel had done) into a system. For him the two perspectives were equally real and equally partial. In portions of *A Vision* he stands above time, and history is projected beneath him as an almost completely external object, obeying the laws of Yeatsian geometry. Elsewhere he explores his concrete relation to Sligo, to his ancestors, and to the immediate history of Ireland—seeing himself as an actor in a drama that combines present and past in a living whole. He gained from the first perspective a clarity of vision and an ability to construct a complex historical pattern; he gained from the second a sense of living drama and of rich and vivid historical filiations. Hence he could admire both the systematic histories of a Petrie, an Adams, or a Spengler, and the fictional and biographical narratives of a Balzac or a Standish O'Grady. And hence he could say, in one moment of paradoxical synthesis of the two perspectives:

History seems to me a human drama, keeping the classical unities by a clear division of its epochs, turning one way or the other because this man hates or that man loves . . . Yet the drama has its plot, and this plot ordained character and passions and exists for their sake.[23]

For the same reason, Yeats's historical symbols fall rather easily into two groups, according to the perspective which gives rise to them. Related to the perspective of creative vision is the more distant historical fact, selected from the cultural heritage precisely because of the symbolic value it may be given. "Dove or Swan," in *A Vision,* is a panorama of persons and events selected in that way. Only secondarily does Yeats elaborate such a symbol in dramatic terms. Related to the existential perspective, on the other hand, are dramatic experiences of Yeats himself, of his friends and family, or even of Ireland present and past, which are felt and understood first in their richness and immediacy and only gradually acquire symbolic status. "Coole Park and Ballylee, 1931" is, in the main, a meditative drama taken from the existential perspective and symbolically developed until it contains wider historical meaning. Conversely, "Long-Legged Fly" presents symbols which have been drawn from the perspective of panoramic vision and then dramatically developed.

Although each perspective somewhat qualifies the other at every point in Yeats's thought, only gradually did the two perspectives and the two groups of symbols become part of a single dramatic vision. In early life Yeats saw only rather tenuous and abstract connections between the larger pattern of history and his own personal experience. Many years later came those vivid moments in which both were in full focus, moments that transformed his thought into a poetic whole. In Part One of this study, therefore, I shall trace the development of his panoramic vision and discuss the dialogical process as it bears upon that vision. In Part Two, I shall trace his somewhat separate elaboration of the experienced historical drama, show how he fused that drama with the panoramic vision, and discuss those poems which render most fully his dialogue with history.

We shall find that Yeats's career supports the advice given by Ralph Waldo Emerson: "The student is to read history actively and not passively; to esteem his own life the text, and books the commentary. Thus compelled, the Muse of history will utter oracles, as never to those who do not respect themselves."[24] Not that Yeats was a model of political wisdom! "We have no gift to set a statesman right," he said;[25] and he often gave evidence of blindness, prejudice, arrogance, and hatred. But through him the Muse of history uttered "oracles" in another way, paradoxically consistent with his subjective distortions. By means of those distortions he dramatized what he called a continual "Last Day," a suprahistorical vision and judgment of man's tragic condition. And the distortions themselves resulted not from meaningless personal whim but from motives shared with his contemporaries—motives which he lifted above the threshold of consciousness into the light of full perception. Indeed, we may be able to say of him, as he said of that Jonathan Swift whom he saw in the looking glass of his later years, that he was a "victim" of his phase of history: such was "his tragedy and his genius."[26]

PART ONE

HISTORY AS VISION

II · THE CYCLES

They will not be patient neither understand that they must begin with an Idea of the world in order not to be prevailed over by the world's multitudinousness: or, if they cannot get that, at least with isolated ideas: and all other things shall (perhaps) be added unto them.

—Arnold to Clough[1]

You are face to face with the heterogeneous, and the test of one's harmony is our power to absorb it and make it harmonious.

—Yeats to Russell[2]

---

i.

IN TRACING THE DEVELOPMENT of Yeats's vision of history we should keep firmly in mind the fact that he was no historian but a poet. He was not, in the academic sense, a disciplined thinker. His passion for truth was what Henry Adams knew only too well as the historian's most serious temptation: "for, if he cares for his truths, he is certain to falsify his facts."[3] Yeats was skilled at finding what he wished to find; and he often oversimplified and distorted the thought of others, moulding it to resemble his own. Nevertheless, he had an acute perception of what related to his needs, a genius for crystallizing thought in image or phrase, and a strict if complicated honesty concerning his deepest intuitions. Moreover, if he was sometimes credulous, he was often shrewdly skeptical. And if he sometimes tortured the thought of others out of all recognizable shape, his artistic alchemy often enabled the fragments to be reborn in a new unity, precise and complex.

Yeats knew this, and with the artist's pride and humility he attributed it to the basic correspondence between mind and world. "Of the many things...that are to change the world," he declared in an early prophecy of a new age, "the artist is fitted to understand but two or three, and the less he troubles himself about the complexity that is outside his craft, the more he will find it all within his craft, and the more dexterous will his hand and thought become."[4] Surely he was correct—at least for the artist whose mind has the passionate breadth and balance of Yeats's own. We can then see the point in Emerson's brash question: "Who cares what the fact was, when we have made a constellation of it to hang in heaven an immortal sign?"[5] For the poet may illuminate universal experience by presenting what Blake, as he applied Aristotle to scriptural history, called "probable impossibilities."[6]

Indeed, granting the defensible subjectivism of Yeats's approach to the world, I can find no very sound reasons for condescension toward his thought. He could say to himself with full seriousness, "Everything that has occupied man, for any length of time, is worthy of our study." It is instructive that he was echoing Pater, who taught him far more than aestheticism, and who had drawn that lesson of true humanism from a Renaissance neo-Platonist and Kabbalist, Pico della Mirandola.[7] As Allen Tate said twenty years ago, "It is still true that Yeats had a more inclusive mind than any of his critics has had."[8] We continue to pool our efforts at understanding and judgment.

It is clear, then, that we have to do not with "objective facts" (assuming they exist) so much as with "poetic constellations." It will therefore be useful to glance at Yeats's understanding of historical symbolism before turning to examine the pattern of cycles that he began to discover in history. To what extent did he himself recognize that such a pattern was largely his own image or shadow projected upon the stream of time? And how did he justify that projection?

His most important teacher in such matters was Blake, of whom his mind had been full "from boyhood up."[9] Blake, as Ellis and Yeats

said, wove "historical incidents and names into mystical poetry,...
under the belief that he was following the highest example, and
that 'prophecy' was the right term for literature so conceived." That
"example" was the Bible as interpreted by Swedenborg, who held
that "the historical books while dealing with facts which occurred
treated them as symbols, as though they had been fable or parable."
Yeats probably knew also that Coleridge had likewise explained how
the "Sacred History becomes prophetic, the Sacred Prophecies historical," because they present "the stream of time continuous as life and a
symbol of eternity." In them, Coleridge said, facts and persons have
"a particular and a universal application," for unlike histories based
on "mechanic philosophy" they are "the living educts of the imagination," that power which "gives birth to a system of symbols, harmonious in themselves, and consubstantial with the truths of which they are
the conductors. These are the *wheels* which Ezekiel beheld, when the
hand of the Lord was upon him ... "[10]

But Blake had also described those wheels, or the cycles of history,
as "seen in Milton's Shadow, who is the Covering Cherub." In other
words, the world of time is the dark reflection of the poetic imagination and also—as Yeats theosophically interpreted the doctrine—the
Shadow of God. For the Covering Cherub is "the self-devouring
serpent, Nature—at once the garment of God and his negation."[11] The
coils of that serpent, the cycles of Western history, are in Madame
Blavatsky's terms the "Glory of Satan" and "the shadow of the
Lord."[12] Envisioning that shadow in its fullness, the poet might
realize his own divinity. Yeats's hermetic order title, *Demon Est
Deus Inversus,* as expounded by Madame Blavatsky, carries that
meaning and provides an important clue to Yeats's lifelong search
for the divine in the demonic, for the more comprehensive self in the
depths of the shadowy adversary to the self.[13]

In moments of excitement Yeats could support his own prophetic
visions or his later "wheels" with such transcendental arguments; but
in more skeptical or defensive moods he granted that he might have
seen but his own shadow. He then deprecated the objective fact and
exalted the artist's heavenly constellation. Poetry arises, he said in
1904, from subjective experience, which the poet must objectify by
mastering "a definite language, a definite symbolism of incident and

scene." He quoted Goethe: "We do the people of history the honour of naming after them the creations of our own minds." And he pointed to Shakespeare's Richard II, who "could never have been born before the Renaissance, before the Italian influence, or even one hour before the innumerable streams that flowed in upon Shakespeare's mind.... He is typical not because he ever existed but because he has made us know of something in our own minds we had never known of had he never been imagined." In 1910 he gave further examples— Dante, Keats, Synge—of poets who by imaginative distortions of history have added to our "being," not our "knowledge." Still later he would call his own cycles of history "stylistic arrangements of experience comparable to the cubes in the drawing of Wyndham Lewis and to the ovoids in the sculpture of Brancusi."[14]

Evident in this position is the early influence of Oscar Wilde, whose *Intentions* had seemed to Yeats a "wonderful book." Art, said Wilde, "is not symbolic of any age. It is the ages that are her symbols." Art is a fine lie, "that which is its own evidence" and which is therefore a kind of truth. Hence the value of Shakespeare's historical plays depends upon "their Truth, and Truth is independent of the facts always, inventing or selecting them at pleasure." And hence to "give an accurate description of what has never occurred is not merely the proper occupation of the historian, but the inalienable privilege of any man of parts and culture." Wilde praised artistic histories from Herodotus to Carlyle, paying special tribute to "the great Raleigh," who wrote "a whole history of the world, without knowing anything whatsoever about the past." Writing in "Dove or Swan" his own history of the Western world, Yeats would later say with more subdued irony that he knew "nothing but the arts and of these little."[15]

Behind such paradoxes lurks Wilde's shrewd perception of what many nineteenth-century historians and men of letters had actually been doing. Matthew Arnold had argued that religion had "materialised itself in the fact, in the supposed fact," and that the fact had failed it—but that the future of poetry was "immense" because "for poetry the idea is everything; the rest is a world of illusion, of divine illusion."[16] Caught in the Arnoldian religious predicament, many historians were semipoetic, locating some variant of the myth of fall and redemption within the stream of history. For medievalists like

Carlyle and Ruskin, the Renaissance repeated the fall of man; for neo-Hellenists it was a time of paradisal freshness, proud individualism, and cultural unity. Michelet, for example, called it "the spring from which the human race recruits its strength, the spring of the soul, which when alone feels itself greater than the world."[17] And Pater, viewing history as an organic process and the work of art as symbolic of its age, disseminated such neo-Hellenism in England. For him the Mona Lisa, fruit of centuries of development, embodied the "idea of humanity as wrought upon by, and summing up in itself all modes of life and thought." And in the style and argument of Joachim du Bellay's treatise on the French language, "the Renaissance became conscious."[18]

Immersed in Pater's work, the early Yeats could easily see Titian as the end of the golden age and Velasquez as "the first bored celebrant of boredom."[19] But he could also share both Wilde's ironic detachment from such mythologized history and his more serious defense of its value. "A Truth in art," said Wilde, "is that whose contradictory is also true. And just as it is only in art-criticism, and through it, that we can apprehend the Platonic theory of ideas, so it is only in art-criticism, and through it, that we can realise Hegel's system of contraries. The truths of metaphysics are the truths of masks."[20] Those remarks anticipate much of Yeats's own later system.

What the masks hide or reveal, of course, is a question in Wilde's aesthetic theory and remained always debatable for Yeats himself. In a world where "facts" are unreliable, what is the ultimate source or meaning of the Arnoldian "idea"? Sometimes, moving toward Platonism or theosophy, Yeats held that art "brings us near to the archetypal ideas themselves, and away from nature, which is but their looking-glass." Sometimes he argued that the "most perfect truth is simply the dramatic expression of the most complete man."[21] Or he could announce that "revelation is from the self, but from that age-long memoried self, that shapes the elaborate shell of the mollusc and the child in the womb, that teaches the birds to make their nest." And he could give that "self" a provisional basis in the psychology of Maxwell, Freud, or Jung, or in the neo-Platonism of Henry More.[22] But he was unwilling finally to reduce such revelation to any clear-cut psychological or metaphysical interpretation. He knew that "wisdom first speaks in images";[23] he took his stand with those poets, psychologists, and philosophers who have held that metaphor and not discursive theory grasps the truth of such revelation most adequately: "Our daily thought was certainly but the line of foam at the shallow edge of a vast luminous sea."[24]

For Yeats, therefore, a symbolic vision of history might have somewhat varying meaning. In any case, however, it should embody and so reveal the desires and conflicts of the poet's entire "being," both conscious and unconscious; and it should therefore bring into the light of understanding hitherto unknown areas in the reader's "being." And on occasion Yeats might hope to establish for the poet's symbolic vision an objective historical validity, to claim for his writings the status which Coleridge granted to scriptural history and prophecy. Indeed, Coleridge's theories of symbolism, of organic correspondence, and of the primary imagination as a "repetition in the finite mind of the eternal act of creation in the infinite I AM"[25] are like the transcendental sanctions for such hope which Yeats himself found in occult, neo-Platonic, and romantic thought.

In following Yeats's dialogue with history, we should be put off neither by extravagant claims to special insight nor by contradictory disavowals of anything but "poetic" intent. Amid his vacillation Yeats was feeling his way—now boldly, now cautiously—within a symbolic mode of cognition based upon an intuited affinity between creative mind and creative universe. He was seeking that kind of truth which for Goethe was "a revelation emerging at the point where the inner world of man meets external reality," which for Wordsworth resulted from "an ennobling interchange / Of action from without and from within," and which led Thoreau to find his "point of interest" somewhere *"between"* himself and external objects. "I would so state facts," said Thoreau, "that they shall be significant, shall be myths or mythologic. Facts which the mind perceived, thoughts which the body thought,—with these I deal." Or as Emerson put it: "The world exists for the education of each man.... He should see that he can live all history in his own person.... He must attain and maintain that lofty sight where facts yield their secret sense, and poetry and annals are alike."[26]

As a young poet, Yeats sought that synthesis of world and mind which, as Goethe said, yields "the happiest assurance of the eternal harmony of existence."[27] But his search was colored by the problems of a later century—and by an increasingly tragic understanding of life. Even at the outset he surmised that complete harmony could exist only in an unfallen realm:

> The woods of Arcady are dead,
> And over is their antique joy...

But he could hope that the discords of the temporal world—of "the cracked tune that Chronos sings"—might have their own pattern, a possible clue to that unfallen harmony.[28] During the 1880's and 1890's, long before transforming such material into major poetry, he was discovering in history a pattern of alternating cycles which seemed to resonate strangely in his own being. Perhaps, as theosophy held, those serpentine coils were a dark reflection of the unfallen creative source; perhaps they were but an image of himself. In any case, the mastery of that vision of history might lead to a transcendence of history. Beyond or through the tragedy of a fallen world, the harmony of existence might be experienced once again.

ii.

Alternating eras entered Yeats's work as early as 1884, in *Mosada*. The Inquisitor in that play sees the world relapse into paganism and prays for yet another era of Christianity. Then, he says, the

> lives of men shall flow
> As quiet as the little rivulets
> Beneath the sheltering shadow of Thy Church,
> And then shall bend, enduring God, the knees
> Of the great warriors whose names have sung
> The world to its fierce infancy again.[29]

One meaning of that alternation is rendered by the central plot, in which the Inquisitor condemns unwittingly the Moorish enchantress who had been his beloved. Those apparent opposites have a hidden affinity. The Inquisitor's militant Christianity therefore rests upon a denial and suppression of its apparent opposite or adversary, which is really its darkly feminine half. And in so rejecting his shadow, the

Inquisitor transforms himself into an even more ominously shadowing force. The historical process simply mirrors and expands that psychological and religious situation. The symbolism, as we shall see, derives partly from Blake; but the psychological process is central to Yeats's own dialogue with history.

By 1888, in *The Wanderings of Oisin,* Yeats added another element to the pattern. Though alternating eras appear in the debate between Oisin and Patrick, most of the poem describes Oisin's cyclical journey to the three islands of the other-world, where he spent one century feasting and hunting, a second century fighting, and a third dreaming. "I did not pick these images because of any theory," Yeats recalled some forty-five years later, "but because I found them impressive, yet all the while abstractions haunted me." Another comment suggested these abstractions: "The choral song, a life lived in common, a futile battle, then thought for its own sake, the last island, Vico's circle and mine, and then the circle joined."[30] Nor was Yeats simply reading into his early work a theory not discovered until many years later; he had been discovering that theory as he wrote the narrative poem itself.

"A passage in *La Peau de chagrin* may have started me," he recalled, and he claimed with considerable exaggeration that throughout the nineties he "knew no ally but Balzac."[31] The relevant passage is probably that describing a journalists' banquet which the hero attends, where an intoxicated debate symbolizes the flux and reflux of history itself and where many arguments suggest an alternation of eras. "Is it my fault," asks one man, "if Catholicism has gone so far as to put a million gods in a bag of flour, if the republic always ends in a Napoleon ... ?" But the debate also symbolizes the cultural dissolution of modern times; and, in a manner recalling Vico, a scholar outlines the fragmentation of society as it passes from its vigorous unitary state to a barbarism of the intellect. We now rely, he says, not upon religion or material force, "but upon intelligence. Is the book as powerful as the sword? is discussion as powerful as action? That is the problem." Though Yeats seems never to have realized the direct relation between Balzac and Vico's thought,[32] Oisin's journey does suggest the cycle as found in *La Peau de chagrin*. The harmonious tribal life on the Isle of the Living recalls Balzac's description

of primitive social unity; the battles by Manannan's decaying tower
on the Isle of Victories may recall the ensuing social fragmentation;
and the dreaming on the Isle of Forgetfulness may recall the substitution of a book for a sword, "thought for its own sake."

That analogy is supported by a related theme in Balzac's novel.
The human will is symbolized by the wild ass's skin, the source of the
hero's achievements, which shrinks as it is used and finally carries its
owner with it into oblivion. By two instinctive processes—we are
told—willing and having one's will, man exhausts the "sources of his
life," whereas "KNOWLEDGE leaves our feeble organism in a state
of perpetual tranquillity."[33] The self-consuming action of the will is
hinted, in Yeats's poem, by the spirit on the Isle of Victories, whose
song implies both personal and historical cycles:

> "With all in all the world I battle wage.
> The strongest of the world, to snatch my prey,
> Came to my tower as age dragged after age.
> Light is man's love and lighter is man's rage—
> His purpose drifts away."[34]

After two centuries, the impulses of love and rage exhausted, Oisin
goes to the Isle of Forgetfulness, where his feeble organism finds
some peace. The mature Yeats would present that self-consuming
action more clearly—at the end of "In Memory of Major Robert
Gregory," in the second of "Two Songs from a Play," and in *The
Trembling of the Veil:* "Our love letters wear out our love; no school
of painting outlasts its founders, every stroke of the brush exhausts
the impulse ... Why should we believe that religion can never bring
round its antithesis?"[35] Hence cycles merge with alternating eras.
Oisin, one life-cycle exhausted, meets St. Patrick; Catholicism puts a
million gods in a sack of flour.

In Balzac's *Séraphita* and *Louis Lambert,* which Yeats must also
have read by his twentieth year,[36] such reversals have yet broader and
more Swedenborgian scope. A man's experience after death is antithetical to that of his life, and the cosmos itself is the pulsing
expiration and inspiration of the omnipotent One.[37] But Yeats found
similar ideas, of course, in theosophy. Sinnett's *Esoteric Buddhism,*
for example, sketched for him the days and nights of Brahma, the

ebbing and flowing of the tide wave of humanity, and the great wheel which begins in Nirvana or the "subjective side of Nature," cycles through the "objective side of Nature" under the impulse of Karma and of Tanka (desire, or Balzac's Will), and finally returns to its Source. That scheme remained central to his thought. "How hard it was," he later recalled, "to refrain from pointing out that Oisin after old age, its illumination half accepted, half rejected, would pass in death over another sea to another island." In 1925, with "subjective" and "objective" significantly reversed, the wheel appeared in *A Vision* as "the one history, and that the soul's."[38]

As that reversal of terms indicates, the wheel did not imply for Yeats the complete superiority of the infinite One over the finite individual. Longing for the eternal but not desiring the annihilation of a Fergus who leaves the realm of action for that of the Druid's "dreaming wisdom," Yeats stressed the occult doctrine that the fall into time is as necessary as the ultimate return. In theosophical terms, all evolution results from the conflict between the individuality of Lucifer (which Yeats would later call *antithetical*) and the transcendence of Christ (which he would call *primary*). Their final reconciliation will be "the crown of man's ultimate return to divinity."[39] Yeats believed that Blake held a similarly ironic view of the cycles, that for him the polar forces of the wheel which the moralistic Swedenborg called evil and good were "really two forms of good," the "personal" and the "impersonal." "When we act from the personal we tend to bind our consciousness down as to a fiery centre. When...we allow our imagination to expand away from this egoistic mood, we merge in the universal mood."[40] In *Mosada,* the Inquisitor sees the world return to its egoistic "fierce infancy." And Blake's "Mental Traveller" sets forth the entire personal and historical cycle: the fierce infant bound to a rock becomes an aged man with abstract mind and then returns to his fierce infancy.

Yeats visualized this Blakean wheel (which results from the primal fall and fragmentation of the Divine Man) as the journey around the compass made by Urizen and Luvah, the reasoning and emotional moods. That journey, which is also a solar wheel of day and night, is "a hieroglyphic for human life," he said, and "for the life of creeds and societies."

The day-time is essentially a period of war, and Urizen rises as the sun into the zenith, personal, thinking, destructive; contending, first with his opposite vegetative instinct, or Tharmas, and then, at symbolic noon, having driven before him the emotional clouds of Luvah, becoming a power of active, struggling, uninspired life . . . ; and having now grown weary and feeble, through too great success in his contest with those desires and emotions, which are at once his enemies and that upon which he builds all his activity . . . he sinks westward down into the half-animal life of old age and of sickness, and as he falls curses his new opposite, always youthful Los, who forever beats upon his anvil in the East . . . forming new suns, new lives.[41]

So Oisin had journeyed through emotional clouds, ironically successful battles, and feebleness, returning to curse his opposite in Ireland. More systematically the *Will*, in *A Vision*, would war against its opposites while rounding the wheel.

But what of the Ireland to which Oisin returns? As Blake said in *The Four Zoas:* "The day for war, the night for secret religion . . ."[42] And in *Europe* the Christian era, as Yeats said, is a "sleep of eighteen hundred years . . . during which man was a dream." For then the "clouds of Luvah" cover the world: "Inspiration, because it is essentially active and law-breaking, has died out, and 'thou shalt not' is said to be written over the chimneys of its house. Rules of life, born of Luvah, Pity, that is pity for the troubles of the mere vegetative body, spread everywhere, and the soul sleeps in a passive materialism."[43] At the beginning of such a night Blake's primal man fell "prostrate before the wat'ry shadow" of Luvah. So the Inquisitor of *Mosada* expects men's lives to flow like rivulets beneath "the sheltering shadow" of the Church, and so Oisin finds Irish chieftains caught like fish in St. Patrick's net of wrong and right.[44] But, as another warring day follows that night, Oisin may hope (with the reinforcement of Irish tradition) that the heroes are not dead but merely in exile. By 1903 Yeats indicated clearly that the conflict between Oisin and Patrick illustrates the Blakean "day and night of religion," the alternation of "a period when the influences are those that shape the world" with one "that would lure the soul out of the world, out of the body." More systematically in *A Vision* the warring pagan *antithetical* eras would alternate with the Christian and rational *primary* eras.[45]

Such are the main historical elements that lie, however dimly and fragmentarily, behind the excess of imagery and symbolism in *The Wanderings of Oisin*. At that time Yeats was groping for his language, his desire for order hampered by the very richness of his imagination. That is why the revision for the collected *Poems* of 1895 further clarifies this symbolism. The cycle of life had been obscured by his naming the first island that of the "Living" and his suggesting that an "Isle of Youth" could not be found; now the first island became that of "Dancing" and the hidden refuge from the cycle became the "Island of Content." Yeats also rewrote the song of the spirit on the Isle of Victories so that soul and tower, now in clearer parallel, are subject to the moon; and the spirit will wage war "till the moon has taken all." Helped by Blake's lunar symbolism of twenty-seven heavens or churches, or by similar theosophical ideas, he took another step toward *A Vision*.[46]

A note added to this version also points to a developing symbolism. After vaguely referring to the traditional three islands, Yeats said: "A story in *The Silva Gadelica* describes 'four paradises,' an island to the north, an island to the west, an island to the south, and Adam's paradise in the east." In later editions he kept only that statement, as an implicit reference to his Irish source, although *Silva Gadelica* had not appeared until 1892 and the story it contains has no clear relation to his previously written poem.[47] He had selected those elements that suggest a geographical and biblical symbolism: increasingly Oisin's journey seemed like Urizen's journey around the points of the compass. In fact, he had said of Blake's lunar cycle that the liberation of Luther (the twenty-seventh church) "was so merely material or 'Northern,' that where his work ended that of Adam needed to begin again 'in eternal circle' "[48]—just as he later remarked that after the incomplete illumination of old age Oisin must pass "over another sea to another island." And at least by now he had learned from his reading of Jacob Boehme and others that Oisin's journey was a symbol for the alchemical *rota* or *opus circulatorium,* the cyclical transformation of the four elements, the four seasons, and other quaternities. In that analogy of the revolving universe and of the microcosmic cycles within man, the motifs of elements and cardinal points are often replaced by corresponding journeys, such as those of Osiris, Hercules, and Enoch.

Yeats himself was now acquainted with the symbolic *peregrinatio* to the four quarters in Michael Maier.[49]

Although, as critics have noted, obscurities remained in *The Wanderings of Oisin,* some needed not excision but the clarification that only years of thought would bring. Life on the three islands is not adequately correlated with the conflict between Oisin and Patrick; but that incoherence troubled Yeats's account of the cycle and the alternating eras in Blake, and was solved only by complicated geometry in *A Vision.* Oisin's islands, too, are ambiguously a refuge from life and a mirror of it, and he is spurred on by strangely mingled longings—for Niamh, for the past, and for death. But that motive is itself the paradoxical Will or Tanka, which impels the soul through the cycles of a life that mirrors eternity, in order to lead it back to its vaguely remembered source. In a story of 1896 Yeats further clarified that motive, with the perhaps unexpected help of Leonardo da Vinci: "The hope and desire of returning home to one's former state, is like the moth's desire for the light; and the man, who, with constant longing awaits each new month and new year—deeming that the things he longs for are ever too late in coming—does not perceive that he is longing for his own destruction." That "noble sentence," taken with some modification from Leonardo's notebooks, illustrates for Owen Aherne "the pathway which will lead us into the heart of God." Nor did Yeats radically alter its meaning: the original sentence is clearly based upon an understanding of the alchemical *rota.*[50]

With increasing clarity Yeats would see how, mixing memory and desire, the vision of a transcendence of life impels us ironically through life's cycles. In 1913 a character in "The Hour Before Dawn," who sleeps as Oisin slept on the third island, would paraphrase Leonardo's sentence; and in 1921 "The Wheel," another paraphrase, would come to Yeats spontaneously. In 1926 he would imagine an old man learning that the landscape of this world is "not solid, that all he sees is a mathematical line drawn between hope and memory." In 1929, recalling the Kabbalistic "death of the kiss" and referring to the end of both personal and historical cycles, he would say: "The last kiss is given to the void."[51] If Oisin, chasing Niamh, did not know that formula, Crazy Jane, in "Crazy Jane and Jack the Journeyman," would be better instructed. And the hermit Ribh would give in

"Meru" (1934) a more powerfully ambiguous vision of the wheel around which Tanka impels all souls and all civilizations. As he forged the inconsistencies of *The Wanderings of Oisin* into luminous if paradoxical wholes, Yeats would have reason to be "persuaded that our intellects at twenty contain all the truths we shall ever find."[52]

iii.

But allies other than Balzac, Blake, and the theosophists helped Yeats to find those alternating cycles in history. The 1895 revision of *The Wanderings of Oisin,* for example, echoes a passage that had become for many Victorians an archetype of the reversal of eras. Yeats tells how Manannan, his "dark hall" completed,

> cried to all
> The mightier masters of a mightier race;
> And at his cry there came no milk-pale face
> Under a crown of thorns and dark with blood,
> But only exultant faces.

Precisely that strange interruption had stopped the laughter of the gods in Zeus's hall, as Heine had recounted the tale: "Suddenly there came gasping towards them a pale Jew, dripping with blood, a crown of thorns on his head; bearing a great cross of wood on his shoulder; and he cast the cross on the high table of the gods, so that the golden goblets trembled and fell, and the gods grew dumb and pale, and ever paler, till they melted in utter mist." Heine had then described, in effect, Luvah's or Patrick's religion of pity for the vegetative body: "...the world became grey and gloomy.... Olympus became a hospital, where flayed, roasted and spitted gods went wearily, wandering around, binding their wounds and singing sorrowful songs. Religion no longer offered joy, but consolation; it was a woeful, bleeding religion of transgressors. Pity is the last consecration of love; it may be, love itself."[53]

Among those who shared Heine's preoccupation with that religious conflict and agreed that "as the heart of the poet is the central point of the world, it must, in times like these be miserably divided and torn,"[54] most important for Yeats—once again—was Pater. The wavering loyalties which Pater described in *Marius the Epicurean* he saw also in Botticelli's grey-tinted figures, who are "saddened perpetually by the shadow upon them of the great things from which they shrink" and who are "neither for Jehovah nor for his enemies." Similarly the pagan bards of Yeats's "The Old Men of the Twilight" (1895) are sentenced by St. Patrick to "become grey herons and stand pondering in grey pools and flit over the world in that hour when it is most full of sighs, having forgotten the flame of the stars and not yet perceived the flame of the sun." Lionel Johnson, too, Yeats saw as a maker of a "twilight world" inhabited by those who have "renounced the joy of the world without accepting the joy of God," and he would later ask: "Why are these strange souls born everywhere today? with hearts that Christianity, as shaped by history, cannot satisfy." Quite consciously Yeats was wandering in the limbo, the cultural interregnum, of Arnold's "Stanzas from the Grande Chartreuse."[55]

He sought to harmonize paganism and Christianity in the Rosicrucian peace that broods throughout his early poetry. But such symbolism had already entered Ibsen's *Emperor and Galilean: A World-Historic Drama,* which Yeats probably read in the early nineties.[56] The "momentous figures" of this play, written by what Yeats called "the earlier and ... greater" Ibsen,[57] embody the historical conflict between the first empire, "founded on the tree of knowledge," and the second, "founded on the tree of the cross." But the opposites might be reconciled: "The third is the empire of the great mystery; that empire which shall be founded on the tree of knowledge and the tree of the cross together, because it hates and loves them both, and because it has its living sources under Adam's grove and under Golgotha."[58] Ibsen himself had declared in his famous Stockholm speech of 1887 that "the ideals of our time, as they pass away, are tending toward that which ... I have designated as 'the third empire.'" Soon, in his romances of 1896, Yeats would suggest such an empire, giving in "The Tables of the Law" his interpretation (as George Sand in *Spiridion* had given hers) of Joachim of Flora's seminal concept of the "third era."[59]

Indeed, on every hand Yeats could find descriptions of alternating eras and organic cycles. In Byron's *Childe Harold,* in Shelley's *Hellas,* in Arnold's "Dover Beach," he could glimpse a disillusioning flux and reflux. On the continent Goethe had declared the sole theme of world history to be the ebb and flow of Belief and Unbelief and the Saint-Simonians had talked of alternating "organic" and "critical" epochs.[60] In England Arnold suggested in "The Function of Criticism" alternating periods of creation and criticism or expansion and consolidation, and Carlyle declaimed: "As in long-drawn systole and long-drawn diastole, must the period of Faith alternate with the period of Denial; must the vernal growth, the summer luxuriance of all Opinions, Spiritual Representations and Creations, be followed by, and again follow, the autumnal decay, the winter dissolution." Carlyle also described ages of what Yeats would call "Unity of Being," when all men "were animated by one great Idea," and other ages in which religion had split into philosophies and "disunion and mutual collision in all provinces of Speech and Action" increasingly prevailed. The time of Socrates, for example, was characterized by a yielding to the "spirit of speculation"; that of Shakespeare was the brief and belated blossom of Catholicism or the "spiritual flower-time" after the long and stormy English spring; and that of Samuel Johnson was "wholly divided." All world-history was "the story of the Phoenix, which periodically, after a thousand years, becomes a funeral pyre of its own creation."[61]

Though often contemptuous of Carlyle, Yeats may have absorbed much from one whom he called "the chief inspirer of self-educated men in the 'eighties and the early 'nineties."[62] But so great was Carlyle's influence and so pervasive were the ideas he helped to transmit that Yeats did not need to learn from him directly. Ruskin, Morris, Standish James O'Grady, Edward Carpenter, and William Magee (who signed himself John Eglinton) were all more congenial sources of such ideas. "In the time of Chaucer," said Magee, for example, "the English nation is as fair as a rosebud, and its poets babble of spring, but a couple of centuries later, when Queen Elizabeth was pondering whether she could not in some way restrain London's further growth, its expanded petals were falling away in a shower of dramas and epics." The same change Yeats later called "the falling asunder of the human mind, as an opening flower falls asunder." He said, "...Chaucer's personages had disengaged themselves from Chaucer's crowd, forgot their common goal and shrine, and after sundry magnifications became each in turn the centre of some Elizabethan play . . ."[63]

But most important, perhaps, was an earlier account of modern fragmentation, which Yeats reviewed in 1893. "When I began to write," he has said, "I avowed for my principles those of Arthur Hallam in his essay upon Tennyson." That "little known and profound essay" of 1831 defined for him "more perfectly than any other criticism in English the issues in that war of the schools which is troubling all the arts."[64] In the Elizabethan age, Hallam had said, the poet was at one with society and there was a "reciprocity of vigor between different orders of intelligence." But a "period of degradation" followed, and the nineteenth century was engaged in a complicated return to the sources of imaginative power. Sensitive, Reflective, and Passionate Emotion, once intermingled, were now in conflict, each "striving to reproduce the regular power which the whole had once enjoyed."[65] That account supported Yeats's growing conviction that the world "was now but a bundle of fragments" and influenced his later description of the rise of aestheticism, with its romantic "melancholy" and its "return of the mind upon itself."[66] Hallam had also argued that the "*objective* amelioration" brought by modern machinery would cause a "decrease of *subjective* power" as the "higher feelings" were absorbed into the "palpable interests of ordinary life." In 1893, long before Hallam's italicized terms became the governing concepts in the wheel of *A Vision,* the knight in Yeats's "Out of the Rose" heard "how men would turn from the light of their own hearts, and bow down before external order and outer fixity, and that then the light would cease, and none escape the curse except the foolish good man who could not, and the passionate wicked man who would not, think."[67] That vision of increasing objectivity, of Blake's Urizen entering the North, Yeats would elaborate until, in revolt against "outer fixity," he himself would voice the defiance of "The Wild Old Wicked Man."

Certainly Yeats was not alone in asking, "Is not all history but the coming of that conscious art which first makes articulate and then destroys the old wild energy?"—and in believing that this historical curve might be charted with some geometrical precision. Emerson had also said, "There is a moment in the history of every nation, when, proceeding out of . . . brute youth, the perceptive powers reach their ripeness and have not yet become microscopic . . ."[68] And Sinnett had quoted J. W. Draper's comparison of individual and national life and his conclusion that there "is a geometry that applies to all nations as an equation of their curve of advance." Whether or not Yeats read Draper's full account of the five stages in each European cycle, he did discover in 1896 the work of J. S. Stuart-Glennie, who had his own cyclical theory, according to which a new phase begins every five hundred years.[69]

Moreover, Emerson's rather Pythagorean theory, which led him to call Plato the momentary balancer of Asia and Europe, the unbounded and the bounded, was shared by Pater, for whom Phidias and Aeschylus assumed that crucial role. Their perfection, "attainable only through a certain combination of opposites," was a precarious balance of the Asiatic and European, the Ionic and Doric, the centrifugal and centripetal forces in history. So it would be in Yeats's "Dove or Swan." Pater also held that "in the Athens of Plato's day, as he saw with acute prevision, those centrifugal forces had come to be ruinously in excess of the centripetal"—and Yeats would later write of his own time, in "The Second Coming":

> Turning and turning in the widening gyre
> The falcon cannot hear the falconer;
> Things fall apart; the centre cannot hold . . .[70]

It is hardly surprising that in *Per Amica Silentia Lunae,* just before being visited by the "instructors" who spoke through his wife, Yeats wrote this sentence: "I do not doubt those heaving circles, those winding arcs, whether in one man's life or in that of an age, are mathematical, and that some in the world, or beyond the world, have foreknown the event and pricked upon the calendar the life-span of a Christ, a Buddha, a Napoleon . . ." Ideas of that sort, as John Stuart Mill had said, "were the general property of Europe."[71]

But Yeats added another clause, also the fruit of long meditation: "I do not doubt . . . ," he said, "that every movement, in feeling or in thought, prepares in the dark by its own increasing clarity and confidence its own executioner." That is, in brief, the compensatory psychological process he glimpsed behind the alternating cycles of history. In simple form, it is evident in his own myths: Inquisitor and Moorish enchantress, Patrick and Oisin—these are projected opposites doing necessary battle within a single soul. But that clause may also point to the way in which, as Yeats believed, a poet or prophet may foreknow the event. By raising to full consciousness that ironic dialogue of swan and shadow—of egocentric assertion and unconscious counterassertion, of confident feeling and executioner in the dark—he may come to understand not merely himself and his myths but also that contemporary history of which he forms an integral part. However, to trace in detail that path to prophetic knowledge—and thereby to glimpse the source of Yeats's amazing growth and of the power and ethical relevance of his later poetry—we must turn to a different aspect of his early vision of history. We must turn from the cycles to the apocalypse.

III · THE APOCALYPSE

Crows o'er the gods   the Golden-combed . . .
and crows yet another   beneath the earth,
a dark red cock   in the halls of Hell. . . .
Loud blows Heimdal,   the horn is aloft,
and Odin speaks   with Mimir's head. . . .
Hidden things I know;   still onward I see
the great Doom of the Powers,   the gods of war....
the World-serpent writhes   in Jötun rage;
he lashes the waves. . . .
The sun is darkened,   Earth sinks in the sea. . . .
                              —*Völuspa*[1]

Our history speaks of opinions and discoveries, but in
ancient times . . . history spoke of commandments and
revelations. [Men] looked as carefully and as patiently
towards Sinai and its thunders as we look towards
parliaments and laboratories.
                              —"Magic"[2]

---

i.

ALREADY IN THE EIGHTIES AND NINETIES the life of the seasons contained for Yeats, as he put it years later, "the symbolical syntax
wherein we may write the History of the World."[3] But he did not
rest in a Spenglerian vision of cyclical fate. As for Leonardo, the
seasonal cycle or alchemical *rota* must reveal the quintessence. Then
eternal and temporal, Christ and Lucifer, Deus and Demon, might be

reconciled. Then God might burn Nature with a kiss, as in "The Man who Dreamed of Faeryland," but without annihilation. Yeats would envision that paradoxical state in "News for the Delphic Oracle," a poem in which Oisin himself reaches a fitting haven at the end of his author's own long cyclical journey. But even in *The Wanderings of Oisin* the poetic rendering of the cyclical journey itself may suggest that state.

Here we must seriously engage Yeats's occultism. Those who judge that tradition by its third-rate apostles and ignore its psychological implications may well conclude that Yeats's "religion" had no consequent ethics, that his escape from the nineties resulted from some external cause, or that he strangely combined great powers of self-transcendence with a need to dabble in systems of dubious repute. But those are only half-truths. The central paradox of Yeats's career is that of spiritual alchemy. Because the alchemist desires an impossible apocalypse, symbolized by the transmuting of all things into incorruptible gold, he undertakes his Great Work—an arduous yet possible self-transformation, a lifelong search for wholeness and unity with the cosmic forces. So it was with Yeats. Precisely because the young aesthete longed to transmute or escape the temporal world, he began hesitantly to transform himself into one who could accept that world. The results of that alchemy were not obvious in his poetry until after 1902, but the fire had been lit years before.

Since 1884 at least, Yeats had begun to grasp that paradox of romantic aspiration and realistic achievement. The "last Arcadian" says that salvation from the cycles of time may be found in poetry: "Words alone are certain good." When he adds that the "very world itself may be / Only a sudden flaming word," he may imply the sanction that Yeats was beginning to find for his aestheticism.[4] That "flaming word" or Logos is the circle of Eternity, which the temporal cycles imperfectly mirror. The poet may reconstitute that circle and attain the apocalypse by transmuting the cycles into the golden realm of the imagination, by perceiving in the particulars of the fallen world the lineaments of the universal. Hence Oisin's journey to those three islands which so strangely mingle time and eternity is a symbol of the apocalypse attained. And the alchemical *rota* or heroic circular journey reveals the quintessence—which is, according to

Leonardo's "noble sentence," precisely that romantic aspiration or longing, composed of transcendental memory and desire, which ironically leads Oisin and all men through the cycles of this life. Such aesthetic alchemy had also, as Yeats knew, the sanction of Balzac's Louis Lambert, who dreamed that "perhaps, the day will come when the inverse meaning of ET VERBUM CARO FACTUM EST will be the gist of a new Gospel which will say: AND THE FLESH SHALL BE MADE THE WORD, IT SHALL BECOME THE WORD OF GOD."[5]

In extreme form, that is the goal of Yeats's panoramic vision of history: the reversal of fall and incarnation, the transmutation of flesh into Word, and the correlative deification of the poet, who sees all history as his reflection. However, the progress toward that goal is complicated by the existential movement in Yeats's dialogue with history—as the poet recognizes his human finitude, undergoes the dramatic experience of life in time, and provokes encounters with an anti-self who may teach him all that he does not yet know. In fact, that existential complication is integral to the apocalyptic doctrine itself. For, though the early Yeats often wished to evade it and critics of gnosticism often wish to ignore it, the practical consequence of that doctrine is clear. If the poet would transcend the world by transmuting all flesh, he must explore and realize in art the full circle of human potentialities. Most immediately he must pursue that which seems his opposite, adversary, or shadow, but is really unconscious within him. The Inquisitor of *Mosada* rejects that dark enchantress and is condemned to endure uncomprehendingly the flux and reflux of history. The poet in quest of the apocalypse must accept her. That fuller recognition and understanding of history's dark forces and of the correlated forces within his own being will mean for him both self-annihilation and growth.

Here again Blake was of great help. Though he "dared to see that the serpent must always keep its tail in its mouth, and creed follow creed, no matter how bitter be our longing for finality," he too postulated an aesthetic salvation from the cycles. As Yeats understood it, Christ, or the poetic imagination, might draw man out of the wheel of birth. "Imagination is eternal—it knows not of death—it has no Western twilight and Northern darkness. We must cast our life, thought after thought, desire after desire, into its world of freedom, and so escape from the warring egotisms of elements and years."[6] Despite Yeats's world-weary tone, this apocalyptic longing must lead not away from nature but through it. All thoughts, all desires, must be imaginatively rendered. As "Christ put on the temporal body, which is Satan,...that it might be consumed, and the 'spiritual body revealed,'" so poetry "puts on nature that nature may be revealed as the great storehouse of symbolism, without which language is dumb."[7] One can escape the world only by fully accepting it. As a symbol of Christ's redemptive descent Blake had presented Milton's descent to accept and so transform his opposite, his feminine emanation and shadow—image of his "dark mind," his wives and daughters, and the cycles of history.

A semi-Blakean apocalypse entered Yeats's fiction as early as 1893, in "The Heart of the Spring." There an old man learns "that there is a moment...which trembles with the Song of the Immortal Powers, and that whosoever finds this moment and listens to the Song shall become like the Immortal Powers themselves." It is the moment of the lark's song in Blake's *Milton*—that of Christ's descent into the wheel and Milton's redemption of his shadow—which Yeats had diagrammed in his Blake study.[8] And throughout the nineties he considered ways of finding that moment, listening to the circular melody, and re-creating it in art.

In doing so, he was, in his own view, gradually discovering what Spengler would later call "the secret rhythm of all things cosmic," of which artistic imitation is born. In 1896 he said, "The more a poet rids his verses of heterogeneous knowledge and irrelevant analysis, and purifies his mind with elaborate art, the more does the little ritual of his verse resemble the great ritual of Nature" and the poet become, "as all the great mystics have believed, a vessel of the creative power of God." That belief—and not his alleged lack of "allies"—is the reason Yeats largely "kept silent" during these years about all concerning his theory of history which he "could not get into fantastic romance."[9] He did not wish to analyze or argue the cycles; he wished to make his work a "ritual" that would copy the same eternal pattern. Though such an effort could not strengthen his direct grasp of history, it could develop the symbolism through which he would later explore history. Moving for the time being in a realm free from the more intractable complexities of historical fact, his vision could elaborate itself according to its own laws and so gain that self-sufficiency it needed, he believed, in order to qualify as "truth."

Furthermore, that elaboration implies more than mere "purification" of the mind. The circular ritual of Nature implies wholeness as well. In the alchemical technique of *imaginatio* the mind is a well-sealed vessel into which nothing irrelevant may enter—and also from which nothing may escape.[10] The alchemist must fully explore the contents of that vessel, both conscious and unconscious; he must discover the *rota* or cosmic rhythm within. Yeats identified himself with that quest: "certain of us are looking everywhere for the perfect alembic that no silver or golden drop may escape." Nor was he afraid of eccentricity in that effort. He knew that Poe, for example, had created "personages and lyric emotions, which startle us by being at once bizarre and an image of our own secret thoughts." That was possible because the mind is a "microcosm, mirroring everything in universal nature."[11]

With confidence, therefore, Yeats elaborated his personal microcosm, finding his complexity within his "craft." He hoped to say with Paracelsus, "In this crust of bread I have found all the stars and all the heavens."[12] The apocalyptic romances that resulted from his effort—"Rosa Alchemica," "The Tables of the Law," and "The Adoration of the Magi"—may offend us today by their unctuous and allusive style and by their fantastic content, which seems so far from the "realities" of twentieth-century life. But they are more successful than we usually admit: the young James Joyce even thought one worthy of the Russian masters.[13] And they are of cardinal importance in Yeats's canon. As "visions of history" they are mythical, but as symbolic confrontations of that shadow which Yeats elsewhere projected upon a more recognizable past, they are profoundly realistic. They represent a crucial stage of that dangerous search for wholeness —the descent into the depths and the trumpeting up for judgment— which made possible his lifelong growth and his remarkable prophetic poetry.

ii.

On the surface, "Rosa Alchemica" announces a post-Christian era (Blake's pagan day, the resurgence of Heine's and Pater's exiled gods), in which the Order of the Alchemical Rose will make possible for its initiates the transcendence of all history. Before meeting Michael Robartes, who introduces him to the Order, the narrator already yearns for such transcendence. He imagines himself another Pater (with touches of Huysmans' des Esseintes[14]), who sympathizes with "everything which has moved men's hearts in any age" and experiences all human passions "without their bitterness and without satiety." "I had gathered about me," he says, "all gods because I believed in none, and experienced every pleasure because I gave myself to none, but held myself apart, individual, indissoluble, a mirror of polished steel."[15] But, though critics have often confused the narrator with the author, the story itself treats this earnest discipleship with some irony. In fact, it remarkably suggests Nietzsche's attack upon the "mirroring and eternally self-polishing soul" who "no longer knows how to affirm, no longer how to deny,"[16] and Yeats's own assertion of 1909 that "the ideal of culture expressed by Pater can only create feminine souls. The soul becomes a mirror not a brazier."[17]

This critical irony can antedate Yeats's reading of Nietzsche in 1902 because it is not applied from a vantage point outside his occult doctrine: it inheres in the very nature of spiritual alchemy. The narrator tells of the alchemical book he has already written, "a fanciful reverie over the transmutation of life into art, and a cry of measureless desire for a world made wholly of essences."[18] But the alchemy of this story implies a psychic transformation more profound and more dangerous than he has yet imagined. Despite his apocalyptic yearnings he still believes—in the words of *The Hour-Glass*—

> that truth is learnt
> When the intellect's deliberate and cold,
> As it were a polished mirror that reflects
> An unchanged world; not when steel dissolves
> Bubbling and hissing, till there's nought but fume.

He has yet to discover that when the steel "all fumes up," the visionaries "walk as when beside those three in the furnace / The form of a fourth."[19] In other words, there is a truth that may be learned only by accepting one's own transformation. Then steel mirror may turn brazier, lamp, or luminous drop of gold. Then, in alchemical numerology, three may become four, or the part the whole, and man may partake of the circle of Eternity.

This the narrator dimly perceives when, upon meeting Robartes, he hears voices proclaiming the breaking of the mirror and rises through companies of aesthetic essences into "that Death which is Beauty herself." "All things that had ever lived seemed to come and dwell in my heart, and I in theirs..." But he has seen only a faint image of the alchemical fire to which Valentinus compared the fire of the Last Day, where all is dissolved that the divine substance may waken.[20] To attain the perspective of the whole or eternity, a man must accept the annihilation of that rigid part which he is. The ego must assimilate all that it has rejected. Full initiation therefore requires a further yielding to the force that threatens to dissolve the narrator's "fixed habits and principles"—the force that, with King Lear, he calls *hysterica passio*.[21]

He must journey to the West, the direction of dying life and awakening vision. Arriving at the temple, an old customhouse "set out on the very end of a dilapidated and almost deserted pier" on a remote Connemara headland, he imagines "that the sea, which kept covering it with showers of white foam, was claiming it as part of some indefinite and passionate life, which had begun to war upon our orderly and careful days, and was about to plunge the world into a night as obscure as that which followed the downfall of the classical world."[22] In slightly different form that grey sea had worn away Manannan's tower in *The Wanderings of Oisin,* had defeated the maddened Cuchulain, and later became the "blood-dimmed tide" of "The Second Coming." It is perhaps an inevitable symbol of the flux of history and also of what Melville (as Yeats may have known) called the encompassing "horrors of the half known life."[23] Jung, like Yeats, sees it as referring to the subliminal psychic life or *Anima Mundi.* Indeed, he has described its Dionysian aspect in words that apply strikingly to this romance: "Dionysus is the abyss of impassioned dissolution, where all human distinctions are merged in the animal divinity of the primordial psyche—a blissful and terrible experience. Humanity, huddling behind the walls of its culture, believes it has escaped this experience, until it succeeds in letting loose another orgy of bloodshed."[24] In "Rosa Alchemica" the waves, "part of a teeming, fantastic inner life," embody powers "greater or less than man"; and the immortal woman who soon dances with the narrator is "more or less than human." These powers may absorb men: the narrator's soul is drunk up by the woman, and the personality of Robartes "had dissolved away like salt in water." But the temple stands as a mediating and controlling form "between the pure multitude of the waves and the impure multitude of men."[25]

In order to become the luminous mask or *persona* of those interior yet transcendent powers, the initiate must immerse himself in the entire round of moods (the multifoliate rose) denied by the conscious order of the Christian era. He may then enter the magical dance whose rhythm enacts "the circle of Eternity, on which alone the transient and the accidental could be broken, and the spirit set free."[26] But, forced to descend into the Dionysian abyss, the narrator flees from the terrifying shadow that is the projection of his own darker longings. Finding that the "lonely, majestical multitude" of Yeats's poem exert the power of one "whose name is legion," he retreats from gnostic vision to a timid Christian moralism.[27]

His conflict is symbolically expanded by a historical antithesis important for the later poetry. The forces of dissolution evoke that realm where all things may be transmuted by the golden smithies of the Byzantine Emperor. Divinities on the temple walls are "wrought in a mosaic not less beautiful than the mosaic in the Baptistery at Ravenna."[28] (When the romance was reissued in 1924, Yeats changed the glitter of the alchemical peacocks from that of jewels to that of Byzantine mosaic.[29]) Resisting those forces, the narrator thinks of his "wide staircase, where Swift had passed joking and railing, and Curran telling stories and quoting Greek in simpler days..."[30] But he is far weaker than the Anglo-Irish speaker of "Blood and the Moon," who later declares that

> This winding, gyring, spiring treadmill of a stair is
> my ancestral stair;
> That Goldsmith and the Dean, Berkeley and Burke have
> travelled there.

Wishing to transcend the world, the narrator of "Rosa Alchemica" moves toward Yeats's Byzantium; lacking courage equal to desire, he clings to an effete version of classical order.

He is torn between the historical opposites which Pater had called the "centrifugal" and "centripetal" or "Asiatic" and "European," and which Nietzsche, as Yeats would soon learn, had called the "Dionysian" and "Apollonian." Yeats already knew their occult analogues, the "Transfiguration" and "Incarnation," and he would later sum up all these connotations in his terms *primary* and *antithetical*. Then, echoing his poem "The Magi," he would concisely describe the predicament experienced by the narrator of "Rosa Alchemica": "When the old *primary* becomes the new *antithetical*, the old realisation of an objective moral law is changed into a subconscious turbulent instinct. The world of rigid custom and law is broken up by 'the uncontrollable mystery upon the bestial floor.' "[31]

Because Yeats sought to transcend those opposites, to attain the full circle of psychic wholeness, his narrator's *fin-de-siècle* temptations embody his own creative potential. Taken seriously, the desire to experience all human passions must lead beyond Pater, just as spiritual alchemy must lead beyond aesthetic reverie. So too, any classical order worthy the name must be erected upon a full experience of the Dionysian abyss. As the narrator flees from the responsibility of meeting and assimilating Robartes, his shadow-self, the slow fire of Yeats's alembic reveals the dross of such earlier *personae* as the speaker of that flaccid apocalyptic poem "The Valley of the Black Pig." Hence the narrator's timorous but fascinated gaze upon the turbulent Western sea in "Rosa Alchemica" is part of Yeats's own controlled assimilation of that subconscious turbulence. And hence that narrator can later give way to the more masterful yet raging Lear of the great poems: "Hysterica passio, down thou climbing sorrow!"

Yeats was learning what Blake's Milton meant when, recognizing the selfhood and descending to dissolve it and to redeem the shadow, he urged men "to despise death & to go on / In fearless majesty annihilating Self."[32] He was learning also what Boehme meant, in his many discussions of psychic transformation. The "craving of every essence," said Boehme, "makes in its turn a mirror, to see and to know itself in the mirror. And then the craving seizes this (namely the mirror), brings it into its imagination, and finds that it is not of its life. Hence opposition arises and loathing, so that the craving would discard the mirror, and yet cannot." Yeats's parrot then rages "at his own image in the enamelled sea" or the narrator of "Rosa Alchemica" half-wishes to break his mirror-image. "And therefore," Boehme continued, "the craving seeks the limit of the beginning, and passes out of the mirror. Thus the mirror is broken, and the breaking is a *turba,* as a dying of the formed or comprehended life." And Boehme summarized the process on the cosmic level—for each creature is itself a mirror of the eternal: the Eternal Nature "seeks the limit of the malignity, and would abandon it."[33] That is the process whereby the evil of the selfhood is explored, defined, and transcended —or, in Blake's phrase, given "a body...that it may be cast off for ever."[34] Boehme's conception of that process, evident in Yeats's alchemical technique in this romance, would reappear years later in Yeats's own formulation of "measurement" and "judgment" as the primary functions of apocalyptic art.

iii.

In "The Tables of the Law" Owen Aherne has found the lost introduction to Joachim of Flora's *Eternal Gospel,* the book "in which the freedom of the Renaissance lay hidden." It has "swept the commandments of the Father away" and "displaced the commandments of the Son by the commandments of the Holy Spirit."[35] The *Fractura Tabularum* of this gospel recalls the prophetic fury of Orc, in Blake's *America:*

> "The times are ended; shadows pass, the morning 'gins
> to break;
> "The fiery joy, that Urizen perverted to ten commands,
> "What night he led the starry hosts thro' the wide
> wilderness,
> "That stony law I stamp to dust..."[36]

But its *Lex Secreta* presents as the "true inspiration of action" Yeats's aesthetic alchemy:

Just as poets and painters and musicians labour at their works, building them with lawless and lawful things alike so long as they embody the beauty that is beyond the grave; these children of the Holy Spirit labour at their moments with eyes upon the shining substance on which Time has heaped the refuse of creation; for the world only exists to be a tale in the ears of coming generations; and terror and content, birth and death, love and hatred and the fruit of the Tree are but instruments for that supreme art which is to win us from life and gather us into eternity like doves into their dove-cots.[37]

Again such aesthetic formulas lead to the more disturbing perceptions that mark genuine growth. Because extracting the quintessence from the *rota* of all moods is more difficult than quoting Leonardo's "noble sentence" about it, Aherne also finds the new revelation overwhelming. But whereas the narrator of "Rosa Alchemica," whose ego temporarily drowned in the sea of moods, had suffered what Jung calls psychic annihilation, Aherne suffers the complementary fate of inflation: his ego attempts an impossible identification with those transcendent forces. In Boehme's terms, the partially transformed creature mistakenly identifies itself with that Eternal Nature of which it is a limited reflection. This is especially clear in a somewhat later version of the story, which develops the material more fully. Feeling "a divine ecstasy, an immortal fire in every passion," Aherne sees everywhere "its image, as in a mirror," and thinks he is "about to touch the Heart of God." But then he feels himself "caught in the glittering folds of an enormous serpent" and "falling with him through a fathomless abyss." Because he has "looked out of the eyes of the angels," his world ironically remains the cyclical serpent of multiplicity, Blake's satanic labyrinth. He now believes that man can only approach the Heart of God "through the sense of separation from it which we call sin," and that, because he has discovered the law of his being, he can no longer sin.[38]

That is a common predicament in our age. But this story, unlike Eliot's rather similar discussion of satanism in his essay on Baudelaire[39] or Tate's prayer in "The Last Days of Alice," does not offer an orthodox Christian solution. The gnostic God sees in the glittering satanic folds of the temporal world a dark yet beautiful reflection of his own image. So it was with Aherne in the first flush of ecstasy. But, because a finite ego cannot endure isolation in a mirroring labyrinth (which is Hérodiade's situation, not that celebrated in "First Principles"), it has what Yeats would call in *The King's Threshold*

> The hunger of the crane, that starves himself
> At the full moon because he is afraid
> Of his own shadow and the glittering water ... [40]

Still later, in *Calvary,* this passage would merge with Aherne's statement, "I ceased to be among those for whom Christ died," to form an enigmatic song:

> Motionless under the moon-beam,
> Up to his feathers in the stream;
> Although fish leap, the white heron
> Shivers in a dumbfounded dream.
>
> God has not died for the white heron.
>
> Although half famished he'll not dare
> Dip or do anything but stare
> Upon that glittering image of a heron,
> That now is lost and now is there.

Lunar symbolism would then define "subjective" or *antithetical* man as but one phase in the complete round of being:

> But that the full is shortly gone
> And after that is crescent moon,
> It's certain that the moon-crazed heron
> Would be but fishes' diet soon. [41]

"What can a swan need but a swan?" "The Tables of the Law" offers an early answer. For when a swan or a heron—or Aherne—deifies himself, he cuts himself off from the Heart of God, starves himself, and therefore induces in himself a fear of "his own shadow and the glittering water" very like that fear known by the narrator of "Rosa Alchemica," who faltered a stage earlier on the spiral initiatory path, and also like that known by the yet simpler Inquisitor of *Mosada.* If implicitly denied, the portion of the Self which is beyond the ego exacts its compensation: what is rejected attacks. Aherne therefore longs to return, simply and impossibly, to the state of a finite *primary* man whose relation to his God can be spelled out by the letter of the law. Yeats himself, observing error and compensation, alchemical action and reaction, moved forward on his winding stair. Because his romance was not only a prophecy of a new era but also an apocalypse, depicting the full circle of opposites, he was enabled to fight these battles again with greater force and comprehension.

iv.

Years later, remembering his expectation of an influx from Joachim of Flora's Holy Spirit, Yeats said that the new era was to have been born from "all that our age had rejected, from all that my stories symbolized as a harlot, and take after its mother."[42] This symbol, dominant in "The Adoration of the Magi," is also semi-Blakean and gnostic. Yeats read Blake's Christ as a dual personage: the son of his mother, he brought the restrictive law of the Christian night; the Son of his Father, He is the lawless poetic imagination. Hence Blake could say in *The Everlasting Gospel,*

> The Mother should an Harlot been,
> Just such a one as Magdalen . . .[43]

The next era, thought Yeats, would take after the harlot-mother of the new incarnate principle.

Blake's harlots are also "emanations or 'shadows' " which "seek to be united to states other than those from which they were radiated." Verses like

> The harlot's cry from street to street
> Shall weave old England's winding sheet

refer "far more," said Yeats, to such emanations "than to their embodied types. The children they bring forth are spectral desires to desolate the world."[44] But, though she now weaves a winding sheet of materialism and restrictive Christianity, at the apocalypse the harlot may unite with her true state. As Blake put it in *Milton,* no longer "a wandering Harlot in the streets," she shall join her "Lord & Husband." In other words, that aspect of man which has been repressed, exiled, and thus perverted—the Moorish enchantress of *Mosada*—must find its place in his transcendent unity. In alchemy, *meretrix* the whore is the *prima materia,* the dark or unconscious *corpus inperfectum* that must be redeemed.[45]

Blake's Orc stamps the "stony law" into dust so that

"...pale religious letchery, seeking Virginity,
"May find it in a harlot, and in coarse-clad honesty
"The undefil'd, tho' ravish'd in her cradle night and morn;
"For everything that lives is holy, life delights in life..."[46]

Filtered through Yeats's early aestheticism, that is what happens in
"The Adoration of the Magi." The three naive sages from the west
of Ireland, seeking a dying woman in Paris who will reveal the secret
names of the gods, believe themselves led astray by devils when they
find her to be a harlot—"because Wisdom could not have alighted in so
foolish a neighborhood."[47] But she is indeed Sophia or Wisdom
herself—and Yeats here indicates his understanding of the gnostic use
of this symbol.

According to the book of Enoch, Sophia descended from heaven to
earth but was rejected by men and now awaits the Messianic age.
Elsewhere, however, we learn that she was, as a harlot, married by
the gnostic prophet Simon Magus. She was not only identified with
Helen, with the moon, and with the mother of all, but was also
called the "lost sheep" whom Simon had descended from heaven to
release from the flesh—even as, according to another text, she was
enabled to reascend by the aid of Jesus or the true light.[48] In Kabbalistic terms, she is the Holy Shekinah, the fallen or exiled Presence
of God, whose reunion with God is the apocalyptic event but who
may be "lifted up" in daily redemptive acts of men who microcosmically undergo that apocalypse. Yeats himself, in "The Rose of the
World," had associated that divine harlot with Helen and Deirdre
and had echoed the description of her given in Proverbs 7:22-31. In
1909 his astrological comment on Simon Magus indicated his awareness of the psychological meaning of that gnostic myth:

There is an astrological sense in which a man's wife or sweetheart is
always an Eve made from a rib of his body. She is drawn to him
because she represents a group of stellar influences in the radical horoscope. These influences also create an element in his character, and his
destiny, in things apart from love or marriage. Whether this element
be good or evil she is therefore its external expression. . . . Sometimes
a man may find the evil of a horoscope in a woman, and in rescuing
her from her own self may conquer his own evil, as with Simon

Magus who married a harlot. Others may find in a woman the good that conquers them and shapes them. All external events of life are of course an externalisation of character in the same way, but not to the same degree as the wife, who may represent the gathering up of an entire web of influences . . . . We are mirrors of the stellar light and we cast this light outward as incidents, magnetic attractions, character-isations, desires.[49]

By that time, of course, he also knew Patmore's view that the "external man and woman are each the projected *simulacrum* of the latent half of the other," and that the saint sees in a woman "only the projected shadow of one half of his own personality"[50]—a view quite in harmony with Jung's descriptions of *anima* projection. But in Blake's work the creation of Eve has roughly analogous meaning, and he describes the emanation or shadow of Milton as taking both the sixfold form of his wives and daughters and the form of the cycles of history. In Yeats's own life there would likewise occur, at the time of his marriage, a simultaneous condensation and expansion of the shadow into the form of a woman and the form of a historical myth. Even in 1917 he knew far more than he would admit when he said, "I even wonder if there may not be some secret communion, some whispering in the dark between Daimon and sweetheart."[51]

It is not strange, therefore, that in "The Adoration of the Magi" the old men should be rewarded when they finally confront that harlot or shadow which embodies Sophia herself. One falls into a trance, crows like a cock, has a vision of the previous incarnation at Bethlehem, and receives a Hermetic prophecy that reverses the traditional Christian reading of Virgil's *Fourth Eclogue.* The harlot then expounds some of the divine wisdom. Though her exposition is anti-climactic, partly because of Yeats's reticence, it deals with the four sacred objects of Ireland, which, like the alchemical *rota,* the cyclical journey, and the dialogue of opposites, symbolize the full circle of psychic and cosmic wholeness. (And that, incidentally, is why Yeats also introduced those four objects into his stories of Red Hanrahan, as part of a modified Grail legend.)

Though more exclusively a dance of symbols than "Rosa Alchemica" and "The Tables of the Law," "The Adoration of the Magi" also explores the tensions discerned by the prophetic intuition that Yeats believed the basis of poetry. Literature, he said, can never be made "by anything but by what is still blind and dumb within ourselves." The poet must "explore especially what has been long forbidden, ... not only 'with the highest moral purpose,' like the followers of Ibsen, but gaily, out of sheer mischief, a sheer delight in the play of the mind."[52] He must court and accept the dark part of that mind, the shadow or harlot; he must redeem the projected emanation. Even the light play of symbols may be part of that work, and so point forward to a more serious realization.

v.

The symbolism and meaning of these apocalyptic romances are foreshadowed (as any disciple of Blake and Morris would have known) in the *Völuspa,* where the twin cocks, divine and diabolic, announce Odin's speech with Mimir's head and introduce a vision of the great Doom of the Powers and the sinking of the Earth into the sea. Odin's dialogue with the miraculous head of Mimir (or Mimir's Well), which a rationalist mythographer calls the world-fructifying union of sun and ocean,[53] was for the Norse poet the god's mysterious quest for wisdom. And for Yeats—who sent his narrator to the Western abyss, portrayed the sun-hero Cuchulain fighting the waves and journeying to the Hawk's Well, and considered Odin the archetype of the questing and self-crucifying prophetic poet[54]—that dialogue must have been the fiery imagination's glimpse of its own more comprehensive nature in the shadowy waters that seem contrary to it. Yeatsian *personae* often recoil from that perception and regard the sea as their mere adversary; or (at what later is called the "Fifteenth Phase") they may assume their perception to be final and so attain a lonely and still "fallen" deification. But Yeats himself, standing partly outside his creations, knew that the *hysterica passio* cannot be so simply rejected or assimilated. Pursuing a slower alchemy, he maintained through vacillation the perilous balance of ego and unconscious —or human and transcendental—that he described in his introduction to Lady Gregory's *Gods and Fighting Men:* the "gods are indeed more wise and beautiful than men; but men, when they are great men, are stronger than they are, for men are ... the foaming tide-line of their sea."[55]

Increasingly, then, Yeats learned that the golden age for which he longed may come (as in the *Völuspa*) only after the immersion in a darker and more turbulent realm, and that finally we cannot distinguish its paradisal completeness from death. So Leonardo's "longing" or "quintessence" furthers the mundane life it seems to reject. Of course, many things contributed to Yeats's growth; and he was too skeptical to have, strictly speaking, a "religion" with "consequent" ethics. But alchemical dialogue with the shadow-self includes the possibility of skepticism and invites the continuing assimilation of compensatory elements. It is no accident that in a letter of 1902 Yeats urged upon the young James Joyce, who admired these romances, the virtues required by his Great Work: "The qualities that make a man succeed do not show in his work, often, for quite a long time. They are much less qualities of talent than qualities of character—faith (of this you have probably enough), patience, adaptibility (without this one learns nothing), and a gift for growing by experience, and this is perhaps rarest of all."[56] He was discovering that the knife-edge of alchemy is a possible path.

But there remains a crucial question about any path that leads toward "completeness" rather than "perfection." Though a less gnostic branch of alchemy (to which Blake is somewhat closer) conceives of the Great Work as a psychological *imitatio Christi,* Yeats clearly sought to reconcile Christ and Lucifer, the self-giving and the self-asserting. In the course of a severe and often profound critique of Jung's similar gnosticism, Buber has declared: "The soul which is integrated in the Self as the unification in an all-encompassing wholeness of the opposites, especially of the opposites good and evil, dispenses with the conscience as the court which distinguishes and decides between the right and the wrong."[57] But that sentence, which is at least debatable as it applies to Jungian psychology, cannot accurately describe Yeats's path. A strict conscience remained within his paradoxical wholeness; indeed, he gradually strengthened his "Vision of Evil." Witness the violent self-damnation and self-justification of his later poem "The Choice": he elected as artist to rage in the dark. I shall discuss the fuller import of that semi-Blakean choice to "put on Satan" in Part Two, when I turn to Yeats's existential perspective upon history and consider certain of his great meditative poems. It is enough here to suggest how the romances of 1896 contain in embryo the power and the ethical relevance of that later poetry.

Their traditional symbolism presents what Jung calls the "immediate religious experience" of one who, "no longer shielded by walls or by communities," approaches "the zone of world-destroying and world-creating fire."[58] In the revised version of "The Tables of the Law," the narrator fears that the Eleusinian spirits will fling their torches upon him, "so that all I held dear, all that bound me to the spiritual and social order, would be burnt up, and my soul left naked and shivering among the winds that blow from beyond this world and from beyond the stars." He is rather like a Blakean spectre, whose body is woven on the Looms of Cathedron and who fears the time when the resistless wheels will "unwind the soft threads & reveal / Naked of their clothing the poor spectres before the accusing heavens."[59] But what he fears is that process of self-annihilation which is the poet's vocation. "Our souls that were once naked to the winds of heaven," Yeats wrote in 1901, "are now thickly clad, and have learned to build a house and light a fire upon its hearth, and shut-to the doors and windows."[60] The poet must learn to become again "unaccommodated man"; like King Lear he must stand on the heath, amid threatening and inspiring winds, and cry, "Unbutton here!" As early as 1892 Yeats praised that tragic and visionary development as he saw it in Tennyson, whose growth "was accompanied ever by a shedding off of hopes based upon mere mechanical change and mere scientific or political inventiveness, until at last his soul came near to standing, as the soul of a poet should, naked under the heavens."[61]

So standing, the poet may further his own self-transformation and also enable himself to write prophetically of "the great Doom of the Powers." For the anti-self speaking out of the void may bring visions that are what Yeats called "symbolical histories" of the "dominant moods and moulding events in this life," or (in a psychologically more acute phrase) "symbolical shadows of the impulses that have made them."[62] The resulting poems may belong to that older type of history written when men "looked as carefully and as patiently towards Sinai and its thunders as we look towards parliaments and laboratories." This may sound fantastic. But Emerson, as Yeats surely knew, had similarly described the power of "The Poet":

> It is a secret which every intellectual man quickly learns, that beyond the energy of his possessed and conscious intellect he is capable of a new energy (as of an intellect doubled on itself), by abandonment to the nature of things; that beside his privacy of power as an individual man, there is a great public power on which he can draw, by unlocking, at all risks, his human doors, and suffering the ethereal tides to roll and circulate through him; then he is caught up into the life of the Universe, his speech is thunder, his thought is law ...[63]

One may suspect that Emerson underestimated the risks of unlocking those "human doors," which Yeats (also thinking of "Sinai and its thunders") called "the doors...of those less transitory minds," the genius of the family, that of the tribe, and that of the world.[64] For behind that bouyant Emersonian faith, as behind all that is smugly esoteric in these romances, looms the shadow that Yeats saw in Blake, then in Nietzsche, and in others on to his own day—a shadow of impulses that have made the disastrous "moulding events" in this century. Yeats had reason to think that the poet might be a microcosm of his era. He had glimpsed in himself the Dionysian abyss ignored by a humanity "huddling behind the walls of its culture"—the dark compensation for effete moralism and arid rationalism that would assume its most terrible historical proportions only after his own death in 1939.

In other words, not the occult doctrine in itself but the experience of its psychological meaning led Yeats to believe "that the dark portion of the mind—the subconscious—had an incalculable power, and even over events," and to assert later that Ireland was during these early years "preparing, in that dark portion of the mind which is like the other side of the moon, for insurrection and anarchic violence."[65] As Jung has said, in commenting on the self-murder and self-fertilization symbolized in Nietzsche's poem "Between Birds of Prey" and in Odin's sacrifice to himself: "if a man reckons the unconscious as part of his personality, then one must admit that he is in fact raging against himself. But, in so far as the symbolism thrown up by his suffering is archetypal and collective, it can be taken as a sign that he is no longer suffering from himself, but rather from the spirit of his age."[66] Yeats became convinced of a similar view. Hence the parrots, swans, and birds of prey who rage at their own image lead, in the course of a lifetime, to Yeats's own perception of his likeness to that Swift whose "tragedy" and "genius" both lay in the fact that he was a "victim" of his age. But even in the nineties Yeats knew that for such victims the Dionysian abyss may become a well of wisdom. Like Odin, they may learn the secrets of the runes; like Vala, they may prophesy "the great Doom of the Powers."

That knowledge also informs Yeats's search for "personality"—for he sought "personality" through a complex dialogue with the compensatory inner voice. That voice or daimon, as Jung has said, "makes us conscious of the evil from which the whole community is suffering. ... But it presents this evil in an individual form, so that one might at first suppose it to be only an individual characteristic."[67] Speaking perhaps through a Michael Robartes, it is a Lucifer to whom one must consciously but partly yield, in order that illumination and doubling of strength may take place. "Only the man who can consciously assent to the power of the inner voice," according to Jung, "becomes a personality; but if he succumbs to it he will be swept away by the blind flux of psychic events and destroyed." From this point of view, the "great and liberating thing about any genuine personality" is that "he voluntarily sacrifices himself to his vocation, and consciously translates into his own individual reality what would only lead to ruin if it were lived unconsciously by the group."[68]

If Yeats did not live to see that ruin, he was aware of the psychic depths beneath his so-called naive protofascism. Where his characters succumbed, he consciously assented. The shattering of the stony law and the descent into the raging Western sea are more than literary devices, and there is more than Yeatsian flourish in his question: "Why should we honor those that die upon the field of battle, a man may show as reckless a courage in entering into the abyss of himself."[69] The abyss glimpsed in the apocalyptic romances of 1896 he would explore and master in such poems as "The Second Coming," "Nineteen Hundred and Nineteen," "Meditations in Time of Civil War," and "Parnell's Funeral"—poems which render and judge an evil that can be fully known only by one who has conversed with an interior Lucifer.

The early Yeats was discovering that the apocalypse—an image of wholeness transcending the fragmented temporal world and self—could be nothing other than a full rendering of the opposites within that world and that self. Hence his alchemical path, his way of being wise as a serpent and harmless as a dove, led not to the cancelling out of right and wrong but to the agony and exhilaration of self-knowledge. An ambiguous way of ethical action, it was yet a contemplative way that enabled the poet to transform himself into his own tragic character. Like his own image of Parnell,

> Through Jonathan Swift's dark grove he passed, and there
> Plucked bitter wisdom that enriched his blood.[70]

And if, as he viewed history from the panoramic perspective, that Yeatsian character too often spoke like an ape of the Absolute—what more dare we ask for our edification? He was translating into his individual reality the ruinous forces of our time.

IV · THE DARK MOON
AND THE FULL

To such a pitch of folly I am brought,
Being caught between the pull
Of the dark moon and the full.
        —"The Double Vision of Michael Robartes"

From man's blood-sodden heart are sprung
Those branches of the night and day...
        —"Vacillation"

In a word, it is Mercury, the laughter of fools and
the wonder of the wise.... This is that substance
which at present is the child of the sun and moon;
but originally both his parents came out of his belly.
He is placed between two fires, and therefore is ever
restless.
—Thomas Vaughan[1]

---

i.

ALTHOUGH CYCLE AND APOCALYPSE assumed fairly clear form in
Yeats's mind during the nineties, from 1889 to 1919 his judgments
of history and his hopes for a new era moved through three phases
suggestive of a Hegelian dialectic. That was because, as spiritual
alchemist, he knew the soul to be a mercurial synthesis of opposites.

Restlessly following the spiral path "between two fires," Yeats first
sought a Dionysian transcendence of form, then an Apollonian reconstitution of form, and then paradoxical syntheses of both impulses.
Necessarily, the three stages on his path were reflected in his shifting
vision of history.

During the first stage, his hopes for a new era were significantly
contradictory. He wished it to combine qualities that he described in
1889, foreshadowing his *primary* and *antithetical* eras, as belonging to
"Ireland and youth" and "England and old age." He admired a
national culture, in which literature was "Greeklike" and "as young
as nature," with a single "wild and pungent Celtic flavor" and a
sympathetic and self-abnegating melancholy. But he also admired, if
reluctantly at first, a cosmopolitan culture, in which literature was "as
old as mankind," the complex possession of a few, with many separate
passions and a subjective, brooding melancholy.[2] Hence, though he
longed to blend Irish nationalism with the medievalism of Ruskin
and Morris and a romantic return to nature, he also longed for a more
cosmopolitan and esoteric era, a "greater renaissance."[3] Blake, he
said, "was the first to announce" this "successor" of the Christian era
and "the first to claim for the imagination the freedom which, Mr.
Pater has told us, was won for the heart by the Renaissance." Blake
also seemed to "foreshadow those French mystics who have taken
upon their shoulders the overcoming of all existing things, and say
their prayers 'to Lucifer, son of the morning, derided of priests and
kings.' "[4] For in the "new romanticism" of Villiers de L'Isle-Adam
and Maeterlinck, a movement "against the external and heterogeneous," Yeats saw the dawn of Blake's pagan day. "Let us wait in
silence," Maeterlinck had said; "perhaps ere long we shall be conscious
of 'the murmur of the gods.' "[5] So viewed, the new era became a
virtual apocalypse.

However, as Yeats listened for the murmur of the gods or dreamed
of Thoreau's beanrows, he was also expecting great violence. Madame
Blavatsky had said that Europe was on the eve of "a cataclysm which
her own cycle of racial Karma" had "led her to." Yeats himself
collected prophecies of war from various countries and, after Cleve-
land's report to Congress on the Venezuelan crisis in 1895, wrote to

Florence Farr: "Has the magical armageddon begun at last?" He had seen an article

> announcing inevitable war and backing it up with excellent argument from the character of Cleveland. The war would fulfil the prophets and especially a prophetic vision I had long ago with the Mathers's, and so far be for the glory of God but what a dusk of the nations it would be? for surely it would drag in half the world.[6]

Throughout his life a similar ambiguity would pervade his expectations of violence.

His attempts to reconcile such differing hopes were vague. He could abruptly and rather unconvincingly relate the Celtic element in literature to contemporary symbolism. Or he could simply declare that Europe would soon enter "an age of imagination, of emotion, of moods, of revelation."[7] That dim future might somehow harmonize medieval unity and Renaissance freedom, or even peace and war. It might symbolize the entire wheel of history, the full round of moods, as experienced in an eternal moment. For that multifoliate rose was the apocalyptic goal toward which, through its very contradictions, Yeats's early historical thought was moving.

That is clear in his poetry, where theories of history merge to produce a complexity quite different from the usual nineties expression of world-weariness. Ernest Dowson's "Epilogue," for example, stands prettily on the page:

> Let us go hence: the night is now at hand;
> The day is overworn, the birds all flown;
> And we have reaped the crops the gods have sown;
> Despair and death; deep darkness o'er the land,
> Broods like an owl...
>
> . . . .
>
> Let us go hence, somewhither strange and cold,
> To Hollow Lands where just men and unjust
> Find end of labour, where's rest for the old,
> Freedom to all from love and fear and lust.
> Twine our torn hands! O pray the earth enfold
> Our life-sick hearts and turn them into dust.[8]

But "The Valley of the Black Pig" opens a remarkable symbolic vista:

The dews drop slowly and dreams gather: unknown spears
Suddenly hurtle before my dream-awakened eyes,
And then the clash of fallen horsemen and the cries
Of unknown perishing armies beat about my ears.
We who still labour by the cromlech on the shore,
The grey cairn on the hill, when day sinks drowned in dew,
Being weary of the world's empires, bow down to you,
Master of the still stars and of the flaming door.

Though "some talk" of MacGregor Mathers' (or the vision reported
to Florence Farr) may lie behind this poem,[9] that is but one of its
elements. Yeats was consciously "seeing all in the light of European
literature" and finding his "symbols of expression in Ireland."[10] Title
and setting recall peasant prophecies of a great battle "to break at last
the power of their enemies";[11] but that Irish victory, paradoxically
becoming an earthly defeat, here symbolizes a European apocalypse.

The dew-drenched vision suggests the end of all cycles, when a
heroic Fergus may barter power for knowledge and become nothing,
knowing or being all. The speaker desires just such a distancing of
turmoil as occurs in the poem's muted violence, and he welcomes the
annihilation that will follow this Armageddon. Though elsewhere
Mongan speaks directly of the "Boar without bristles" which comes
"from the West" (and which kills Adonis and Diarmuid in the Greek
and Irish myths of the year),[12] that destructive beast is here obliquely
called both conqueror of visible light and ruler of the element of fire.
"Where there is nothing...there is God"—or, as Madame Blavatsky
had said, "Darkness, in its radical, metaphysical basis, is subjective and
absolute light."[13] Hence the Irish Black Pig becomes the gnostic
primal darkness, a paradoxical lightbearer or Lucifer who opposes
(with Blake and the "French mystics") the priests and kings of "the
world's empires." Perhaps there is a further semi-Blakean symbolism.
The speaker seems a forced builder of the cromlech or Druid serpent-
temple, image of the closed-in brain of man and of the cyclical empire
of this world, formed when "The ever-varying spiral ascents to the
heavens of heavens / Were bended downward." He prays to one
rather like Blake's destructive initiator of a new era, "flaming Orc,"
whose name, derived from "Orcus," also means "pig" in Irish.[14] But

in this passive vision the Black Pig, like Orcus in early myth, is less a grim or exultant reaper than a god who gently bears men to rest.

Yeats had rapidly expanded his syncretic myth for the wheels of history, of which the Black Pig forms a part. He correlated theosophically John Rhys's *Celtic Heathendom* with Sir James Frazer's *Golden Bough* and concluded that

> the battle between the Tribes of the goddess Danu, the powers of light . . . and the Fomor, the powers of darkness . . . was the establishment of the habitable world, the rout of the ancestral darkness; that the battle among the Sidhe for the harvest is the annual battle of summer and winter; that the battle among the Sidhe at a man's death is the battle of life and death; and that the battle of the Black Pig is the battle between the manifest world and the ancestral darkness at the end of all things; and that all these battles are one, the battle of all things with shadowy decay.[15]

He often alluded to the sunset or shadowy victory that may hide a transcendence of all limiting earthly form. Niamh had longed for the end of the solar cycle in *The Wanderings of Oisin*,[16] and Oisin's third island was the underwater land of the Fomor. Cuchulain (whom Rhys had called a sun-hero) warred "with the bitter tide; / And the waves flowed above him, and he died."[17] In the 1895 revision of "The Madness of King Goll" the Fomorian sorceress Orchil "shakes out her long dark hair / That hides away the dying sun." In "Rosa Alchemica" the immortal woman binds her hair about the narrator and drinks him up. And in "The Binding of the Hair," as crows sweep out of the darkness "like fragments of that sleep older than the world," the beheaded Aodh (or "fire") sings for Queen Dectira. Cuchulain's mother Dechtere, Rhys had said, is "the light that overspreads the sky" after the sun "has just sunk below" the horizon.[18] The transcendent death was also a return to the mother-mistress.

In more directly historical symbolism, the new era of "Rosa Alchemica" combines Blake's pagan day, the return of Heine's and Pater's exiled gods, a quasi-Byzantine setting, the victory of "that mood which Edgar Poe found in a wine-cup," and the Irish resurgence and theosophical Armageddon of "The Valley of the Black Pig."[19] But the fact that the narrator himself is overwhelmed by the *hysterica passio* of that contradictory era indicates that there, as elsewhere in Yeats's early work, the immediate force of the transcendental

yearning is critical and destructive. Existing form is broken down;
the ego is dissolved. It is the initial stage, as I have suggested, in
Yeats's alchemy of the imagination: the corruption from which, according to Avicenna, the new birth may come.[20]

What is evident in that story is fitfully apparent in all of Yeats's
early work. It may seem to describe no more than a romantic leap
into the void or into the Celtic twilight:

> Out-worn heart, in a time out-worn,
> Come clear of the nets of wrong and right;
> Laugh, heart, again in the grey twilight,
> Sigh, heart, again in the dew of the morn.[21]

But its negative force is important: it rejects the claustral and exhausted temporal world and self that have thus far been experienced.
And hidden in the paradoxical emotions associated with that twilight or
void where "God stands winding His lonely horn" is the turbulent
sea most directly faced and presented in "Rosa Alchemica," the
Dionysian abyss. The encounter with that abyss—muted by a
lush conventional rhetoric that serves both as a means of escaping the
"time out-worn" and a protection against the full force of the abyss
itself—is part of the ego's strengthening dialogue with all that it has
excluded or has yet to discover. That dialogue enabled Yeats's later
conservatism to be no timorous rigidity or death but a new birth. He
was learning, before he read Nietzsche, that a strong Apollonian
citadel requires a psychological advance: a radical self-criticism ("the
overcoming of all existing things") and a partial organizing of the
subliminal or Dionysian chaos.

ii.

During the first decade of this century, the alchemical *solve* yielded
to the *coagula,* the boundless to the bounded, and apocalyptic visions
to a conservative order. Yeats discovered that poets must now leave
the heaven of "essences" (to which the narrator of "Rosa Alchemica"
had momentarily risen) and go "downward, taking the soul with
us until all is simplified and solidified again." He was entering the
second stage in the progress of the alchemical Mercury as described by
the "Tabula Smagdarina": "He rises from earth to heaven and

descends again to earth and receives into himself the power of above and below."[22]

The movement downward, which increased Yeats's ability to grapple with the everyday world, also changed his social ideals. As late as 1901 he still sought with William Morris and George Russell to maintain a tradition that "permits even common men to understand good art and high thinking, and to have the fine manners these things can give." He attacked the "new and ignoble" tradition, "perfected and in part discovered by the English-speaking people, that has made great wealth and great poverty" and that "has made already the understanding of the arts and of high thinking impossible outside of a small cultivated class."[23] But during the next few years intellectual values seemed to him increasingly to depend upon a social aristocracy, partly because he was being forced by his theater work into a battle with the bourgeois mind. His visit to America in 1903 brought a momentary loss of tension. Perhaps disarmed, as Matthew Arnold had been, by a numerically but not proportionately larger "saving remnant," he reverted to his former idealism:

> Everywhere in America ... one finds people who are of one's own tribe, liberated souls.... The words of Morris and of Ruskin have found hearers who have listened better because of Thoreau and Emerson; and everywhere one finds one's own table of values.... I had got to think it a necessary part of modern life that my tribe should be very small and that I should look at most men with a little hostility because of their hatred for what I love and their love for all that I hate.[24]

But in Ireland he insisted more and more upon the courtly virtues. "We will not forget how to be stern," he wrote in 1904, "but we will remember always that the highest life unites, as in one fire, the greatest passion and the greatest courtesy." And he found such virtues in the life of the big houses, "Where passion and precision have been one / Time out of mind."[25] The changing political climate had also brought disillusionment. By 1908 he decided that the idealism of the "poor Irish clerk or shopboy," which he had praised in 1901, was "gone, with Fenianism and its wild hopes"—a thought he would later put into "September 1913."[26]

Of course, he could claim that his aristocratic temper itself had been partly formed by John O'Leary's Fenianism, which had been opposed "from the first, though not strongly from the first," by the bourgeois mind that had "made a new nation out of Ireland."[27] But now he stressed aspects of his earlier background that he had once minimized or even rejected. In 1890 he had accused Standish O'Grady of "that love of force common among a certain type of literary men"; in 1904, attacking his own early "region of shadows," he said that he felt "towards it as O'Grady feels towards it sometimes.... As so often happens with a thing one has been tempted by and is still a little tempted by, I am roused by it to a kind of frenzied hatred which is quite out of my control."[28] In 1896 he had thought Blake foreshadowed the "French mystics"; in 1903, revising his essay, he was reminded rather "of Nietzsche, whose thought flows always, though with an even more violent current, in the bed Blake's thought has worn."[29] When discovering Nietzsche in 1902 he had said, "I have not read anything with so much excitement since I got to love Morris's stories which have the same curious astringent joy." But his relish for the astringency was greater than before. He admired increasingly the "strength" that made such a poet as Synge "delight in setting the hard virtues by the soft, the bitter by the sweet, salt by mercury, the stone by the elixir."[30] Of the alchemical opposites that symbolized his ideal balance, it was now the bitter, the salt, that he most needed.

As always, he projected his own progress upon the screen of history. He was no longer in sympathy with his essay "The Autumn of the Body" because in the nineties he had mistaken

> for a permanent phase of the world what was only a preparation. The close of the last century was full of a strange desire to get out of form, to get to some kind of disembodied beauty, and now it seems to me the contrary impulse has come.... The Greeks said that the Dionysiac enthusiasm preceded the Apollonic and that the Dionysiac was sad and desirous but that the Apollonic was joyful and self sufficient.[31]

Though Nietzsche's *Birth of Tragedy* had contributed to that pronouncement of 1903, Dionysian and Apollonian are the "two movements" of the soul ("one to transcend forms and the other to create forms") that Yeats had long known, the "influences" that he had defined in common occult terms as "the Transfiguration on the Mountain and the Incarnation."[32] Nor did he distort Nietzsche's concept of the Dionysian so much as might appear. Though as an unattained transcendence it had often been "sad and desirous" for Yeats, the more exhilarating and terrifying *hysterica passio* of "Rosa Alchemica" would now gain force throughout his career.

Nietzsche also supported the Blakean conception of alternating eras,[33] but the imminent pagan day now seemed to Yeats more Apollonian than Dionysian. With greater violence had come a yet greater desire for a stable order. Partly for that reason, he supplemented Nietzsche with Balzac, going beyond his few favorite volumes to read the entire *Comédie humaine*. Balzac's philosophy interested him "almost more than his drama."[34] "... Nietzsche might have taken," he said later, "and perhaps did take, his conception of the superman in history from his *Catherine de Medici* ..." But Balzac also offered a conservative synthesis: he

> is the only modern mind which has made a synthesis comparable to that of Dante, and, though certain of his books are on the Index, his whole purpose was to expound the doctrine of his Church as it is displayed, not in decrees and manuals, but in the institutions of Christendom.[35]

Now amid greater tension Yeats still wished to reconcile freedom and unity.

As he moved toward a new artistic and social ideal, he was seeking restlessly the historical moments when it might have been realized. In 1899 he had said that the drama has one day of greatness "when the emotions of the cities still remember the emotions of sailors and husbandmen and shepherds" and "another day, now beginning, when thought and scholarship discover their desire." A "Priesthood" like that of pagan esoteric drama might now "spread their religion everywhere and make their Art the Art of the people." But a year later he had lost faith in that priesthood. Only at the "awakening," he now said, in ancient Greece, Elizabethan England, or contemporary Scandinavia, do "great numbers of men" seek in art "a right understanding of life and destiny." They know "that the old revelations are insufficient, and that all life is revelation beginning in miracle and enthusiasm, and dying out as it unfolds itself in what we have mistaken for progress." Though Scandinavia was "passing from her moments of miracle," there was hope for Ireland, a new country rising up against the decaying English metropolis.[36] By 1904 his new focus

was evident. Cervantes, Boccaccio, and the Greek dramatists all "had
the same mind. It is we who are different." The change, which
"followed the Renaissance and was completed by newspaper government and the scientific movement," he described in Blakean terms as
"man falling into his own circumference." Now, rejecting the weari-
ness of life in Maeterlinck as well as in Ibsen, he demanded a theater
where the aristocratic soul might contemplate itself: "joyful, fantastic,
extravagant, whimsical, beautiful, resonant, and altogether reckless."
By 1905, comparing a recent decline with Roman decadence, he could
ask: "Is not that desire for what belongs to common life, whether it
comes from Rome or Greece or England, the sign of fading fires, of
ebbing imaginative desire?"[37]

In "Poetry and Tradition" (1907), taking his stand with a dash of
that recklessness which Castiglione had praised, he sketched an
idealized vision of the Italian Renaissance. And by 1908 he clearly
postponed the miraculous moment of a civilization (the Blakean
moment of divine influx that he had once diagramed)[38] from morning
to noonday, foreshadowing its central place in *A Vision*. "This
moment is impossible until public opinion is ready to welcome in the
mind of the artist a power, little affected by external things, being self-
contained, self-created, self-sufficing, the seed of character." He was
demanding the freedom of that Apollonian principle which he would
later call the subjective or *antithetical* intellect. "Generally up to that
moment," he continued, describing what would become early *primary*
phases, "literature has tried to express everybody's thought, history
being considered merely as a chronicle of facts, but now at the instant
of revelation [the Fifteenth Phase of *A Vision*] writers think the
world is but their palette, and if history amuses them it is but, as
Goethe says, because they would do its personages the honor of
naming after them their own thoughts."[39]

"Rosa Alchemica" had harked back in Swinburnean fashion to a
time before the world had grown grey from Christ's breath, but "At
Galway Races," a poem of 1908, now praised a later cultural peak,
"Before the merchant and the clerk / Breathed on the world with
timid breath." The lunar resurrection of the body prophesied by that
poem required a conservative synthesis like that in Balzac's work.
Hence in 1909 Yeats placed Arthur Hallam's defense of pure poetry,

which had so excited him in the nineties, as a necessary phase in the reaction against a degraded classical morality. He now saw that "the literary element in painting, the moral element in poetry, are the means whereby the two arts are accepted into the social order." Having passed through revolt and purification, the arts were "about to restate the traditional morality." That implied a partial reconciliation of Hellenism and Christianity. The West, Yeats said with approval, had been dominated by Incarnation and hence by power and body; the East he associated implicitly with Transfiguration, with "scorn of the flesh, contemplation of the formless." The Incarnation also implied Greek statues and "that ancient canon discovered in the Greek gymnasium, which, whenever present in painting or sculpture, shows a compact between the artist and society." He correlated that canon of beauty with Blake's "resurrection into unity" and also with Dürer's rediscovery of the ideal form of Adam through measurement of ancient statues.[40] Those diary notes of 1909 would lead directly to the symbolic development in "Dove or Swan" of Phidian Athens and the Renaissance as parallel moments of the "first Adam," and to later poems, "The Statues" and "Under Ben Bulben." Yeats wished now, as he implied in 1910, to "discover thoughts that tighten the muscles, or quiver and tingle in the flesh, and so stand like St. Michael with the trumpet that calls the body to resurrection."[41] For what was the apocalypse now but the reconstitution of ideal Apollonian form?

iii.

During the next decade, vacillating between the opposites with increasing rapidity, Yeats had moments of optimism about the future. In 1913, for example, he said that in the visual arts " 'the fall of man into his own circumference' seems at an end."[42] But the resurrection was still more a hope than an actuality. A poem of that year indicates most exactly how far he had come from his earlier art of Transfiguration:

> Now as at all times I can see in the mind's eye,
> In their stiff, painted clothes, the pale unsatisfied ones
> Appear and disappear in the blue depth of the sky
> With all their ancient faces like rain-beaten stones,

And all their helms of silver hovering side by side,
And all their eyes still fixed, hoping to find once more,
Being by Calvary's turbulence unsatisfied,
The uncontrollable mystery on the bestial floor.

"The Magi," like "The Valley of the Black Pig," transcends historical theorizing—but with striking differences. The speaker himself is no longer a weakly yearning soul; yet, because he need not be specially dream-awakened, his own fate is clearly in question. More important, no longer does life desire death. Yeats has turned from the divine beast of the ancestral darkness to the bestial mystery that begins a new cycle. Hovering, fading, yet strangely solid, the Magi suggest the elements to which life is reduced when the vital synthesis is lost—"the soul a vapour and the body a stone."[43] An indefinite multitude ("all . . . all . . . all"), they imply an era of Transfiguration. As their prototypes sought a reincarnation of Zarathustra and found Christ, so they now seek a new miracle of incarnate life. Fragmented faculties long to return from circumference (sky and stone) to center—to the carnal mystery that is powerfully evoked by the charged abstractions of the last two lines. After the shock of "turbulence," which upsets the incantatory rhythm, the connotations move rapidly from spiritual to bestial, *agape* to *eros,* death or transfiguration to copulation or birth. Years of modifying a Blakean symbolism have brought Yeats closer to the poet who described "pale religious letchery, seeking Virginity" and finding a newborn terror, because "life delights in life."[44] Though the new birth might still be an abstract evocation, the unsatisfied passion had changed its object. Yeats now stood with his St. Michael.

However, because no opposite can gain complete victory, another poem of late 1913 pits the new stress upon life against the former stress upon escape from the wheel. The sleeper of "The Hour before Dawn" envisions not the St. Michael who calls the body to resurrection but his earlier opposite:

For all life longs for the Last Day
And there's no man but cocks his ear
To know when Michael's trumpet cries
That flesh and bone may disappear,

And souls as if they were but sighs,
And there be nothing but God left.

The sleeper's counterimage, repudiating that *primary* wisdom, pummels him, heaps up stone on stone, prays, curses, and goes through that round of life again and again, thanking God only when clouds are "brightening with the dawn."

That dialogue of opposites became increasingly complex as Yeats moved toward the climax of his vision of history. In 1915 "Ego Dominus Tuus" presented, as the heroic discipline behind that disillusioned art which is "a vision of reality," the search for a shadow or anti-self which may conduct the poet to knowledge of his fuller being and, implicitly, to the possibility of rebirth and deliverance from the stream of time in which he is reflected. *Per Amica Silentia Lunae* (1917) developed that thought further and related it to others drawn from the 1909 diary. Both the Middle Ages and the Renaissance were founded on imitation: "St. Francis and Caesar Borgia made themselves over-mastering, creative persons by turning from mirror to meditation upon a mask." That is, we should remember, no ordinary imitation or playing of a role: it is a strengthening dialogue between one's own will and "that other Will," that harlot or Lucifer, the unconscious potential of one's being which speaks through the mask. "The more insatiable in all desire, the more resolute to refuse deception or an easy victory, the more close will be the bond, the more violent the antipathy." The dialogue may even be experienced as a duel: "I sometimes fence for half an hour at the day's end, and when I close my eyes upon the pillow I see a foil playing before me, the button to my face. We meet always in the deep of the mind, whatever our work, wherever our reverie carries us, that other Will." Yeats was making explicit the psychological process that underlay his alchemical romances of 1896. The "heaving circles" of history itself, he could now say, seemed to result from that tension of conscious and unconscious: "every movement, in feeling or in thought, prepares in the dark by its own increasing clarity and confidence its own executioner."[45]

In the same year the "instructors" brought greater clarity and complexity to ideas that Yeats had been developing for over three

decades. Given the fact that Milton's emanation or shadow contained
the cycles of history, and given Yeats's own comment in 1909 on the
marriage of Simon Magus, it must have seemed to him astrologically
and psychologically appropriate that these "instructors" should speak
through his bride. An entire web of projected influences—what he
would now call a "Body of Fate"—was suddenly gathered up into
a single shadow. By the end of November the lunar phases had been
outlined; in December came the gyres which charted European
history.[46]

Characters from the romances were appropriately revived in 1918 to
expound the new wisdom. "The Phases of the Moon" ironically
presents the relation between self and anti-self as seen from the other
side. Robartes and Aherne laugh at Yeats's ignorance, but he is
celebrating the attainment of knowledge, thrusting exultantly at "that
other Will." The apparently *antithetical* Robartes describes the souls'
approach to the *primary* matrix at Phase 1 without sympathy. But at
Phase 15, presumably the fulness of incarnation, the souls attain a
beauty

> Too lonely for the traffic of the world:
> Body and soul cast out and cast away
> Beyond the visible world.

In that *antithetical* consummation, however, the soul does not escape
from the Blakean closed-in cave of the mind, the Satanic labyrinth;
rather it trembles "into stillness," dies "into the labyrinth of itself!"
It is only one extreme of the wheel, not the apocalypse. And Robartes
can say enigmatically even of the Saint's phase:

> The burning bow that once could shoot an arrow
> Out of the up and down, the wagon-wheel
> Of beauty's cruelty and wisdom's chatter—
> Out of that raving tide—is drawn betwixt
> Deformity of body and of mind.

Why "once could shoot"? Only "when we are saint or sage," said
Yeats, "and renounce Experience itself, can we, in imagery of the
Christian Cabbala, leave the sudden lightning and the path of the
serpent and become the bowman who aims his arrow at the centre of

the sun."[47] But the poet himself must renounce that goal; for the sake of his art he must remain in the "ring where everything comes round again." He must make "his home in the Serpent's mouth,"[48] and thus explore the daimonic cycles of history. So for Robartes the bow that once could shoot an arrow out of life remains drawn in the tension of desire. Yet by depicting the entire "wagon-wheel," by fully exploring and representing fallen reality, the poet may attain at least an image of that final release.

Yeats's position here interestingly approximates that of Schopenhauer, with whose work and whose Eastern sources he had long had some acquaintance. For Schopenhauer the poet was similarly "chained to the contemplation of the play":

> he remains beside it, does not get tired of contemplating it and representing it in copies; and meanwhile he bears himself the cost of the production of that play . . . That pure, true, and deep knowledge of the inner nature of the world becomes now for him an end in itself: he stops there. Therefore it does not become to him a quieter of the will, as . . . it does in the case of saint who has attained to resignation; it does not deliver him for ever from life, but only at moments, and is therefore not for him a path out of life, but only an occasional consolation in it . . .[49]

But Schopenhauer had said that "his power, increased by this contemplation and at last tired of the play," will lay "hold on the real": the artist will become the saint.[50] Yeats too saw the poet and tragic hero approaching that consummation at the very end. In 1909, for example, he had seen Hamlet "lingering on the storm-beaten threshold of sanctity," and Shakespeare himself seeking "for wisdom in itself at last, and not in its passionate shadows."[51]

But the ambiguities of that approach must be reserved for later discussion; those of Robartes' position appear again in "The Double Vision of Michael Robartes" (1919), which develops similar material more dramatically. His first vision, by the dark of the moon, is that of *primary* monism:

> Under blank eyes and fingers never still
> The particular is pounded till it is man.
> When had I my own will?
> O not since life began.

His second, by full moon, presents the *antithetical* side of the antinomy
of necessity and freedom. He sees the Sphinx and Buddha ("heraldic
supporters guarding the mystery of the fifteenth phase"),[52]

> And right between these two a girl at play
> That, it may be, had danced her life away,
> For now being dead it seemed
> That she of dancing dreamed.

The human become art, she is no cold artifact but a self-contained
center of activity and contemplation. Yet she is beyond the world—an
Apollonian incarnation that has become one with Dionysian transfiguration:

> Body perfection brought,
>
> For what but eye and ear silence the mind
> With the minute particulars of mankind?
> Mind moved yet seemed to stop
> As 'twere a spinning top.
>
> In contemplation had those three so wrought
> Upon a moment, and so stretched it out
> That they, time overthrown,
> Were dead yet flesh and bone.

However, Robartes does not himself possess this Blakean moment
that Satan's watch fiends cannot find.[53] He remains caught between
the dark moon and the full, though able to arrange his vision in a
song and thus transcend the wheel to which he is subject. The
paradox of his double vision has a specific historical basis. In "A
People's Theatre," also of 1919, Yeats described the increasing physical
and spiritual objectivity of modern times. He imagined the "objective" force as one of two gyres—base to apex and apex to base—the
"two great energies of the world that in Shakespeare's day penetrated
each other" but that have since fallen apart and each come "to greater
freedom." Were it not for the "subjective" gyre "turning inward in
exact measure with the outward whirl of its fellow, we would fall in
a generation or so under some tyranny that would cease at last to be
a tyranny, so perfect our acquiescence." All "visible history" must now

be in harmony with that objectivity, but "the sudden changes, or rather the sudden revelation of future changes, are not from visible history but from its anti-self."

> Blake says . . . that things must complete themselves before they pass away, and every new logical development of the objective energy intensifies in an exact correspondence a counter-energy, or rather adds to an always deepening unanalysable longing. That counter longing, having no visible past, can only become a conscious energy suddenly, in those moments of revelation which are as a flash of lightning. Are we approaching a supreme moment of self-consciousness, the two halves of the soul separate and face to face?[54]

That is the moment reflected in Robartes' split soul. After seeing the objective tyranny, he is granted a revelation of the "always deepening unanalysable longing" that has haunted his dreams. Oppressed by the "commonness of thought," he glimpses in the frenzied sea of revelation the goal of all his sensual and spiritual yearnings. As in "Rosa Alchemica," where Robartes had been a full initiate, the new era seems a virtual apocalypse. However, a vague adumbration of future transcendence has become a firm poetic realization of a life beyond life. Yeats was beginning to reap the fruits of that mercurial ascent and descent advised by the Smaragdine Tablet.

Moreover, that "supreme moment of self-consciousness, the two halves of the soul separate and face to face," is a stage in the development of that distinctively Yeatsian tragedy, which I shall describe later, where the two halves are fused in a single intense moment. Here again there is a striking similarity to Schopenhauer, who had said of the "sublime":

> Then, in the undismayed beholder, the two-fold nature of his consciousness reaches the highest degree of distinctness. He perceives himself, on the one hand, as an individual, as the frail phenomenon of will, . . . helpless against powerful nature, dependent, the victim of chance, a vanishing nothing in the presence of stupendous might; and, on the other hand, as the eternal, peaceful, knowing subject, . . . itself free and apart from all desires and necessities . . .[55]

With Yeatsian modifications, that is the dual nature which Robartes symbolically projects, and which dictates the two positions—that of dramatic experience and that of panoramic vision—in Yeats's dialogue with history.

Another essay of 1919, "If I Were Four and Twenty," further reveals Yeats's position between two fires. Recommending "Unity of Being" to Ireland, he praised recent French literature which expressed "emotional agreement with some historical or local group." "Intellectual agreements, propagandas, dogmas, we have always had, but emotional agreements, which are so much more lasting and put no constraint upon the soul, we have long lacked." Péguy, Jammes, and Claudel, merging past and present and religious and secular, seemed to reconcile unity and freedom. But Yeats's recommendation moved with strange ease toward a more ominous vision. Perhaps "we are restless because we approach a realization that our general will must surrender itself to another will within it, interpreted by certain men, at once economists, patriots, and inquisitors." He then suggested a personal and metaphysical basis for the ambiguity:

> As all realization is through opposites, men coming to believe the subjective opposite of what they do and think, we may be about to accept the most implacable authority the world has known. Do I desire it or dread it, loving as I do the gaming table of Nature where many are ruined but none is judged, and where all is fortuitous, unforeseen?[56]

After that, his final restatement of "Unity of Being" (the swan to that shadow, as in his late letter to Dorothy Wellesley) seems little more than an idealization of the harsher unity he expected.

At one point in the essay he had focused the conflict of unity and freedom, with which he had struggled so long, by means of Balzac's theory of social strife. That theory, he claimed hyperbolically, had changed all his thought. It was a broad view (apparent "only, I think, when one has mastered his whole vast scheme") of a social order created and sustained by "two struggles, that of family with family, that of individual with individual." If our imagination

> has been most affected by individual struggle we insist upon equality of opportunity ... and consider rank and wealth fortuitous and unjust; and if it is most affected by the struggles of families, we insist upon ... social privilege, upon the rights of property.[57]

Yeats kept that theory as one way of rising above momentary political passions: it helped, for example, to form his later outline of "Race Philosophy," which rejects communism and fascism and elaborates the conflict in a series of antinomies. Balzac, he would say, "saved me from Jacobin and Jacobite."[58]

But he was saved only in more balanced moments. He could alternate attacks against censorship with pleas for indoctrination and even for the use of marching men. Like other prophets of twentieth-century violence, he had both a healthy sense of an ideal unity and a dangerous need to replace it with its totalitarian shadow. But, sharing impulses that have bred fascism and sensitive to the values which those impulses deny, he could transcend vacillation in his best poetry and focus that conflict in a remarkably full and intense "vision of reality." That is true of another poem of 1919, which demands comparison with "The Valley of the Black Pig" and "The Magi":

> Turning and turning in the widening gyre
> The falcon cannot hear the falconer...

The strangely compelling quality of those opening lines of "The Second Coming" arises partly from the fact that the orderly operation of centrifugal force (mimed in the assonance pattern) produces uncontrollable disorder. Because the falcon cannot resist the momentum of the gyre movement, it becomes a dangerous agent of violence—a central paradox of determinism and freedom in Yeats's vision of history.

> Things fall apart; the centre cannot hold;
> Mere anarchy is loosed upon the world,
> The blood-dimmed tide is loosed, and everywhere
> The ceremony of innocence is drowned;
> The best lack all conviction, while the worst
> Are full of passionate intensity.

The central problem posed by that forceful summary, according to R. P. Blackmur, is its apparently double source: in Yeats's "magical" system of prophecy and in his observation of the modern world. By what coincidence did both lead to the same conclusion?[59] However, an understanding of Yeats's dialogue with history causes that problem largely to disappear, for the "magic" that I have been describing was not a separate field of investigation but a means of coping with a psychic reality which includes, as one aspect, the correlated schisms in state and soul. Yeats did not simply combine an external analysis of contemporary history with concepts drawn from his "instructors" —or (for that matter) from Pater's account of the gain of centrifugal over centripetal in Plato's day, or from the Delphic Oracle's description of "the bitter waves of blood-drenched life,"[60] or from his own description of the inundating sea in "Rosa Alchemica." He presented with new understanding the psychological and ethical opposites long implicit in his own subjective dialogues.

> The best lack all conviction, while the worst
> Are full of passionate intensity.

Though the language may derive from Shelley,[61] the lines render and judge an evil known through conversation with an interior Lucifer.

This speaker, of course, focuses more clearly upon the social macrocosm than earlier speakers have done, because Yeats's alchemical path has spiraled toward greater inclusiveness. From that basis in mordant perception can now arise the vision itself—with its stammering beginning, its sweeping and somberly weighted climax, and its terrifyingly certain and yet uncertain conclusion:

> And what rough beast, its hour come round at last,
> Slouches towards Bethlehem to be born?

Though the beast has symbolic ancestors—Blake's Orc awakening after eighteen centuries of sleep, the Black Pig visiting blissful destruction upon an exhausted world, the uncontrollable mystery on the bestial floor—it paradoxically transcends them all. It is no herald of an ideal era but the compensatory image which *Spiritus Mundi* or the unconscious sends to one who, himself a mixture of the uncertain "best" and the passionate "worst," hopes for a Second Coming. It slouches as an incompletely specified "shape," its blank and pitiless gaze and its slow thighs conveying more, in juxtaposition to the cradle of Bethlehem, than do all Yeats's systematic explanations.[62] But we are not left with flaccid resignation. The final lines are spoken by one who can maintain his questioning stance even when nearly overpowered by that image erupting from the abyss of himself and of his time.

"Do I desire it or dread it ... ?" Yeats could ask. But he could also say in 1936, "I am not callous, every nerve trembles with horror at what is happening in Europe, 'the ceremony of innocence is drowned.' "[63] There was reason for both question and protest; and the nature of every man's conscious and unconscious complicity would long be a subject for meditation. Following a visionary dialectic between two fires, Yeats had related the depths of his mind and the modern world. "Something more profound, more rooted in the blood than mere speculation ...," as he later said of Balzac, "constrained him to think of the human mind as capable, during some emotional crisis, or ... by an accident of genius, of containing within itself all that is significant in human history and of relating that history to timeless reality."[64] Under such constraint, always qualified by skepticism, Yeats had completed his own long series of historical sketches. He could now present the brilliant and subtly modulated panorama of "Dove or Swan," in which Western history itself ebbs and flows under the influence of the dark moon and the full.

V · DOVE OR SWAN

I must Create a System or be enslav'd by another
Man's.

—Blake[1]

Some system of cycles there must always be for every
historical student, as every man's shadow must fall
somewhere on his own landscape; but, as his shadow
moves with every movement he makes, so his cyclical
view of history will shift and dissolve, decompose and
recompose itself anew ...

—R. G. Collingwood[2]

i.

THE "INSTRUCTORS" HAD HELPED to clarify a pattern that might otherwise have become a mere blur of revisions. Hence, after they had played their catalytic and revelatory role, it seemed to Yeats that the chaos was transmuted:

What they undertook to do
They brought to pass;
All things hang like a drop of dew
Upon a blade of grass.[3]

As he had said three decades earlier, "the grass blade carries the universe upon its point"; that microcosmic dewdrop is itself an image of the philosopher's stone, which being projected upon metals may turn them to gold.[4]

A major product of that alchemy is the panorama of Western history set forth in the section of *A Vision* entitled "Dove or Swan." That panorama was useful to Yeats as an intermediate stage between the raw data of history and the dense symbolism of his poetry, but it is also important in itself. The nature of that importance is underlined by a striking coincidence of which Yeats learned in 1926. As he had been drawing his diagrams of history in 1918, the first edition of Spengler's *Decline of the West* had been going through the press. "Here is a very strange thing," he wrote to Sturge Moore, "which will show you what I meant when I wrote of individual man not being shut up in a bottle." Surely, he thought, there had been some occult communication? "I can almost say...that there is no difference in our interpretation of history (an interpretation that had never occurred to anybody before) that is not accounted for by his great and my slight erudition."[5] Yeats exaggerated, but the similarities are substantial. Of course, the means of communication were more various than he wished to allow: his long acquaintance with symbolic visions of history, from Blake and Coleridge to Pater and Wilde, and his direct or indirect absorption of cyclical theory from such seminal thinkers as Joachim of Flora, Vico, Goethe, Saint-Simon, Carlyle, and Nietzsche—these meant that Yeats already understood much that helped to shape Spengler's own synthesis. However, why Yeats and Spengler should be almost magnetically attracted to such material is yet another question—and one which the strikingly similar metaphorical psychologies of Yeats and Jung may help to elucidate. Though occult systems or accounts of subjective dialogue with the shadow-self cannot (as Yeats knew) ultimately explain our experience, they may serve (as he also knew) to organize many of its most elusive elements and to lead to yet further experiential discoveries. He was fundamentally correct in refusing to accept that metaphor of the closed bottle.

Later on, granting the existence of "errors of historical detail" in Spengler's work, he maintained that it "is, if it were nothing more, magnificent as a work of imagination." And Spengler's own comments on the meaning of such an imaginative work apply with precision to Yeats's "Dove or Swan." Whereas the realm of the Become, Spengler said, is amenable to the techniques of science and is rendered in the

Newtonian nature-picture, the realm of the Becoming, "the organism of a pure history-picture,...is intuitively seen, inwardly experienced, grasped as a form or symbol and finally rendered in poetical and artistic conceptions." It is in effect a rendering of the macrocosm, which Spengler defined succinctly: "actuality as the sum total of all symbols in relation to one soul."[6] Such for Yeats was his *Vision* with its panorama of history.

ii.

"Dove or Swan" is, in fact, a typically romantic achievement: a vision of history as art. And the geometry underlying it is no less typically romantic than its historical symbolism. Wordsworth, comparing his early interest in mathematics to that of a shipwrecked man drawing his diagrams upon the sand, had concluded:

> So was it then with me, and so will be
> With Poets ever. Mighty is the charm
> Of those abstractions to a mind beset
> With images and haunted by herself.

Wordsworth's "clear synthesis" was "an independent world, / Created out of pure intelligence."[7] But such a world need not be a mere escape. Surveying his own career in "The Circus Animals' Desertion," Yeats would ask:

> Those masterful images because complete
> Grew in pure mind, but out of what began?

And his answer—"the foul rag-and-bone shop of the heart"—did not involve a completely new perception. In a veiled account of the coming of the "instructors," the wife of Kusta ben Luka also draws diagrams upon the sand, but

> Those terrible implacable straight lines
> Drawn through the wandering vegetative dream

are the lineaments of an ideal world engaged in a perpetual transaction with the real.

> All those abstractions that you fancied were
> From the great Treatise of Parmenides...
> Are but a new expression of her body.[8]

In other words, unconscious manifestations of the will may have universal meaning. Yeats's account of diagrams upon the sand puts in more contemporary psychological terms what Shelley's Cythna had told Laon:

> "My mind became the book through which I grew
>   Wise in all human wisdom, and its cave,
> Which like a mind I rifled through and through,
>   To me the keeping of its secrets gave—
>   One mind, the type of all, the moveless wave
> Whose calm reflects all moving things that are...
>
> "And on the sand would I make signs to range
>   These woofs, as they were woven, of my thought;
> Clear, elemental shapes, whose smallest change
>   A subtler language within language wrought:
>   The key of truths which once were dimly taught
> In old Crotona."

So, in Blake's phrase, the "vegetable glass" of Nature mirrors the eternal realm.[9]

If, as Yeats's occult tradition had also maintained, the will is transcendental and the world is its mirror or shadow, the poet who interprets such unconscious manifestations may be an ideal historian. The "body" of Kusta ben Luka's wife may express his shadow, his Daimon, his *Body of Fate,* and the cycles of history—even as Blake had described those cycles as "seen in Milton's Shadow, who is the Covering Cherub."[10] In fact, Schopenhauer had compared the "mere, pure historian, who works only according to data," to "a man, who without any knowledge of mathematics, has investigated the relation of certain figures, which he has accidentally found, by measuring them." The poet, however, "is like the mathematician, who constructs these relations *a priori* in pure perception, and expresses them not as they actually are in the drawn figure, but as they are in the Idea, which the drawing is intended to render for the senses."[11] If so, what Coleridge had called Ezekiel's wheels, though dictated by twentieth-century "instructors," might be such an ideal vision.

Ignoring some philosophical differences, Yeats supported his hopes with Croce's study of Vico, which he read in 1924. For Vico an indissoluble connection between subject and object is a prerequisite of knowledge. Therefore only God can know the world of nature, while the demigod man can know *his* creation, history: "Man creates the human world, creates it by transforming himself into the facts of society; by thinking it he recreates his own creations, traverses over again the paths he has already traversed, reconstructs the whole ideally, and thus knows it with full and true knowledge." Vico had even maintained that in an age of "barbarism of the intellect" the necessary antidote to imaginative exuberance should be sought in linear geometry rather than in logic.[12]

Croce noted that nineteenth-century idealism had made Vico's "demigod Man into a God, lifted human thought to the level of universal mind." But Yeats, of course, had long known that deification as taught in an older tradition. Milton's Shadow or the Covering Cherub is "the self devouring serpent," both "the garment of God and his negation"—or, as Madame Blavatsky had put it, both the "Glory of Satan" and "the shadow of the Lord."[13] Envisioning that shadow in its fullness—tracing the coils of that serpent in the cycles of Western history—the poet might realize his own divinity.

Of course, Yeats entertained those hopes with self-irony. But even in more skeptical moods he would have agreed with Collingwood that every historical student must have some "system of cycles," just as his "shadow must fall somewhere on his own landscape." Fastening upon some "peculiarly luminous point" and "trying to study it as it actually came into being," the student necessarily gives a period a "fictitious unity" and sets it in a "fictitious isolation"—but he thereby gives it intelligible form.[14] That is a function of Yeats's cycles as of Vico's or Spengler's. We may ask of any such system: how inclusive and coherent is this shadow upon the landscape of history? And though "Dove or Swan" is a poetic vision rather than a full-scale interpretation of the past, Yeats's geometry itself suggests a remarkable inclusiveness as well as coherence.

His twenty-eight-phase lunar cycle is an attempt to do justice to the antinomies of unity and plurality, objectivity and subjectivity, necessity and freedom, in their historical manifestations.[15] That wheel, like those of Boehme and Blake, "is every completed movement of thought or life, twenty-eight incarnations, a single incarnation, a single judgment or act of thought."[16] It begins in unity with the matrix of Nature at the dark of the moon (complete *primary* or "solar"), moves toward self-conscious individual life at full moon (complete *antithetical* or "lunar"), and then, with the shattering of individual unity, lapses back into the matrix, now conceived as God. When charting history the wheel ordinarily describes a millennium or an "era" of two millennia. The pagan era, beginning about 2000 B.C., is dominantly *antithetical*—"multitudinous," subjective, aristocratic. It is founded upon a spiritual influx coming through Zeus's swan to Leda, from whose two eggs hatched the Heraclitian opposites of Love and War. The first millennium of that era, unknown in detail, rounds its wheel and declines into Asiatic barbarism by 1000 B.C.; the second reaches its full moon or Phase 15 during the time of Phidias and then declines into barbarism as it approaches the new influx (dominantly *primary*—"single," objective, equalitarian), which comes through the dove to Mary. The first millennium of the Christian era reaches its full moon in Byzantium about A.D. 560 and declines into the stagnant life of the eleventh century; the second reaches its full moon during the Renaissance and is now declining toward another "multitudinous" revelation.

But since there are wheels within wheels, the picture is more subtly shaded than any summary can suggest. Every period is half of a period which contains it. Hence every Phase 15 is a Phase 8 or 22 (a point of vital conflict) in a larger wheel; and hence the periods are alternately *antithetical* and *primary,* like the brightening and darkening fortnights in Brahminical symbolism. There are also overlapping wheels. Christ's coming at the beginning of our era (which is a "solar" or religious "month" in the Great Year) is the revelation at Phase 15 of the era of classical civilization (a "lunar" or secular "month," from about 1000 B.C. to A.D. 1050). Yeats thus avoided the Spenglerian view that civilizations are hermetically sealed entities. He also introduced with some humor the precession of the equinoxes in order "not to suggest, as Vico did, civilisation perpetually returning to the same point."[17] And his visualization of the wheel as two interlocking cones or gyres, each winding and unwinding a thread of time—one of which corresponds to the "religious" and "vital" impulse, the other to the "political" and "secular" impulse—helped to present the internal dynamics of each phase.

This geometry, of which I suggest only the barest rudiments, is far more complex than that of most historical system-builders. It allows for conflict and continuity, recurrence and novelty. It allows for uncertainty, because the number of wheels is theoretically infinite, and for a freedom like that which the Brahman knows, because the "particulars" of history "are the work of the *thirteenth sphere* or cycle which is in every man and called by every man his freedom."[18] Though such complexity does not actually enter the panorama of "Dove or Swan" at every point, Yeats's system was no mere Procrustean bed. Its main outlines helped to control his imagination; its myriad complications invited him always to discover yet further delicate shading within the bold pattern of history which he set forth. The system thus enabled him clearly yet subtly "to hold in a single thought reality and justice,"[19] to present a panoramic judgment of Western achievements in the light of ideals most fully realized at the "peculiarly luminous points" which he called "full moon."

iii.

After being given the geometry, Yeats turned to fresh historical authorities for help in breathing life into the dry symbolic bones. Any agreement now excited him and renewed his faith in his own undertaking. The ease with which he assimilated the work of three important writers indicates not only his unacademic and rather uncritical syncretism but also the typical form of his vision of history and its unusual breadth.

He found in Flinders Petrie's *The Revolutions of Civilisation* the seasonal analogy that he had frequently met in the nineties. The summer of the Renaissance was ending, but an understanding of the Great Year might give courage for the future. Yeats could agree with Petrie that a cultural cycle begins in rigid archaism, "attains its flexible maturity and then sinks into rigid age."[20] And Petrie's use of sculpture as an index of cultural development must have been stimulating and corroborative. However, though both considered Periclean Athens a cultural peak, Petrie followed it with only one European cycle, whose greatest achievements range from 1250 (sculpture) to

1600 (literature). Byzantine art would be for him a rigid archaism. But the cycles result from a point of view: Yeats valued not only the "westward moving" (humanistic or dominantly *antithetical*) ideals of Hellenic and Renaissance culture, but also the "eastward moving" (transcendental or dominantly *primary*) ideal of Byzantium.[21]

Nor did he fully share the vision of Henry Adams, though in 1921 he wrote with characteristic excitement: "I have read all Adams and find an exact agreement even to dates with my own 'law of history.'" However, Adams saw not gyres but a long parabolic curve charting the acceleration of Western culture. The first important change, he thought, occurred with Constantine's conversion in 310, and increasingly great changes of phase followed about 1600 (from the religious to the mechanical), 1900 (to the electric), and 1917 (to the ethereal). After 1921 acceleration would become inconceivably great.[22] This at least reinforced Yeats's pattern at certain points: the victory of the new *primary* impulse, at Phase 8 of the first millennium; the fragmentation of Europe after Phase 15 of the second millennium; and the rapidly approaching end of our era. Also important to Yeats, no doubt, were Adams' frequent contrasting of thirteenth-century unity and twentieth-century multiplicity, his comparison of civilization to a comet approaching its perihelion, and his very Yeatsian remarks upon the motive forces of history:

> the theory will have to assume that the mind has always figured its motives as reflections of itself, and that this is as true in its conception of electricity as in its instinctive imitation of a God. Always and everywhere the mind creates its own universe, and pursues its own phantoms; but the force behind the image is always a reality,—the attractions of occult power.[23]

In *The Origin of Christian Church Art,* by Josef Strzygowski, that "most philosophical of archeologists,"[24] Yeats found an account of the conflict between Northern abstract and Southern representational art that seemed to reinforce the historico-geographical symbolism that he had taken over, with modifications, from Blake. Northern art was for Yeats *primary,* and Southern was *antithetical.* He thought too that Strzygowski described the "symbolic East" when he attributed to Eastern nations "conceptions that dazzle and astonish by an impression of power," and the "symbolic West" when he presented it as "that which absorbs and uses, and is a kind of matrix."[25] But the fourfold symbolism was a tenuous interpretation, to which Yeats did not always hold. Usually—and with support from Strzygowski—he combined East and North in "symbolic Asia," the force of spirit or *primary* transcendence, and West and South in "symbolic Europe," the force of body or *antithetical* immanence.[26]

The wheel of each era, said Yeats, "must be thought of as the marriage of symbolic Europe and symbolic Asia, the one begetting upon the other. . . . Christ or Christendom was begotten by the West upon the East. This begetting has been followed by a spiritual predominance of Asia. After it must come an age begotten by the East upon the West that will take after its Mother in turn." This view was partly supported by Strzygowski, who had "repeatedly called attention to the fact that Hellas died early in the embrace of the East." Yeats said that after Alexander "Greek civilisation, formalised and codified, loses itself in Asia." He agreed that Christ came "at a time of intellectual and spiritual satiety."[27] Then, according to Strzygowski, began a "new age," which "first relapsed into the ways of the old Semitic East, then gradually found its true course in that artistic sense of the Northern peoples and the pastoral nomads which drew its inspiration from Iran." This art triumphed over the Western "Christian classical art" and maintained its growth until about A.D. 400.[28]

That account appears to support Yeats's vision of an Asiatic and Byzantine millennium. Indeed, though Strzygowski did not admire the later imperial Byzantium,[29] his preference for abstract, Asiatic art contrasts sharply with Petrie's preference for European art that celebrates the idealized human form. But Yeats, because of the breadth of his own synthesis, could rejoice in the support of both authorities. His initial simplification of their work could contribute to the final complication of his own. Less historian than poet, he read not to criticize but to create.

iv.

No summary of its geometry or examination of a few of its sources, however, can adequately suggest the rich texture of "Dove or Swan."

For that we must turn to the detailed organization and stylistic rendering of Yeats's vision. He believed that

> Our towns are copied fragments from our breast;
> And all man's Babylons strive but to impart
> The grandeurs of his Babylonian heart.

His panorama of Babylons built and destroyed therefore projects upon a temporal landscape that apocalyptic moment—the moment of the multifoliate rose—in which the soul "contemplates all the events of its memory and every possible impulse."[30] He says in effect with Emerson: "I believe in Eternity. I can find Greece, Asia, Italy, Spain and the Islands,—the genius and creative principle of each and of all eras, in my own mind." Or with Thoreau: "All the events which make the annals of our nations are but the shadows of our private experiences. Suddenly and silently the eras which we call history awake and glimmer in us, and *there* is room for Alexander and Hannibal."[31]

That is why, though "Dove or Swan" seems to move back and forth between Yeatsian myth and rather neo-Hellenic history, it remains a coherent reverie. The mood sometimes suggests Pater, but rarely here are purple passages disconcertingly separate from more abstract discussion. All is condensed and fused. The style combines that of prophetic vision (so confident in its smooth flow, its ellipses, its uncanny use of co-ordination) and that of individual speculation (tentative and searching in its qualifications, its reliance upon personal experience, its confessions of ignorance). It is an ironically balanced prose, rich in provocative comparisons and aphorisms.

Occasionally, it is true, Yeats's prose moves toward a self-indulgent aloofness: "Each age unwinds the thread another age had wound, and it amuses one to remember that before Phidias, and his westward-moving art, Persia fell, and that when full moon came round again, amid eastward-moving thought, and brought Byzantine glory, Rome fell; and that at the outset of our westward-moving Renaissance Byzantium fell . . ."[32] We may then recall Kierkegaard's admonition that

> world-history is the royal stage where God is the spectator, where He is not accidentally but essentially the only spectator, because He is

the only one who *can* be. To this theater no existing spirit has access. If he imagines himself a spectator here, he merely forgets that he is himself an actor on the stage of the little theater

—that of the ethical drama of the individual.[33] In terms of Yeats's subjective dialogue, such indulgence results from the ego's claim to power over that which is revealed to the visionary self. It is, as I have suggested, a constant temptation—one which may cause the prophetic poet to lapse into the state of Hérodiade amid that monotonous land, the mirror-image of her pride, and one which is dramatized in the fall of Aherne in "The Tables of the Law." But usually in "Dove or Swan" Yeats maintains a finer balance: it is the panoramic or God's-eye view of history—but the landscape is seen as through a glass somewhat darkly.

Among its richest and most balanced parts are those describing the three periods of full moon. As the Greek full moon approaches, Yeats calls attention to the "horizontal dance" of opposites (*primary* and *antithetical,* Eastern and Western) which combine in the moment of apparent perfection:

> Side by side with Ionic elegance there comes after the Persian wars a Doric vigour, and the light-limbed dandy of the potters, the Parisian-looking young woman of the sculptors, her hair elaborately curled, give place to the athlete. One suspects a deliberate turning away from all that is Eastern, or a moral propaganda like that which turned the poets out of Plato's Republic, and yet it may be that the preparation for the final systematisation had for its apparent cause the destruction, let us say, of Ionic studios by the Persian invaders, and that all came from the resistance of the *Body of Fate* to the growing solitude of the soul. Then in Phidias Ionic and Doric influence unite—one remembers Titian—and all is transformed by the full moon, and all abounds and flows.[34]

Taking his cue from Nietzsche, Pater had described that dance of opposites and its resolution.[35] Shelley had glimpsed that moment of unity in what Yeats had once called the "half-understood vision" at the climax of *Prometheus Unbound,* when "all things flow to all," man becomes "one harmonious soul of many a soul," and the moon's snow is "loosened into living fountains."[36] But the style here fusing such elements is characteristically Yeatsian: a vigorous opening sentence in which the cadences themselves enact the yielding of Ionic to

Doric; a long and tentative sentence which suspends before us various psychological, historical, or mythical causes for this transformation; and a concluding sentence which swiftly combines historical perception and Yeatsian myth, with the help of a casual parenthesis glancing at the Renaissance full moon two millennia later. The total effect is an image of change that combines clarity of foreground with a calculated indistinctness of background—a bold symbol that seems to emerge from the acknowledged complexity of life.

"With Callimachus pure Ionic revives again, as Furtwängler has proved"; and Yeats sketches "in masters and man a momentary dip into ebbing Asia" and then the decline: "Aristophanes' passion-clouded eye falls before what one must believe, from Roman stage copies, an idler glance.... Aristotle and Plato end creative system—to die into the truth is still to die—and formula begins."[37] The ironic balance of that parenthetical aphorism sets the tone for the coming *primary* or "solar" phases. But, as the following passages suggest, the Yeatsian ironies are various. They may, first of all, flower in an almost lyric vision:

> When I think of the moment before revelation I think of Salome— she, too, delicately tinted or maybe mahogany dark—dancing before Herod and receiving the Prophet's head in her indifferent hands, and wonder if what seems to us decadence was not in reality the exaltation of the muscular flesh and of civilisation perfectly achieved. Seeking images, I see her anoint her bare limbs according to a medical prescription of that time, with lion's fat, for lack of the sun's ray, that she may gain the favour of a king, and remember that the same impulse will create the Galilean revelation and deify Roman Emperors whose sculptured heads will be surrounded by the solar disk. Upon the throne and upon the cross alike the myth becomes a biography.

Beginning with dark Salome and the Prophet's head (a solar sacrifice like that when the Fomorian sorceress "Orchil shakes out her long dark hair/That hides away the dying sun") the solar symbolism weaves through this passage of suspended judgment, unifying sacred and secular. The ironic gains and losses that occur when myth becomes biography later informed the densely evocative poem "Veronica's Napkin." After some reading in Mommsen's *The History of Rome,* Yeats envisioned Christ and Caesar more fully as parallel yet antipodal figures.[38]

Again, the irony may become sharper. According to the new *primary* impulse, "God is now conceived of as something outside man and man's handiwork, and it follows that it must be idolatry to worship that which Phidias and Scopas made, and seeing that he is a Father in Heaven, that Heaven will be found presently in the Thebaid, where the world is changed into a featureless dust and can be run through the fingers"—a sardonic twist given to Blake's vision of infinity in a grain of sand. "All must be narrowed to the sun's image cast out of a burning-glass and man be ignorant of all but the image."[39] Yet this is not mere deprecation; and in "Demon and Beast" Yeats had presented that solar consummation more ecstatically, though still with ironic overtones.

Or again, the irony may assume the form of an apparently neutral description. At first the *primary* impulse is completely separate from its antithesis: "All about it is an *antithetical* aristocratic civilisation in its completed form, every detail of life hierarchical, every great man's door crowded at dawn by petitioners, great wealth everywhere in few men's hands, all dependent upon a few, up to the Emperor himself who is a God dependent upon a greater God, and everywhere in court, in the family, an inequality made law." Misled by the poise of the irony here—or else too eager to convict Yeats of protofascism—George Orwell said that these words describe Yeats's anticipated ideal civilization. But the passage continues, "All is rigid and stationary," and the art is significantly that of a conventional realism.[40]

Despite the assumptions of a good many critics, it should be clear that Yeats's historical sympathies and antipathies are not simple, that his prose is constantly shaped by the pressure of ironic qualifications. This is true even when his enthusiasm is obvious:

> I think if I could be given a month of Antiquity and leave to spend it where I chose, I would spend it in Byzantium a little before Justinian opened St. Sophia and closed the Academy of Plato. I think I could find in some little wine-shop some philosophical worker in mosaic who could answer all my questions, the supernatural descending nearer to him than to Plotinus even, for the pride of his delicate skill would make what was an instrument of power to princes and clerics, a murderous madness in the mob, show as a lovely flexible presence like that of a perfect human body.[41]

Here *primary* and *antithetical* merge in a dominantly solar full moon, a subjective yet transcendental and corporate ideal. However, though the final image can suggest Greece and the Renaissance, in this solar era—with its acknowledged power and madness—the human body appears very obliquely in the artifice of mosaic.

Similar qualifications occur throughout Yeats's description of early Byzantium. He imagines that "religious, aesthetic and practical life were one, that architect and artificers—though not, it may be, poets, for language had been the instrument of controversy and must have grown abstract—spoke to the multitude and the few alike." All "were almost impersonal, almost perhaps without the consciousness of individual design, absorbed in their subject-matter and that the vision of a whole people." However, the splendor they created is "no representation of a living world but the dream of a somnambulist." Amidst "an architecture that suggests the Sacred City in the Apocalypse of St. John," their vision fuses pagan and Christian elements in an image of the soul's transcendent ideal:

> this vision, this proclamation of their invisible master, had the Greek nobility, Satan always the still half-divine Serpent, never the horned scarecrow of the didactic Middle Ages.... Could any visionary of those days, passing through the Church named with so un-theological a grace "The Holy Wisdom" ... fail to recognise some one image seen under his closed eyelids? To me it seems that He, who among the first Christian communities was little but a ghostly exorcist, had in His assent to a full Divinity made possible this sinking-in upon a supernatural splendour, these walls with their little glimmering cubes of blue and green and gold.[42]

Human life, seemingly denied, is transmuted into the golden cubes of a transcendental art. In alchemical terms, this is the ascetic's "transfiguration upon the golden ground of Byzantine mosaic." In theosophical terms, the assent of half-divine Son to full divinity is a reconciliation with the half-divine Serpent. It seems a momentary apocalypse, sun and moon, *Deus* and *Demon* reconciled. Under the dome of "The Holy Wisdom," Son and Serpent return to their single form: the Logos, the "Blazing Dragon of Wisdom."[43]

As an image of wholeness, the Byzantium of "Dove or Swan" grew also from the ideal which Yeats saw approximated in pre-Raphaelite painters and in that "master-work of the Romantic movement," the Stockholm Town Hall, where all "that has not come out of the necessities of site and material, no matter in what school the artist studied, carries the mind backward to Byzantium." The many artists, "myth-makers and mask-makers," worked in seemingly perfect freedom and harmony. "All that suggestion of novelty and of the immeasurable past; all that multitude and unity, could hardly have been possible, had not love of Stockholm and belief in its future so filled men of different minds, classes, and occupations that they almost attained the supreme miracle, the dream that has haunted all religions, and loved one another." In those remarks Yeats was not far from Blake's dicta, "The Eternal Body of Man is The Imagination," and "Christianity is Art."[44] However, the builders of Blake's Golgonooza have bosoms that beam "With all colours of precious stones . . . Displaying Naked Beauty,"[45] whereas Yeats's Byzantine artificers ironically display that beauty only through lifeless mosaic.

Renaissance artists, like those of Phidian Athens, would seek a different alchemical *lapis,* that of "profane perfection," symbolizing and promoting not "transfiguration" but "incarnation." (Indeed, in the more defiantly humanistic later years of his life, Yeats would entirely omit Byzantium from his panorama: "Civilisation rose to its high tide mark in Greece, fell, rose again in the Renaissance but not to the same level."[46]) As the gyres run on toward that time, secular and religious impulses again separate.[47] Then, the religious full moon over, the Embodiment of God "shall grow more like ourselves, putting off that stern majesty, borrowed, it may be, from the Phidian Zeus—if we can trust Cefalù and Monreale; and His Mother—putting off her harsh Byzantine image—stand at His side." Here, in symbols that recall Adams' comparison of the Virgin of France and the Virgin of Dreux, appears "the first vague dawn of the ultimate *antithetical* revelation." Mother and Son begin to approximate Venus and Adonis —in accord with a progression like that in Blake's "Mental Traveller." Man, "under the eyes of the Virgin, or upon the breast of his mistress, became a fragment. Instead of that old alternation, brute or ascetic, came something obscure or uncertain that could not find its full explanation for a thousand years."[48] History now moves by way of courtly love toward the deification of the concrete individual.

Yeats sees "in Romanesque the first movement to a secular Europe, but a movement so instinctive that as yet there is no antagonism to the old condition."[49] And having relocated most medieval virtues in Byzantium, he has come far enough from his youthful admiration for Ruskin and Morris to write: "I do not see in Gothic architecture . . . as did the nineteenth-century historians, ever looking for the image of their own age, the creation of a new communal freedom, but a creation of authority, a suppression of that freedom though with its consent."[50] The "Church grows secular that it may fight a new-born secular world." By 1250 or 1300 the King has mastered chivalry, the Church has mastered Christendom—"reversing the achievement of Constantine, for it was now the mitre and the crown that protected the Cross." Dante "writes the first sentence of modern autobiography, and in the *Divina Commedia* imposes his own personality upon a system and a phantasmagoria hitherto impersonal; the King everywhere has found his kingdom." Then, Yeats adds—characteristically fusing causes of very different kinds—the transcendental Image, "itself encouraged by the new technical method, the flexible brush-stroke instead of the unchanging cube of glass, and wearied of its part in a crowded ghostly dance, longs for a solitary human body."[51]

But the Renaissance also had the defects of its qualities. Full moon of the millennium and Phase 22 of the era, it was "the breaking of the Christian synthesis" just as the age of Phidias was "the breaking of the Greek traditional faith."[52] That made possible a "reconciliation of Paganism and Christianity" quite different from that in Byzantium —a reconciliation which

> meant to the mind of Dürer . . . that the human norm, discovered from the measurement of ancient statues, was God's first handiwork, that "perfectly proportioned human body" which had seemed to Dante Unity of Being symbolised. The ascetic, who had a thousand years before attained his transfiguration upon the golden ground of Byzantine mosaic, had turned not into an athlete but into that unlabouring form the athlete dreams of: the second Adam had become the first.[53]

Correlated with Biblical typology, Dürer's great work becomes an apt symbol: reconstitution of the first Adam through measurement (associated with power and body) is the rediscovery of the humanistic norm, in contrast to the ascetic's imitation of Christ, the second Adam, and its correlated art of transfiguration.

Later, in "Long-Legged Fly" and "Under Ben Bulben," Yeats would associate the first Adam with the vigor of the Sistine Chapel frescoes; but here Phase 15 itself brings those artists whom he had especially admired in early life—Botticelli, Crivelli, Mantegna, and Leonardo da Vinci—who "make Masaccio and his school seem heavy and common by something we may call intellectual beauty or compare perhaps to that kind of bodily beauty which Castiglione called 'the spoil or monument of the victory of the soul.'" (". . . when she with heavenly influence beareth rule over martiall and grosse nature," added Castiglione's Bembo, "and with her light overcometh the darknesse of the body.")[54] Yeats later developed the intuition appropriate to this moment of transcendental humanism in the mind's history, "the premonition of some perfection born out of itself": "Does not one discover in the faces of Madonnas and holy women painted by Raphael or da Vinci, if never before or since, a condition of soul where all is still and finished, all experience wound up upon a bobbin? Does one not hear those lips murmur that, despite whatever illusion we cherish, we came from no immaturity, but out of our own perfection like ships that 'all their swelling canvas wear'?" The "bobbin" is Yeatsian in its homeliness and its geometrical allusion, but it helps to focus Pater's vision of La Gioconda as "a beauty wrought out from within upon the flesh, the deposit, little cell by cell, of strange thoughts and fantastic reveries and exquisite passions." For she who had been Leda and St. Anne embodied the old "fancy of a perpetual life, sweeping together ten thousand experiences."[55]

The limitations of this art are suggested by its dreamlike nature, and are delicately underlined by the contrasting art of the next gyre. Then "the forms, as in Titian, awaken sexual desire—we had not desired to touch the forms of Botticelli or even of Da Vinci—or they threaten us like those of Michael Angelo, and the painter himself handles his brush with a conscious facility or exultation. The subject-matter may arise out of some propaganda as when Raphael in the Camera della Segnatura, and Michael Angelo in the Sistine Chapel, put, by direction of the Pope, Greek Sages and Doctors of the Church, Roman Sybils and Hebrew Prophets, opposite one another in apparent equality." The willfulness evident in that dictated synthesis will increasingly affect even those who resist the modern search for mere "*primary* information" and seek to establish "*antithetical* wisdom": "Blake, Coventry Patmore at moments, Nietzsche, are full of a morbid excitement. . . . They were begotten in the Sistine Chapel and still dream that all can be transformed if they be but emphatic." Even now Yeats might have included his own name on that list.[56] In old age, his shadow on the landscape of history shifting as he moved, he would turn to this later point in the Renaissance to find reflected the sexual desire, the force, the conscious facility and exultation of his own poetry.

The gyres run on, charting the fragmentation and abstraction of the last three centuries—toward Phase 23, "the first where there is hatred of the abstract, where the intellect turns upon itself," and where Yeats finds Pound, Eliot, Joyce, and Pirandello; toward that tyranny of the general will, that frozen decadence, after which the age will reverse itself. Again will come the "brood of Leda, War and Love; history grown symbolic, the biography changed into a myth." Then man "will no longer separate the idea of God from that of human genius, productivity in all its forms." But that new era, for all of Yeats's evident approval, will be no true Eden or New Jerusalem, "seeing that the day is far off when the two halves of man can define each its own unity in the other as in a mirror, Sun in Moon, Moon in Sun, and so escape out of the Wheel."[57] Before that true apocalypse —when swan and shadow are completely reconciled and the subjective dialogue with history may end—man continues the cyclical enactment of all his potentialities.

v.

Like most romantic visions of "eternal ideal history,"[58] "Dove or Swan" seems deterministic if taken literally or finally. That could hardly be otherwise, for the external and panoramic nature of the vision prevents Yeats from rendering more than the harsher side of the antinomy of freedom and necessity. Apparent freedom of action re-emerges when, in his poetry, he views history from the "inside," as dramatic experience. But even this external view of history implies another kind of freedom, central to Yeats's poetic theory: that known in contemplation. As I have indicated, the full rendering of the cycles implied for even the early Yeats an aesthetic apocalypse. In

"Dove or Swan" he projected upon a temporal landscape that apocalyptic moment in which the soul "contemplates all the events of its
memory and every possible impulse." By this time he had explored
more fully that movement from will to intellect which is experienced
by the poet or visionary who passes through the realm of the cycles into
that of the apocalypse.

In *The Unicorn from the Stars,* for example, Martin Hearne (whose
name relates him to Yeats's other visionary birds) is inspired by a
"frenzy" to transform the world but then learns, "What I have to
pierce is the wild heart of time. My business is not reformation but
revelation." In "Dove or Swan" Nietzsche too has the "morbid excitement" of one who would transform the world, but "when the doctrine
of the Eternal Recurrence drifts before his eyes, [he] knows for an
instant that nothing can be so transformed."[59] That movement appears, with gradually increasing clarity, in all of Yeats's work: the
will, abandoning itself, yields to intellect; desire yields to self-knowledge. Appropriately, the second edition of "Dove or Swan" omits
all description of the future and cuts short the panorama at this point:

> I can recognise that the limit itself has become a new dimension,
> that this ever-hidden thing which makes us fold our hands has begun
> to press down upon multitudes. Having bruised their hands upon that
> limit, men, for the first time since the seventeenth century, see the
> world as an object of contemplation, not as something to be remade,
> and some few, meeting the limit in their special study, even doubt if
> there is any common experience, doubt the possibility of science.

Strictly speaking, this is a *primary* insight, coming with the last quarter
of the moon. Henry Adams had said that history would "bring
Thought to the limit of its possibilities in the year 1921."[60] In concluding position, however, this statement recalls Schopenhauer, whose
doctrine of the artist's release from the wheel of will into free contemplation probably helped to shape Yeats's own as it had shaped
that of an earlier poetic historian: "Contemplation . . . ," said Burckhardt, "is not only the right and duty of the historian; it is also a
supreme need. It is our freedom in the very awareness of universal
bondage and in the stream of necessities."[61]

But Yeats went beyond that doctrine in an important respect. Contemplation, though not willful, is not passive or static. In fact, if we

renounce the desire to remake the world, we may learn how to change it in the only possible way. For when the ego abdicates, it frees a deeper self which is "not I"—a self which can say, "we would not change that which we love,"[62] and which can therefore allow the forces of a continual creation to flow through it. Most artists seem to have recognized this as a paradoxical fact of experience. Some in the Occident have explained it in Christian terms; Yeats himself explained it in various ways, depending upon his momentary philosophical bearings. In his later years he often relied upon an organic philosophy derived partly from Coleridge—and hence his concluding reference in "Dove or Swan" to the seventeenth century. The "mischief began," he said elsewhere, "at the end of the seventeenth century when man became passive before a mechanized nature." Paradoxically, that "mechanic philosophy" which produced the revolutionary faith in "levers" also, as Coleridge had said, "turned the human mind into the quicksilver at the back of a mirror."[63] But just as such mechanical action to transform the world implies a mental passivity, so true contemplation is intensely active. It is an organic part of the creative processes of the cosmos. Yeats believed, therefore, that in the artist the mirror must again "turn lamp," enabling him to become in his contemplative moment both "predestinate and free, creation's very self."[64] In such phrases he reformulated that alchemical shattering of the objective mirror and distilling of the luminous drop of gold which had concerned him since the time of his apocalyptic romances, and which properly symbolized both the artist's transcendence of the cyclical world and his imaginative growth within that world.

In this context "Dove or Swan" may assume its full meaning as a romantic vision. Emerging from a long exploration of the symbolic uses of historical "fact," given a basic structure by an ambiguously psychological and metaphysical geometry, and amplified with material gleaned from a wide variety of poetic, philosophical, and historical works, "Dove or Swan" dramatizes Yeats's central belief that the acceptance of history is at one with freedom and creativity. Of course, he did not accept an "objective" history, a chronicle of facts as perceived by historians whose minds had become mirrors. He transmuted such facts—not through a desire to remake the world, but as the consequence of assuming a "subjective" or fully human point of view. If his vision has the necessarily limited scope of his own mind, it has also the fullness and equanimity which result from his having accepted an "ideal history": the full round of human potentialities, the various forms of action, passion, and contemplation. That ideal history—a complex image of the rich and yet limited human condition—he projected symbolically upon the temporal landscape of "Dove or Swan."

When "man has withdrawn into the quicksilver at the back of the mirror," said Yeats, "no great event becomes luminous in the mind."[65] But in "Dove or Swan" the mirror has turned lamp. Events become luminous: they have the radiance of indefinitely suggestive symbols, microcosms of the visionary's total universe. The smithies of "Byzantium" have broken the flood, the gong-tormented sea of time, and subdued it to the golden forms of the mind. "Entering into the imagination," as Yeats had once called the Blakean apocalypse, was no longer a passive communion with the essences of art; it was an imaginative grasp of the tensions of life. For Yeats, therefore, this vision of Ezekiel's wheels was no grim fatalism. It brought the freedom of contemplation and heralded a surge of creative activity beyond any that he had yet known.

VI · THE LIDLESS EYE

Never did eye see the sun unless it had first become
sunlike...
          —Plotinus[1]

                              ...these eyes
By water, herb and solitary prayer
Made aquiline, are open to that light.
          —"Ribh at the Tomb of Baile and Aillinn"

---

i.

THOUGH YEATS HAD FOUND "a good net for a herring fisher," a
system that might be successfully dipped into the sea of life,[2] the
detailed vision of "Dove or Swan" was but a momentary achievement—
as he had foretold, in effect, when describing Phase 17. In that phase,
where he placed himself, mental images "flow, change, flutter, cry out,
or mix into something else." The *Will* is falling asunder. "The separated fragments seek images rather than ideas, and these the intellect
... must synthesise in vain, drawing with its compass-point a line that
shall but represent the outline of a bursting pod." A poet of Phase 17
(whose *Body of Fate* is "loss" and whose *Mask* is "simplification by
intensity") may if successful become a Dante who sees "all things set
in order."[3] Yeats, however, gained but a series of fragmentary
glimpses.

Nevertheless, poems that do not attempt a full God's-eye view of
history may be the solider for their skepticism, irony, and humility.

In them the perspective of dramatic experience may qualify and deepen that of panoramic vision. They may even be utterances arising from that precarious moment when the speaker has become "naked under the heavens," when he has earned the right to glimpse from his angle of vision the panorama which "Dove or Swan" claims to present in full. And because the visionary's ego is then more completely in abeyance, Kierkegaard's warning against imagining a human access to the royal stage of world history may seem nearly irrelevant. It is not Yeats that speaks but his art that speaks through him.

When he then attributed the piercing vision and simplified point of view to dramatic characters, he was not merely objectifying and distancing his own ideas. As he asked Sean O'Casey in 1928:

> Do you suppose for one moment that Shakespeare educated Hamlet and King Lear by telling them what he thought and believed? As I see it, Hamlet and Lear educated Shakespeare, and I have no doubt that in the process of that education he found out that he was an altogether different man to what he thought himself, and had altogether different beliefs.[4]

That assertion emerged from his own long educative dialogue with the shadow or anti-self. Three decades earlier Michael Robartes had cried: "There is Lear, his head still wet with the thunder-storm, and he laughs because you thought yourself an existence who are but a shadow, and him a shadow who is an eternal god . . ."[5] Characters or "moods" had often spoken to that effect, sardonically reversing the egocentric conception of swan and shadow. By the 1920's Yeats was well prepared to understand Pirandello's somewhat similar studies of the ironic dialogue between character and author, mask and life, mirror and ego—just as he would have understood Jung's later remark: "It is not Goethe who creates *Faust*, but *Faust* which creates Goethe."[6]

However, though believing that literature results from "a dumb struggling thought seeking a mouth to utter it,"[7] Yeats obviously did not believe the poet to be merely passive. He could describe the conscious intellect as operating negatively: "I hold as Blake would have held also, that the intellect must do its utmost 'before inspiration is possible.' It clears the rubbish from the mouth of the sybil's cave but it is not the sybil."[8] But he also saw its positive function: "A dramatist can help his characters to educate him by thinking and studying everything that gives them the language they are groping for through his hands and eyes, but the control must be theirs, and that is why the ancient philosophers thought a poet or dramatist Daimon-possessed."[9] Even a poet of Phase 17 (for whom "expression of *Daimonic* thought" is relatively easy) may therefore play dramatic roles in his personal life. "A good scenario . . . puts words into the mouths of all its characters while we sleep."[10] The poet, he said, after arduously fitting himself for a role, may, like the player of the *Commedia dell' Arte,* while improvising "discover or reveal a being which only exists with extreme effort, when his muscles are as it were all taut and all his energies active."[11] At such moments of active receptivity, the moods may speak through him.

Playing his role of "simplification by intensity," Yeats could say to himself, "I know nothing but the novels of Balzac, and the Aphorisms of Patanjali";[12] but he could also lend a voice to Old Tom, the Hermit Ribh, and other moods. These visionary speakers, for all their differences, have a certain family identity, which is evident most quintessentially in the saints or fools. They are "Eastern" or "solar" types, whose "eye is fixed upon the sun and dazzles."[13] They are related not to the lunar swan which rides the storm or drifts on the darkening flood but to its alchemical opposite, the eagle, which Yeats had called the "lidless eye that loves the sun."[14] They represent, in other words, not so much the active soul or *Will* which is conscious of its immersion in the realm of opposites as the contemplative soul or *Creative Mind* which has partly transcended that realm through identification with the source of being. The "*Will* has a natural desire for the *Mask* and the *Creative Mind* a natural perception of the *Body of Fate*; in one the dog bays the Moon, in the other the eagle stares on the Sun by natural right."[15]

Saint and fool may therefore become revelatory microcosms, reflecting from their point of view the panorama of history. The saint who possesses intellect, said Yeats, "will use it but to serve perception and renunciation. His joy is . . . to permit the total life, expressed in its humanity, to flow in upon him and to express itself through his acts and thoughts." The saint will even assert: "Man does not perceive the truth; God perceives the truth in man." The yet more plastic fool, the traditional "Child of God," would "at his best . . . know all wisdom if he could know anything."[16] However, when such characters and their near relations speak in these poems, they are not merely *primary* or Eastern, not merely abstracts of *Creative Mind*. Active *Masks* sought by Yeats's own *Will,* and seeking to speak through that *Will,* they necessarily and fortunately have some delight in conflict, some relish for Western humanism. Their utterances, therefore, not only provide fresh views of the panorama of history but also shed light on the nature of Yeatsian "vision" itself—that process of creative perception, ambiguously human and divine, active and passive, which harmonized for him the egocentric and the transcendent.

ii.

An extreme form of the microcosmic vision of history is the gnomic utterance, such as "Fragments," which conveys the "emotion of multitude" by presenting "the little limited life of the fable, which is always the better the simpler it is, and the rich, far-wandering, many-imaged life of the half-seen world beyond it."[17]

> Locke sank into a swoon;
> The Garden died;
> God took the spinning-jenny
> Out of his side.

As Locke sinks into Blake's "Single vision & Newton's sleep" he causes the death of several Gardens. The doctrine of the *tabula rasa,* reducing the mind to quicksilver at the back of the mirror, spells death to the Grove of Academia, where Plato's heirs maintained the existence of a more active perception, and to the garden of Platonic forms itself (More's Soul of the World), which, as Yeats knew, Spenser could still celebrate as the Garden of Adonis.[18] This post-Renaissance reenactment of the loss of Eden results, in Blakean and Platonic fashion, from the division into sexes: "Such was that happy garden-state," Marvell had said in "The Garden," "While man there walked without a mate . . ." Though elsewhere imagining "the 'primary qualities' torn from the side of Locke" while "some obscure person somewhere" invented the spinning jenny,[19] Yeats here wittily merges the two events—for the "primary qualities," abstracted and incarnated by what Whitehead called the "fallacy of misplaced concreteness," form that mechanical Nature which man has wed and exploited but which (like a Blakean "emanation" or harlot) threatens to overwhelm him with her own demonic force.[20] Yeats had read Whitehead's statement that every university now organizes itself in accordance with Locke's views, but he had much earlier read Blake's:

> I turn my eyes to the Schools & Universities of Europe
> And there behold the Loom of Locke, whose Woof rages dire,
> Wash'd by the Water-wheels of Newton: black the cloth
> In heavy wreathes folds over every Nation . . .[21]

That loom (a harlot weaving old England's winding sheet) is imaged in Yeats's spinning jenny, even as Blake's Urizen (whose compass-point, like that of the intellect in Phase 17, charts the fall into division) is imaged in the God of this poem.[22]

But, as the second fragment indicates, the poem's real source is not literary:

> Where got I that truth?
> Out of a medium's mouth,
> Out of nothing it came,
> Out of the forest loam,
> Out of a dark night where lay
> The crowns of Nineveh.

A fanciful claim to authority? Yes, but also an evocation of that indescribable matrix which accounts for the gnomic wit and exhilaration of the first fragment. The poet's truth has come from that fruitful void which, in defiance of Lockean psychology, is the repository of all things dead and the source of all things reborn. Hence the poem itself, in a very Yeatsian paradox, is made possible by the continuing life of that principle whose "death" it describes. And hence the speaker, accepting that "loss" which is part of his modern fate, also knows in delighted contemplation the mystery of a continuous creativity.

Such paradoxes allow Yeats's visions of history to balance truths and countertruths with more breadth of judgment than most critics' descriptions of *primary* and *antithetical* imply—as in the equally gnomic "Veronica's Napkin":

> The Heavenly Circuit; Berenice's Hair;
> Tent-pole of Eden; the tent's drapery;

Symbolical glory of the earth and air!
The Father and His angelic hierarchy
That made the magnitude and glory there
Stood in the circuit of a needle's eye.

Some found a different pole, and where it stood
A pattern on a napkin dipped in blood.

Ecstatic contemplation of one pole yields to laconic recognition of another, with perhaps an undertone of poignancy. Yet here too is the "emotion of multitude." In Ibsen's *Emperor and Galilean* the Christians had sung of those two poles with simpler fervor:

Doomed is the world's proud cedar-tree,
The axe shall its roots dissever;
The palm He planted on Calvary,
Blood-watered, shall bloom for ever.[23]

For Yeats (as for Ibsen) the first tree is both Hebraic and pagan: tent pole of the paradisal garden, the world-tree Yggdrasil, polestar, the pole of the revolving earth itself—as Yeats had learned long ago from Goblet d'Alviella and Madame Blavatsky.[24] It is also the pole of Blake's paradisal world, the glory created by the angelic forces of the imagination: "The sky is an immortal Tent built by the Sons of Los."[25] It bears as drapery or foliage the Heavenly Circuit of Plotinus,[26] the macrocosm flowering—as Buddha or Ribh would know— from the "Inexhaustible Point."[27] The second tree, however, is a bare pole on which the God Himself is crucified. Though now the "myth becomes a biography," the "tree has to die before it can be made into a cross."[28]

Again, tent pole and drapery of the first tree suggest Frobenius' image of the Cavern, "identified in the Hermetic Fragments with the Heavens," which Yeats associated with the *antithetical,* time-oriented culture of Father and hierarchical multitude of angels. The bare pole and the ensuing apostolic journeys of those who "found" there a "pattern" of life suggest Frobenius' image of the Altar and radiating roads, which Yeats associated with the *primary,* space-oriented culture of the equalitarian imitators of the Son.[29] Even the minute particulars in this poem carry out the ironic contrasts. Father and angelic hierarchy, though infinitely small, were anthropomorphic images which "stood," and from them flowed power. Later, though the divine became human, the pole alone "stood"; the God was suspended, the human image reduced to a "pattern." Whereas the fruit of one tree included among its riches Berenice's Hair, miraculous image of violence committed and mortal love made eternal, the fruit of the other was Veronica's Napkin, miraculous image of violence undergone and divine love become mortal.

It is "only by ancient symbols," said Yeats, ". . . that any highly subjective art can escape from the barrenness and shallowness of a too conscious arrangement, into the abundance and depth of nature. The poet of essences and pure ideas must seek in the half-lights that glimmer from symbol to symbol as if to the ends of the earth, all that the epic and dramatic poet finds of mystery and shadow in the accidental circumstance of life."[30] So it is in "Veronica's Napkin," and Berenice's Hair brings further "abundance" to the poem partly by its recall of Yeats's own celebrations of enduring love in a cyclical cosmos. That image explicitly enters "Her Dream," where the concluding lines—

> And after nailed upon the night
> Berenice's burning hair

—answer an interrogatory conceit of Henry More's:

> That famous star nail'd down in Cassiopee,
> How was it hammer'd in your solid sky?[31]

It is implicit elsewhere, as in "He Wishes His Beloved Were Dead," where like the Heavenly Circuit the hair is "bound and wound/About the stars and moon and sun," and more obliquely in "His Bargain," where "all the windings" of that hair are eternal, not merely subject to the windings of "Plato's spindle."[32] Something like it even glimmers in "Who Goes with Fergus?" where the landscape becomes a feminine macrocosm:

> . . . the shadows of the wood,
> And the white breast of the dim sea
> And all dishevelled wandering stars.

And that "half-light" glimmers on to Pope, who had written:

Not Berenice's locks first rose so bright,
The heav'ns bespangling with dishevell'd light.[33]

Far more dramatic, as visions of alternating eras and of the interaction of human and divine, are "Two Songs from a Play." The
musicians of *The Resurrection,* unfolding and folding the curtain, rend
the veil between us and the drama of death and rebirth at the heart
of time:

> I saw a staring virgin stand
> Where holy Dionysus died,
> And tear the heart out of his side,
> And lay the heart upon her hand
> And bear that beating heart away . . .

The climax of beating repetition gives almost tactile force to that
violently destructive rescue by an unnamed virgin who is no mere
Athene but includes some qualities of Demeter and even of the
murderous Hera (all of whom in other legends perform this role of
saving the heart to make possible rebirth).[34] And the lines echo
Blake's account of that myth of mistress, mother, and murderess:

> She binds iron thorns around his head,
> She pierces both his hands & feet,
> She cuts his heart out at his side
> To make it feel both cold & heat.[35]

But the musicians' song quickly moves from such empathic participation to release in a distanced vision—a shift characteristic of Yeats's
double perspective on history:

> And then did all the Muses sing
> Of Magnus Annus at the spring,
> As though God's death were but a play.

In the second stanza, from that lofty vantage point, the meaning
of the "play" appears. Shelley had modified the tenor of Virgil's
Fourth Eclogue by introducing, at the end of the final chorus of *Hellas,*
the horrifying vista of endless cycles. But this song has anticipated
and emotionally assimilated that fate—just as "The Nineteenth Century and After" has transformed the melancholy "grating roar/Of

pebbles which the waves draw back," in Arnold's "Dover Beach," to the "keen delight" of "The rattle of pebbles on the shore/Under the receding wave."

> Another Troy must rise and set,
> Another lineage feed the crow,
> Another Argo's painted prow
> Drive to a flashier bauble yet.

The tone renders the Muses' transcendence of human heroism and also a passionate identification with it—and does so, strangely enough, in the very driving force of the contemptuous epithets. Such resonance is one indication of the Yeatsian fusion here of *Creative Mind* and *Will*, contemplative acceptance and active desire.

But the visionary gaze returns from the distant future to the immediate sacred drama, now seen clearly, with Christ as the reborn Dionysus and the maternal and destructive qualities of the virgin now dominant:

> The Roman Empire stood appalled:
> It dropped the reins of peace and war
> When that fierce virgin and her Star
> Out of the fabulous darkness called.

"Appalled" has the ambiguity given it by Blake in "London," where "the Chimney-sweeper's cry/Every black'ning Church appalls": the Empire pales before the goddess who has prepared its pall or winding sheet and whose call from the darkness may therefore suggest that of the harlot, heard "thro' midnight streets."

The closing song gradually shifts from that divine drama to a complementary human one:

> In pity for man's darkening thought
> He walked that room and issued thence
> In Galilean turbulence;
> The Babylonian starlight brought
> A fabulous, formless darkness in;
> Odour of blood when Christ was slain
> Made all Platonic tolerance vain
> And vain all Doric discipline.

Blake had told how Albion or "Dark'ning Man walk'd on the steps of fire before his halls" and Luvah rose "a Shadow from his wearied intellect"; and how later, terrified by this night of religion, Albion cried: "Why roll thy clouds in sick'ning mists? . . . O cruel pity!"[36] Seen as Orc, Luvah is the "new born terror," the turbulent initiator of a new era, wearing "dark robes of blood, or cloud," and also associated with the starlight that symbolizes Urizen's "darkened intellect," abstract and mathematical.[37] But this stanza is no simple condemnation of man's idolatry. Christ's pity, however limited and limiting, is a genuine sympathy for man's falling condition. Like "Veronica's Napkin," the stanza closes with an intense objective statement that strangely subsumes both the Christian attitude and its antithesis. The divine sacrifice made vain the merely natural virtues of Greek culture and offered a superior mode of salvation—yet the images also evoke the spectacle of a sober and restrained culture maddened like some beast by the odor of blood. The Asiatic or centrifugal, in its spirituality and bestiality, has defeated the European or centripetal.

The second stanza seems to contemplate a purely human process of reversal:

> Everything that man esteems
> Endures a moment or a day.
> Love's pleasure drives his love away,
> The painter's brush consumes his dreams;
> The herald's cry, the soldier's tread
> Exhaust his glory and his might . . .

With that preparation the stress may shift, ending the song (with a paradox like that of "Fragments") not in a lament for exhaustion but in a celebration of that mysterious source which is continuously feeding a Phoenix conflagration:

> Whatever flames upon the night
> Man's own resinous heart has fed.

The marvelous word "resinous" evokes the hot richness of the flame, the dense and aromatic source, the pine tree of Attis, the Tree of Life flowering from the heart of Adam Kadmon (the generic "Man's . . . heart" reinforcing that effect), and the torches of the Bacchantes who celebrate this Dionysian drama of death and rebirth that is now seen as immanent in all history.[38]

It has been argued that the closing lines are, in their stress upon human creativity, "slightly out of key with the insistence of the rest of the two songs on divine miracle."[39] But there is a clear if elliptical progression from the initial sacred drama, through the divine-human interaction, to the final human drama. The Muses sang "As though God's death were but a play" partly because, from the necessary and yet limited perspective of the closing lines, the songs dramatize a metaphorical projection of the life that flows through man. The "play," however, is more than play; the metaphor points to something more than metaphor. The "beating heart" of the first song and the "resinous heart" of the second are partial images for the same inexplicable force. To the complaint that this is a mystery, that Christ or Dionysus must be either God or Man, the play itself retorts by disposing of those rational heresies (in effect, the Docetist and Ebionite) held by Greek and Hebrew, and ending with the conviction that "there is always something outside knowledge, outside order." As Heraclitus said, "God and man die each other's life, live each other's death."[40] No less than the orthodox Christian, Yeats needed the symbol of incarnation to focus the paradoxes of a world in which every act is also a suffering, every creation a discovery, every death a rebirth.

iii.

That divine-human polar reality at the heart of all power and knowledge, at the unknowable center of the cycles of history, is glimpsed from yet different points of view in other poems. "Leda and the Swan" begins, like "Two Songs from a Play," with overwhelming empathic participation: "A sudden blow: the great wings beating still . . ." After subjecting us to that incursion of a starkly physical power, the octave prolongs the hovering moment of anticipation and moves from direct perception into questions that heighten our awareness of the swan's nature even as they imply the speaker's imperfect apprehension of the event:

> How can those terrified vague fingers push
> The feathered glory from her loosening thighs?

> And how can body, laid in that white rush,
> But feel the strange heart beating where it lies?

Another violent movement carries us into the wider perspective of history:

> A shudder in the loins engenders there
> The broken wall, the burning roof and tower
> And Agamemnon dead.

The alien ecstasy of creation produces—and *is,* proleptically—man's shudder at the violence of destruction. The richly human middle term in that generative series (Helen, Clytemnestra, the Dioscuri) is brutally dropped from view, and the act of generation itself reverberates in the emotional arc of its consequences—"broken wall," "burning . . . tower," and "Agamemnon dead." This moment, in Blake's phrase, "Is equal in its period & value to Six Thousand Years," for

> all the Great
> Events of Time start forth & are conciev'd in such a Period,
> Within a Moment, a Pulsation of the Artery.[41]

Heine had said, "Under Leda's productive hemispheres lay in embryo the whole Trojan world, and you could never understand the far-famed tears of Priam, if I did not first tell you of the ancient eggs of the Swan."[42] But for this speaker, man is less a self-confident creator than a questioning victim:

> Being so caught up,
> So mastered by the brute blood of the air,
> Did she put on his knowledge with his power
> Before the indifferent beak could let her drop?

Postcoital indifference merges with the indifference of that destructively creative power toward the vessels of its impulse, and the climactic question almost answers itself by being asked. The visionary speaker, at least, feels the power that courses through history without being able to understand it.

But may Leda, in suffering a more complete violation than that suffered by this speaker, have been momentarily opened to fuller vision? When the walls are broken, the veils rent, light may flood the soul. The speaker's question therefore points beyond himself toward more completely visionary harlots, fools, and saints. We are left here, however, with the feel of that "strange heart beating" and that still more uncannily autonomous "shudder"—a physical yet more-than-physical spasm that is the source of all life and death. Physical "beating"—of wings or heart or loins—renders, as in "Two Songs from a Play," that violently assaulting mystery of incarnation ("brute blood of the air") which produces all dramas of incarnation.

A quieter poem about Western history, "Wisdom," approaches the divine-human center through a witty argument concerning creative perception. This speaker seems to stress man's own conscious powers —yet irony already appears in his bold statement that the artifacts themselves and not the artists are active:

> The true faith discovered was
> When painted panel, statuary,
> Glass-mosaic, window-glass,
> Amended what was told awry
> By some peasant gospeller;
> Swept the sawdust from the floor
> Of that working-carpenter.

The last phrase merges the faith and its artistic discovery: as the Carpenter was discovered by one of comparable craft, so the richer, "amended" image was disclosed by a more subtly endowed art.

> Miracle had its playtime where
> In damask clothed and on a seat
> Chryselephantine, cedar-boarded,
> His majestic Mother sat
> Stitching at a purple hoarded
> That He might be nobly breeched . . .

That "Miracle" recalls the assent of the half-divine Son to full divinity as described in "Dove or Swan," and the transmutation of Christ into the child Wisdom by this artistic alchemy is analogous to the ascetic's "transfiguration upon the golden ground of Byzantine mosaic" under the dome of another "Wisdom," Hagia Sophia. But the event resists historical placement. Because the poem may rely upon a seventeenth-century painting in the Italian Renaissance tradition, T. R. Henn has placed it in the Renaissance.[43] The poem, however, does not describe a painting: after introductory reference to various media, it leads us (much as the conclusion of "Lapis Lazuli" does) through the idea of an artifact into a visionary realm. Moreover, the Mother in the painting Henn cites is neither "majestic" nor clothed in "damask," nor is her seat "chryselephantine." Such details carry us toward the East. When Yeats speaks of the "stern majesty" of religious figures, he has Byzantium in mind, and a majesty "borrowed, it may be, from the Phidian Zeus." And the Phidian Zeus itself was "chryselephantine, its main fabric cedar."[44] Pater had discussed that ornamental art at length, as exemplifying the Ionic or Asiatic influence which, in Phidias, was harmonized with the Doric or European. Just so, the diction of the wittily formal pronouncement of "Wisdom"—which presents an eclectic historical apocalypse—harmonizes "miracle" and "play-time," "chryselephantine" and "cedar-boarded," "majestic" and "stitch-ing," "nobly" and "breeched."

But one more Eastern detail carries the poem beyond the Renaissance, Byzantium, or Phidian Greece. This Mother resides

> In starry towers of Babylon
> Noah's freshet never reached.

That condescending allusion recalls Blake's assertion that Noah, Shem, and Japhet represent "Poetry, Painting & Music, the three Powers in Man of conversing with Paradise, which the Flood did not Sweep away."[45] Art—as "conversation" or dialogue—is simultaneously a human creation and a transcendental revelation, by which man gains access to a realm beyond the flood of space and time. In Babylon's towers man therefore glimpses, through his own creative effort, his own majestic creators—a familial Trinity which Ribh could worship, residing like the Kabbalistic Supernals in their transcendental Ark:[46]

> King Abundance got Him on
> Innocence; and Wisdom He.
> That cognomen sounded best
> Considering what wild infancy
> Drove horror from His Mother's breast.

The poem's casual levity has moved toward a piercing profundity—
"got" catching up the paradox of transcendental "blood" treated in
other poems, and "That cognomen sounded best" wittily pointing the
relativity of all symbols for the unknowable creative process. The concluding lines, like the art they describe, banish horror without taming
the world's intensity. For Yeats as for Blake wildness or "excess" is
an active force known in and through art. The traditional infant
Lamb of faith becomes, in effect, a young Lion inhabiting Blake's
realm of higher Innocence—or the "Blazing Dragon of Wisdom" itself.

Similar paradoxes appear in "Sailing to Byzantium," in which a
voyage to a specific point in history is a Plotinian voyage beyond all
history, and in which monuments of the soul's magnificence reveal
sages standing in God's holy fire. The generic "Soul" comes to seem
both egocentric and transcendent, and the carefully unspecified golden
"form" for which the speaker yearns suggests both human construct
and Platonic idea. As an imagined transmutation of the active and
passionate speaker into the realm of transcendental contemplation, that
form also invites comparison with the iconography of the Mundaka
Upanishad: "Like two birds of golden plumage, inseparable companions, the individual self and the immortal Self are perched on the
branches of the selfsame tree. The former tastes of the sweet and
bitter fruits of the tree; the latter, tasting of neither, calmly observes."
By the end of the poem the speaker has almost reached the point
where the two birds—soulbird and sunbird, the yearning old man and
the golden form—become one: in the striving yet contemplative voice
that sings of "what is past, and passing, and to come" within *this*
"artifice of eternity." The poem thus evokes that Phoenix nest upon
the Tree of Life (as Yeats described it in another passage dealing
with the same cluster of symbols) which holds "the passion that is
exaltation and the negation of the will."[47] It fuses what he, like
Schopenhauer, called the two halves of the soul.

"Byzantium," of course, elaborates yet more richly these ambiguities of craft and inspiration, creation of new life and death to this
life, in that realm inhabited by

image, man or shade,
Shade more than man, more image than a shade

as by

> Miracle, bird or golden handiwork,
> More miracle than bird or handiwork . . .

In each poem the speaker moves on his winding path or whirlpool-turning[48] toward the timeless, through the sea of generation toward the condition of fire, which descends to meet him by way of its own gyre or winding path. Then may occur on the pavement of Byzantium what Blake had described as occurring in his "Holy City":

> From the clotted gore & from the hollow den
> Start forth the trembling millions into flames of mental fire,
> Bathing their limbs in the bright visions of Eternity.

That archetypal image of spiralling mutual approach, embodied in a long tradition of ritual and iconography, is an apt symbol for the paradoxes of Yeats's creative perception. The meeting point of the two gyres may suggest that combination of incarnation and transfiguration which occurs when the poem itself translates the turbulent *rota* of history into passionate stillness, the "gong-tormented sea" of "mire and blood" into "an agony of flame," or Blake's "Bloody Deluge" into "living flames winged with intellect."[49]

iv.

The "mood" or character who most fully illustrates such paradoxes is the Hermit Ribh, an Irish Christian before the coming of St. Patrick, one "whose Christianity had come from Egypt, and retained characteristics of those older faiths that have become so important to our invention."[50] Like Emerson's Plato or Pater's Phidias, he balances West and East, lunar and solar, *Will* and *Creative Mind*. Yeats, of course, who balanced Balzac and Patanjali in his mind, offered ample opportunity for Ribh to speak through him. In 1929 he wrote that Frobenius, about whom Pound had been talking,

> has confirmed a conception I have had for many years, a conception that has freed me from British liberalism and all its dreams. The one heroic sanction is that of the last battle of the Norse Gods, of a gay struggle without hope. . . . Science is a criticism of Myth. There would be no Darwin had there been no Book of Genesis, no electron but for the Greek atomic myth; and when the criticism is finished there is

not even a drift of ashes on the pyre. Sexual desire dies because every touch consumes the Myth, and yet a myth that cannot be so consumed becomes a spectre.

I am reading William Morris with great delight, and what a protection to my delight it is to know that in spite of all his loose writing I need not be jealous for him. He is the end, as Chaucer was the end in his day, Dante in his, incoherent Blake in his. There is no improvement: only a series of sudden fires, each though fainter as necessary as the one before it. We free ourselves from obsession that we may be nothing. The last kiss is given to the void.[51]

That letter strangely modulates, as Yeats describes a process which *A Vision* assigns to the increasingly *primary* phases, from the gay struggle to retain the doomed heroic individuality into the quieter acceptance of that "last kiss"—the Kabbalistic death of the kiss in which the individual returns to the God of negative theology. Under both the Western and the Eastern attitudes, and sustaining their paradoxical union, is an acceptance of the historical process—in Western civilization or in a single life—which makes possible the creation of the new through the relinquishment of the old. In this Yeats is close to Blake:

> . . . he who kisses the joy as it flies
> Lives in eternity's sun rise.[52]

It is that sunrise which, in his own richly ironical way, Ribh sees with eyes that have been made "aquiline"—or, as Plotinus had it, "sunlike"—sharing in essence that light which they perceive and thus, like the eagle's lidless eye, staring on the sun by natural right.

In "Ribh at the Tomb of Baile and Aillinn," that light emanates from an ambiguously sexual and spiritual source: the conflagration of the "intercourse of angels" who are transfigured lovers. It is the light of the apocalyptic resolution of opposites—man and woman, love and death, body and spirit, human and divine—the completeness attainable only beyond purification by tragedy, in the element of both light and dark fire. This sun of man's being, behind both swan and shadow, corresponds to what Yeats called his own "mood between spiritual excitement, and the sexual torture and the knowledge that they are somehow inseparable," and it has often been described by alchemical formulas which bear a striking similarity to Yeats's version of the myth of Baile and Aillinn.[53] But Ribh himself is not quite beyond the realm in which one must say "somehow inseparable": the light is broken by the leaves, and the aquiline eye (as becomes increasingly clear in later songs) implies not simply the eagle's "natural right" but also the soaring individual will that struggles toward such vision.

In "Ribh Denounces Patrick" and "Ribh in Ecstasy" the solar visionary describes that spiritual and sexual energy which creates him —of which he is the fallen shadow and to which he now has but intermittent access. His momentary ecstasy—as he states in "Whence Had They Come?"—is shared by all, when "Dramatis Personae" speak through them. And those "moods" play out the drama of history:

> Whence had they come,
> The hand and lash that beat down frigid Rome?
> What sacred drama through her body heaved
> When world-transforming Charlemagne was conceived?

The heaving drama in the body of Rome, whose frigidity had prepared in the dark its own violator, is one with the shudder within Leda's body, at an earlier point in the history of man's passionate subjection to the power that flows through him.

The cyclical form of that history is presented by Ribh in "The Four Ages of Man":

> He with body waged a fight,
> But body won; it walks upright.
>
> Then he struggled with the heart;
> Innocence and peace depart.
>
> Then he struggled with the mind;
> His proud heart he left behind.
>
> Now his wars on God begin;
> At stroke of midnight God shall win.[54]

Some four decades earlier, we recall, Yeats had described that cycle ("a hieroglyphic for human life" and "for the life of creeds and societies") as followed by Blake's Urizen, and in 1934 he attributed a similar vision of European history to Balzac.[55] But Ribh's emphasis is distinctive. For him all development is a losing struggle, followed by death into a new matrix. Hence a series of defeats can move ironically through enforced humility toward that consummation which had been described in "Ribh Considers Christian Love Insufficient." That poem had also moved from assertion of self to loss of self—turning Ribh's diligent hatred against the theological projections of the self in a way that has long been exploited as a psychological technique in Bhakti Yoga, a way that Emerson too could understand: "When we have broken our god of tradition and ceased from our god of rhetoric, then may God fire the heart with his presence."[56]

> Then my delivered soul herself shall learn
> A darker knowledge and in hatred turn
> From every thought of God mankind has had.
> Thought is a garment and the soul's a bride
> That cannot in that trash and tinsel hide:
> Hatred of God may bring the soul to God.

The "stroke of midnight" may then announce the soul's divine marriage and death into true life: "How can she live till in her blood He live!" But the full cost has been exacted, and the last couplet of "The Four Ages of Man" is even less optimistic in tone: the defeat for the ego or selfhood is final.

Ribh's view of that consummation was foreshadowed in 1909 when Yeats described Hamlet as "lingering on the storm-beaten threshold of sanctity," and Shakespeare himself as seeking "for wisdom in itself at last, and not in its passionate shadows." Again in 1917 he said:

I shall find the dark grow luminous, the void fruitful when I understand I have nothing, that the ringers in the tower have appointed for the hymen of the soul a passing bell.
The last knowledge has often come most quickly to turbulent men, and for a season brought new turbulence.[57]

Ribh is such a man: engaged in the wars of the fourth age, awaiting the midnight ringers in the tower, he wryly describes in the third person his own progress.

He has almost attained that imaginative resurrection symbolized in Blake's *Milton* by the raising of Lazarus, after which, Yeats had said, the Covering Cherub (or the Serpent of history, Milton's Shadow) "persists only as something recognized as wholly apart from life and imagination, awaiting the day when it can be cast out as no

longer needed for a resting-place for the soul." It is both "the body
of Christ put off upon the Cross and the tomb where that body
rests." It is no longer seen as a cycle of twenty-seven Churches, but
divides into four: "Paul, Constantine, Charlemagne—head, heart,
loins—correspond to the three days of His repose in the tomb, and
Luther to the day of his resurrection from the dead."[58] Hence Ribh
tersely presents the tomb of this life in four ages (though his sequence
runs "loins, heart, head, soul") and not, as the unregenerate Michael
Robartes had presented the wheel, with fond contemplation of twenty-
eight phases.

Ribh can say of those four states, as Blake's Los had said: "behold,
they stand before us / Stretch'd over Europe & Asia! come O Sons,
come, come away!"[59] His farewell in "Meru" is again a curious
mixture of Eastern and Western, and again both elements had a
long history in Yeats's own mind. Though he had noted in 1934
that at some religious full moon one could "find some cavern upon
Meru, and so pass out of all life," Madame Blavatsky had acquainted
him with that mountain long before—as symbol of Heaven, mythically
located at the North Pole, and corresponding to the seventh occult
principle or pure Soul.[60] In his own work such movement Eastward
out of life had often been very easy. The Wise Man of *The Hour
Glass* declares:

> We perish into God and sink away
> Into reality—the rest's a dream.

But he must also have known Thoreau's more vigorously Western
view of that willed yet destined course:

> Let us . . . work and wedge our feet downward through the mud and
> slush of . . . appearance . . . , through church and state, through poetry
> and philosophy and religion, till we come to a hard bottom and rocks
> in place, which we can call *reality*. . . . The intellect is a cleaver; it
> discerns and rifts its way into the secret of things. . . . My instinct
> tells me that my head is an organ for burrowing, as some creatures
> use their snout and forepaws, and with it I would mine and burrow
> my way through these hills.

In 1909, seeing Eastern intelligence as dangerous to the tasks of Western life, Yeats had said, "All civilisation is held together by the
suggestions of an invisible hypnotist—by artificially created illusions.

The knowledge of reality is always in some measure a secret knowledge. It is a kind of death."[61] Now, however, the "mood" groping through Yeats's vacillations and qualifications has found its full language:

> Civilization is hooped together, brought
> Under a rule, under the semblance of peace
> By manifold illusion; but man's life is thought,
> And he, despite his terror, cannot cease
> Ravening through century after century,
> Ravening, raging, and uprooting that he may come
> Into the desolation of reality:
> Egypt and Greece, good-bye, and good-bye, Rome!
> Hermits upon Mount Meru or Everest,
> Caverned in night under the drifted snow,
> Or where that snow and winter's dreadful blast
> Beat down upon their naked bodies, know
> That day brings round the night, that before dawn
> His glory and his monuments are gone.

Ribh is perilously balanced. His valediction pays tribute to a heroically destructive endeavor that is willed, yet hated, and predestined. The sonnet's octave moves like the fatal logic it describes: premise, premise, and conclusion. But after the second premise, with its alliterative expansion and starkly abstract goal, the conclusion erupts in a strangely gay farewell to the glory that was Greece and the grandeur that was Rome. Partly the joy of the Eastern sage released from the wheel, it is also the heroic banter of the Norse gods in their final struggle—or of Yeats's rather un-Sophoclean chorus: "a gay goodnight and quickly turn away."[62] Then in the sestet logic and farewell yield to a vision informed with Western ideals and Eastern pessimism, as we are led ineluctably back from physical experience to historical perception. The barrel-hoops of civilization are one with the cycles of nature; and that early vision of "unwinding the soft threads" and standing "naked under the heavens" has acquired a remarkable new force.

We may now see why Ribh revises another ancient symbol, the passage from the lunar wheel of history into the Sun itself upon which the aquiline eye gazes. "Although the wise *Magi* and *Mathematicians* have made a Sphere, and described the Wheel, yet that is not enough," Boehme had said. The "wheel hath a much more subtle understanding, and cannot be made in any Circle after this manner: for it goes into itself towards the Heart of the Sun..." Florence Farr had learned how the soul is

> whirled about
> Wherever the orbit of the moon can reach,
> Until it plunge into the sun

where it may

> Forget its broken toys
> And sink into its own delight at last.[63]

That solar apocalypse, which Yeats calls the "Sphere" in *A Vision*, Ribh calls "There"—the term by which (in the MacKenna translation) Plotinus refers to the Divine Sphere: "the sun, There, is all the stars; and every star, again, is all the stars and sun." There, as Boehme said, "life windeth itself *inwards* to the Sun":[64]

> There all the barrel-hoops are knit,
> There all the serpent-tails are bit,
> There all the gyres converge in one,
> There all the planets drop in the Sun.

But the rendered meaning of "There" (like that of Ribh's intercourse of angels) catches up the solidity, energy, and sensual force of history in the very transcendence of history. That is evident in the rough vigor of the opening diction and in the strategic emphasis upon the verbs—knit, bit, converge, drop—with their kinetic and even sexual connotations. Though as saint, Ribh imaginatively transcends "the recurring and the beautiful, all the winding of the serpent," as poet he makes "his home in the serpent's mouth."[65] Hence he can also say in "He and She" that "All creation shivers"—a word ecstatically poised between pain and delight—with the sweet lunar cry, "I am I, am I."

When Ribh can accept in contemplation the total process of history, he may know the miracle of creative freedom; for when the ego abdicates, the forces of a continual creation may flow through the visionary. That process Ribh presents in a poem that has been little understood, "What Magic Drum?":

He holds him from desire, all but stops his breathing lest
Primordial Motherhood forsake his limbs, the child no longer
 rest,
Drinking joy as it were milk upon his breast.

Through light-obliterating garden foliage what magic drum?
Down limb and breast or down that glimmering belly move
 his mouth and sinewy tongue.
What from the forest came? What beast has licked its young?

On one level, that "child" or creation is any genuine vision—not, like Shelley's, a "system of thought ... constructed by his logical faculty to satisfy desire," but, like Blake's, "a symbolical revelation received after the suspension of desire."[66] As another writer nourished by Ribh's Eastern tradition has put it: "There must be the cessation of all search, and only then is there a possibility of the coming into being of the nameless." That cessation is a kind of death, through which the dark grows luminous, the void fruitful. "All things," Ellis and Yeats had said, "before they can create are compelled to die in Western twilight, for life exists merely through willing and joyous or unwilling and mournful sacrifice of life."[67] The "he" of this poem —quite possibly Ribh himself, described in the third person because one cannot of such a moment say "I"—becomes the vehicle of "primordial Motherhood" not through unwilling sacrifice, like Leda or "frigid Rome," but through a willing suspension of desire, an acceptance of limitation and a consequent opening to the forces beyond. He therefore experiences the incursion of that transcendental "blood" not as a destructive rape, a breaking of the individual walls, but as an awe-inspiring intimation of magic force and creative power visiting the self from the unknown forest and complementing that motherhood which momentarily resides within the self. Such a myth, it should be clear, has direct relations to Yeats's own visionary dialogue with history. And further implications of the process it describes will appear later, when we turn to the concluding visions in "Meditations in Time of Civil War" and "Nineteen Hundred and Nineteen."

v.

The historical range of that wholeness glimpsed by Ribh is combined in "Long-Legged Fly" with a yet more complex rendering of the paradox that extreme attention constitutes the creative faculty in man. Here the dramatic relativity of viewpoint is enriched sixfold: three subjective moments in history—when the lidless eye is fixed upon that "nothing" known by the medium of "Fragments"—are viewed by three somewhat external speakers. But the strategy of the poem is gradually to merge the three moments and the three voices, so that the final refrain (in tone as in reference) suggests the various historical dimensions implicit in the eternal moment of the silent mind, Blake's "Moment" within which "the Poet's Work is Done."

That civilisation may not sink,
Its great battle lost,
Quiet the dog, tether the pony
To a distant post;
Our master Caesar is in the tent
Where the maps are spread,
His eye fixed upon nothing,
A hand under his head.
Like a long-legged fly upon the stream
His mind moves upon silence.

That the topless towers be burnt
And men recall that face,
Move most gently if move you must
In this lonely place.
She thinks, part woman, three parts a child,
That nobody looks; her feet
Practise a tinker shuffle
Picked up on a street.
Like a long-legged fly upon the stream
Her mind moves upon silence.

That girls at puberty may find
The first Adam in their thought,
Shut the door of the Pope's chapel,

Keep those children out.
There on that scaffolding reclines
Michael Angelo.
With no more sound than the mice make
His hand moves to and fro.
Like a long-legged fly upon the stream
His mind moves upon silence.

The poem almost reverses the structure of "Leda and the Swan." In each stanza the almost teleological opening clause evokes a vista of historical consequences, past for us but future for the speakers. The following imperatives pull us rapidly into the drama enacted at the initial moment of the historical pattern, and the description of that drama leads to a refrain which presents, in what at first seems half-mockery, its most inward reality. The "long-legged fly" contrasts especially with the first speaker's somewhat adulatory vision of his master and his precariously floating civilization. It stresses, through an incongruity the speaker himself may not fully grasp, the apparent insignificance of the mind's initial movements.

But the more sophisticated speaker of the second stanza chooses to dramatize that very insignificance: hence, though proleptically paraphrasing Marlowe, he allows Helen herself to remain anonymous. The "tinker shuffle," mimed in the verse rhythm, contrasts sharply with the action of the more Pateresque Helen in *A Vision*:

> ...she comes before the mind's eye elaborating a delicate personal discipline.... While seeming an image of softness and quiet, she draws perpetually upon a glass with a diamond.... She will wander much alone as though she consciously meditated her masterpiece that shall be at the full moon, yet unseen by human eyes, and when she returns to her house she will look upon her household with timid eyes, as though she knew that all powers of self-protection had been taken away . . .[68]

But here Helen consciously meditates no masterpiece. The opening clause of purpose is from an external point of view; the creative individual has at such a moment no intent of that order: desire suspended, he is conscious of "nothing," of the "fruitful void," of the child drinking joy, or of the "thinking of the body." If Helen thinks at all in the usual sense, she "thinks...That nobody looks"—while "*her feet* / Practice..." Likewise in the third stanza Michael Angelo "reclines," while "*His hand* moves to and fro." Their limbs have not yet been forsaken by primordial Motherhood. Though in this poem the obvious masterpiece is that of Michael Angelo, even he does not draw upon a glass with a diamond. His hand moves with "no more sound than the mice make"—and the comparison fuses the stanza tonally with the final refrain, which now has its full resonance.

The speaker of that stanza, whose opening line contrasts so outrageously with those of the first two, has the brazenly ironic yet delicate voice of the ageing Yeats himself; he describes neither the war to preserve a civilization nor the love which causes war, but the art which produces and directs such love. The causal regression in each stanza is thus paralleled by the causal regression of the whole poem, and the final stanza most fully develops the theme. Michael Angelo affirms, with Dürer, the Greek "compact between artist and society" of which Yeats had written in 1909. Pater had told how "Spartan women set up in their chambers a Nireus, a Narcissus, or a Hyacinth, that they might bear beautiful children." By 1903 Yeats had related that to Eden and to a more Nietzschean artistic task:

> I said the poets hung
> Images of the life that was in Eden
> About the child-bed of the world, that it,
> Looking upon those images, might bear
> Triumphant children . . .

By 1919 that idea had entered his conservative synthesis: "A single wrong choice may destroy a family, dissipating its tradition or its biological force, and the great sculptors, painters, and poets are there that instinct may find its lamp."[69] For the third speaker of "Long-Legged Fly," and for the poem as a whole, it is the artist who most significantly prevents civilization from sinking.

He does so by re-enacting a normative creation. Michael Angelo creates an image of God creating man in His image, and the artist's re-creation is in order that the first Adam may be again "found" in the human mind. As Pater had said, Michael Angelo's genius concerned itself "almost exclusively with the making of man. For him it is not...the last and crowning act in a series of developments, but the first and unique act, the creation of life itself in its supreme form, off-hand and immediately . . ."[70] But of course Michael Angelo "creates" by reclining on the scaffold with raised hand—a pose which quite properly suggests that of his own Adam, for he too "finds" or partakes of creation. We now fully realize the oblique reference of the refrain: "And the Spirit of God moved upon the face of the waters." In all three minds the Elohim re-enact that creative and reflective movement over water—over that unconscious element which is "the signature of the fruitfulness of the body and of the fruitfulness of dreams."[71]

This poem need not use William Empson's more elevated diction: "King spider, walks the velvet roof of streams." The "long-legged fly" itself, preventing by its tonal distance from *Genesis* any simple deification, includes all the creative power man might desire—and without sacrificing the quiet homeliness which the image first had as one of a cluster of potential symbols observed by Yeats's John Sherman, on the river that was his imaginative possession: "boys riding in the stream to the saddle-girths, fish leaping, water-flies raising their small ripples, a swan asleep."[72]

In that triptych of resurrected creative moments, Yeats renders the aquiline vision to which he aspired in "An Acre of Grass":

> A mind Michael Angelo knew
> That can pierce the clouds,
> Or inspired by frenzy
> Shake the dead in their shrouds;
> Forgotten else by mankind,
> An old man's eagle mind.

Pater had said that with Michael Angelo "the beginning of life has all the characteristics of resurrection; it is like the recovery of suspended health or animation."[73] As Yeats doubtless knew, Michael Angelo himself was committed to a neo-Platonic theory of vision, and his sonnets frequently contain imagery of an aquiline or angelic soaring toward the spiritual sun.[74] The resurrective power and soaring mind make unusually appropriate the emphatic double form that Yeats gives to the artist's name. Yeats himself had long wished, by discovering "thoughts that tighten the muscles, or quiver and tingle in the flesh," to stand like the Angel Michael "with the trumpet that calls the body to resurrection." And another of his Michaels said,

> Michael Angelo's Sistine roof,
> His "Morning" and his "Night" disclose
> How sinew that has been pulled tight,
> Or it may be loosened in repose,
> Can rule by supernatural right
> Yet be but sinew.[75]

Indeed, Michael Angelo fitted with remarkable ease into Yeats's modification of that pervasive iconography which correlates Michael, the eagle, the sun, and a perception which is creative and re-creative. Dante, Chaucer, Blake, and Shelley had so used the eagle, and Henry More (for whom "Great Michael" was the "second *Adam*,... nothing else but the Image of the God of Heaven") had written:

> Whate're my pregnant Muse brings forth to light,
> She'll not acknowledge to be of her kind,
> Till Eagle-like she turn them to the sight
> Of the eternall Word, all deckt with glory bright.[76]

Coleridge, too, had been drawn to such imagery of light and, when attacking the doctrine that the mind is a mere quicksilver at the back of the mirror, had quoted with approval Plotinus' assertion that the eye cannot behold the sun unless it is soliform.[77] And Nietzsche's Zarathustra, who often celebrated a subjective eagle and solar will, wisdom, and joy, had counseled man to "o'erleap his own shadow— and verily! into *his* sun."[78] When Yeats referred to "eagle thoughts" and exhorted the Wealthy Man to "Look up in the sun's eye," he was drawing upon such traditional material.[79]

But he knew the tradition through its occult versions as well. Among the angelic hierarchy Michael is the "Ruler of Solar Fire,"[80] and in Tarot symbolism the Eagle is the "higher and Divine Nature," the "alchemical Eagle of distillation, the Renewer of life."[81] With Isaiah's sanction ("But they that wait upon the Lord shall renew their strength; they shall mount up with wings as eagles")[82] the eagle thus implies both resurrection and the kind of renewal sought by the speaker of "An Acre of Grass." The alchemical eagle itself is an image for the inspiring union of heaven and earth, and hence for the psychology of the poetic process:

> For the eagle leaves her egg; that is to say, the water leaves her limosity in the earth. . . . the Vulcan or earthly sun makes the water ascend to the region of the air, and here the water is spread under the superior fires; for she is exposed to the eye of the sun and to the pointed ejaculations of all the fixed stars and planets—and this in a naked, rarified, opened body.[83]

In Thomas Vaughan's terminology, that is a description of Ribh's attainment of the aquiline or soliform eye, as the visionary becomes "naked under the heavens."

Of course, Yeats's own use of such imagery underwent paradoxical transformations. He earlier used the solar to represent the "highly disciplined or individual kingly mind," the joy of self-sufficiency—qualities that are in some respects lunar in his later thought. His solar characters therefore run a gamut from Cuchulain (who has "looked upon the sun," who has the hawk's "clear eye," and who can say, "he that's in the sun begot this body") and the savage ger-eagle of *Calvary* (who "has chosen his part / In the blue deep of the upper air / Where one-eyed day can meet his stare"), through the aristocratic eagles of *Responsibilities* and that fool whose "self assertive yet self immolating" passion he related in 1904 to "the hot sun," and on to Ribh, the mood speaking in "Demon and Beast," and Tom O'Roughley:

> How but in zig-zag wantonness
> Could trumpeter Michael be so brave?[84]

Actually, because apocalyptic resurrection involves the resolution of opposites—as that "zig-zag" implies—Yeats's solar celebrations always tend to reach out to include complementary lunar qualities. The later poems on the eagle mind rest upon the epistemology of *A Vision* but fuse that with the suggestions of heroic power and discipline in the early symbol. Ribh and Michael Angelo are spiritual aristocrats as well as visionaries.

From this vantage point, it is clear why Yeats speculated that Berkeley (another who had been drawn to such imagery) may privately have come to regard "Light as the creative act of a universal self dwelling in all selves," and why he reproved Berkeley because he dared not say that man in so far as he is himself, in so far as he is a personality, reflects the whole act of God; his God and Man seem cut off from one another. It was the next step and because he did not take it Blake violently annotated "Siris" and because he himself did take it, certain heads—"Christ Blessing" . . . for instance—have an incredible still energy.[85]

The poet who can say with the Kena-Upanishad, "In the lightning, in the light of an eye, the light belongs to Spirit,"[86] recognizes that the solar aspect of his mind must continually aspire to the condition of saint or fool. Subjective self must wed objective eye, or, in alchemical terms, swan must wed eagle. The many interpretations of Yeats's work that stress too simply the antithesis of swordsman and saint neglect this overwhelming and central fact.

Yeats, then, agreed with Browning's statement that the subjective poet

is impelled to embody the thing he perceives, not so much with reference to the many below as to the one above him, the supreme intelligence which apprehends all things in their absolute truth,—an ultimate view ever aspired to, if but partially attained, by the poet's own soul. Not what man sees, but what God sees,—the *Ideas* of Plato, seeds of creation lying burningly on the Divine Hand,—it is toward these that he struggles.[87]

But the complete subjective poet, he believed, must render that struggle itself, the aquiline effort to pierce the clouds, the turbulence on the threshold of sanctity. Yeats himself was certainly not "lost in complete light," though he could quote the Japanese saying: "What the artist perceives through a medium, the saint perceives immediately."[88] And he could imagine a poet who has come to share in the vision of such a saint, a poet "standing in the door of the tower, while about him" breaks "a windy light," who knows how from his artistic faculty there looks out "as from behind a mask that other Who alone of all men, the country-people say, is not a hair's breadth more nor less than six feet high." Yet that poet might have in mind's eye and ear nothing but the secular, "for was it Columbanus or another that wrote 'There is one among the birds that is perfect and one perfect among the fish'?"[89]

The mood speaking in "The Dancer at Cruachan and Cro-Patrick" could hear all creatures acclaiming, proclaiming, declaiming such perfect Creaturehood. The mood speaking in "Tom the Lunatic" focuses upon yet more particular beings. Momentarily relaxing his attention, he has lost his aquiline vision:

> "What change has put my thoughts astray
> And eyes that had so keen a sight?
> What has turned to smoking wick
> Nature's pure unchanging light?"

But regaining that vision, he shakes the dead from their shrouds:

> "Huddon and Duddon and Daniel O'Leary,
> Holy Joe, the beggar-man,
> Wenching, drinking, still remain
> Or sing a penance on the road;
> Something made these eyeballs weary
> That blinked and saw them in a shroud.

> "Whatever stands in field or flood,
> Bird, beast, fish or man,
> Mare or stallion, cock or hen,
> Stands in God's unchanging eye
> In all the vigour of its blood;
> In that faith I live or die."

Tom has become again, if precariously, what Schopenhauer called "that *one* eye of the world which looks out from all knowing creatures." No more than the poet standing in the door of the tower would he be surprised by Meister Eckhart's bold statement, "The eye by which I see God is the same eye by which he sees me," or the statement of Shelley's Apollo: "I am the eye with which the Universe / Beholds itself and knows itself divine..."[90] As that eye, he beholds the eternally living particulars of this world—the "seeds of creation," mare and stallion, cock and hen, "lying burningly on the Divine Hand."[91]

Appropriately, Yeats's final revision of the Delphic Oracle's account of Plotinus' journey was a re-vision in the light of Ribh's sun or Tom's unchanging eye. For if the escape from the whirlpool of history to the element of fire is fully accomplished (as it is not in "The Delphic

Oracle upon Plotinus" or "Sailing to Byzantium") the voyager redis-
covers within the fire itself that sea of generation and destruction, the
"bitterness of life" from which comes all astringent joy. "News for
the Delphic Oracle," because it describes that escape that is no escape,
recapitulates a career of visions of the endured cycles and the desired
apocalypse. Its fusion of sense and spirit in the attraction of another
realm that seems but a heightened version of this one was dimly
apparent in "The Wanderings of Oisin" and in "John Sherman,"
where (perhaps recalling Blake's *Thel*) poetry was defined as "essentially a touch from behind a curtain." Forty-five years later, Yeats
described Moreau's "Women and Unicorns" as "mystery—the mystery
that touches the genitals, a blurred touch through a curtain." As he
tried to give voice to that "dumb struggling thought" that had so
long haunted him, "this came":

> Bird sighs for the air,
> Thought for I know not where,
> For the womb the seed sighs.
> Sinks the same rest
> On intellect, on nest,
> On straining thighs?[92]

Revised to eliminate the question, that could only present a lover's
dramatic conviction, and it accordingly became "The Lover's Song" in
"The Three Bushes." But distanced, the thought could attain a different kind of certainty—as the soliform eye's exultant and ironic vision
of Plotinus' "There," now seen as the final rest or center of all its
modes of being. For Yeats as for Nicolas of Cusa the divine-human
polarity enables and requires the attempt to elevate oneself to that
mysterious point where the opposites are reconciled.[93]

There—where the Golden Race becomes a group of salty old
codgers like the Enobarbus whom the speaker echoes—all the serpent-
tails are bit and all the gyres converge in one:

> There all the golden codgers lay,
> There the silver dew,
> And the great water sighed for love,
> And the wind sighed too.

The ambiguous longing that sent Oisin on his cyclical journey—that
quintessence revealed by the alchemical *rota*—finds its proper consummation, which is not the tomb of "The Wheel":

> Man-picker Niamh leant and sighed
> By Oisin on the grass;
> There sighed amid his choir of love
> Tall Pythagoras.
> Plotinus came and looked about,
> The salt-flakes on his breast,
> And having stretched and yawned awhile
> Lay sighing like the rest.

But of what kind of love does this choir sing? And why has
Rhadamanthus disappeared? The speaker is delightedly teaching his
neo-Platonic oracle about a rather Blakean heaven, and

> what is Antichrist but those
> Who against Sinners Heaven close
> With Iron bars, in Virtuous State,
> And Rhadamanthus at the Gate?[94]

It is a heaven that magnificently combines the sublime and the ridic-
ulous, and that must also run the tragic gamut of existence, for
ecstasy cannot exist without pain:

> Those Innocents re-live their death,
> Their wounds open again.
> The ecstatic waters laugh because
> Their cries are sweet and strange...

Because this poem is a vision of the teleological goal of all love
sighs—of Plotinus' vision and Oisin's infatuation, of the Innocents'
death and the brute dolphins' "plunge"—it is as part of a larger harmony, not as a "bitter" moral contrast,[95] that beyond or within the
tableau of Peleus and Thetis ("Thetis' belly listens"),

> Down the mountain walls
> From where Pan's cavern is
> Intolerable music falls.

Out of the dark heart of Yeats's symbolical sun, there flows that "sensual music" from which the speaker of "Sailing to Byzantium" wished to flee to the refining fire—a music, however, which even in that poem was caught up in an "artifice of eternity" more complete than that for which the speaker yearned. Now, like all that is "intolerable," it heightens ecstasy. In this transcendent sea of generation, which like that of Gemistus Plethon may symbolize "the garden's ground or first original,"[96] the "nymphs and satyrs / Copulate in the foam." It is the end and beginning of all cycles, the comedy beyond tragedy, the old eagle's vision of the Sabbath of Creation—a Yeatsian rendering of that foretold by Boehme when he wrote, "you shall see the *seventh Seal with the Eye of Sol.*"[97]

PART TWO

HISTORY AS DRAMATIC EXPERIENCE

VII · THE LIVING HERITAGE
AND THE MEASURED WAY

All history becomes subjective; in other words there
is properly no history, only biography. Every mind
must know the whole lesson for itself,—must go over
the whole ground. What it does not see, what it
does not live, it will not know.
—Emerson[1]

...every Soul is its own Judgment.
—Boehme[2]

---

i.

AFTER THE PANORAMA of "Dove or Swan," as truncated for the second
edition of *A Vision,* comes a striking confession. "Day after day,"
Yeats tells us, "I have sat in my chair turning a symbol over in my
mind, exploring all its details, defining and again defining its elements, testing my convictions and those of others by its unity, attempting to substitute particulars for an abstraction like that of algebra."
He recalls the prophecies of communists and socialists, of Balzac and
Kagawa, and wonders how completely they harmonize with his own.
"Then I draw myself up into the symbol and it seems as if I should
know all if I could but banish such memories and find everything
in the symbol.... But nothing comes—though this moment was to
reward me for all my toil." However, that is no confession of the

aridity of his system; it is another movement in his constant oscillation between the lofty perspective of creative vision and the earthly perspective of dramatic experience. It is a sudden return to humility before the unpredictable particulars of the flux of history:

> Then I understand. I have already said all that can be said. The particulars are the work of the *thirteenth sphere* or cycle which is in every man and called by every man his freedom. Doubtless, for it can do all things and knows all things, it knows what it will do with its own freedom but it has kept the secret.[3]

We should keep that return in mind as we read the next and final sentence of *A Vision*: "Shall we follow the image of Heracles that walks through the darkness bow in hand, or mount to that other Heracles, man, not image, he that has for his bride Hebe, 'The daughter of Zeus, the mighty, and Hera, shod with gold'?" Heracles the image and Heracles the man are for Yeats as for Plotinus subjective and objective, earthly manifestation and unfallen reality,[4] and they are in some ways analogous to Yeats's first and second Adams. But we should not give a one-sided Christian interpretation to that duality.[5] Yeats had long celebrated both Self and Soul, Oedipus and Christ, the flaming heart of man and the holy fire that may strike him dumb. He ended *A Vision* not with a clear ethical or religious exhortation, but with a question that poses the problem anew. His own previous confession involved a necessary if temporary return from the God's-eye view of history perceived as an eternal constellation to the finite human experience of the stream of time—a return from communion with Heracles the man to recognition of the subjective state of Heracles the phantom, caught amid the Heraclitian tensions, "like black night with bow uncased, and the shaft upon the string, fiercely glancing around like one in the act to shoot."[6]

The duality of Heracles (which is also that of the Dioscuri)[7] becomes, when projected into the macrocosm, that of the two armies of God: "in heaven the hosts of Michael; in the abyss (the manifested world) the legions of Satan. These are the unmanifest and the manifest; the free and the bound (in matter): the virginal and the fallen." But "both are the Ministers of the Father, fulfilling the word Divine." Therefore *"blessed and sanctified is the Angel of Havas,"* or Satan. What Madame Blavatsky calls "the true philosophical and metaphysical interpretation of Samael, or Satan, the adversary in the Kabala,"[8] informs Yeats's work as symbolic structure when he envisions a rosy peace of Heaven and Hell, or is caught in his own civil war between saint and swordsman, or "puts on Satan" as one step in the ethical process (learned in part from Blake and Boehme) of self-measurement and self-judgment.

At this point, then, we turn to investigate in detail the complementary aspect of Yeats's dialogue with history. We turn from his flight with the Angel Michael to his battle in the abyss with the Angel Samael—from *Deus* to *Demon,* from man as gnostic visionary and semidivine creator to man as tragic sufferer and scapegoat. Of course, such antitheses oversimplify the matter. Again and again in the poetry, as I have pointed out, the piercing vision is appropriately clouded by human limitations and gains force from the visionary's sharing and re-creating human experience. Indeed, only when the visionary himself, humble before an as yet unknown truth, opens himself to the winds of heaven and earth, may he become the vessel of that which he can never completely grasp. Hence the panoramic vision of history is qualified pervasively by its opposite. And Yeats's existential perspective upon history is similarly qualified. Samael may rise to share the eagle vision of Michael; tragic experience may lead to exaltation and illumination; history as crucifixion may be redeemed by translation of the temporal fact into the eternal constellation. The two perspectives, the two armies of God, represent the two faces of one reality, whether we call it Being and Becoming or Eternal Word and transitory flesh. However, because a paradoxical unity that is no more than dimly intuited or theoretically affirmed cannot be fully rendered in art, there was at first a decided cleavage between Yeats's world of vision and his world of dramatic experience. Only gradually did the two perspectives merge to enable him to present full-bodied dramatic visions of the tragedy of eternal imagination crucified on the rood of time.

ii.

Like his search for a pattern in history, Yeats's exploration of its drama began early in life. As a boy, he read with excitement in Hugo, Dumas, Scott, and Balzac.[9] (Indeed, Balzac would always be a powerful reminder of the claims of the existential perspective: "whenever I have been tempted to go to Japan, China or India for my philosophy," he said in 1934, "Balzac has brought me back, reminded me of my preoccupation with national, social, personal problems, convinced me that I cannot escape from our *Comédie humaine.*")[10] Later he listened to the conversations of the historian York Powell, who "cared nothing for philosophy, nothing for economics, nothing for the policy of nations; for history, as he saw it, was a memory of men who were amusing or exciting to think about." Yeats's father, too, praised what he called the "historic sense," the loyalty to the "sorrowful and lovable" drama of one's national history.[11]

At its best, that sense will lead a man (as Allen Tate has said) to consider history "a vast body of concrete fact" to which he "must be loyal" and not merely "a source of mechanical formulas."[12] But even within this existential perspective, the early Yeats had to fight off the temptation to discover in the past only what the intellect could most easily master or had already mastered. In 1909, contrasting two kinds of love for Ireland, that of Thomas Davis and that of William Allingham, he summarized the temptation and his resistance:

> In Allingham I find the entire emotion for the place one grew up in which I felt as a child. Davis on the other hand was concerned with ideas of Ireland, with conscious patriotism. His Ireland was artificial, an idea built up in a couple of generations by a few common-place men. This artificial idea has done me as much harm as the other has helped me. I tried to free myself from it, and all my enemies come from my fighting it in others.... One cannot sum up a nation intellectually, and when the summing up is made by half-educated men the idea fills one with alarm.

In sharp contrast to that intellectualized love stood his own childhood nostalgia:

> I remember when I was nine or ten years old walking along Kensington High Street so full of love for the fields and roads of Sligo that I longed—a strange sentiment for a child—for earth from a road there that I might kiss it. I had no politics.... This love was instinctive and left the soul free. If I could have kept it and yet never felt the influence of Young Ireland I had given a more profound picture of Ireland in my work.[13]

That conflict between instinctive love and nationalist passion runs through Yeats's early prose. In 1888 he had shown great sympathy for Allingham's sense of place:

> Perhaps ... to fully understand these poems one needs to have been born and bred in one of those western Irish towns; to remember how it was the centre of your world, how the mountains and the river and the roads became a portion of your life forever; to have loved with a sense of possession even the roadside bushes where the roadside cottagers hung their clothes to dry. That sense of possession was the very centre of the matter.[14]

But he had also sadly accused Allingham of lacking both nationalist fervor and a serious interest in the peasantry—faults common to writers of the Protestant Ascendancy, such as Charles Lever and Samuel Lover.[15] Indeed, the instinctive love itself seemed definitely Anglo-Irish as well as non-national, and Yeats tried at that time to have little sympathy for the Anglo-Irish tradition. In 1890, for example, he referred contemptuously to "the West British minority with their would-be cosmopolitanism and actual provincialism" and asserted that Standish O'Grady's enthusiasm for Irish history was "out of place" in that context.[16] But he was drawn toward the provincialism and cosmopolitanism even as he condemned them. In 1891 he argued that he had presented in "John Sherman" a "typical Irish feeling," Sherman's devotion to the town of Ballagh. It was, he admitted, a "West of Ireland feeling, ... for, like that of Allingham for Bally-shannon, it is West rather than National." But he continued:

> Sherman belonged like Allingham to the small gentry who, in the West at any rate, love their native places without perhaps loving Ireland. They do not travel and are shut off from England by the whole breadth of Ireland, with the result that they are forced to make their native town their world.

He recalled the same feeling in his own and his mother's devotion to Sligo, and he claimed "for this and other reasons that *Sherman* is as much an Irish novel as anything by Banim or Griffin."[17]

Here, as in his multiple historical and apocalyptic hopes of the same period, Yeats's contradictions are not finally weaknesses but strengths. They represent an attempt, through vacillation, to remain true to a reality more complex than that seen from any single point of view.

Indeed, he had glimpsed in 1888 the organic fusion of local, national, and universal toward which he was moving:

> To the greater poets everything they see has its relation to the national life, and through that to the universal and divine life: nothing is an isolated artistic moment; everything fulfills a purpose that is not its own; the hailstone is a journeyman of God; the grass blade carries the universe upon its point. But to this universalism, this seeing of unity everywhere, you can only attain through what is near you, your nation, or, if you be no traveller, your village and the cobwebs on your walls.

With that microcosmic dewdrop in mind, Yeats thought to approach the universe through his immediate experience. "One can only reach out to the universe with a gloved hand—" he said; but the young nationalist concluded too simply, forgetting the village and its cobwebs, "that glove is one's nation, the only thing one knows even a little of."[18] He thus shifted the meaning of those Allingham verses he liked to quote: "A wild west Coast, a little Town .../ Let me sing of what I know."[19]

Through the years he developed that conception of the "glove," which was, historically speaking, his living heritage. From this point of view, in 1930, he criticized Pound's "conception of excellence" as "so international that it is abstract and outside life."

> I do not ask myself whether what I find in Elizabethan English, or in that of the early eighteenth century, is better or worse than what I find in some other clime and time. I can only approach that more distant excellence through what I inherit, lest I find it and be stricken dumb.[20]

By that time, as his comment implies, Yeats's own tradition had become emphatically Anglo-Irish—an allegiance that had its obscure beginnings in his early and uneasy love for the West of Ireland. But at first, unable to commit himself to all the implications of the "gloved hand," he tried to combine it with the more orthodox nationalism of his compatriots. He therefore attempted during his early years in London a direct assimilation of the image of Ireland—primarily through a voracious reading. He sought, however, an image richer and more living than that evoked by the stereotypes and slogans of political writers.

The popular Irish histories, he felt, were "wholly empty of the historical spirit": they offered only a melodrama in which Ireland was virtuous, her enemies evil—a "mystery play of devils and angels."[21] More scholarly histories, though careful and impartial, often deprived the past of all life. If the historian "reason and compare and argue only, he belongs to those who record and not those who reveal." The true historian should be to some extent an imaginative artist.[22] Moreover, believing with Blake that "Houses of Commons and Houses of Lords" are "something Else besides Human Life," Yeats held that the "history of a nation is not in parliaments and battle-fields, but in what the people say to each other on fair-days and high days, and in how they farm, and quarrel, and go on pilgrimage."[23]

One historian was exempt from such criticism. Standish O'Grady had written what Yeats called "the only purely artistic and unforensic histories that we have."[24] In such works as *Red Hugh's Captivity, The Bog of Stars, The Story of Ireland,* and *The Flight of the Eagle,* O'Grady had "written Irish history in a philosophic spirit and as an imaginative art." He was the first, Yeats said, "to have written not mainly of battles and enactments, but of changing institutions and changing beliefs, of the pride of the wealthy and the long endurance 'of the servile tribes of ignoble countenance.' "[25] O'Grady also reinforced Yeats's still uncertain attempt to elevate the sense of place into an attachment of national and religious importance. When in *The Flight of the Eagle* O'Grady evokes the associations clustering about Sliabh Fuad, the Irish mountain becomes, as Yeats said, "a person of the history, a symbol of 'the Gaelic tradition.' " In O'Grady's words, it is in vindication of that mountain, "far more than as champion of the 'Dark Rosaleen' of our modern singer," that the sword of Hugh Roe "is soon to flash in the North."[26]

Yeats considered *The Flight of the Eagle* neither "historical romance" nor "history in our modern sense": though much of it is but inference, all the inference exists for the sake of history. He placed it (as Wilde had placed the work of Carlyle) in a more ancient tradition. It "would have met with no complaints in the day of Herodotus."[27] But he knew of another modern parallel. His own disagreement with O'Grady's politics reminded him that John Stuart Mill had said of Michelet, "The effect of his books is not acquiescence,

but stir and ferment."[28] Yeats surely knew—if only through a reading
of Mill's essay—that the parallel went yet further; for one might say
of the Vichian Michelet, as Yeats said of O'Grady, that he "looked
for the great tides of passion and thought that are the substance of
life."[29] In this indirect way (as also, probably, in his early reading
of Emerson) Yeats was being further prepared for his later reading
of Croce on Vico. Just as he moved toward a Vichian conception of
historical cycles, so he moved toward a Vichian conception of the
historian as one who relives the past, who re-creates in his own mind
what the mind of man had once created.[30]

For other versions of the Irish drama, Yeats turned to more strictly
imaginative literature. Yet closer to the reality of the past than
O'Grady's volumes, he thought, must be the poetry "sung and repeated
at the hearths of the people."[31] He supplemented O'Grady's vision
of the Gael with the work of many translators of that poetry and
continuers of its tradition, including Callanan, Edward Walsh, the
Young Ireland writers, and then Aubrey De Vere, Allingham,
Mangan, and Samuel Ferguson.[32] For a clearer portrayal of the social
milieu he turned to Irish novels, which he read continually while in
London, "seeking in them an image of Ireland that I might not forget
what I meant to be the foundation of my art."[33] In them he found
two "accents": in Croker, Lever, and Lover, that of the Anglo-Irish
gentry, who "lived lightly and gaily"; and in William Carleton and
Michael and John Banim, that of the peasantry, whose writing he
thought "ruder but deeper."[34] At that time he decidedly preferred
the accent of the peasantry. Carleton, in particular, he thought, had
rendered the real substance of life and at his best might be termed
"a great Irish historian." Showing a taste for the humor and wild
vitality that did not enter his own poetry until much later, Yeats
speculated that Carleton was perhaps "the peasant Chaucer of a new
tradition."[35]

But even folk poetry and peasant novels offered conventional,
partial, or otherwise distorted views of Ireland. More important, they
could never present Yeats's own view. That became clear to him
during the late 1890's, when he returned to Ireland, spent some time
at the Gore-Booths', met Lady Gregory, and began his career as

theatre manager. Now he had greater opportunity to compare the image of Ireland which he had derived from its literature with that which stood immediately before him. His verdict was inevitable:

> I only escaped from many misconceptions when, in 1897, I began an active Irish life, comparing what I saw about me with what I heard of in Galway cottages. . . . Somebody has said that all sound philosophy is biography, and what I myself did, getting into an original relation to Irish life, creating in myself a new character, a new pose—in the French sense of the word—the literary mind of Ireland must do as a whole, always understanding that the result must be no bundle of formulas, not faggots but a fire. We never learn to know ourselves by thought, said Goethe, but by action only; and to a writer, creation is action.[36]

He was beginning to understand the full implications of the "gloved hand." Realizing that he must begin with his own life and move in widening circles from the intimately known to the unknown, he returned, in effect, to his village and the cobwebs on his walls. The present image of Ireland was before him: the little towns of the West, Allingham's Ballyshannon and his own Sligo; the peasantry of Galway cottages, with their tales and jests; the residents of the big houses, Lady Gregory, the Gore-Booths; the Abbey, soon to be filled with rioting spectators; the Paudeens of Dublin shops; the artists and teachers, Padraic Pearse, Thomas MacDonagh and others, who would soon help to create the "terrible beauty" of the Easter Rising. He must begin with this image, in all its richness and bitterness, and move backward through time, dramatizing and judging in the light of his own experience, establishing a full imaginative connection between present and past. And the goal of that creative process, as his comment emphasizes, would be not merely historical knowledge but also self-knowledge.

He had noted earlier that according to Blake, "What a man can see from his garden that is his universe . . . , the rest is an illusion of reason."[37] Learning now the fuller meaning of that assertion, he was led toward Thoor Ballylee, where he would establish a personal and possessive relation to Irish history. For the "sense of possession," as he had said of his feeling for Sligo, is "the very centre of the matter."

iii.

The immediate result of getting into an original relation to Irish life was a more obviously autobiographical poetry. Though Yeats had long since turned from the dramatic poetry his father had taught him to admire toward a poetry of personal utterance, his early attempts, as he said, came to "little but romantic convention, unconscious drama. It is so many years before one can believe enough in what one feels even to know what the feeling is."[38] Now, though seeking as before "an always personal emotion . . . woven into a general pattern of myth and symbol,"[39] he drew more heavily upon his daily experience, believed more passionately in his own feelings, and spoke out with a new directness.

Yet this was not an autobiographical poetry in any simple sense. Yeats wished to create in himself "a new character, a new pose." In part, he wished to counter "the new ill-breeding of Ireland, which may in a few years destroy all that has given Ireland a distinguished name in the world," by setting up what he called "a secondary or interior personality created out of the tradition of myself, and this personality (alas, only possible to me in my writings) must always be gracious and simple." It must have "that slight separation from interests which makes charm possible, while remaining near enough for passion."[40] Though he has been criticized adversely for developing "a studied literary pose deriving from Pater,"[41] Yeats was here, as frequently, transforming a period trait into something stronger and more profoundly traditional. The *personae* which gave him a dramatic basis for social criticism are not radically different from those of Pope, and surely Marvell's superb balance of personality (which Yeats mentioned in 1907 as a supreme example of "style," or the sensible impression of the free mind)[42] was also more fully realized in art than in life. It is against such a background that we should place his bold statement of 1909: "Style, personality—deliberately adopted and therefore a mask—is the only escape from the hot-faced bargainers and the money-changers."[43]

"At the Abbey Theatre" aptly illustrates this critical intention. Beneath the grace and politeness of the speaker's address to Douglas Hyde there flickers a critical irony. Hyde's poetic and scholarly potentials were being dissipated, Yeats thought, and his artistic integrity was being threatened if not violated by his methods of wooing the public and building up the Gaelic League.[44]

> You've dandled them and fed them from the book
> And know them to the bone; impart to us—
> We'll keep the secret—a new trick to please.
> Is there a bridle for this Proteus
> That turns and changes like his draughty seas?

After that description, the speaker's veiled impatience with such dandling can come to an ironical climax:

> Or is there none, most popular of men,
> But when they mock us, that we mock again?

If the people are mocked, mocked also are the "popular" and their "tricks."

But the speaker of this poem, personal and topical as it may seem, finds his own voice only through imitating that of Ronsard—a fact which suggests yet other implications of Yeats's search for a new pose. He associated Ronsard with the poetry of "self portraiture" or dramatic experience, in contrast to that of "vision": "Villon always and Ronsard at times create a marvellous drama out of their own lives."[45] Nor was the close imitation of another's drama a self-betrayal. It was, in part, a means of exploring history: what the mind does not live, as Emerson said, it will not know. But it was also a means of gaining a foothold in an ideal society. "We carry in our heads always," Yeats wrote in 1909, "that form of society aristocracies create now and again for some brief moment at Urbino or Versailles."[46] (Indeed, as "Poetry and Tradition" suggests, the new fusion of passion and detachment owes more to Castiglione than to Pater.) Moreover, such imitation could be a means of revitalizing one's art. In 1905 Yeats had said that in order to renew the life of any art

> we go backward till we light upon a time when it was nearer to human life and instinct, before it had gathered about it so many mechanical specialisations and traditions. We examine that earlier condition and think out its principles of life that we may be able to separate accidental from vital things.

William Morris, after studying early printing, made a new type "that had the quality of his own mind about it, though it reminds one of its ancestry"; and Coleridge and Wordsworth, influenced by Percy's *Reliques,* created "a simplicity altogether unlike that of old ballad-writers."[47] Yeats was doubtless reinforced in this belief as in others by Hallam's essay on Tennyson. Of "Oriana" Hallam had said:

> We know no more happy seizure of the antique spirit in the whole compass of our literature; yet there is no foolish self-desertion, no attempt at obliterating the present, but everywhere a full discrimination of how much ought to be yielded and how much retained. The author is well aware that the art of one generation cannot *become* that of another by any will or skill; but the artist may transfer the spirit of the past, making it a temporary form for his own spirit, and so effect, by idealizing power, a new and legitimate combination.[48]

But ultimately, for Yeats, that new "combination" could emerge because imitation provides a language or scenario for the "dumb struggling thought" or "mood" that seeks articulation. As early as 1888, writing to Katharine Tynan, he expressed dislike of "retrospective art," but explained that her poem on St. Francis was not retrospective because "the St. Francis within you spoke."[49] He later combined that belief with another:

> that if a man is to write lyric poetry he must be shaped by nature and art to some one out of half a dozen traditional poses, and be lover or saint, sage or sensualist, or mere mocker of all life; and that none but that stroke of luckless luck can open before him the accumulated expression of the world.[50]

In sum, the poet's shaping of himself, and allowing himself to be shaped, to some traditional form or forms (Yeats did not limit himself to one alone) may enable him to transcend the trivial and incoherent and to make articulate, through the voices of the "past," the voices of his own depths and the depths of others. He seeks a living heritage—one with which he can be in dramatic communication—because he seeks a deepening and refining of his own mind, so that it may utter the spiritual forms common (though with infinite variation) to all men.

Not all of these implications of the "new pose" are clearly present, of course, in the relative slightness of "At the Abbey Theatre." But their existence helps to explain why Yeats could correlate his search for a pose (as he did in his quotation from Goethe) not with escape from self but with the search for self-knowledge. And they provide a useful approach to other poems of this period, in which Yeats more clearly begins to move—partly by means of his new pose—through dramatic and historical experience toward a "tragic" and contemplative transcendence of time that is characterized by self-knowledge and self-judgment.

But, in the context of Yeats's existential perspective upon history, the very notion of a transcendence of time requires some preliminary comment. Although since 1902 Yeats had stressed the Apollonian rather than the Dionysian, Incarnation rather than Transfiguration, "self portraiture" rather than "vision," that was but another tack in the zig-zag progress toward greater completeness. Hence, in both prose and poetry, even meditations upon Apollonian qualities within history tended to move quite beyond history. In 1904, when Yeats described those qualities as created by the "high disciplined or individual kingly mind," the "measurer-out" or "marker-in of limits," he said that such art brings "not merely discipline but joy; for its discipline is ... the expression of the individual soul turning itself into a pure fire and imposing its own pattern, its own music, upon the heaviness and dumbness that is in others and in itself."[51] In the moment of self-expression, the artist transcends the objective pressures of his time; history is consumed in his pure fire. Similarly in 1909, when Yeats praised Greek art, he said that, if carried to its logical conclusion, it would gather up "by a kind of deification a capacity for all energy and all passion, into a Krishna, a Christ, a Dionysus."[52] As he imagines the Apollonian form, it is so filled with the energy Blake called "eternal delight" that it becomes Dionysian. Clearly, the ultimate goal of the "measurer-out" is to pass beyond all measurement. The bounded is a way toward the boundless. This is not, however, the yearning transcendence of the early poetry, but the joyful transcendence of formal accomplishment and of energy in excess.

Nor does it require for Yeats an ideal moment in history, such as that of Phidian Athens. In another essay of 1904, after describing the death of our civilization, he progressively postponed the new era of history until it seemed to enter the realm of myth. As he did so, his hope for a specific future event transformed itself into a confidence in the heroic potential of man. At the end of the essay, praising art that celebrates the active personality, he used images that suggest both temporal defeat and transcendental victory: "when Lucifer stands among his friends, when Villon sings his dead ladies to so gallant a rhythm, when Timon makes his epitaph, we feel no sorrow, for life herself has made one of her eternal gestures, has called up into our hearts her energy that is eternal delight."[53] That statement recalls Nietzsche's view that in Greek tragedy the boundless Dionysian cele-bration of eternal life arises amid the defeat of the Apollonian hero, who is but an individual vessel of that life. But Nietzsche was clari-fying for Yeats a position that Yeats himself had long held. The early study of Blake had stated that "incarnation and crucifixion... are identical." That is, when Christ or the poetic genius enters time, it becomes subject to the conflicts and defeats symbolized by the cross. We recall that "Christ put on the temporal body, which is Satan, on purpose that it might be consumed and the 'spiritual body re-vealed.' "[54] For exactly the same purpose, Yeats's own poetic genius now began to put on the temporal body. His earlier understanding of "Transfiguration" had been hasty and immature. One must fully enter time before transcending it.

In putting on that "temporal body," he developed his earlier Blakean view that we must cast our life into the imagination's "world of freedom, and so escape from the warring egotisms of elements and years," in the direction of Schopenhauer, who had described how the poet becomes his own tragic character and so attains that sublimity which occurs when "the twofold nature of his consciousness reaches the highest degree of distinctness," and he perceives himself as both "the frail phenomenon of will" and "the eternal, peaceful, knowing subject... free and apart from all desires and necessities."[55] "The Double Vision of Michael Robartes," as I have suggested, sym-bolically projects that two-fold nature of the consciousness; and "Sailing to Byzantium," which is a lyric of dramatic experience as well as one of vision, moves toward just such sublimity.

In 1922 Yeats described most clearly his own version of that tragic sublimity, which is attained by poets for whom "contemplation" is no escape from life but "the worst crisis of all." Dante and Villon, he said, "would not, when they speak through their art, change their luck; yet they are mirrored in all the suffering of desire. The two halves of their nature are so completely joined that they seem to labour for their objects, and yet to desire whatever happens, being at the same instant predestinate and free, creation's very self."[56] Such poets have discovered or released a cosmic creativity or "shaping joy" (as Yeats described it in 1907), which delights in nothing more than to fuse in a single image both *Will* and *Mask,* both history and its transcendence. "This joy," he said, "because it must be always making and mastering, remains in the hands and in the tongue of the artist, but with his eyes he enters upon a submissive, sorrowful contemplation of the great irremediable things..."[57]

That "shaping joy" enables the artist to escape morbid self-preoccupation, to balance every motive with its hidden opposite, and so to attain an objective vision of the generic tragedy of life. The "morbid melancholy" of Synge's early work, Yeats said, was possible because "as yet the craftsmanship was not fine enough to bring the artist's joy which is of one substance with that of sanctity." Later, Synge could contemplate "even his own death as if it were another's" and find "in his own destiny but as it were a projection through a burning-glass of that general to men."[58] Such an artist can then realize with Schopenhauer that the

> true sense of tragedy is the deeper insight, that it is not his own individual sins that the hero atones for, but original sin, i.e., the crime of existence itself:
>
> > Pues el delito mayor
> > Del hombre es haber nacido;
> > (For the greatest crime of man
> > Is that he was born;)
>
> as Calderon exactly expresses it.[59]

Or he can exclaim ecstatically, with the speaker of Yeats's "Consolation":

> How could passion run so deep
> Had I never thought
> That the crime of being born
> Blackens all our lot!

Presenting his view in Rosicrucian terms, Yeats described the Rose no longer as the sorrowful wandering beauty which, like the Shekinah or Presence of God, suffers with man the woes of a fallen world, but as the ecstasy known when one's private fate and the world itself are transcended in tragic art. The last words of Timon and Cleopatra move us, he said,

> because their sorrow is not their own at tomb or asp, but for all men's fate. That shaping joy has kept the sorrow pure, for the nobleness of the Arts is in the mingling of contraries, the extremity of sorrow, the extremity of joy, perfection of personality, the perfection of its surrender, overflowing turbulent energy, and marmorean stillness; and its red rose opens at the meeting of the two beams of the cross, and at the trysting place of time and eternity.[60]

Such art weds the Apollonian and the Dionysian. It puts on and consumes the temporal body; it accepts and transcends history. Its ecstasy arises from at least three sources: the artist's joy in experiencing our limited temporal life; his joy in contemplating it, amid defeat, as an "eternal gesture" of "life herself"; and his "shaping joy," which has enabled him to bring to a single focus those contrary joys in the bounded and the boundless. Yeats called such art "tragic"; but his stress upon its joy indicates his continuing belief that the profoundest tragedy points, however obscurely, beyond itself toward a universal comedy.

Characters in his plays occasionally describe that "tragic joy" which, he said in 1904, reaches its climax "when the world itself has slipped away in death." The poet of *The King's Threshold* proclaims that "when all falls / In ruin, poetry calls out in joy." Yeats reworked *The Shadowy Waters* until he could say in 1905 that it was "now upon one single idea—which is in these new lines—

> 'When the world ends
> The mind is made unchanging for it finds
> Miracle, ecstasy, the impossible joy,
> The flagstone under all, the fire of fires,
> The root of the world.' "

But, he added, the play "is only right in its highest moments—the logic and circumstances are all wrong."[61] Though he began to invent such circumstances for his plays, his poems show more clearly his progress toward realizing in "minute particulars" those insights which he could now put abstractly.

"No Second Troy," for example, employs the new Yeatsian "pose" of passion and detachment as a means toward this "tragic" end. In this passionate utterance, almost the speaker's argument with himself, the dominant voice is yet that of detachment and acceptance:

> Why should I blame her that she filled my days
> With misery, or that she would of late
> Have taught to ignorant men most violent ways,
> Or hurled the little streets upon the great,
> Had they but courage equal to desire?

The passion to blame is increasingly submerged—with the effect of Lear's "Hysterica passio, down, thou climbing sorrow!"—until the poem explodes in its last fiery question: "Was there another Troy for her to burn?" Though the beloved may seem vindicated, we do not forget that "counter-truth," that passion being kept down by the sword's point.[62] The very hyperbole of praise uttered by the voice of acceptance includes all that the *hysterica passio* might say against this destructive Helen. The rhetorically triumphant question fully reveals the submerged wound. Like Dante or Villon, Yeats's speaker still seems to labor for his object though accepting, even desiring, whatever happens. The exultant tone of the conclusion partly arises, then, from the wedding of the active and contemplative halves of the self. And because the "shaping joy" has kept the sorrow pure, the speaker's utterance reveals, like his beloved's actions, "a mind / That nobleness made simple as a fire," though with a hidden tension that gives it "beauty like a tightened bow." Here, as in many later poems, the speaker incarnates in his own defeat the nobility he sees in the defeated person upon whom he meditates. His transcendence of time and hers become one.

A similar though quieter effect occurs in "Against Unworthy Praise"; but Yeats soon developed more forceful ways of charging the moment of contemplation with passion, fusing "marmorean stillness" and "overflowing turbulent energy," and thus transcending the limited historical action. In "Friends," a poem of 1911, the dispassionate voice of judgment, finally overwhelmed, can do no more than describe the speaker's own passionate state:

up from my heart's root
So great a sweetness flows
I shake from head to foot.

The final words evoke an image of the limited physical body, which has been charged with an excess of energy and delight. By 1912, in "The Cold Heaven," Yeats translated the entire moment of contemplation into an overwhelming vision: "Suddenly I saw the cold and rook-delighting heaven..." The slight distancing effect of the past tense disappears in the final cry:

Ah! When the ghost begins to quicken,
Confusion of the death-bed over, is it sent
Out naked on the roads, as the books say, and stricken
By the injustice of the skies for punishment?

Again the limited body—now the naked "spiritual body" revealed by incarnation and crucifixion—is "Riddled with light." In 1913 "The Magi" used a similar technique to develop material drawn from a less personal history. In its final line—"The uncontrollable mystery on the bestial floor"—the solidly limited is again transfigured by an excessive energy.

But as Yeats dramatized the active man on the stage of history, writing topical verse in which the speaker argues not with himself but with others, the problem of contemplative transcendence became yet more acute. The rhetorical attack itself must somehow be purged by the "shaping joy." The "gracious and simple" *persona,* with "that slight separation from interests which makes charm possible," could help, of course—but how could such grace and detachment be maintained even as the speaker studies hatred with increasing diligence? Part of the answer is found in Yeats's reference to the Gaelic poet's curse where "delight in ... vehemence" has taken "out of anger half the bitterness with all the gloom." The poet's joy may keep him from being psychologically dependent upon those whom he attacks. As Yeats said of the Irish, "Our minds, being sufficient to themselves, do not wish for victory but are content to elaborate our extravagance, if fortune aid, into wit or lyric beauty." The root motive of such a poetic elaboration is neither hatred of an opponent nor desire for social change, but love of a transcendent ideal, an "impossibly noble life." Its "core," as Yeats said of all great art, is "an overpowering vision of certain virtues, and our capacity for sharing in that vision is the measure of our delight."[63]

So it is, for example, in "Upon a House Shaken by the Land Agitation." The title itself, with a touch of irony, universalizes the topical, and in the first quatrain that house almost disappears in the impossibly noble life it has nourished:

> How should the world be luckier if this house,
> Where passion and precision have been one
> Time out of mind, became too ruinous
> To breed the lidless eye that loves the sun?

We have moved from the present fact to a vision of an endless history, and then to a vision of an eternal virtue—that high disciplined mind symbolized by eagle's eye and sun. Then, amplifying that movement, the poem adds sweetness to strength:

> And the sweet laughing eagle thoughts that grow
> Where wings have memory of wings, and all
> That comes of the best knit to the best? Although
> Mean roof-trees were the sturdier for its fall,
> How should their luck run high enough to reach
> The gifts that govern men, and after these
> To gradual Time's last gift, a written speech
> Wrought of high laughter, loveliness and ease?

Here again the conclusion has a strange depth: that high climax, the goal at the end of Time, shaken by temporal agitation yet clearly transcending it, is the "written speech" of this poem itself. Its "loveliness and ease" have almost refined away the thought of political argument. The speaker does not "wish for victory"; his graceful questions elaborate his vision of "certain virtues." (In that Urbino or Versailles which the speaker carries in his head, it is appropriate that men are governed not by other men, but by "gifts.") We are not tempted to quarrel about whether those virtues have appeared in a particular Irish house; rather, we delightedly share in that vision.

"September 1913" is yet more successful in transcending the occasion, because of the far richer use of the speaker's own personality as

its final meaning. This is most evident in its conclusion. One critic
has said that "although the poem as a whole is the record of a man's
imagined attempt to use all the devices of speech, from conversation
to oratory, in the effort to inculcate a point of view," the "end of the
effort is a satiric taunt that would hardly attain its aim."[64] But that
is exactly the point. Never is the speaker's mind really upon "victory"—
not even in the concluding taunt:

> Yet could we turn the years again,
> And call those exiles as they were
> In all their loneliness and pain,
> You'd cry, "Some woman's yellow hair
> Has maddened every mother's son":
> They weighed so lightly what they gave.
> But let them be, they're dead and gone,
> They're with O'Leary in the grave.

In that stanza breathes an intense tenderness toward those generous
exiles who, though dead, have become haunting presences. It is a
tenderness that dominates the final refrain: "But let them be..." The
"core" of the poem is there revealed as no rhetorical attack but a
compassionate celebration of virtue. "To a Shade" carries this technique a step further. The speaker now addresses one of that "passionate serving kind" who is dead and gone. As the poem moves to its
final expression of concern for the rest and safety of that "unquiet
wanderer," we again transcend the satiric taunt to contemplate a
virtue that really has not died and cannot die. It lives in that still walking shade and in the speaker's own indignant but compassionate
utterance. The theme of such poems is really what Yeats called "something immortal and imperishable within himself," which the speaker
finds mirrored in history.

Another poem of 1913, "To a Friend Whose Work Has Come to
Nothing," brings this technique close to its tragic consummation, that
joy when all falls in ruin. It is easy to distort this poem by paraphrase;
to say, for example, that Yeats urges Lady Gregory to "accept the
difficulty of disdaining her enemies." But the poem itself rises from
consideration of the friend's defeat, her enemies' meanness, her own
honorable breeding, to these final lines:

> Bred to a harder thing
> Than Triumph, turn away
> And like a laughing string
> Whereon mad fingers play
> Amid a place of stone,
> Be secret and exult,
> Because of all things known
> That is most difficult.

The first word, "Bred," is the poem's last clear allusion to aristocratic pride; when we reach that imperative, "Be secret and exult," it has been charged with more important meanings. For the language defines and enacts the rose blooming on the cross. The laughing string, like the poem itself, is enabled to give us its sweet music by the very insanity of the historical forces that play upon it. That place of stone is its crucifixion and its transcendence—the "flagstone under all," the "root of the world." And the final motive offered for such tragic joy is not enmity, disdain, or even pride, but the fascination of what's difficult. Shelley had said in the *Defence of Poetry* that heroes may be poetic ideals even though "remote from moral perfection," because the "vices" of a poet's contemporaries, the peculiar errors of age or class, are but "the temporary dress in which his creation must be arrayed, and which cover without concealing the eternal proportions of their beauty."[65] Yeats was now developing a technique whereby the poem itself, as it fuses action and contemplation, refines away that temporary dress and finally reveals the eternal proportions.

iv.

In transcending history, Yeats's poems clearly transcend to some degree the vices which belong to that realm. Their core is not anger or contempt for a temporal opponent but a kind of love, the celebration of an eternal virtue. But their ethical position cannot adequately be described (as critics have often attempted to describe it) in terms of a semi-Nietzschean heroic vitalism. The speakers of these poems may also rise through the realm of arrogance and violence—the realm of "warring egotisms"—and enter that of charity, self-judgment, and peace. Yeats often sanctions such terms, and his poetry fulfills their implications—at first hesitantly, and then with magnificence.

The early Yeats, we must recall, had drawn from Shelley and Blake the view that true art, created by the imagination and not by the self-deceiving will, reveals the nature of man and the cosmos. The "world as imagination sees it is the durable world"; the "laws of art" are the "hidden laws of life." And the "sympathy with all living things, sinful and righteous alike, which the imaginative arts awaken, is that forgiveness of sins commanded by Christ." It follows that most didactic literature is not art; it is not forgiveness but accusation of sin, "not of the Father but of Satan, the accuser." True art is also symbolic, expressive, apocalyptic; whereas false art is "mimetic, not from experience but from observation, and it is the mother of all evil, persuading us to save our bodies alive at no matter what cost of rapine and fraud." In 1901 Yeats could still say that "behind the momentary self, which acts and lives in the world, there is that which cannot be called before any mortal Judgement seat," that great literature is therefore "the Forgiveness of Sin," and that "when we find it becoming the Accusation of Sin, as in George Eliot, who plucks her Tito in pieces with as much assurance as if he had been clockwork, literature has begun to change into something else."[66]

When Yeats began to celebrate the temporal body, much of that view remained intact. The temporal is the vehicle of the spiritual; the poems transcend the self that acts in the world to celebrate the eternal lineaments of all selves. Furthermore, Yeats now meant by the "body" that Blakean wholeness of being which is inseparable from a joyous acceptance of life, and which is inconsistent with self-righteous or repressive moralism, political abstraction, or any hatred or violence born of a defensive incompleteness. "In a country like Ireland," he said in 1904, where abstractions "have taken the place of life, men have more hate than love, for the unhuman is nearly the same as the inhuman, but literature, which is a part of that charity that is the forgiveness of sins, will make us understand men no matter how little they conform to our expectations."[67]

However, as Yeats's speakers committed themselves increasingly to the temporal, engaging in satirical attacks and celebrating an aristocratic order that is maintained by violence, they drew upon themselves a more severe refining away of dross than occurs in "September 1913" or "To a Friend Whose Work Has Come to Nothing." For

Yeats could not restrict in his poetry that acute ethical sensibility evident in his analyses of Irish politics and his assessments of George Russell, John Shawe-Taylor, and John Synge. In 1909 he said that style is "self-conquest"; in 1910 he referred to "that purification from insincerity, vanity, malignity, arrogance, which is the discovery of style." And he was developing a newly purgatorial conception of the tragic character. This he saw in the "tragic ecstasy" of Synge's Deirdre: "at last when Deirdre, in the paroxysm before she took her life, touched with compassionate fingers him that had killed her lover, ... we too were carried beyond time and persons to where passion, living through its thousand purgatorial years, as in the wink of an eye, becomes wisdom."[68] In "the twinkling of an eye, at the last trump," the corruptible puts on incorruption—and Yeats has come very close to the ethical implications of that saying. If we translate this into the world of his own poetry, we see that as the aristocratic and satirical poet is "carried beyond time" he must recognize in himself the voice of satanic pride and accusation. His poem must become a self-judgment.

Of course, Yeats could put this view in deceptively romantic terms. "To speak of one's emotions," he said in 1910, "without fear or moral ambition, ... to be utterly oneself, that is all the Muses care for." But note his example: "Villon, pander, thief and man-slayer, is as immortal in their eyes, and illustrates in the cry of his ruin as great a truth as Dante in abstract ecstasy, and touches our compassion more."[69] Those last two phrases make Yeats's approval quite different from Swinburne's praise for one whose "gift of writing admirable songs ... has perhaps borne better fruit for us than any gift of moral excellence."[70] A lack of fear and moral ambition is not amoralism: it is the prerequisite for honest self-judgment. Hence Yeats could add: "All art is the disengaging of a soul from place and history, its suspension in a beautiful or terrible light to await the Judgment, though it must be, seeing that all its days were a Last Day, judged already." Blake had said that a "Last Judgment" occurs whenever "any Individual Rejects Error & Embraces Truth." Yeats saw in Synge "an unmoved mind where there is a perpetual Last Day, a trumpeting, and coming up to judgment."[71] That was his own increasingly clear ideal.

Again he was really discovering the full meaning of his earlier apocalyptic theory. Taken in an ethical sense, his statement that the poetic genius puts on "the temporal body, which is Satan, on purpose that it might be consumed," points not only to an alchemical dialogue with Lucifer of the kind implicit, as I have suggested, in his early romances, but also to that later poem "The Choice," which holds that the poet who chooses "perfection of the work" must "refuse / A heavenly mansion, raging in the dark." He must himself experience "the day's vanity, the night's remorse." In order to avoid the self-deceiving rhetoric of moral accusation, he must explore the fallen world in his own person and raise it, through purgatorial contemplation, to a Last Judgment. That is the meaning of Blake's ethic, as Yeats had seen it: "each man ... is by nature evil, and must be continually changed into his direct contrary, and ... this is not restraint but self-annihilation, and is the only gate of eternal life." It is also the meaning of Boehme's doctrine that the Eternal Nature seeks, in the "mirror," the "limit of the malignity, and would abandon it." According to Boehme's cosmic cycle, the unmanifest Desire becomes incarnate in the egocentric variety of Nature so that it may then transform itself into a "crystalline, clear Nature" purged of self-will.[72] In that process, "every Soul is its own Judgment." That harmony of self-realization and self-sacrifice, of variety and unity, is the goal of Yeats's own alchemical and poetic work.

That is one reason for his frequent suggestion (as in the comment on Synge) that the "artist's joy" is "of one substance with that of sanctity." But he could also draw support for that position from a more orthodox Christian writer. In 1901 he said, "there is only one perfection and only one search for perfection, and it sometimes has the form of the religious life and sometimes of the artistic life; and I do not think these lives differ in their wages, for 'The end of art is peace'...." He was paraphrasing Coventry Patmore, and Patmore (whose synthesis of Aquinas and Swedenborg was often congenial to Yeats) is in part behind his distinction in 1913 between the soul revealed in art and that revealed in moral rhetoric: "A soul shaken by the spectacle of its sins, or discovered by the Divine Vision in tragic delight, must offer to the love that cannot love but to infinity a goal unique and unshared; while a soul busied with others' sins is soon melted to some shape of vulgar pride."[73] The peace of art, according to Patmore, is that which Aquinas called the "tranquillity of order" and considered identical with joy. It involves, "in its fullest perfection, at once the complete subdual and the glorification of the senses, and the 'ordering of all things strongly and sweetly from end to end.'" Such art, expressing a soul's unique "beauty and felicity," combines purity and passion. For "virtues are nothing but ordered passions, and vices nothing but passions in disorder."[74]

Yeats's poetry moves toward that glorification and subdual of the senses by combining in various ways the speaker's "tragic delight" and his purgatorial recognition of his own vices. As he is "carried beyond time," he orders his passions by recognizing their disorder. In Blake's terms, he gives falsehood a body that it may be cast out. He discovers and measures, in the mirror of a self-reflective art, what Boehme called the "limit of the malignity," and so transcends it. Sometimes this is explicit. In *Responsibilities,* after "September 1913" and "To a Friend Whose Work Has Come to Nothing," Yeats placed, as a deliberate counterweight, "Paudeen." There the speaker rises from his blind, stumbling indignation at stupidity and spite to the perception, born in upon him by the "luminous wind,"

> That on the lonely height where all are in God's eye,
> There cannot be, confusion of our sound forgot,
> A single soul that lacks a sweet crystalline cry.

The recognition of Boehme's "crystalline Nature" in others purifies the darkly egocentric speaker himself. After the next satirical poem, "To a Shade," Yeats placed the wry admission—humbler even than its original prose idea—of "When Helen Lived."[75]

But Yeats soon tried to merge the active voice of social criticism with the contemplative voice of self-purgation. This occurs, still uneasily, in the poem of 1914 that closes *Responsibilities.* It begins with the illumination brought by that wind among the reeds which speaks of a transcendental realm:

> While I, from that reed-throated whisperer
> Who comes at need, although not now as once
> A clear articulation in the air,
> But inwardly, surmise companions

Beyond the fling of the dull ass's hoof
—Ben Jonson's phrase—and find when June is come
At Kyle-na-no under that ancient roof
A sterner conscience and a friendlier home,
I can forgive even that wrong of wrongs,
Those undreamt accidents that have made me
—Seeing that Fame has perished this long while,
Being but a part of ancient ceremony—
Notorious, till all my priceless things
Are but a post the passing dogs defile.

Amazingly enough, the syntactical heart of that tour de force of invective is the statement, "I can forgive." Forgive what? Not persons but "accidents": the impersonal process of history which has caused the speaker's plight but which, now accepted, can be seen as merely "accidental" because not essential to his being. He accepts his lot and blames no one for producing it, though he notes the existence of some asses and dogs; and he honestly recognizes that his minimal forgiveness is possible only while he is supported by the surmised "companions" and by that "sterner conscience" and "friendlier home." In other words, he defines quite exactly the proud and precarious nature of his moral equilibrium. We see that, ethically as well as aesthetically, the goal of the power that measures is to transcend all measurement. For the speaker—that "interior personality" created out of the tradition of Yeats himself, here finding its voice in part by imitating those of Jonson and Erasmus—judges his limited self in the light of an inward voice or luminous wind that he but imperfectly incarnates.

Again in "The People" the speaker is the voice of a passion and detachment explicitly related to the Renaissance. But as he yearns for the world of Castiglione's courtier, he finds himself frustrated by moral responsibility as well as by historical circumstance:

"What have I earned for all that work," I said,
"For all that I have done at my own charge?
The daily spite of this unmannerly town,
Where who has served the most is most defamed,
The reputation of his lifetime lost

Between the night and morning. I might have lived,
And you know well how great the longing has been,
Where every day my footfall should have lit
In the green shadow of Ferrara wall;
Or climbed among the images of the past—
The unperturbed and courtly images—
Evening and morning, the steep street of Urbino
To where the Duchess and her people talked
The stately midnight through until they stood
In their great window looking at the dawn;
I might have had no friend that could not mix
Courtesy and passion into one like those
That saw the wicks grow yellow in the dawn..."

Told by his "phoenix" that, despite her ill treatment at the hands of the crowd, she had never complained of the people, all he could reply was:

"You, that have not lived in thought but deed,
Can have the purity of a natural force,
But I, whose virtues are the definitions
Of the analytic mind, can neither close
The eye of the mind nor keep my tongue from speech."
And yet, because my heart leaped at her words,
I was abashed, and now they come to mind
After nine years, I sink my head abashed.

That phoenix, Maud Gonne, was but one of several manifestations of the ethical anti-self with whom Yeats held conversations on this subject. Dialogues with George Russell had helped to shape his sense of the necessary conflict between the pride of intellect and art and the humility of love and service. The "most fundamental of divisions," he concluded, is between the "religious genius," to which "all souls are of equal value," and the "intellect," which "can only do its work by saying continually 'thou fool.' "[76] The problem had acquired historical dimension in silent dialogues with Patmore (whose comment on the conflict between the people and the man of genius may also lie behind "The Dolls") and with Plutarch: "it is much the same everywhere; nothing is ever persecuted but the intellect, and the one thing

Plutarch thought one should never complain of is the people. They are what they are and it is our work to live our lives in their despite."[77] Yet in honestly recognizing this problem, the analytic mind of Yeats's poetic speaker measures its own moral limitations and, in doing so, transcends them. Yeats agreed with Shelley: "The wise want love; and those who love want wisdom." But he knew that antithesis as a subjective conflict: "Why does the struggle to come at truth take away our pity, and the struggle to overcome our passions restore it again?"[78] From that conflict emerges a poetry of wisdom which may often discover its want of love.

Such poems as "Paudeen" and "The People" indicate, then, one important direction in which Yeats's quasi-autobiographical poetry began to move. He began to dramatize the history of his time in utterances that combine proud assertion and honest admission, social criticism and tragic purgation:

> Out of Ireland have we come.
> Great hatred, little room,
> Maimed us at the start.
> I carry from my mother's womb
> A fanatic heart.[79]

He moved toward the role of the scapegoat, the historical victim, taking upon himself—in his great meditative poems—the sins of his time. He would have ample reason to cry, in "Parnell's Funeral":

> Come, fix upon me that accusing eye,
> I thirst for accusation.

If he would also write "profane" poems, the finest of them attack only a repressive and hypocritical spirituality, and they measure their profanity by a more inclusive light. There is, of course, that famous conclusion:

> Homer is my example and his unchristened heart.
> The lion and the honeycomb, what has Scripture said?
> So get you gone, Von Hügel, though with blessings on
> your head.

Homer is *my* example: Yeats refers to the vocation of the poet. Art, as he said in 1913, is "sanctity's scapegrace brother." (Nor is that brotherhood merely—as some critics' comments on "Vacillation" imply—a matter of sentimental reverence: "I think that before the religious change that followed on the Renaissance men were greatly preoccupied with their sins, and that to-day they are troubled by other men's sins, and that this trouble has created a moral enthusiasm so full of illusion that art, knowing itself for sanctity's scapegrace brother, cannot be of the party.")[80] Even the scapegrace poet, "because he may not stand within the sacred house but lives amid the whirlwinds that beset its threshold, may find his pardon."[81] That is so because he takes upon himself the Satanic body, declares it, measures it, and consumes it. Only so may the unregenerate lion yield its honey. Only so may the poet, in the phrase Patmore had quoted, order "all things strongly and sweetly from end to end." As Yeats said of the Irish, "If we were ... bitter beyond all the people of the world, we might yet lie—that too declared and measured—nearest the honeyed comb."[82]

Of course, that process of salvation through self-knowledge may itself be used by the ego as a basis for a new pride:

> I am content to follow to its source
> Every event in action or in thought;
> Measure the lot; forgive myself the lot!
> When such as I cast out remorse
> So great a sweetness flows into the breast
> We must laugh and we must sing,
> We are blest by everything,
> Everything we look upon is blest.[83]

But that pride itself is again known and rendered—in the consciously rhetorical phrase "such as I," as in the allocation of this speech to "My Self" in opposition to "My Soul." And at the end of the volume, after several more turns of the winding stair, yet another countervoice, though conceding that "Repentance keeps my heart impure," will have its say:

> But what am I that dare
> Fancy that I can
> Better conduct myself or have more
> Sense than a common man?[84]

It is surely with such implications as these in mind that Yeats revised "To Ireland in the Coming Times" for reprinting in 1925 to suggest that he was engaged in not the saint's but the poet's disciplined dialogue with the psychic forces of the subliminal world—with the "elemental creatures" that

> hurry from unmeasured mind
> To rant and rage in flood and wind.

"Unmeasured" was introduced in revision not merely to describe the boundless in contrast to the bounded but also to enable a shift in the following lines from "austere" to "measured":

> Yet he who treads in measured ways
> May surely barter gaze for gaze.

In the bartering of gazes or the silent dialogue with those creatures whose name is legion and who represent an interior Lucifer, the poet's measured tread or dance, shaped by his joy, becomes a self-measurement and a transcendence of self. And because in the stream of subliminal shadows one's own shadow mingles with those of one's nation and those of all mankind, both dialogue and measurement have more than personal significance. That is why, as Yeats explored the world of personal drama created by his getting into "an original relation to Irish life," and as he moved outward through the "glove" of the immediate into Irish history, he began to create a profoundly ethical poetry—a poetry not of sanctity but of tragic self-knowledge.

VIII · THE SPIRITUALIZED SOIL

And every Space that a Man views around his dwell-
ing-place
Standing on his own roof or in his garden on a mount
Of twenty-five cubits in height, such Space is his
Universe.
                          —Blake[1]

A man walked, as it were, casting a shadow, and yet
one could never say which was man and which was
shadow, or how many the shadows that he cast. Was
not a nation, as distinguished from a crowd of chance
comers, bound together by this interchange among
streams or shadows...?
                          —*The Trembling of the Veil*[2]

---

i.

AS YEATS NOW MOVED OUTWARD through the glove of immediate
experience into the drama of history—discovering and creating
his own tradition, and measuring the self that did so—he became
increasingly interested in his family heritage. One immediate encouragement to such interest was his absorption in Balzac during 1908-9.[3]
Though Balzac's world contained a necessary balance between the
family and the individual, it was the family (as Yeats believed) which
created "the more noble and stable qualities, those that are spread

through the personality and not isolated in a faculty." As he summarized in 1919:

> For a long time after closing the last novel one finds it hard to admire
> deeply any individual strength that has not family strength behind it.
> He has shown us so many men of talent, to whom we have denied
> our sympathy because of their lack of breeding, and has refused to
> show us even Napoleon apart from his Corsican stock, as strong roots
> running backward to the Middle Ages.[4]

But whatever the immediate encouragements, Yeats's new interest in
the family developed naturally from his early attachment to Sligo and
his later attempt to establish a possessive relation to Ireland as a
whole. Extending such a relation into the past, he found the family
line to be the most accessible and often the most rewarding path.

In the prologue to *Responsibilities,* for example, the family leads
toward a wider historical drama:

> Pardon, old fathers, if you still remain
> Somewhere in ear-shot for the story's end,
> Old Dublin merchant 'free of the ten and four'
> Or trading out of Galway into Spain;
> Old country scholar, Robert Emmet's friend,
> A hundred-year-old memory to the poor ...

This last appositional phrase combines with the direct address to cause
the old scholar to be both alive and a memory (almost to be alive
because a memory) in a semilegendary realm that the speaker himself
had entered with his early phrase, "story's end." Metaphor operates
similarly in another poem, "In Memory of Alfred Pollexfen," which
describes the merging of family tradition into folk history, perpetuated
by

> the lips of common men
> Who carried in their memory
> His childhood and his family.

These shades carried in memory are real presences—like those of
"September 1913" and "To a Shade"—because the true locus of history, from the existential perspective, is the living human mind. The
active power of such presences—though deprecated as "childish" by

the more sophisticated part of the consciousness—is clear in "Under
Saturn":

> Although my wits have gone
> On a fantastic ride, my horse's flanks are spurred
> By childish memories of an old cross Pollexfen,
> And of a Middleton, whose name you never heard,
> And of a red-haired Yeats whose looks, although he died
> Before my time, seem like a vivid memory.

As the slippery syntax indicates ("memories ... of a ... Yeats whose
looks ... seem like a vivid memory"), from this perspective history is
a vista of memory—personal memory shading into that of family and
folk—leading back to the image of one who died long ago. A step
further and one might reach or seem to reach *Anima Mundi* or the
Great Memory. A present mind may then seem to gain access to a
world of actions immanent in both present and past. Hence in "The
Tower" images of men-at-arms are experienced as present realities:

> Before that ruin came, for centuries,
> Rough men-at-arms, cross-gartered to the knees
> Or shod in iron, climbed the narrow stair,
> And certain men-at-arms there were
> Whose images, in the Great Memory stored,
> Come with a loud cry and panting breast
> To break upon a sleeper's rest
> While their great wooden dice beat on the board.

And hence the ageing Yeats would often meditate upon some episode
in his family history and allow the meditation "to expand until the
mind of my family merges into everybody's mind."[5] The particulars
of time seemed a glove through which he might reach the eternal
forms of the imagination.

The concept of the Great Memory is, then, partly a means of
articulating and controlling that experience of the dramatic interpenetration of past and present. Analogies to this are evident not only
in the thought of Vico, Michelet, or Emerson, but also in the practice
of other artists: Browning's reliving, in *The Ring and the Book,* of
past events which are themselves the re-enactment of an archetypal
drama; the exploration by Henry James's characters of a "visitable

past"; or the hallucinatory exploration of such a past by Faulkner's characters—as when in *Absalom, Absalom!* Quentin Compson and his friend Shreve relive the ride of Henry Sutpen and Charles Bon on a Christmas Eve before their time.

But, as all these writers imply, a man may visit the past or be visited by it only when he stands in firm imaginative relationship to a specific locale. "The Tower" indicates the importance for Yeatsian meditation of a consequent technique, which is less an Ignatian "composition of place" than an alchemical invocation of spirits[6]:

> I pace upon the battlements and stare
> On the foundations of a house, or where
> Tree, like a sooty finger, starts from the earth;
> And send imagination forth
> Under the day's declining beam, and call
> Images and memories
> From ruin or from ancient trees,
> For I would ask a question of them all.

The speaker begins with an act that puts him in sympathetic relation to the spirits he would invoke; in pacing upon the battlements he has already stepped into the past. Further, and still before any explicit invocation, he opens himself fully by staring upon objects that suggest the source of historical and natural continuity. The "foundations" are a present evidence of beginnings as well as endings; and the partly humanized tree, also suggesting ruin yet starting from the earth at this moment, informs him of a continuing and available power residing in or behind such natural shapes.

The passage is not merely rhetorical preparation. It exemplifies the fusion of subject and object, of the world of human values and its natural matrix, toward which Yeats continually moved and for which he had found support in Claudel as in Balzac. He admired Claudel's *L'Otage,* in which the besieged aristocrat Coufontaine declares that, as the earth has given his family its name, so he gives to the earth his humanity. He takes pride in the family oak, now uprooted, whose roots were firmly embedded, half in the Roman foundation of the chateau, half in the clay and flint of its native place.[7] In 1919, when Yeats explained to his fellow Irishmen the importance of Balzac and

Claudel, he turned also to the Russian theologian Vladimir Soloviev. A wayside well planted about with roses, a sight Yeats had not seen before in Ireland, had brought to mind "the curious doctrine of Soloviev, that no family has the full condition of perfection that cannot share in what he calls 'the spiritualisation of the soil.'" Yeats suggested that Soloviev's doctrine is "derivable, perhaps, from the truth that all emotional unities find their definition through the image, unlike those of the intellect, which are defined in the logical process." But he knew that he might be finding his own thoughts in Soloviev's argument. "Soloviev is a dry ascetic, half-man, and may see nothing beyond a round of the more obvious virtues approved by his Greek Church." Hence Yeats provided his own definitions:

> I understand by "soil" all the matter in which the soul works, the walls of our houses, the serving up of our meals, and the chairs and tables of our rooms, and the instincts of our bodies; and by "family" all institutions, classes, orders, nations, that arise out of the family and are held together, not by a logical process, but by historical association, and possess a personality for whose lack men are "sheep without a shepherd when the snow shuts out the sun."[8]

Soloviev maintained that the moral destiny of man is "to transfigure and spiritualise material nature";[9] and a similar apocalyptic idea lies behind Yeats's own phrase, "the spiritualisation of the soil," which he attributed to Soloviev. In 1901, recalling myths of the marriage of the Divine Man and Physis, he had suggested that "here in Ireland the spirit of man may be about to wed the soil of the world."[10] He had long held that view, and he had considered "that union with created things" to be the prelude to "the soul's union with the uncreated spirits."[11] In 1906 he again elaborated its apocalyptic implications:

> I am orthodox and pray for a resurrection of the body, and am certain that a man should find his Holy Land where he first crept upon the floor, and that familiar woods and rivers should fade into symbol with so gradual a change that he may never discover, no, not even in ecstasy itself, that he is beyond space, and that time alone keeps him from Primum Mobile, Supernal Eden, Yellow Rose over all.[12]

Behind that partial translation of temporal into eternal we may see the transformation of self and cosmos which, for Blake, would create the New Jerusalem; behind Blake, behind Boehme and alchemy, we may glimpse gnostic theories of the creative and transfiguring imagination, which, through Greek Orthodoxy, helped to mold the thought of Soloviev. Yeats's perception of a similarity was no accident.[13]

When, therefore, the spirit of man weds the soil of the world, it may create those emotional unities which make possible a richly organic social life, and it may also redeem a fallen world. It may enable man to transcend what Yeats had called in 1893 this "world of whirling change, where nothing becomes old and sacred," and re-enter the Eden in which everything is "steeped in the heart," so that every powerful emotion may find at once "noble types and symbols for its expression."[14] Just as Yeats's panoramic vision of history seeks to transmute the flesh into the Eternal Word, so his dramatic experience of history moves toward the union of past and present in a dramatic whole, toward a transcendence of the division between subject and object, and toward the consequent attainment of a resurrection into unity. The goal is again a world of symbolic correspondences that might yield assurance of the eternal harmony of existence.

But the goal envisioned is not quite the goal attained. Without a complementary vision of evil, that ideal would be for Yeats as slight and shadowy as the optimism of Morris or Shaw:

> To the Garden City mind the slightness and shadowiness may seem that of the clouds at dawn; but how can it seem to us in Ireland who have faith—whether heathen or Christian—who have believed from our cradle in original sin, and that man lives under a curse, and so must earn his bread with the sweat of his face, but what comes from blotting out one half of life?[15]

For Yeats that evil comprised not simply the moral weakness of man, but all the antinomies which limit the realization of desire and yet intensify passion. The struggle between the individual will and the social order, said Yeats, makes Balzac's "common soldiers, his valets, his commercial travellers, all men of genius." He doubted if law had for Balzac "any purpose but that of preserving the wine when the grapes had been trodden, and seeing to it that the treaders know their treads."[16] Claudel too had used that metaphor in *L'Otage* to describe the heroic virtues produced when the aristocratic order meets adversity. Sygne cries to her cousin, Coufontaine, "O Georges, toute notre race en ce jour a été mise sous le pressoir," and he answers, "O vin sacré issu de ce quadruple coeur!"[17] The family, the vine of France, the grapes of wrath, and the Eucharist itself merge in a tragic spiritualization of the soil.

Likewise, in each poem celebrating Yeats's family tradition, the very mode of utterance—apology, question, challenge, elegy—embodies a recognition of the counterforces of isolation and fragmentation within the self, within society, and within the cosmos as a whole. From the refusal to indulge in the deceptions or self-deceptions of rhetorician or sentimentalist arises a "vision of reality" more poignant and more passionate than any celebration of an ideal harmony. "In Memory of William Pollexfen," for example, though celebrating family continuity, moves through a sequence of deaths to a cry that renders at once both community and loss:

> At all these death-beds women heard
> A visionary white sea-bird
> Lamenting that a man should die;
> And with that cry I have raised my cry.

Cosmic unity is inseparable from the tears of things. "Under Saturn," too, presents the active shades in memory as moods that disturb the speaker's emotional balance—indeed, as unfavorable astral influences. But they are unfavorable because betrayed: the poem moves to an evocation of the child's "entire emotion" for his native place which is inseparable from a sense of isolation and guilt:

> You heard that laboring man who had served my people. He said
> Upon the open road, near to the Sligo quay—
> No, no, not said, but cried it out—"You have come again,
> And surely after twenty years it was time to come."
> I am thinking of a child's vow sworn in vain
> Never to leave that valley his fathers called their home.

In those last four lines the sense of guilt itself modulates, in a characteristically Yeatsian way, from an active passion to the quiet burden of self-knowledge.

More complex in its handling of such conflicts is the prologue to *Responsibilities*. It begins with explicit apology, thus rendering the speaker's sense of separation from his heritage; but the omission at the outset of any specific guilt succeeds in throwing primary emphasis upon the dramatic continuity of that heritage. Moreover, the heritage itself is of a paradoxical breadth: the poem moves from the solid virtues of merchant and scholar to the largesse of "Soldiers that gave, whatever die was cast," to the more startling nonchalance of the "Old merchant skipper that leaped overboard," and on to the "daily spectacle" of the "silent and fierce old man," William Pollexfen,

> that stirred
> My fancy, and set my boyish lips to say,
> "Only the wasteful virtues earn the sun."

Whatever the *boyish* lips may have said, the context firmly weds for the mature speaker both solid and wasteful giving, both the humble act and the grand gesture, as seen in men who have variously accepted their fate. Only then can the full apology have its proper force:

> Pardon that for a barren passion's sake,
> Although I have come close on forty-nine,
> I have no child, I have nothing but a book,
> Nothing but that to prove your blood and mine.

That "Pardon," like the "forgive" in the closing lines to *Responsibilities,* has been strangely qualified. The poem measures both the speaker's limitation—his failure to maintain the solid virtues and to transmit yet further his inherited stamina—and his acceptance of that limitation. For his "barren passion" is itself a "wasteful virtue" and a result of the "die's cast." Even his wastefulness has a peculiar solidity: the deprecated "book" makes articulate the hitherto silent gestures of soldier and skipper and even the undefined "daily spectacle" of the fierce old man. It transmits within its own half-legendary world the qualities that seem (since the beginning of the "story") always to have belonged to such a world. In the restraint, irony, and well-grounded pride of his apology, as in the breadth of his admirations, the speaker himself thus incarnates the inheritance that he addresses.

If this is a mere "book," it is one which mirrors life with a strange fullness. In fact, these lines set the stage for a dramatic interplay throughout *Responsibilities* between "book" and "child," "doll" and "baby," "art" and "life." Every poem must resolve that tension, often through explicit discussion of the tension itself, and so become a more complete art than the "book" it deprecates or the "priceless things" it wryly defends—an art of living images. The creation of such images, of course, has begun long before the actual "composition" of poems. Yeats wrote of William Pollexfen: "Even today when I read *King Lear* his image is always before me and I often wonder if the delight in passionate men in my plays and in my poetry is more than his memory."[18] It *was* more, as the prologue to *Responsibilities* suggests: for the memory itself is partly a function of that delight—partly a shadow cast by the passionate self of the poet. The speaker mirrors his inheritance partly because that inheritance, as he sees it, has emerged in consciousness as a complex image of his state. The poems can so richly reconcile life and art because they arise in a mind that views history as a realm of "interchange among streams or shadows," where "one could never say which was man and which was shadow"—a realm of shades more than men, more images than shades, where discovery and creation, receiving and giving, are inextricably mingled.

ii.

The dialogue between self and shadows—whether antiselves or projections of the self—produced in "Meditations in Time of Civil War" a rich orchestration of personal and historical conflicts. The poem is a complex act of creation and self-judgment in the realm of the spiritualized soil.

"Surely..." The dialogue enters with that stress on the very first word, as the speaker yearningly considers "Ancestral Houses." Already the opening sentence contains the seeds of its own negation:

> Surely among a rich man's flowering lawns,
> Amid the rustle of his planted hills,
> Life overflows without ambitious pains...

Gradually the image of the fountain emerges, establishing the correspondence of spirit and soil which underlies the entire poem. But the pale abstractness of the setting, in which the fountain alone "rains down life," already calls into question the reality of that social ideal. The retort is deserved: "Mere dreams, mere dreams!" But a surprising counterassertion follows:

> Yet Homer had not sung
> Had he not found it certain beyond dreams
> That out of life's own self-delight had sprung
> The abounding glittering jet . . .

It is the intuition of a radical self-sufficiency and vitality, which has been too hastily projected into the inadequate landscape of ancestral houses. The allusion to Homer suggests the reason for the inadequacy: sweetness must come from strength. Life cannot merely overflow "without ambitious pains"; the "abounding glittering jet" results from a pent-up force that can surmount obstacles. The dream must be revised: it is precisely the ambitious pains of violent and bitter men that

> might rear in stone
> The sweetness that all longed for night and day,
> The gentleness none there had ever known . . .

Instead of an effortless fountain, a monumental synthesis of opposites: but though "in stone," such a synthesis is momentary, a historical climax which bears the seeds of its own destruction. The eighteenth-century elegance, mimed in the verse itself, renders ambitious pains unnecessary and dries up the fountain:

> O what if levelled lawns and gravelled ways
> Where slippered Contemplation finds his ease
> And Childhood a delight for every sense,
> But take our greatness with our violence?

Where then may the speaker himself seek the transfiguration of the fallen world? He turns from the world dreamed of to the world possessed, from "Ancestral Houses" to "My House." At the time he was writing this sequence, 1921-22, Yeats was relating the "sense of possession" he had felt in Sligo to his concept of "Unity of Being":

All that moves us is related to our possible Unity; we lose interest in the abstract and concrete alike; only when we have said, "My fire," and so distinguished it from "the fire" and "a fire," does the fire seem

bright. Every emotion begins to be related, as musical notes are related, to every other.[19]

In "My House" we see a measure of historical continuity, but also
strength and even violence:

> An ancient bridge, and a more ancient tower,
> A farmhouse that is sheltered by its wall,
> An acre of stony ground,
> Where the symbolic rose can break in flower,
> Old ragged elms, old thorns innumerable,
> The sound of the rain or sound
> Of every wind that blows...

Isaiah had prophesied the spiritualization of a soil very like this stony
ground: "The wilderness and the solitary place shall be glad for
them; and the desert shall rejoice, and blossom as the rose." Blake had
envisioned in such a place the marriage of Heaven and Hell:

> Roses are planted where thorns grow,
> And on the barren heath
> Sing the honey bees [20]

But in the harsh Yeatsian landscape even the symbolic rose must
break in flower.

Here the speaker does not inherit the glory of the rich; he re-enacts
the founding of a house:

> Two men have founded here. A man-at-arms
> Gathered a score of horse and spent his days
> In this tumultuous spot,
> Where through long wars and sudden night alarms
> His dwindling score and he seemed castaways
> Forgetting and forgot;
> And I, that after me
> My bodily heirs may find
> To exalt a lonely mind,
> Befitting emblems of adversity.

The isolated modern poet's need to forge his own tradition may itself
be a condition of great achievement: his spiritual inheritance is that
of adversity, with its attendant opportunities. Yet the comparison of

founders ominously reduces the man-at-arms to the speaker's own proud and introverted isolation. Such was not the condition of those violent, bitter men who could rear in stone the sweetness and gentleness that all had longed for. In a wilderness where art is divorced from power and communion, the symbolic rose threatens to be more dream than reality.

That lurking conflict is already evident in the first stanza of "My House." This is a poem of interior landscapes, one in which "familiar woods and rivers...fade into symbol." The speaker might say with Wordsworth,

> bodily eyes
> Were utterly forgotten, and what I saw
> Appeared like something in myself, a dream,
> A prospect in the mind

—or feel with Coleridge that the object of Nature is "the dim awaking of a forgotten or hidden truth of my inner nature."[21] Hence, as we move from "Old ragged elms, old thorns innumerable," to

> The stilted water-hen
> Crossing stream again
> Scared by the splashing of a dozen cows...

we should suspect an ironic self-image, as yet unexplored. The second stanza takes up that stilted isolation, presenting as another spiritual ancestor Milton's Platonist, atop his winding stair, in his "chamber arched with stone," withdrawn from the crude traffic of the world:

> Benighted travellers
> From markets and from fairs
> Have seen his midnight candle glimmering.

The ironic parallels are as yet but implicit; the speaker has not allowed himself to examine his proud isolation in full daylight.

Asking why such blindness is possible, we note a further implication in the Platonist who, the speaker imagines,

> toiled on
> In some like chamber, shadowing forth
> How the daemonic rage
> Imagined everything.

Both he and his spiritual heir, though lonely creators of emblems, castaways from the world of markets and fairs, are yet at home in a lighted chamber, communing with the world soul, while others are "benighted." But they do not commune with the "holy calm" that overspread Wordsworth's soul and caused him to see the landscape as a prospect in the mind. The demiurgic power as this speaker experiences it is a "daemonic rage," the transcendental corollary of his own bitter violence and of the "long wars and sudden night alarms" that isolate him as they once isolated the first founder in this spot. Again the poem's complex theme modulates from reassuring unity to division and fragmentation. But the conflicts in "My House" are submerged, apparent only because the speaker is shadowing forth more complete emblems of his own condition than he yet admits.

He turns now to another possession, the table whereon he shadows forth that daemonic rage. Into his world of adversity, isolation, and cyclical change comes "Sato's gift, a changeless sword," placed by pen and paper

> That it may moralise
> My days out of their aimlessness.

But for a poet aware of the virtues of change as well as its dangers, that is a vexing symbol:

> In Sato's house,
> Curved like new moon, moon-luminous,
> It lay five hundred years.
> Yet if no change appears
> No moon; only an aching heart
> Conceives a changeless work of art.

Though a world of tortured change needs an image of the changeless, does not that image itself imply a fallacious ideal, a static culture, empty and unproductive?[22] No, the speaker surmounts his objection by imagining in the East an unchanging tradition maintained by centuries of mental alertness, inspired by transcendental longings:

> Soul's beauty being most adored,
> Men and their business took
> The soul's unchanging look;

For the most rich inheritor,
Knowing that none could pass Heaven's door
That loved inferior art,
Had such an aching heart
That he, although a country's talk
For silken clothes and stately walk,
Had walking wits; it seemed
Juno's peacock screamed.

There, in contrast to the milieu of "Ancestral Houses," the grandson was no "mouse," the "inherited glory of the rich" was not an empty shell, the peacock did not merely stray "with delicate feet upon old terraces" while Juno was ignored by the "garden deities."

But is that peacock scream, that apocalyptic annunciation,[23] more than another illusion? Whether dream or past reality—and it is slightly distanced by the ironic diction of this section—it can now do no more than stimulate this speaker's aching heart. Is that not function enough? An ambiguous answer emerges in the next section, "My Descendants." Returning to the cyclical world of the West, to the lunar inheritance which for better or worse he must enjoy and transmit, the speaker presents himself as one who "must nourish dreams" —but is he obligated or condemned to do so? And are they unsubstantial fantasies or symbolic roses, evasion or transfiguration of life?

Having inherited a vigorous mind
From my old fathers, I must nourish dreams
And leave a woman and a man behind
As vigorous of mind, and yet it seems
Life scarce can cast a fragrance on the wind,
Scarce spread a glory to the morning beams,
But the torn petals strew the garden plot;
And there's but common greenness after that.

But if his descendants should lose that ambiguous flower, he would, enraged, hasten the very cyclical destruction that haunts him:

May this laborious stair and this stark tower
Become a roofless ruin that the owl
May build in the cracked masonry and cry
Her desolation to the desolate sky.

No longer dare he hope that his "bodily heirs" may find, to their advantage, "Befitting emblems of adversity." He may be both founder and last inheritor—

> The Primum Mobile that fashioned us
> Has made the very owls in circles move

—and he will therefore take consolation only in the goods of the moment:

> And I, that count myself most prosperous,
> Seeing that love and friendship are enough,
> For an old neighbor's friendship chose the house
> And decked and altered it for a girl's love . . .

Though still unable to refrain from adding another phrase which contemplates at least some bare monument to the present—

> And know whatever flourish and decline
> These stones remain their monument and mine

—in his minimal optimism he has now abandoned even the immortality of the "changeless work of art." Surely here at least the speaker may find the self-sufficiency for which he longs: no mere dream, but the reality of "life's own self-delight."

Yet in glimpsing the depths of his isolation, he has begun to reach outward: "Seeing that love and friendship are enough." That evocation of a sweetness and gentleness not "in stone," as in ancestral houses, but memorialized by these "stones," translates the entire problem to a different plane. The isolation itself called into question, the speaker turns from house and descendants to "The Road at My Door."

> An affable Irregular,
> A heavily-built Falstaffian man,
> Comes cracking jokes of civil war
> As though to die by gunshot were
> The finest play under the sun.

He turns from lunar tragedy to solar comedy, from lofty poetic isolation to the gay cameraderie of a modern man-at-arms—or (in terms of what Yeats called Shakespeare's dominant myth, and was one of his own) from that porcelain vessel, Richard II, saluting his native soil with ostentatious sentiment and telling sad stories of the death of kings, to those vessels of clay, Falstaff and Prince Hal, with their rough humor and affection.[24] Adversity and violence need not imply isolation, nor can the poet dismiss this comedy as trivial:

> A brown Lieutenant and his men,
> Half dressed in national uniform,
> Stand at my door, and I complain
> Of the foul weather, hail and rain,
> A pear tree broken by the storm.

It is not a symbolic rose that has broken, and the contrast of persons recalls the unacknowledged difference in "My House" between the introverted speaker and the first founder in that tumultuous spot. By night the Platonist in his tower had seemed romantically superior to the travellers; by day the retiring and complaining poet becomes a half-comic, half-pathetic pastoral foil to the new military hero.[25] He is, in fact, like that "shadow" noted earlier, the stilted waterhen "Scared by the splashing of a dozen cows."

> I count those feathered balls of soot
> The moor-hen guides upon the stream,
> To silence the envy in my thought;
> And turn towards my chamber, caught
> In the cold snows of a dream.

What dream has been nourished? In this solitary place what narcissus has broken in flower? The implied answer is developed in "The Stare's Nest by My Window," and it will lead, in "I See Phantoms...," beyond the humility of perception to a new reconciliation: an ironic acceptance of the poet's vocation.

> The bees build in the crevices
> Of loosening masonry, and there
> The mother birds bring grubs and flies.
> My wall is loosening; honey-bees,
> Come build in the empty house of the stare.

He no longer imagines a sweetness that bitter men might rear in stone, nor does he hope defiantly for the destruction of his tower and for owls to "build in the cracked masonry." He now sees that sweetness may reside in the very loss he had feared—the very loosening of his wall. This is an inevitable discovery—or rather, rediscovery, for the breaking of protective walls, the nakedness before the winds of heaven, had long been known to Yeats as a prerequisite of poetic vision. Although the invoked honey bees recall those in Porphyry's cave of the nymphs—souls who are "eminently just and sober" and who, "after having performed such things as are acceptable to the gods," will reascend from the world of generation[26]—they also, and perhaps more importantly, recall those which Blake imagined as singing on the barren heath, on the desert that blossoms as the rose. Yeats had once read that prophecy thus: "Freedom shows beauty like roses, and sweetness like that given by the honey of bees, in the road where morality had only revealed a desert or a heath."[27] Given Blake's understanding of negative and restrictive morality (a disguise for the impulse to tyrannize, to wall others in or out), the sweetness which comes with the abandonment of such morality is not opposed to that ("both cathartic and preservative"[28]) produced by Porphyry's bees. For the speaker of this poem such sweetness can come only with freedom from his own self-confinement. Though able, in Shelley's symbolic language, to imagine his tower as contrary in meaning to a dark cave,[29] he now sees that the cloistered permanence of his "chamber arched with stone" is what it always was, the cavern of the mind of which Blake had written: "For man has closed himself up, till he sees all things thro' narrow chinks of his cavern."[30] As this speaker states it, now fusing visions of himself and of society:

> We are closed in, and the key is turned
> On our uncertainty; somewhere
> A man is killed, or a house burned,
> Yet no clear fact to be discerned:
> Come build in the empty house of the stare.

He shares Eliot's waste land—

> We think of the key, each in his prison
> Thinking of the key, each confirms a prison
> Only at nightfall, aethereal rumours
> Revive for a moment a broken Coriolanus

—and the waste land of Claudel's Coufontaine:

> Là-bas on dit qu'il y a eu je sais quoi,
> Les villes de bois qui brûlent, une victoire vaguement
> gagnée. L'Europe est vide et personne ne parle sur la terre.[31]

But the besieged dynastic house or prison is not, from this speaker's humbled position, the abbey of Coufontaine or even "some marvellous empty sea-shell"; it is an empty starling's nest.

Not through coincidence or mere rhetorical artifice does he fuse here the isolation and vastation sprung from his own mind and those imposed by violence from without. He has moved from a romantic parallel between poet and man-at-arms to a humiliating acknowledgment of their differences, and now to an agonized perception of their moral identity:

> A barricade of stone or of wood;
> Some fourteen days of civil war;
> Last night they trundled down the road
> That dead young soldier in his blood:
> Come build in the empty house of the stare.

> We had fed the heart on fantasies,
> The heart's grown brutal from the fare;
> More substance in our enmities
> Than in our love; O honey-bees,
> Come build in the empty house of the stare.

The poet's barricade of self-sufficiency and his consequent self-brutalization are, in his introverted realm, equivalent to the nationalist-inspired civil war that rages about him. "Was not a nation...bound together by this interchange among streams or shadows...?" His fantasies that bitterness and violence might bring sweetness, his glorying in adversity, and his rage against his descendants have earned his indictment. But the indictment itself is a partial release from the prison: hence the initial statement, in the first person singular, "My wall is loosening," leads to community in isolation, "We are closed in," and then to a perception of shared guilt, a moral identification of self and those beyond all barricades, "We had fed the heart on fantasies..." In the final cry to the honeybees the arrogant dream of self-sufficiency is transcended; the perception that "love and friendship are enough" has flowered, purged of its complacency.

The poet can now climb his winding stair, not to a chamber arched with stone, but to the top of a *broken* tower, where he is possessed by a vision:

I climb to the tower-top and lean upon broken stone,
A mist that is like blown snow is sweeping over all,
Valley, river, and elms, under the light of a moon
That seems unlike itself, that seems unchangeable,
A glittering sword out of the east. A puff of wind
And those white glimmering fragments of the mist sweep by.
Frenzies bewilder, reveries perturb the mind;
Monstrous familiar images swim to the mind's eye.

Every "Space that a Man views around his dwelling-place / Standing on his own roof ... is his Universe." But as the animating wind makes clear, this universe is no longer a confining mental chamber. The speaker is naked to the winds of heaven. He leans upon the very ruin of self-sufficiency; sweeping over the landscape are the "cold snows of a dream" shared by those beyond the broken barricades. Though he sees by a light whose ominously unchangeable source is a bizarre transmutation of his own earlier ideal, "A glittering sword out of the east," and though the "monstrous" images that come are also damningly "familiar," this is no private fantasy but a vision based upon his own complicity in the engulfing horror.

The first group of phantoms objectifies the brutality and hatred he has just recognized:

"Vengeance upon the murderers," the cry goes up,
"Vengeance for Jacques Molay." In cloud-pale rags, or in lace,
The rage-driven, rage-tormented, and rage-hungry troop,
Trooper belabouring trooper, biting at arm or at face,
Plunges towards nothing, arms and fingers spreading wide
For the embrace of nothing ...

But he is no longer a lofty Platonist, shadowing forth the "daemonic rage"; he glimpses the abyss within himself:

> and I, my wits astray
> Because of all that senseless tumult, all but cried
> For vengeance on the murderers of Jacques Molay.

The next group, phantoms of the "heart's fullness," provides an emotional antithesis:

> Their legs long, delicate and slender, aquamarine their eyes,
> Magical unicorns bear ladies on their backs.
> The ladies close their musing eyes. No prophecies,
> Remembered out of Babylonian almanacs,
> Have closed the ladies' eyes, their minds are but a pool
> Where even longing drowns under its own excess;
> Nothing but stillness can remain when hearts are full
> Of their own sweetness, bodies of their loveliness.

But this is not an ethical antithesis: these apparitions are not the invoked honeybees. Here one aspect of the self-sufficiency and self-delight which the speaker first projected into the fountain of "Ancestral Houses" achieves final definition: not a fountain but a pool, not an abounding jet of life but an eternal stillness of self-contemplation. However beautiful, it is the deathly goal of Narcissus. For the living speaker these ladies and unicorns can image not a solution but one term of a predicament.

Indeed, they are strangely similar to their antitheses, the rage-driven troop: "even longing drowns under its own excess." Because the vision has moved from one blindness to another, from the ravenous imperception of Breughel's blindmen careering into the abyss to the closed eyes of Moreau's narcissistic women and unicorns,[32] it can now move easily, through an inversion of details further stressing that affinity, to a harshly empty synthesis:

> The cloud-pale unicorns, the eyes of aquamarine,
> The quivering half-closed eyelids, the rags of cloud or of lace,
> Or eyes that rage has brightened, arms it has made lean,
> Give place to an indifferent multitude, give place
> To brazen hawks.

Predatory rage and static self-satisfaction merge in a yet more terrible blindness:

> Nor self-delighting reverie,
> Nor hate of what's to come, nor pity for what's gone,
> Nothing but grip of claw, and the eye's complacency,
> The innumerable clanging wings that have put out the moon.

Such is the consummation the speaker envisions in modern history, such the consummation of his own ethical dialectic. Yet, though inescapably of his time, he is partly freed by the vision itself. He does not fully yield to the rage of the avenging troop, and he cannot now adopt the transcendent narcissism of aquamarine or closed eyes. The poem renders a precarious solution: not the imagined escape from the prison of self through freedom in love, but the open-eyed self-recognition of the half-trapped poet.

> I turn away and shut the door, and on the stair
> Wonder how many times I could have proved my worth
> In something that all others understand or share;
> But O! ambitious heart, had such a proof drawn forth
> A company of friends, a conscience set at ease,
> It had but made us pine the more.

The "ambitious pains" which vexed him at the beginning of the poem cannot be escaped. The dialogical movement here as throughout the meditation—"But O! ambitious heart"—renders the speaker's alertness to the continual temptations to self-containment. It renders, therefore, his actual if momentary freedom from such self-containment. Because all images of fulfilment carry their own irony, he must accept the problematic human state, with its attendant guilt and dissatisfaction. And if life cannot in any facile way be self-delighting—

> The abstract joy,
> The half-read wisdom of daemonic images,
> Suffice the ageing man as once the growing boy.

The irony of "suffice," which has led critics to comment upon Yeats's vacillation between action and contemplation or upon his "unfortunate" dabbling in the occult, can be fully weighed only in the context of this rich meditation on what may and what may not suffice the heart. That irony implies no dismissal of the poetic task as "mere dreams." Nor is the speaker now Shelley's "visionary prince" priding himself, through romantic irony, on "mysterious wisdom won by toil."[33] He is rather the fortunate victim of the "daemonic images" we have just seen, which are for him the burden of self-knowledge. He no longer strives for the goal of action or that of fantasy—a substitute for action.

> The rhetorician would deceive his neighbours,
> The sentimentalist himself; while art
> Is but a vision of reality.[34]

The complex irony in that "but," as in the "suffice" of this poem, partly answers any objection that "Meditations in Time of Civil War" does not move to a clear ethical transcendence of the speaker's problem, as glimpsed in "The Stare's Nest at My Window." A willed vision of what the honeybees might bring would be factitious; the poet can realize only what he is. The rest may come of its own accord when, through being perceived, the psychic walls begin to crumble. Ribh would say, "He holds him from desire"—and, indeed, the final section of this poem has rendered just such a "symbolical revelation received after the suspension of desire" as "What Magic Drum?" describes. "Does not all art come," Yeats wrote, "when a nature, that never ceases to judge itself, exhausts personal emotion in action or desire so completely that something impersonal . . . starts into its place, something which is as unforeseen, as completely organised, even as unique, as the images that pass before the mind between sleeping and waking?"[35] Such are the "daemonic images" of this last section; such, in a larger sense, is the entire poem.

Despite Yeats's frequently quoted remarks about virtue as dramatic, the wearing of a mask,[36] this poem renders his understanding of the fact that attention is the mother of virtue as it is of art. Though the speaker wears various masks of poetic or moral ambition, engages in the deceits of rhetorician and sentimentalist, he closely watches the self that does so. From that watching, that attention, spring both the ethical development of the speaker and the poem itself. For the poem, the "vision of reality," is of that mask-wearing self, and it is therefore, like the poems of Villon, finally "without fear or moral ambition" though decidedly ethical in its substance. In 1905, arguing against didactic art, art composed with the intent to persuade, Yeats had said:

If we understand our own minds, and the things that are striving to utter themselves through our minds, we move others, not because we have understood or thought about those others, but because all life has the same root. Coventry Patmore has said, "The end of art is peace," and the following of art is little different from the following of religion in the intense preoccupation that it demands. Somebody has said, "God asks nothing of the highest soul except attention"; and so necessary is attention to mastery in any art, that there are moments when we think that nothing else is necessary, and nothing else so difficult.[37]

Yeats clearly understood another of Patmore's statements: "Attention to realities, rather than the fear of God, is 'the beginning of wisdom'..." Given the bold prophetic note sounded by his art, we can see that he also might say with Patmore: "Indeed, it is difficult to say how far an absolute moral courage in acknowledging intuitions may not be of the very nature of genius and whether it might not be described as a sort of interior sanctity which dares to see and confess to itself that it sees, though its vision should place it in a minority of one."[38]

In "Meditations in Time of Civil War," as in the apocalyptic romances of the nineties, a partial yielding to the daemonic voice enables the poet to perceive and judge those powers within him which, unconsciously obeyed, would lead and have led to historical catastrophe. But this poem of dramatic experience shows more clearly the complex interior dialogue through which suffering moves toward illumination, as the daemonic is incorporated into the precarious equilibrium of personality—and so transformed. The last sentence of the poem, ironically echoing Wordsworth's "Ode on the Intimations of Immortality,"[39] reinforces this conclusion. Wordsworth had said:

> Shades of the prison-house begin to close
>   Upon the growing Boy,
> But He beholds the light, and whence it flows,
>   He sees it in his joy...

And in compensation for the complete loss of that light, Wordsworth had found "soothing thoughts that spring / Out of human suffering," a "faith that looks through death," a "philosophic mind." But the Yeatsian speaker, aware of the Wordsworthian atrophy so rationalized, ironically affirms in his own life a lack of change, and so points to a more genuinely continuing growth:

> The abstract joy,
> The half-read wisdom of daemonic images,
> Suffice the ageing man as once the growing boy.

Though his continuing joy is "abstract," an inevitable limitation arising from his turning inward to the source of daemonic images, the light shining through those images has led him to perceive the existence of his own prisonhouse, his chamber arched with stone, and to prevent it from closing upon him irrevocably. It has led him also to see that the "philosophic mind," with *its* "eye's complacency" is another form of the spiritual atrophy that tempts through every image that asks to be taken as a final truth, another phantom illustrating the multiform blindness which he precariously escapes. Perception must "suffice," and full perception warns that our wisdom is momentary and but "half-read."

The symbolic rose, which here *breaks* in flower so diversely, cannot be forced. It must bloom in the midst of civil war: a unity of being that maintains the abounding jet of life must arise from the perception of disunity. No individual may complacently possess that fountain of life's self-delight. He may know it only through continuing openness, continuing vulnerability. Yeats had recognized as much, in a passage of 1917 which foreshadowed this poem:

> A poet, when he is growing old, will ask himself if he cannot keep his mask and his vision without new bitterness, new disappointment ...
>
> Surely, he may think, now that I have found vision and mask I need not suffer any longer. He will buy perhaps some small old house, where, like Ariosto, he can dig his garden, and think that in the return of birds and leaves, or moon and sun, and in the evening flight of the rooks he may discover rhythm and pattern like those in sleep and so never awake out of vision. Then he will remember Wordsworth withering into eighty years, honoured and empty-witted, and climb to some waste room and find, forgotten there by youth, some bitter crust.[40]

And the speaker of "Meditations in Time of Civil War" had guessed as much, near the beginning of the poem: "Homer had not sung ..." The *Iliad* offers no Goethean assurance of the eternal harmony of existence; indeed, Homer taught Goethe that in our life on earth we have, properly speaking, to enact Hell. The rose, finally, is the meditation itself, the spiritualization of that tragic soil, the vision of that state. For both the poet and the man, Yeats was discovering, the "peace" of that vision is the paradoxically active means of transfiguring the wheel of destiny.

IX · POET OF ANGLO-IRELAND

Preserve what is living and help the two Irelands,
Gaelic Ireland and Anglo Ireland so to unite that
neither shall shed its pride.
                        —*Pages from a Diary*...[1]

I prefer that the defeated cause should be more vividly described than that which has the advertisement of
victory. No battle has been finally won or lost.
                        —*Wheels and Butterflies*[2]

---

i.

WHEN, IN THE LATE NINETIES, Yeats placed himself in a personal
relation to Ireland, he not only moved toward a more autobiographical poetry and a dramatic relation to history but also took
an important step toward a specific historical allegiance that would
deeply affect his poetry. His early attachment to Sligo, his family
heritage, his fruitful reliance upon Coole Park—all pointed toward
the Anglo-Irish tradition. But the nationalism that had conflicted with
his early provincial attachment yet more decidedly conflicted with
any attachment to Anglo-Ireland.

As Yeats recalled in 1930, the question was complicated by his
early romanticism. Anglo-Ireland was part of the eighteenth century
and, though such nationalists as John O'Leary and J. F. Taylor praised

that century and "seemed of it," Yeats himself had first "ignored it" because he wanted "romantic furniture" and then "hated it" because political opponents "used it to cry down Irish literature that sought audience or theme in Ireland."[3] He turned away from Goldsmith and Burke because he considered them "a part of the English system," and he turned away from Swift because he acknowledged no verse between Cowley and Smart, no prose between Sir Thomas Browne and Landor.[4] There were yet further complications. His early sympathy for the peasantry was not only nationalistic and romantic, but also religious and economic. At seventeen, "bored by an Irish Protestant point of view that suggested by its blank abstraction chloride of lime," he had sought out the peasant's pagan and Catholic lore.[5] For him as for his father, Protestantism brought to mind the stereotype of the Belfast man, epitome of puritanical commercialism.[6] Moreover, Yeats was then one who could praise the noble tradition which had made "neither for great wealth nor great poverty" and condemn the "new and ignoble" tradition of the vulgar rich, "perfected and in part discovered by the English-speaking people," which had made the arts all but impossible.[7] He could also attack the wealthy as decayed gentry. In 1889, for example, he had criticized Robert Louis Stevenson's Chevalier Burke, in *The Master of Ballantrae,* as a false portrayal of the typical Irishman:

> He is really a broken-down Norman gentleman, a type found only among the gentry who make up what is called "the English Garrison." He is from the same source as the Hell Fire Club and all the reckless braggadocio of the eighteenth century in Ireland; one of that class who, feeling the uncertainty of their tenures, as Froude explains it, lived the most devil-may-care existence.... They are bad, but none of our making; English settlers bore them, English laws moulded them. No one who knows the serious, reserved and suspicious Irish peasant ever held them in any way representative of the national type.[8]

By 1891, after much study of the eighteenth century in preparation for a historical essay never published,[9] Yeats was only a little less antagonistic to the Anglo-Irish gentry. It is a class, he said, "that held its acres once at the sword's point, and a little later were pleased by the tinsel villany [sic] of the Hell Fire Club." Its existence had been "a pleasant thing enough for the world. It introduced a new wit—a humor whose essence was dare-devilry and good-comradeship, half real, half assumed." But for Ireland it had been "almost entirely an evil." Not the least of its sins had been "the creation in the narrow circle of its dependents of the pattern used later on for ... 'the stage Irishman.'" The quality of the humor aside, Yeats agreed with William Carleton that the peasant "is not appeased because the foot that passes over him is shod with laughter."[10] In the novels of Croker, Lover, and Lever, Yeats saw the image of this gentry, usually with "a hospitable, genial, good soldier-like disposition," but with "no more sense of responsibility, as a class, than have the *dullahans, thivishes, bowas,* and *water sheries* of the spirit-ridden peasantry." That lack of responsibility explained why the Anglo-Irish had never had a poet: "Poetry needs a God, a cause, or a country." Maria Edgeworth was consequently the only novelist of the gentry to receive Yeats's full praise:

> She constantly satirized their recklessness, their love of all things English, their oppression of and contempt for their own country. . . . Her novels give, indeed, systematically the mean and vulgar side of all that gay life celebrated by Lever.[11]

It is no wonder that Yeats's *Representative Irish Tales,* which contains these comments, was reviewed by one periodical, as Yeats said later, "under the idea that it was written by a barbarous super-republican American."[12]

But after the turn of the century, when Yeats began to formulate his own conservative synthesis, his view of the aristocracy changed markedly. He was both pursuing his anti-self and discovering his own heritage. By 1904 he treated with respect and admiration not only the ancient Irish and Norman-Irish aristocracy but also the Anglo-Irish of the eighteenth century. The stories retold in Lady Gregory's *Gods and Fighting Men,* he said,

> helped to sing the old Irish and Norman-Irish aristocracy to their end. They heard the hereditary poets and story-tellers, and they took to horse and died fighting against Elizabeth or against Cromwell; and when an English-speaking aristocracy had their place, it listened to no poetry indeed, but it felt about it in the popular mind an exacting and ancient tribunal, and began a play that had for spectators men and women that loved the high wasteful virtues.

He no longer saw foreign exploiters wearing the mask of harsh comedy. The English were at least trying to learn an ancient role from their conquered spectators.

> I do not think that their own mixed blood or the habit of their time need take all, or nearly all, credit or discredit for the impulse that made our modern gentlemen fight duels over pocket-handkerchiefs, and set out to play ball against the gates of Jerusalem for a wager, and scatter money before the public eye; and at last, after an epoch of such eloquence the world has hardly seen its like, lose their public spirit and their high heart and grow querulous and selfish as men do who have played life out not heartily but with noise and tumult. Had they understood the people and the game a little better, they might have created an aristocracy in an age that has lost the meaning of the word.

Yeats now criticized the Anglo-Irish primarily not for cruelty and irresponsibility but for lack of depth and complexity in their passion. In order to "create a great community," he would now re-create the old aristocratic foundations of life—but "not as they existed in that splendid misunderstanding of the eighteenth century."[13]

As he clarified his aristocratic ideal, he distinguished it from its debased versions. Though he was pursuing an anti-self, that anti-self was no character portrayed by Lever or Lover. Even in 1904 he saw the nineteenth-century querulousness and selfishness as twice removed from the ancient ideal. And when, during the 1920's, he finally accepted the Anglo-Irish tradition as his own, he could define it all the more firmly. No longer was Chevalier Burke typical of the gentry as a whole—broken-down Norman gentlemen, eighteenth-century braggadocios, and nineteenth-century English Garrison. A gulf had opened between the age of Swift and the gay and vulgar life chronicled in the novels Yeats read in his youth. After the French Revolution, he said, the "Protestant Ascendancy with its sense of responsibility" gave place to the "Garrison, a political party of Protestant and Catholic landowners, merchants and officials." These "loved the soil of Ireland"—"the merchant loved with an ardour, I have not met elsewhere, some sea-board town where he had made his money, or spent his youth"—but

> they could give to a people they thought unfit for self-government, nothing but a condescending affection. They preferred frieze-coated

humourists, dare-devils upon horseback, to ordinary men and women; created in Ireland and elsewhere an audience that welcomed the vivid imaginations of Lever, Lover, Somerville and Ross.[14]

For the moment Yeats could dissociate even his immediate parental stock from the Protestant Ascendancy with which he poetically identified himself.

Paradoxically, his complete allegiance to Anglo-Ireland was made possible by the establishment in 1922 of the Irish Free State. Nine years later Yeats described its effect with his usual vivid oversimplification. The "mere existence" of the new Irish state, he said, had delivered artists from "obsession." No longer distracted by political nationalism, they could now give full attention to their work.

> Freedom from obsession brought me a transformation akin to religious conversion. I had thought much of my fellow-workers—Synge, Lady Gregory, Lane—but had seen nothing in Protestant Ireland as a whole but its faults, had carried through my projects in face of its opposition or indifference, had fed my imagination upon the legends of the Catholic villages or upon medieval poetry; but now my affection turned to my own people, to my own ancestors, to the books they had read.[15]

Though the transformation had really been long in developing, his memory stressed this essential truth: with Protestant Ireland now but a component of a free Irish state, he could change his allegiance without seeming, to himself or others, to desert the nationalist cause.

But political reasons had not disappeared from his mind. The Anglo-Irish, he thought, had much to teach a young state seeking political stability. Momentarily forgetting the praise O'Leary and Taylor had given the eighteenth century, he said: "Now that Ireland was substituting traditions of government for the rhetoric of agitation, our eighteenth century had regained its importance." And religion was still of political significance to him, though the "obsession" was different:

> It seemed that we the Protestants had a part to play at last that might find us allies everywhere, for we alone had not to assume in public discussion of all great issues that we could find in St. Mark or St. Matthew a shorthand report of the words of Christ attested before a magistrate. We sought religious conviction by a more difficult research . . .[16]

He was perhaps remembering that in 1925, after his speech on divorce in the Irish Senate, a passionate and ironic plea for tolerance, one senator had angrily retorted that the Gospel according to St. Matthew was historically accurate and, furthermore, should be the law of the land.[17] Catholic censorship had of course plagued Yeats ever since the controversy over *The Countess Cathleen*. But before Irish Independence he had argued (with some reason) that such confusion of art with homiletics derived from English bourgeois puritanism and was therefore grotesquely out of place in Ireland under the apparent protection of the Roman Church.[18] Now, as Protestantism came to mean the heroism of Parnell rather than the calculation of the Belfast man, and as Catholicism came to mean a crude intellectual tyranny in modern Ireland rather than a rich medieval culture, Yeats's historical analysis and his strategy changed. If, as he came to believe, in his country the Church *was* Babbitt,[19] co-operation was impossible.

It is clear that Yeats had changed not his passion but its object. With rebellious pride the growing boy had defended the Catholic peasantry against the Anglo-Irish gentry; with that same pride the ageing man defended the heirs of those Anglo-Irish against the new Catholic rulers of the Irish Free State. The boy had learned, with his Fenianism, the righteous indignation and aristocratic integrity of John O'Leary; the man saw O'Leary's spiritual ancestry in the people of Jonathan Swift. In 1925, concluding his senate speech on the divorce question, Yeats said:

> I think it is tragic that within three years of this country gaining its independence we should be discussing a measure which a minority of this nation considers to be grossly oppressive. I am proud to consider myself a typical man of that minority. We against whom you have done this thing, are no petty people. We are one of the great stocks of Europe. We are the people of Burke; we are the people of Grattan; we are the people of Swift, the people of Parnell. We have created the most of the modern literature of this country. We have created the best of its political intelligence. Yet I do not altogether regret what has happened. I shall be able to find out, if not I, my children will be able to find out whether we have lost our stamina or not. You have defined our position and given us a popular following. If we have not lost our stamina then your victory will be brief, and your defeat final, and when it comes this nation may be transformed.[20]

Nearly three decades before, Yeats had written to George Russell: "Absorb Ireland and her tragedy and you will be the poet of a people, perhaps the poet of a new insurrection."[21] That counsel he had really directed to himself—and now, political circumstances reversed, directed to himself again. For one who continually sought emblems of adversity, who rejoiced in the fallen world from which he tried to escape, the repetition of the tragedy was not altogether matter for regret.

ii.

Such, in brief, was Yeats's revaluation of the Anglo-Irish heritage that he was to explore during the rest of his life. Establishing a possessive relation to that strand of history, he had in 1917 acquired the Norman tower at Ballylee, "a permanent symbol of my work plainly visible to the passerby." His theories of art, he said, depended upon just such "rooting of mythology in the earth."[22] Partly because its main theme is not the Anglo-Irish heritage itself, "The Tower" (1925) illustrates how, uniting the pride of the two Irelands, Yeats had gradually rooted his own mythology in that soil of the past.

"What shall I do with this absurdity ... ?" After the vigorous complaint against old age, posing the problem of the "Excited, passionate, fantastical / Imagination" that is "derided by / A sort of battered kettle at the heel," the speaker of "The Tower" enters upon a tortuous and elliptical reverie. Far from bidding the Muse "go pack," he invokes images and memories from the spiritualized soil, "For I would ask a question of them all." But he does not ask the question in this dialogue with history until ten stanzas later. Meanwhile we follow, with fascination and some perplexity, what seems but brilliant improvisation, a Yeatsian preponderance of means over ends like that apparent (but merely apparent) in "All Souls' Night."

The personages invoked, however, all testify to the richly varied past that is now the speaker's possession. Mrs. French is a figure from that cruel eighteenth-century comedy which Yeats once, with Carleton, utterly rejected. The ballad-poet Raftery had composed in the eighteenth-century tradition a tribute to one Mary Hynes, the remaining foundation of whose house the speaker has just stared upon. In *The Celtic Twilight* Yeats had re-created their story and its setting with quiet sympathy.[23] There too he had mentioned the man "drowned in the great bog of Cloone" because of Raftery's song. Red Hanrahan is even more completely a possession: Yeats created him as Raftery had created the moonlit image of Mary Hynes, and "drove him drunk or sober" across the countryside as Raftery had driven the men bewitched by his song. But Hanrahan too came from the eighteenth century: the original name Yeats gave to that poet and hedge-schoolmaster, O'Sullivan Rua, suggests his prototype, the Irish peasant poet, Eoghan Ruadh Ó Suileabháin.[24] Finally, the "ancient bankrupt master of this house" is (like the first founder in "Meditations in Time of Civil War") parallel to the speaker himself, save that he has "finished his dog's day."

These and some lesser figures now inhabit a common limbo. Accessible to the speaker's call, they are his present re-creations, who stand ready to instruct him. Both creatures and masters, they are possessed by the speaker and they possess him. That is so because they variously embody the power and the predicament of the excited, passionate, fantastical imagination: an outrageous power, maiming, blinding, maddening, murdering—the "horrible splendour of desire." If the farmer was Mrs. French's victim, so the drowned man was Raftery's, so Hanrahan was Yeats's; and perhaps the ancient bankrupt master of the Norman tower was, like Raftery, Yeats, Hanrahan, and all imaginative men, victim not only of circumstance but also of that very imagination which now has made him "fabulous." Down the centuries we see "Rough men-at-arms," images of that same "horrible splendour of desire," who

> Come with loud cry and panting breast
> To break upon a sleeper's rest
> While their great wooden dice beat on the board.

It is precisely that splendor which the speaker himself now defiantly elects, in full knowledge of its destructive power, as his highly traditional goal:

> the tragedy began
> With Homer that was a blind man,
> And Helen has all living hearts betrayed.
> O may the moon and sunlight seem

> One inextricable beam,
> For if I triumph I must make men mad.

Only such triumph now seems possible to the ageing poet under "the day's declining beam," deserted as the blind man is by all things belonging to "the prosaic light of day," condemned to the moonlit realm of the imagination. Here, yet more violently than in "Meditations in Time of Civil War," the predicament reverses that of Wordsworth's "Ode on the Intimations of Immortality," where the speaker is troubled by the fading of the visionary light "into the light of common day."

If, when Yeats's speaker finally asks his question—

> Did all old men and women, rich and poor,
> Who trod upon these rocks or passed this door,
> Whether in public or in secret rage
> As I do now against old age?

—it now seems anticlimactic, that is because already the undeniable fact of age pales before the splendor of the fantastical imagination that remains. The embodied spirits stand before him, mute witnesses to his predicament, yet witnesses now far more to the continuing power that resides within him. And the calculated anticlimax is surmounted by a strange turn of events:

> Go therefore; but leave Hanrahan,
> For I need all his mighty memories.

The speaker retains out of that company the one who is most completely his creature and his master. His own mighty memories are not enough; he needs a memory's memory. Yet that paradoxical declaration of dependence leads not to a genuine question but to a final taunt:

> Old lecher with a love on every wind,
> Bring up out of that deep considering mind
> All that you have discovered in the grave,
> For it is certain that you have
> Reckoned up every unforeknown, unseeing
> Plunge, lured by a softening eye,

Or by a touch or a sigh,
Into the labyrinth of another's being;

Does the imagination dwell the most
Upon a woman won or a woman lost?
If on the lost, admit you turned aside
From a great labyrinth out of pride,
Cowardice, some silly over-subtle thought
Or anything called conscience once;
And that if memory recur, the sun's
Under eclipse and the day blotted out.

As he evokes longingly the "great labyrinth" unexplored, he establishes a precarious victory over the transcendent image of Hanrahan which he has created. He tortures Hanrahan now as long ago with his own horrible splendor of desire. Even for Hanrahan experience must have been limited; he—like Homer, Raftery, and the speaker himself—is sentenced to the world of the blind.

However, a strange though characteristic irony enters here. The speaker is forcing upon Hanrahan, who has reckoned up or measured his experience, a more disturbing self-measurement. Hanrahan's explorations and hence his being have been limited by his own ego—directly through "pride" or "cowardice," or indirectly through the masks of intellect or conscience. He has been limited by the "fear or moral ambition" which always threaten creative activity, for desire—as this taunt obliquely recognizes—also demands surrender of self. We must, of course, see in the speaker's taunt to Hanrahan his own self-knowledge and self-judgment. In other words, his own often wildly egocentric celebration of desire here moves to a yet further recognition of its pitfalls: the limitation of fulfilment inherent in the ego's anxious possession of that world which it has created and known. Appropriately, therefore, his phrasing approaches Blake's description of how "Los could enter into Enitharmon's bosom & explore / Its intricate Labyrinths" only when "the Obdurate heart was broken."[25] The bearing of this recognition upon his own problem of clinging to life and thus inhibiting the exploration of death will emerge implicitly in the rest of the poem.

Grasping the implications of this long review of images and memories, and moving on to the concluding testament, declaration of faith, and plan for the future, we may be struck by a similarity to another great dramatic monologue, by a poet whom the early Yeats admired. Despite many differences, Tennyson's "Ulysses" contains the same initially perplexing fusion of complaint, elegy, and defiant assertion—a fusion that renders, in heroic opposition to the finitude of human life, the infinitude of the creative and exploring mind. In both poems the selection of an ageing speaker heightens that contrast; the firm possession of a labyrinthine past makes more poignant the precarious tenure of the present and the vastness of all that is yet unexplored. Against all odds both protagonists try to project the achievements of the past into the present and on into an open future. But the speaker of "The Tower," himself a bitterly realistic poet for all his fantastic assertions, is explicitly concerned with the problem that Ulysses merely exemplifies—the problem that Yeats, in his long preparation for the poem, had once defined: "It may be," he had said in *The Celtic Twilight,* "that in a few years Fable, who changes mortalities to immortalities in her cauldron," will have changed blind Raftery to a perfect symbol of "the magnificence and penury of dreams."[26]

In the second part of "The Tower" the speaker has evoked those aspects of his Anglo-Irish heritage which best symbolize the horrible splendor of the imagination wrought to its highest pitch. In his realism he dryly accepts, in his defiance he ironically exalts, Mrs. French, "Gifted with so fine an ear," as well as "beauty's blind rambling celebrant." Having dramatically vindicated the imagination in the face of all that is temporal, having seen also that anxious possession of the world created and known is a bar to further creation and exploration, he may now rest in a more serene faith in the independence of the imagination and in a "pride" that is not the ego's apprehensive desire to possess and dominate but the whole being's exultant sense of creative giving. He may therefore evoke without irony a quite different aspect of the Anglo-Irish heritage—that which Yeats had celebrated in his Senate speech of the same year:

> It is time that I wrote my will;
> I choose upstanding men
> That climb the streams until
> The fountain leap, and at dawn

> Drop their cast at the side
> Of dripping stone; I declare
> They shall inherit my pride,
> The pride of people that were
> Bound neither to Cause nor to State,
> Neither to slaves that were spat on,
> Nor to the tyrants that spat,
> The people of Burke and of Grattan
> That gave, though free to refuse—

If Houses of Lords and Houses of Commons are something other than human life, certain individuals who are politically active may yet be, as they are here, "what Blake called 'naked beauty displayed.' ... The great men of the eighteenth century were that beauty; Parnell had something of it, O'Leary something..."[27] Fisherman, fountain, dawn, with their connotations of natural richness and vitality, of Irish landscape and ceremony of innocence, help to define the beneficent pride of Anglo-Ireland, which is now (in an act consonant with its own nature) bequeathed at a moment of exultant self-giving to that new age for which Yeats had always hoped—an age "that will understand with Blake that the Holy Spirit is 'an intellectual fountain,' and that the kinds and degrees of beauty are the images of its authority."[28] That "beauty" implies no mere aestheticism but rather what Yeats in 1902 had called "the pure joy that only comes out of things that have never been indentured to any cause" and that is a prerequisite for the "impartial meditation about character and destiny we call the artistic life."[29]

As this phrase in "The Tower" moves toward its final sustained cadence, it introduces further images of the authority of that fountain which is the possession of no person; "pride" becomes yet more clearly impersonal—the pride of a natural largesse (of morn, horn, showers, hour) which works through individuals:

> Pride, like that of the morn,
> When the headlong light is loose,

—antithetical to that moment in "The Second Coming" which the line echoes: "The blood-dimmed tide is loosed"—

> Or that of the fabulous horn,
> Or that of the sudden shower
> When all streams are dry,
> Or that of the hour
> When the swan must fix his eye
> Upon a fading gleam,
> Float out upon a long
> Last reach of glittering stream
> And there sing his last song.

As the shower modulates into the song of the swan (which, like Tennyson's dying Merlin, follows the gleam[30]), we recall that this very testament is such a shower or song in the arid landscape of decrepit age. The penury of the imagination, almost eclipsed by its magnificence, now appears only in such implications, or in the momentary defiance which the thought of the swan and his fading world brings:

> And I declare my faith:
> I mock Plotinus' thought
> And cry in Plato's teeth,
> Death and life were not
> Till man made up the whole,
> Made lock, stock and barrel
> Out of his bitter soul,
> Aye, sun and moon and star, all.
> And further add to that
> That, being dead, we rise,
> Dream and so create
> Translunar Paradise.

As the word "bitter" recognizes, these consciously defiant articles of faith are what in 1930 Yeats called "all that heroic casuistry, all that assertion of the eternity of what nature declares ephemeral."[31] Yet in the poem they are truths of the imagination: "For if I triumph I must make men mad." The speaker is earning his right (declared in "To a Young Beauty") to attend that late but select dinner of which Landor once spoke, with Landor himself and with Donne, who also had proudly declared, "Death be not proud."

Turning to the future, he demonstrates through yet further shifts of tone, the imaginative validity of his argument. When Tennyson's Ulysses cast his thoughts beyond the sunset, he strangely merged death, a newer world, and a reliving of the past. But even more than for Ulysses, for this speaker penury and magnificence now meet and are reconciled in serene ambiguity:

> I have prepared my peace
> With learned Italian things
> And the proud stones of Greece,
> Poet's imaginings
> And memories of love,
> Memories of the words of women,
> All those things whereof
> Man makes a superhuman
> Mirror-resembling dream.

He has prepared his peace in the mirroring world of the imagination; but though he had referred to a future translunar Paradise, this peace is a present reality. The lines also state that he has made his peace with the things of the world which he must abandon. The slackening verse movement indicates that the speaker is beginning to rest after his orgy of creation, as Eternal Man rested on the seventh day, the mirroring imagination sufficient unto the moment.[32] The simile that follows re-creates this moment, but with a difference. It moves from daws who "chatter and scream, / And drop twigs layer upon layer"— the life process of "preparing"—to the mother bird who

> will rest
> On their hollow top,
> And so warm her wild nest.

The simile further devalues preparatory life and the materials it accumulates, as opposed to the culminating moment; and it presents that peaceful and extended moment as one of brooding yet "wild" creativity.

A new vista of contemplative activity has opened. The speaker now must—and can—"leave both faith and pride" to others. It is, as he says, both a bequeathing and also now a quiet abandonment by one whose metal has been broken. From one point of view, we may say that, magnificence having been created, penury can be accepted. But penury has also been seen as a creative state itself. The obdurate heart broken, another labyrinth can be entered and explored. Hence there is little trace, in the final phrase of this testamentary song, of the proud credo uttered a moment before. The phrase begins by asserting the creative force inherent in any act of the imagination:

> Now shall I make my soul,
> Compelling it to study
> In a learned school...

But it modulates to something quite different from the last song of the defiant swan:

> Till the wreck of body,
> Slow decay of blood,
> Testy delirium
> Or dull decrepitude,
> Or what worse evil come—
> The death of friends, or death
> Of every brilliant eye
> That made a catch in the breath—
> Seem but the clouds of the sky
> When the horizon fades;
> Or a bird's sleepy cry
> Among the deepening shades.

The speaker approaches Keats's view that the world is the "vale of Soul-making," a "School" in which each soul learns its "Identity."[33] But he leaves carefully unspecified the content of school and soul. He presents only, in all realism, the prospect of a fading world. More strictly, evil and loss no longer seem important; but as the metaphors suggest, with them fades all that is temporal. The lines render, in a quiet mode, that "tragic joy" which, Yeats had said in 1904, reaches its climax "when the world itself has slipped away in death." A similar thought had come to Yeats on the occasion of Synge's death: "He had no need of our sympathies. It was as though we and the things about us died away from him and not he from us."[34] But in

"The Tower" that darkening of the world of mirroring realities, that fading of the gleam on which the swan fixes its eye, is the final act of the eternal imagination. The poem has moved to the acceptance of death, and to the creation of death in that acceptance. The horrible splendor of desire—the creative and destructive, illuminating and blinding power of the imagination—here attains its final ethereal harmony: "a bird's sleepy cry / Among the deepening shades."

iii.

In re-creating history the speaker of "The Tower" moves beyond history. Following him, we have seen some ways in which Yeats was now grounding his concepts and symbols in the soil of Anglo-Ireland. But he wished to discover yet further relations between the people of Burke and the defiant swan, the Italian things, and the stones of Greece. In 1930 he wrote in his diary:

> How much of my reading is to discover the English and Irish originals of my thought, its first language, and where no such originals exist, its relation to what original did. I seek more than idioms, for thoughts become more vivid when I find they were thought out in historical circumstances which affect those in which I live, or, which is perhaps the same thing, were thought first by men my ancestors may have known.[35]

He was delighted to find Anglo-Irish prototypes for his own theory of history and his own conservatism. Swift's *Discourse of the Contests and Dissensions between the Nobles and Commons in Athens and Rome,* he thought, led up to Edmund Burke "so clearly that one may claim that Anglo-Ireland recreated conservative thought in one as in the other. Indeed the *Discourse* with its law of history might be for us what Vico is to the Italians, had we a thinking nation."[36] In a moment of excitement he took a yet more extreme position. The *Discourse,* he said,

> is more important to modern thought than Vico and certainly fore-shadowed Flinders Petrie, Frobenius, Henry Adams, Spengler, and very exactly and closely Gerald Heard. It needs interpretation, for it had to take the form of a pamphlet intelligible to the Whig nobility. He saw civilisation "exploding"—to use Heard's term—just before the final state, and that final state as a tyranny, and he took from a Latin writer the conviction that every civilisation carries with it from the first what shall bring it to an end.[37]

Burke borrowed or rediscovered Swift's insight into historical process, Yeats concluded, while Coleridge borrowed "all but that inevitable end."[38]

Discovering such English and Irish originals—studying "the rebirth of European spirituality in the mind of Berkeley, the restoration of European order in the mind of Burke"[39]—Yeats found thoughts becoming more vivid not merely because he had established a historical relation to those thinkers but also because he was not studying "thought" alone. He would agree in part with the description of such study given by R. G. Collingwood, who also learned from Vico and Croce:

> I plunge beneath the surface of my mind and there live a life in which I not merely think about Nelson but am Nelson, and thus in thinking about Nelson think about myself.... If what the historian knows is past thoughts, and if he knows them by re-thinking them himself, it follows that the knowledge he achieves by historical enquiry is not knowledge of his situation as opposed to knowledge of himself.... He must be, in fact, a microcosm of all the history he can know.[40]

But Yeats would go yet further. It is characteristic that, attributing a similar Vichian theory of historical knowledge to Swift, he introduced a characteristically passionate complication: it is to Vanessa that Swift says, in *The Words upon the Window-Pane,* "When I rebuilt Rome in your mind it was as though I walked its streets."[41] He was studying whole men—and learning, in that study, about a microcosmic whole man in the present.

That is why he could say, "I have before me an ideal expression in which all that I have, clay and spirit alike, assist; it is as though I most approximate towards that expression when I carry with me the greatest amount of hereditary thought and feeling, even national and family hatred and pride."[42] He elaborated that goal when revising these diary notations for publication in *Wheels and Butterflies*:

> Swift haunts me; he is always just around the next corner. Sometimes it is a thought of my great-great-grandmother, a friend of that Archbishop King who sent him to England about the "First Fruits," sometimes it is S. Patrick's, where I have gone to wander and meditate, that brings him to mind, sometimes I remember something hard or harsh in O'Leary or in Taylor, or in the public speech of our states-

men, that reminds me by its style of his verse or prose. Did he not speak, perhaps, with just such an intonation? This instinct for what is near and yet hidden is in reality a return to the sources of our power, and therefore a claim made upon the future. Thought seems more true, emotion more deep, spoken by someone who touches my pride, who seems to claim me of his kindred, who seems to make me a part of some national mythology, nor is mythology mere ostentation, mere vanity if it draws me onward to the unknown; another turn of the gyre and myth is wisdom, pride, discipline.[43]

These eighteenth-century men—and especially Berkeley and Swift —were therefore complex masks with whom Yeats might converse and from whom he might learn of "what is near and yet hidden." Each stood before him as both reflection and shadow: projection of his own consciously held position and also of potentialities within himself that he had not yet fully discerned. Each stood also as "cosmic" reflection and shadow: intimation of an ideal passion and ideal unity, and embodiment of the tensions of the fallen world. Early in the century, before his complete allegiance to Anglo-Ireland, Yeats had suggested the use to which he would put these figures: "There is scarcely a man who has led the Irish people, at any time, who may not give some day to a great writer precisely that symbol he may require for the expression of himself."[44] But he had more fully suggested their meaning even earlier, in 1896, when Swift alone had seemed to him to transcend a fallen century. He had said then of Swift:

> He did not become ... a great light of his time because of the utility of his projects or of any high standard of honest thinking—for some of his most famous projects were expressions of a paradoxical anger, while others he defended with arguments which even he could not have believed—but because he revealed in his writings and in his life a more intense nature, a more living temperament, than any of his contemporaries. He was as near a supreme man as that fallen age could produce, and that he did not labour, as Blake says the supreme man should, "to bring again the golden age" by revealing it in his work and his life, but fought, as with battered and smoke-blackened armour in the mouth of the pit, is to the discredit of "the century of philosophers": a century which had set chop-logic in the place of the mysterious power, obscure as a touch from behind a curtain, that had governed "the century of poets."

But even that fighting in the mouth of the pit—which Yeats was increasingly to see as a substantial part of his own vocation—was, he had said in 1896, a way of revealing "a more powerful and passionate, a more divine world than ours." For Swift had "given the world an unforgettable parable by building an overpowering genius upon the wreckage of the merely human faculties."[45] The parable was of central importance to an admirer of *King Lear* who would later write "Sailing to Byzantium" and "The Tower" and would dramatize in *The Words upon the Window-Pane* the ageing Swift's dread of madness as a *hysterica passio* of historical dimensions.

That play itself is more than a spiritualist tour de force or an ingenious device for bringing historical drama into a modern setting. Like "The Tower," it renders the sense of a dramatic interpenetration of past and present. Indeed, the Swift who haunted Yeats, who was always just round the next corner, was audible to him also: "I can hear Swift's voice in his letters speaking the sentences at whatever pace makes their sound and idiom expressive. He speaks and we listen at leisure."[46] Mediumship was an apt vehicle for what Yeats himself experienced as a psychological reality, a source of power "near yet hidden." Hence the scenario of the Anglo-Irish past, like that of *A Vision* or that of the early romances, might lend to the moods a voice. The dramatic perspective of *The Words upon the Window-Pane* recalls that of *On Baile's Strand*: the madness and death of the heroic are seen from the vantage-point of the unheroic and utilitarian milieu which mirrors ourselves and which has helped to drive the hero over the edge of sanity. But what once appeared in the context of Irish myth has now been discerned in the experienced drama of history.

Like Swift, Berkeley was for Yeats a complex mirror of ideal and reality. The great enemy of the abstract, he wished to "create a philosophy so concrete that the common people could understand it." "Descartes, Locke and Newton took away the world and gave us its excrement instead," said Yeats. "Berkeley restored the world"—"the world that only exists because it shines and sounds."[47] In so describing a reparation of the fall presented in "Fragments," Yeats was not applauding Berkeley's idealism as it is usually conceived:

Sometimes when I think of him what flitted before his eyes flits before mine also, I half perceive a world like that of the Zen priest in Japan or China, but am hurried back into abstraction after but an instant.[48]

Similarly in *A Vision,* turning in reaction against his own abstract system toward "a reality which is concrete, sensuous, bodily," Yeats recalled passages "written by Japanese monks on attaining Nirvana."[49] For Zen, Nirvana is no escape from the wheel except as it is an immediate and concrete apprehension of that harmony which the wheel merely symbolizes. It is no release from individual consciousness except as it is a moment of enlightenment in which the error of abstraction which posits cut-off individuals disappears. It is thus cognate with the goal of spiritual alchemy and is an "affirmation" that transcends the opposites, a "word" that cannot be refuted. Zen shares with Yeats the view that "You can refute Hegel but not the Saint or the Song of Sixpence."[50]

"You ask me what is my religion and I hit you across the mouth."[51] That Zen retort might well have been uttered by the young Berkeley whom Yeats envisioned, "solitary, talkative, ecstatic, destructive." Such a temperament, Yeats thought, Berkeley also showed in later years "though but in glimpses or as something divined or inferred" behind the complacent mask of the mature bishop, which he wore because, in a time "terrified of religious scepticism and political anarchy," it "hid from himself and others his own anarchy and scepticism."[52] Yeats was here glimpsing a tension within his own conservative "pose," though he had more complex dramatic and psychological techniques for realizing and so transcending it. Thinking of Berkeley's isolation, Yeats also thought of his own father "and of others born into the Anglo-Irish solitude."[53] Such men he saw as isolated from Ireland ("scattered men in an ignorant country"[54]), isolated by their genius in a time of imaginative ebb tide (for Berkeley the "first great imaginative wave had sunk, the second had not risen"[55]), and isolated both physically and spiritually from England. Considering this last fact, Yeats saw in them the best elements of an Irish culture in which "solitaries flourish," a culture which has the "sense for what is permanent."

Born in such community Berkeley with his belief in perception, that abstract ideas are mere words, Swift with his love of perfect nature, of the Houyhnhnms, his disbelief in Newton's system and in every sort of machine, Goldsmith and his delight in the particulars of common life that shocked his contemporaries, Burke with his conviction that all states not grown slowly like a forest tree are tyrannies, found in England an opposite that stung their own thought into expression and made it lucid.[56]

Like Yeats himself, they were caught between contraries, goaded into passionate thought and action, and enabled to play a triumphantly liberating role—that of "hardship borne and chosen out of pride and joy."[57] Their soil too had been spiritualized by tragedy. "The historical dialectic," Yeats said, "trampled upon their minds in that brutal Ireland, product of two generations of civil war...; they were the trodden grapes and became wine."[58]

As a quasi-ideal culture, eighteenth-century Ireland suggested the Renaissance and Periclean Athens. Yeats saw "in Bolingbroke the last pose and in Swift the last passion of the Renaissance."[59] Professionalism was not yet a curse. "Unity of being was still possible though somewhat over-rationalised and abstract, more diagram than body": the fall described in "Statistics" was just beginning. But when "Swift sank into imbecility or madness his epoch had finished in the British Isles."[60] Thus far, Yeats's description suggests his Phase 18, from 1550 to 1650 (the picture of Europe after 1650 is much less favorable in "Dove or Swan"[61]); but Swift's epoch was also a delayed and imperfect Phase 15:

> I seek an image of the modern mind's discovery of itself, of its own permanent form, in that one Irish century that escaped from darkness and confusion. I would that our fifteenth, sixteenth, or even our seventeenth century had been the clear mirror, but fate decided against us.[62]

Hence a submerged analogy with Phase 15, that time when the shadow of history becomes a clear mirror, runs through Yeats's vision of the Enlightenment. Corbet, in *The Words upon the Window-Pane,* gives the conventional interpretation: "That arrogant intellect free at last from superstition." But Yeats calls that "the young man's overstatement full of the unexamined suppositions of common speech," and he adds:

> I saw Asia in the carved stones of Blenheim, not in the pride of great abstract masses, but in that humility of flower-like intricacy—the partic-

ular blades of the grass; nor can chance have thrown into contiguous generations Spinoza and Swift, an absorption of the whole intellect in God, a fakir-like contempt for all human desire ...; the elaboration and spread of Masonic symbolism, its God made in the image of a Christopher Wren; Berkeley's declaration, modified later, that physical pleasure is the *Summum Bonum,* Heaven's sole reality, his countertruth to that of Spinoza.... Spinoza and the Masons, Berkeley and Swift, speculative and practical intellect, stood there free at last from all prepossessions and touched the extremes of thought ...[63]

That is the "horizontal dance" of opposites, *primary* and *antithetical,* Asiatic and European, which Yeats noticed in "Dove or Swan" only as Phase 15 approaches and recedes.[64] It is the clear mirror, the mind's discovery of "its own permanent form"—a repetition of that self-discovery which, according to Hegel, took place in fifth-century Greece. For Yeats, Berkeley fought the "Irish Salamis," which resulted in the "birth of the national intellect."[65]

Though the fusion of extremes was incomplete, though there was no real full moon when "all abounds and flows," it was a near miss. The Anglo-Irish would seem

the Gymnosophists of Strabo close at hand, could they but ignore what was harsh and logical in themselves, or the China of the Dutch cabinet-makers, of the *Citizen of the World*: the long-settled rule of powerful men, no great dogmatic structure, few great crowded streets, scattered unprogressive communities, much handiwork, wisdom wound into the roots of the grass.[66]

And the epoch passed, like that of Greece, with a sinking into the *primary.* The "mechanicians mocked by Gulliver" prevailed; the "moment of freedom could not last":

Did not Rousseau within five years of the death of Swift publish his *Discourse upon Arts and Sciences* and discover instinctive harmony not in heroic effort, not in Cato and Brutus, not among impossible animals ... but among savages, and thereby beget the sans-culottes of Marat? After the arrogance of power the humility of a servant.[67]

Anglo-Ireland seemed thus to combine transcendental ideal and fallen reality. Yeats cast two crosslights upon it, revealing the virtues of Phidian Athens and the Renaissance as well as the tragic conflicts of modern Ireland. If, in his prose, the vision lacks complete coherence, it nevertheless testifies to his continual attempt to hold in a single thought reality and justice. The poetry itself brings that double vision into a single paradoxical focus.

iv.

In the two poems celebrating Swift, Goldsmith, Berkeley, and Burke, that double vision is evident as a living tradition is viewed from the dramatic perspective. "The Seven Sages" begins with a trivial boasting, a parody of Yeats's own celebration of his family memories:

> *The First.* My great-grandfather spoke to Edmund Burke
>   In Grattan's house.
> *The Second.*   My great-grandfather shared
>   A pot-house bench with Oliver Goldsmith once.
> *The Third.* My great-grandfather's father talked of music,
>   Drank tar-water with the Bishop of Cloyne.
> *The Fourth.* But mine saw Stella once.

Yet what is trivial? Tar water? Berkeley's *Siris,* as Coleridge said, "beginning with Tar ends with the Trinity, the omne scibile forming the interspace." Yeats himself said: "And the tar water, and the cures it worked, what a subject for a discourse! Could he not lead his reader—especially if that reader drank tar water every morning—from tar to light?"[68] For these Anglo-Irish, logic is one with passion, and the loftiest intellectual achievement is rooted in the humblest biographical facts. The question of the fifth sage may then not arise from the inconsequence of senility:

> *The Fifth.*   Whence came our thought?
> *The Sixth.* From four great minds that hated Whiggery.
> *The Fifth.* Burke was a Whig.
> *The Sixth.*   Whether they knew or not,
>   Goldsmith and Burke, Swift and the Bishop of Cloyne
>   All hated Whiggery; but what is Whiggery?
>   A levelling, rancorous, rational sort of mind
>   That never looked out of the eye of a saint
>   Or out of a drunkard's eye.
> *The Seventh.*   All's Whiggery now,
>   But we old men are massed against the world.

Quite aware of the liberties he takes with history, the sixth sage praises both an intensely subjective vision and the objective ability to share the unusual vision of another. And though the seventh applies his redefined epithet much as the old soldier in Tate's "To the Lacedemonians" applies another such—

> All are born Yankees of the race of men
> And this, too, now the country of the damned

—the sages embody a somewhat more dryly comic heroism. As the poem proceeds, however, their "massed" opposition gains in dignity and richness. They carry on the magnanimity of dissent in "Burke's great melody," the love for the common life in what "Oliver Goldsmith sang," the savage indignation chiseled on the "tomb of Swift," and the persuasive utterance of Berkeley, leading "from tar to light":

> a voice
> Soft as the rustle of a reed from Cloyne
> That gathers volume; now a thunder-clap.

Once more an apparently inconsequent remark leads us back to origins:

> *The Sixth.* What schooling had these four?
> *The Seventh.*   They walked the roads
>   Mimicking what they heard, as children mimic;
>   They understood that wisdom comes of beggary.

Though the poem returns to the apparently trivial, the last word has the resonance of a tradition maintained in spite of, and because of, adversity. It has the resonance, too, of the understanding in "The Tower" that magnificence arises from penury, and the understanding in "Meditations in Time of Civil War" that the honeybees may "build in the crevices / Of loosening masonry." "Beggary" is the state of "fruitful void," known by the wise fool or by the visionary poet who has become again "unaccommodated man" and stands "naked under the heavens." It is here celebrated by minds magnanimous in victory, heroic in defeat, firm in apparent eccentricity, yet humble before the simplest facts of experience.

In "Blood and the Moon," because the speaker is no simple sage but the owner of the tower, the double vision is more complex, and a more painful wisdom comes of a more extreme beggary.

> Blessed be this place,
> More blessed still this tower;
> A bloody, arrogant power
> Rose out of the race
> Uttering, mastering it,
> Rose like these walls from these
> Storm-beaten cottages—
> In mockery I have set
> A powerful emblem up
> And sing it rhyme upon rhyme
> In mockery of a time
> Half dead at the top.

In Vichian manner he re-erects the tower that rose out of the race, paradoxically both expression and master of Ireland. As he blesses that tower, his emblem joins spirit and blood in a fruitful if precarious marriage that mocks his own less vital, more incoherent time.

Then, after recalling towers that variously combined wisdom and directing power, he sings his own symbol of the compelling harmonies of life:

> I declare this tower is my symbol; I declare
> This winding, gyring, spiring treadmill of a stair is
>   my ancestral stair;
> That Goldsmith and the Dean, Berkeley and Burke have
>   travelled there.

That firm pronouncement, with its relish for the bitter and salt of effort and repetition on the winding path of nature, gives body to the nostalgia of the narrator of "Rosa Alchemica," who had boasted of his "wide staircase, where Swift had passed joking and railing, and Curran telling stories and quoting Greek."[69] In various ways the following triplets balance wisdom and power, spirit and clay:

> Swift beating on his breast in sibylline frenzy blind
> Because the heart in his blood-sodden breast had dragged
>   him down into mankind,
> Goldsmith deliberately sipping at the honey-pot of his mind,

—prophetic illumination because of enforced suffering and compassion, balanced by judicious mental delectation—

> And haughtier-headed Burke that proved the State a tree,
> That this unconquerable labyrinth of the birds, century
> after century,
> Cast but dead leaves to mathematical equality;

—proud logic supporting the organic richness and force of a body politic that transcends the dead level of rationalist structures—

> And God-appointed Berkeley that proved all things a dream,
> That this pragmatical, preposterous pig of a world, its
> farrow that so solid seem,
> Must vanish on the instant if the mind but change its theme;

—a magical, whimsical power of the mind to annihilate the gross solidity of flesh. From sibylline frenzy to subjective mind's ascendancy, it is a rich chord: Anglo-Ireland "free at last from all prepossession" and touching the "extremes of thought." The precarious harmony is that of the "winding, gyring, spiring treadmill" of life itself, with its continual shifts and counterstresses:

> *Saeva Indignatio* and the labourer's hire,
> The strength that gives our blood and state magnanimity
> of its own desire;
> Everything that is not God consumed with intellectual fire.

Far more precarious, however, than the unity of that blessed and bloody tower is the speaker's possession of it. Hence, indeed, the note of forced rhetoric in his mocking and his celebration; for, despite his declaration, he is of the time which he mocks. His emblem is at most a passionate mental re-enactment of that eighteenth-century power. It is proper, therefore, that his series was climaxed not by Swift but by Berkeley, whose consuming intellectual fire leads toward the more extreme perception of the speaker himself. Stepping now outside his mentally possessed tradition, he returns to his own time. The opposites so variously unified begin to fall apart in his mind:

> The purity of the unclouded moon
> Has flung its arrowy shaft upon the floor.

Seven centuries have passed and it is pure,
The blood of innocence has left no stain.
There, on blood-saturated ground, have stood
Soldier, assassin, executioner,
Whether for daily pittance or in blind fear
Or out of abstract hatred, and shed blood,
But could not cast a single jet thereon.
Odour of blood on the ancestral stair!
And we that have shed none must gather here
And clamour in drunken frenzy for the moon.

Spirit and blood no longer meet and interpenetrate in the miracle of various life. The lunar shaft is inviolable; on the ancestral stair is blood shed for base motives. The speaker, now barred from the realm of physical power, can but clamor in drunken frenzy for that of spirit. His stair is no longer the gyre of life but a deathly limbo between blood and the moon. It is as though the sequence hoped for in "The Magi" were reversed.

As the speaker now turns his gaze upward from the bestial floor toward the sky, the opposites fall further apart. A Blake engraving captioned "I Want! I Want!" depicts a ladder leaning against the moon, a small figure at the base beginning its climb; Yeats's "John Sherman" mentions a brooch in the form of "a ladder leaning against the moon and a butterfly climbing up it."[70] Symbols of the soul's impossible ascent, they may have led Yeats to use here the dying butterflies in the waste room atop Thoor Ballylee, as the speaker's clamor for the moon leads to a half-mocking perception of beauty in death:

Upon the dusty, glittering windows cling,
And seem to cling upon the moonlit skies,
Tortoiseshell butterflies, peacock butterflies,
A couple of night-moths are on the wing.
Is every modern nation like the tower,
Half dead at the top?

He then turns upon his argument and denies the wisdom of Swift's heart, of Goldsmith's honeypot, of Burke's haughty head, even of Berkeley's mind, which fully controlled a living world:

> No matter what I said,
> For wisdom is the property of the dead,
> A something incompatible with life; and power,
> Like everything that has the stain of blood,
> A property of the living; but no stain
> Can come upon the visage of the moon
> When it has looked in glory from a cloud.

That abrupt and arrogant reversal is tinged, he knows, with "drunken frenzy" and bitter mockery. It is as though he would justify both the separation of the opposites which he must endure and his own deathly yearnings. He is still caught, like his modern tower, in a realm that is neither blood nor moon. But is his frenzy utterly different from that which emerged from Swift's middle state? As the victim of his historical moment, he has at least the wisdom appropriate to his condition: half-dead, barred from full life or death, he knows himself. And in knowing himself, in holding reality and justice in a single thought, he does in fact take another step on the winding stair of life.

The strength of this poem, like that of "Meditations in Time of Civil War," could not exist without the speaker's vigorous honesty. Despite a rather common critical assumption based upon our usual blindnesses, self-dramatization does not preclude self-knowledge. Hence, though the detailed conflicts of "Blood and the Moon" derive from a historical predicament, its final meaning is of the Dantesque order that Yeats saw in all art worthy the name: "the disengaging of a soul from place and history, its suspension in a beautiful or terrible light to await the Judgment, though it must be, seeing that all its days were a Last Day, judged already."[71]

v.

Beginning with a direct personal relation to Ireland, moving in widening circles through the re-experienced drama of the past, Yeats could reach a universal history—the Renaissance, Phidian Athens, all the antinomies of *primary* and *antithetical* or of blood and the moon. Fleetingly in personal meditation, enduringly in the poems, he merged dramatic experience and panoramic vision in a full-bodied yet comprehensive reality.

Now that I am old and live in the past I often think of those
ancestors of whom I have some detailed information. Such and such
a diner-out and a charming man never did anything; such and such
lost the never very great family fortune in some wild-cat scheme;
such and such, perhaps deliberately for he was a strange, deep man,
married into a family known for harsh dominating strength of character. Then, as my mood deepens, I discover all these men in my
single mind, think that I myself have gone through them all at this
very moment, and wonder if the balance has come right; then I go
beyond those minds and my single mind and discover that I have
been describing everybody's struggle, and the gyres turn in my
thought.[72]

The experienced and re-experienced drama leads toward the panoramic vision. That statement of 1938 alludes to a richness of content
that results from years of meditation, and it conforms to Yeats's understanding of Vico's theory of historical knowledge. But the basic technique of the meditation itself, like so many of his "truths," had been
with Yeats since his twenties. He had presented it in his Blake study
as the means of redeeming fallen man, of creating the apocalypse
through the power of imagination:

The mood of the seer, no longer bound in by the particular experiences
of his body, spreads out and enters into the particular experiences of
an ever-widening circle of other lives and beings, for it will more and
more grow one with that portion of the mood essence which is common to all that lives. The circle of the individuality will widen out
until other individualities are contained within it, and their thoughts,
and the persistent thought-symbols which are their spiritual or mental
bodies, will grow visible to it. He who has thus passed into the impersonal portion of his own mind perceives that it is not a mind but all
minds. Hence Blake's statement that "Albion," or man, once contained all "the starry heavens," and his description of their flight from
him as he materialized. When once a man has re-entered into this,
his ancient state, he perceives all things as with the eyes of God.[73]

But that "truth" possessed so early was now tested by passion and
reinforced by the experience of others. Whether or not Yeats had
noted Emerson's remark that "Dante's praise is that he dared to
write his autobiography in colossal cipher, or into universality," he
himself saw others do much the same thing:

Swift seemed to shape his narrative of history upon some clairvoyant
vision of his own life, for he saw civilisation pass from comparative

happiness and youthful vigour to an old age of violence and self-contempt, whereas Vico saw it begin in penury like himself and end as he himself would end in a long inactive peace.[74]

Hegel and Balzac, he thought, also "saw history as a personal experience." He knew, of course, that each personal vision must, to some degree, be unique: "When I allow my meditation to expand until the mind of my family merges into everybody's mind, I discover there, not only what Vico and Balzac found, but my own particular amusements and interests."[75] History as vision is limited by one's own mental breadth and depth; history as dramatic experience is limited by the extent to which one has, in one's own life, gone over the whole ground. But to seek history in any other way, Yeats believed, is to compile anatomies of last year's leaves and not to see or create a living forest.

That understanding of history informs most of Yeats's major poems. But one, "Coole Park and Ballylee, 1931," shows with unusual clarity the meditative process widening out from immediate personal experience toward the panoramic vision. Its rapid yet oblique movement depends upon Yeats's gradually developed "universalism" or "seeing of unity everywhere," attained through the "glove" of intimately possessed particulars. The emblems of the poem are not postulated so much as discovered, for the speaker meditates upon a concrete world that presses in upon him, demanding significant articulation.

> Under my window-ledge the waters race,
> Otters below and moor-hens on the top,
> Run for a mile undimmed in Heaven's face
> Then darkening through "dark" Raftery's "cellar" drop,
> Run underground, rise in a rocky place
> In Coole demesne, and there to finish up
> Spread to a lake and drop into a hole.
> What's water but the generated soul?

Though recalling Porphyry on the cave of the nymphs, or Yeats on the streams of Shelley's Alastor and the Witch of Atlas,[76] the stanza does not flatly apply some neo-Platonic system. The final question expresses the sudden illumination toward which the specific meditation has moved. The abstract equivalence is but the simplest and most certain part of that illumination—enough to focus tentatively its matrix of particulars. ("I prefer to include in my definition of water a little duckweed or a few fish. I have never met that poor naked creature H_2O."[77]) We go over the course again in retrospect: the soul's pristine vigor, the strange doubleness of its psychic life (moor hen and otter), its swift youthful accomplishment; then adversity or seeming death (the darkness of Raftery's "cellar"[78] suggesting that of the "dark man" himself), forcing the soul downward into the realm of otters but not preventing its eventual creative victory as it rises "in a rocky place" (which recalls, among other things, the "place of stone" in "To a Friend Whose Work Has Come to Nothing"); there, finally, its serene fulfilment and death. But to spell out must not be to limit this "clairvoyant vision"—to deny, for example, a longer temporal course depicted, which prepares for the poem's later widening of focus: the stream which moves past the Norman tower, past the "strong cellar" of the ballad-poet Raftery, to Coole demesne, the residence of Lady Gregory. Though the subject of the meditation will not achieve final definition until the end of the poem, its area is already clear: the accomplishment and the transience of a soul and of a tradition.

The complex stream has led the speaker from his post of observation, his window ledge, to Coole demesne and its suggestions of imminent death. He turns from that thought, but cannot turn from either the mood or the site, both of which seem engendered by the thought.

> Upon the border of that lake's a wood
> Now all dry sticks under a wintry sun,
> And in a copse of beeches there I stood,
> For Nature's pulled her tragic buskin on
> And all the rant's a mirror of my mood:
> At sudden thunder of the mounting swan
> I turned about and looked where branches break
> The glittering reaches of the flooded lake.

The "dry sticks" suggest the end of a life and of an era, the arriving of the "wintry sun" of solar *primary*. The immediate Yeatsian response, where such "branches *break*/ The glittering reaches," is tragic "rant": the soul's defiant effort to "rise in a rocky place," to transmute a final hole to a temporary cellar. As in "Nineteen Hundred and Nineteen," the "thunder of the mounting swan" echoes that response. Yet even that image must in turn be altered by the overwhelming sense of transience:

> Another emblem there! That stormy white
> But seems a concentration of the sky;
> And, like the soul, it sails into the sight
> And in the morning's gone, no man knows why;
> And is so lovely that it sets to right
> What knowledge or its lack had set awry,
> So arrogantly pure, a child might think
> It can be murdered with a spot of ink.

An emblem of what? Yeats, in an often-cited letter, said, "a symbol of inspiration, I think."[79] But we should not ignore his own uncertainty: here as elsewhere the poem refuses to be caught in the net of any simple abstract equivalent. Stormy, even divine power and beauty, arrogant purity—yet seemingly more transient than the soul itself: whether it is that soul, comes to the soul, mirrors the soul, or is created by the soul, it suggests the momentary fulfilment of spirit that redeems the imperfect temporal world.

Twice in this stanza the stream of thought carries the speaker toward the idea of death; once he pulls back, with a third "And," to start his celebration anew—but again, irresistibly, a quality suggests its negation. The oblique rendering of the transience of poetic power, human life, and historical tradition can no longer be maintained. The unstated cause of the "mood," evaded repeatedly, demands utterance. The fact to be confronted is not "sudden thunder" but "dry sticks":

> Sound of a stick upon the floor, a sound
> From somebody that toils from chair to chair...

The theme of personal mortality finds its specific focus, crucially unnamed, and the earlier implications of the end of an era, the end of a period of artistic accomplishment, begin to unfold:

Beloved books that famous hands have bound,
Old marble heads, old pictures everywhere;
Great rooms where travelled men and children found
Content or joy; a last inheritor
Where none has reigned that lacked a name and fame
Or out of folly into folly came.

After describing further that spot where persons as well as trees and gardens were rooted, that placid lake filled by the turbulent stream of time, the speaker turns to the rootless and superficial present, and his mood deepens. This is a more complex adversity—"all that great glory spent." The "glittering reaches of the flooded lake" of history too are dimming. The only glory now possible would be that song celebrated in "The Tower," when the swan fixes his eye upon a fading gleam; but the swan can no longer sing:

We were the last romantics—chose for theme
Traditional sanctity and loveliness;
Whatever's written in what poets name
The book of the people; whatever most can bless
The mind of man or elevate a rhyme;
But all is changed, that high horse riderless,
Though mounted in that saddle Homer rode
Where the swan drifts upon a darkening flood.

As the "Last Arcadian" once mourned the death of the "woods of Arcady," one who *was* a last romantic now mourns "dry sticks" on Coole estate. But the gain in richness and depth is considerable. The growing boy knew that the intimately possessed particulars of life might lead toward the universal; but John Sherman, standing by the riverside of his youth, saw little more than "familiar sights—boys riding in the stream to the saddle-girths..., a swan asleep."[80] The ageing man, standing in imagination by the final lake, looks through such sights, transmuted, upon the landscape of the past. That "darkening flood"—which so marvelously widens and deepens the water imagery—is not the lesser adversity, the "darkening" drop into Raftery's cellar which helped to create "dark" Raftery's "book of the people"[81]—or helped "dark" Milton "build the lofty rhyme." No stream rises; no swan mounts. Pegasus is riderless, and we see no wings. The stream of generation has moved from that double image of youthful vitality, "Otters below and moor-hens on the top," to a double image of its dying fall, drifting swan upon shadow.

The speaker, ostensibly surviving his own significant life, looks back from a "last inheritor" at Coole Park into an indefinite past, from himself and others who were the last romantics to Raftery, Milton, and Homer. It seems a vision not of the cycles of history but of a radical fall. Yet winter does lead to spring, a riderless horse may be ridden, a drifting swan may mount. Even in despair the emblems cannot deny the force of life that produces a continual dialogue between Yeats and the temporal world. Indeed, in this final stanza the meditation itself rises to great lyricism as it claims its impossibility. No more than Lycidas does this swan of a past era float upon his watery bier unwept. Song mourning the lack of song belies itself. Yeats, who knew that no battle has ever been finally lost, knew also that tradition may live in the lament for its passing.

X · RESURRECTED GODS

> The best wine is the oldest, the best water the newest.
> —Blake[1]

> The old images, the old emotions, awakened again
> to overwhelming life, like the Gods Heine tells of,
> by the belief and passion of some new soul are the
> only masterpieces.
> —"Art and Ideas"[2]

i.

TWO OTHER POEMS about the darkening flood of history, "Nineteen Hundred and Nineteen" and "The Statues," combine the perspectives of dramatic experience and panoramic vision yet more extensively. Each utterance arises from the pressure of history in modern Ireland; in each the speaker sees his dramatic moment as part of a long historical process. But in "Nineteen Hundred and Nineteen," as in some apocalyptic visions of the nineties, the speaker contemplates the end of an era, tries to come to terms with the destructive forces of history, and even longs for annihilation; whereas in "The Statues," as in Yeats's forging of a conservative synthesis after 1902, the speaker gathers strength from the past and asserts the continuing power of the intellect over those destructive forces. The two poems dramatize recurrently opposed attitudes in Yeats's dialogue with history.

Because the title of "Nineteen Hundred and Nineteen" reminds us of the Black-and-Tan terrorizing of the Irish countryside, we know

at the outset that the panoramic perspective of the first stanza cannot
be objective but must be shaped by the speaker's awareness of his
own situation:

> Many ingenious lovely things are gone
> That seemed sheer miracle to the multitude,
> Protected from the circle of the moon
> That pitches common things about. There stood
> Amid the ornamental bronze and stone
> An ancient image made of olive wood—
> And gone are Phidias' famous ivories
> And all the golden grasshoppers and bees.

He points to Phidian Athens with a familiarity of tone born of his
own sense of intimacy and even "possession"—but also with a strange
note of deprecation that is not simply aristocratic nonchalance. We
see the ideal harmony of Doric and Ionic or European and Asiatic:
the strength and solidity of "bronze and stone" and the brilliance and
intricacy of ivory and gold. But the Asiatic qualities of "ingenious
lovely things" are dominant. Bronze and stone are "ornamental";
"ivories" hardly suggests the monumental quality of the chryselephantine Zeus or Athene; and the "golden grasshoppers and bees," yet
more delicate, provide the climax. The golden honeycomb of Daed-
alus, according to Pater, symbolizes the Asiatic element in the Greek
synthesis; the golden grasshoppers, according to Thucydides, are
symptomatic of the Athenians' degeneration from Spartan to Ionic
qualities, as they laid aside their arms and adopted the luxurious
ways of peace.[3] In this speaker's retrospective view, then, Athenian
art seems to indicate a self-deceptive and effete ornamental culture.
In the second stanza the basis for that departure from the vision of
"Dove or Swan" emerges, as a bitter irony erupts:

> We too had many pretty toys when young:
> A law indifferent to blame or praise,
> To bribe or threat; habits that made old wrong
> Melt down, as it were wax in the sun's rays;
> Public opinion ripening for so long
> We thought it would outlive all future days.

> O what fine thought we had because we thought
> That the worst rogues and rascals had died out.

Something like Thucydides' critique is being sharply directed at modern British culture:

> All teeth were drawn, all ancient tricks unlearned,
> And a great army but a showy thing;

—but no genuinely peaceable society had emerged:

> What matter that no cannon had been turned
> Into a ploughshare? Parliament and king
> Thought that unless a little powder burned
> The trumpeters might burst with trumpeting
> And yet it lack all glory; and perchance
> The guardsmen's drowsy chargers would not prance.

The taste for military display suggests that violence had merely gone underground, had hidden in the deeper recesses of the self. But now the fragile and the frivolous have been swept away, and with them the facile and self-deceptive dreams of wisdom and beauty. The drawn teeth have been sown again; the seemingly drowsy psychic forces lurking below the consciousness have erupted:

> Now days are dragon-ridden, the nightmare
> Rides upon sleep: a drunken soldiery
> Can leave the mother, murdered at her door,
> To crawl in her own blood, and go scot-free;
> The night can sweat with terror as before
> We pieced our thoughts into philosophy,
> And planned to bring the world under a rule,
> Who are but weasels fighting in a hole.

With that last line, the uglier subliminal forces have been admitted even within the speaker and his fellows. The sinister shadow—"that dark portion of the mind which is like the other side of the moon" and which has prepared for "anarchic violence"[4]—has become dominant: "the nightmare / Rides upon sleep." The speaker is aware through direct experience of the destructive riding or treading of that *mara* (whether horse, fate, Lamia, or terrible mother) which, as vehicle of the erupting adverse unconscious forces, may assume social as well as individual form.[5]

The speaker of "The Gyres" will be able to cry, "What matter though numb nightmare ride on top ... ?" This earlier speaker, though finding no such clear "tragic joy," takes at least a step toward that exultation known when all falls in ruin:

> He who can read the signs nor sink unmanned
> Into the half-deceit of some intoxicant
> From shallow wits; who knows no work can stand,
> Whether health, wealth or peace of mind were spent
> On master-work of intellect or hand,
> No honour leave its mighty monument,
> Has but one comfort left: all triumph would
> But break upon his ghostly solitude.

Here, as later in "Meditations in Time of Civil War" and "Coole Park and Ballylee, 1931," the word "break" has a strange richness, suggesting both temporal loss and a partial transcendence of that loss. But how firm is that "ghostly solitude"? Is it a citadel upon which the waves of triumph would beat ineffectually, upon which the sword of triumph would be shattered—or a more fragile sanctuary which would be easily disturbed by triumph? Instead of answering such questions, the speaker immediately doubts the adequacy of his enigmatic comfort and retreats to despair:

> But is there any comfort to be found?
> Man is in love and loves what vanishes,
> What more is there to say?

But even that attempt at laconic acceptance does not quite succeed: there *is* more to say. The voice of a bitter disillusionment must add, pointing to an Athens that now carries the significance of modern Ireland as well:

> That country round
> None dared admit, if such a thought were his,
> Incendiary or bigot could be found
> To burn that stump on the Acropolis,
> Or break in bits the famous ivories
> Or traffic in the grasshoppers or bees.

The worst having been faced if not accepted, the speaker turns in Part II to a richer image than "the circle of the moon" to render the movement of history. For a moment he rises above the dramatic situation into the realm of panoramic vision alone:

> When Loie Fuller's Chinese dancers enwound
> A shining web, a floating ribbon of cloth,
> It seemed that a dragon of air
> Had fallen among the dancers, had whirled them round
> Or hurried them off on its own furious path;
> So the Platonic Year
> Whirls out new right and wrong,
> Whirls in the old instead;
> All men are dancers and their tread
> Goes to the barbarous clangour of a gong.

When historical flux is seen as artistic form, then, as in "Dove or Swan," change may be accepted and fate may be creatively danced. But though this speaker entertains such a possibility, for him the sense of coercion by the whirling dragon is still dominant. And in the last line his vision of the human dance lapses easily into an image of gong-tormented life.

The "dragon of air" becomes, in Part III, the wind of night and of winter. But after the brief contemplation *sub specie aeternitatis,* the speaker has a quiet detachment. Comfort is again in sight; he offers, in effect, a definition of "ghostly solitude."

> Some moralist or mythological poet
> Compares the solitary soul to a swan;
> I am satisfied with that,
> Satisfied if a troubled mirror show it,
> Before that brief gleam of its life be gone,
> An image of its state;
> The wings half spread for flight,
> The breast thrust out in pride
> Whether to play, or to ride
> Those winds that clamour of approaching night.

In a world of stormy flux the dialogue with the "troubled mirror" of history may at least bring self-knowledge, an image of the soul's "state." Turning on the ambiguity of that word, the stanza evokes now a condition of nobility, the easy yet defiant stateliness of the swan's "play" and its rising to meet and "ride" the opposing winds. No longer "ridden" by dragon or nightmare, the soul uses adversity to further its own flight. As hinted earlier ("He who can read the signs nor sink unmanned..."), adversity may bring greater vitality than do the "ingenious lovely things" of a supposedly ideal era. The speaker is now holding down *hysterica passio* at sword's point. Triumph would but "break" upon his solitude both because it is relatively weaker and because it would calm the winds which aid the soul's flight. But, as "To a Friend Whose Work Has Come to Nothing" warns, this "harder thing / Than Triumph" is "of all things known / ... most difficult." Because of that difficulty, in the next two stanzas the "ghostly solitude" is progressively redefined and finally overwhelmed.

> A man in his own secret meditation
> Is lost amid the labyrinth that he has made
> In art or politics;
> Some Platonist affirms that in the station
> Where we should cast off body and trade
> The ancient habit sticks,
> And that if our works could
> But vanish with our breath
> That were a lucky death,
> For triumph can but mar our solitude.

The solitary soul is not solitary enough. Like Milton's fallen angels, it is "in wandering mazes lost," its hell the Blakean Satanic labyrinth of this life. Even death may not dissipate those self-created complexities to which it mistakenly clings, those ironically triumphant triumphs which now "can but mar" (no longer "break upon") its solitude. The sense of present self-sufficiency is waning. In a similar situation an earlier Yeatsian speaker could imagine a dreamy leap from the Satanic "nets" into a "grey twilight" where "God stands winding His lonely horn."[6] But here:

> The swan has leaped into the desolate heaven:
> That image can bring wildness, bring a rage

To end all things, to end
What my laborious life imagined, even
The half-imagined, the half-written page...

The swan is riding the winds of the storm, but its heaven is desolate. This is not detachment or even solitary triumph but that converse of clinging which masks the continuing impulse to cling: a destructive rage born of frustration.

Hence, though the image suggests that terrible yet ecstatic hour in "The Phases of the Moon" when "all is fed with light and heaven is bare," or that moment when Forgael can cry, "I plunge in the abyss,"[7] the mood remains close to that of the owl in "Meditations in Time of Civil War," who will cry her "desolation to the desolate sky." The speaker exhibits what Rachel Bespaloff has seen in Achilles, a Dionysian "passion for destruction growing out of a hatred for the destructibility of all things."[8] Instead of an acceptance of suffering and an attendant joyous freedom, the speaker knows a desire for annihilation, for the Buddhistic negation of the will which Nietzsche considered the most dangerous temptation for the Dionysian man.[9] Hence this very stanza relapses into the self-mockery that has colored the entire poem:

O but we dreamed to mend
Whatever mischief seemed
To afflict mankind, but now
That winds of winter blow
Learn that we were crack-pated when we dreamed.

The attempt at transcendence a failure, the poem subsides in Parts IV and V into the exhaustion of that mood. The speaker develops the implications of the earlier perception—from which he had turned away in desiring to contemplate a nobler image of his "state"—that he and his fellows are like "weasels fighting in a hole": they themselves "Shriek with pleasure" if they show the "weasel's twist, the weasel's tooth." Like Petrie, who had mocked the learned "child who could not understand the winter" of the historical cycle,[10] he mocks the great, the wise ("They never saw how seasons run"), and the good; but he concludes by reducing himself to a status lower

than that of the incendiary and bigot who "traffic in the grasshoppers
or bees":

> Mock mockers after that
> That would not lift a hand maybe
> To help good, wise, or great
> To bar that foul storm out, for we
> Traffic in mockery.

The "troubled mirror" of the historical moment is now showing the
soul a mocking, raging, destroying image that cannot be denied. The
dancers of history seem no longer mere victims of dragon or barbarous gong but accomplices. Despite its slighter drama, "Nineteen
Hundred and Nineteen" contains an ethical and psychological dialectic very like that of "Meditations in Time of Civil War": a thrust
and counterthrust of assertion and painful recognition that leads
toward an understanding of the soul's true state. That is why, personal emotions exhausted, self-complicity in the cultural failure acknowledged, the speaker has the impersonal vision of Part VI. Again "a
nature, that never ceases to judge itself, exhausts personal emotion
in action or desire so completely that something impersonal . . . starts
into its place, something which is as unforeseen, as completely organised, even as unique, as the images that pass before the mind between
sleeping and waking . . ."[11]

Dragons, nightmare, soldiery, and dancers are caught up in a
visionary coda:

> Violence upon the roads: violence of horses;
> Some few have handsome riders, are garlanded
> On delicate sensitive ear or tossing mane,
> But wearied running round and round in their courses
> All break and vanish, and evil gathers head:
> Herodias' daughters have returned again,
> A sudden blast of dusty wind and after
> Thunder of feet, tumult of images,
> Their purpose in the labyrinth of the wind;
> And should some crazy hand dare touch a daughter
> All turn with amorous cries, or angry cries,
> According to the wind, for all are blind.

Though these images recall Symons' "The Dance of the Daughters of Herodias,"[12] both literary reference and meaning are richer than that echo implies. Symons' poem itself relies upon a Yeatsian, and European, convention:

> Is it the petals falling from the rose?
> For in the silence I can hear a sound
> Nearer than mine own heart-beat, such a word
> As roses murmur, blown by a great wind.
> I see a pale and windy multitude
> Beaten about the air ...

That apocalyptic multitude had already been envisioned in Yeats's "The Hosting of the Sidhe":

> *The winds awaken, the leaves whirl round,*
> *Our cheeks are pale, our hair is unbound ...*

Like Symons' daughters of Herodias, the Sidhe embody the fatal lure of immortal passion and beauty, present also in the "great wind" of Yeats's "The Secret Rose." Yeats had long known of their millennial connotations: "Sidhe is also Gaelic for wind...," he said in 1899. "They journey in whirling winds, the winds that were called the dance of the daughters of Herodias in the Middle Ages, Herodias doubtless taking the place of some old goddess."[13] Yeats was often deliberately vague in his prose notes, and he probably knew then what he did not write until 1934: that Wilde's *Salome* partly derives from Heine's depiction of Herodias in *Atta Troll*, which in turn may derive from "some Jewish religious legend for it is part of the old ritual of the year."[14] Directly or indirectly, he might have met this Aradia, Habundia, or Diana as described by Jacob Grimm or Charles Leland.[15] In any case she entered his own myth of the triform goddess who is mother, mistress, and murderess of the solar hero. Now Herodias' daughters return as the frenzy of destructive passion, the collective nightmare, that ever brings the fall of a civilization. Loie Fuller's dancers (who had presented a Salome dance)[16] become the Sidhe; the dragon of air becomes a dusty wind.

Such images are also prophetic. "When I think of the moment before revelation," Yeats would write in "Dove or Swan," "I think of Salome..."[17] And Pater had written of Leonardo's women, in whom Yeats found the lunar beauty of the Sidhe:

> Daughters of Herodias, ... they are not of the Christian family.... They are the clairvoyants, through whom, as through delicate instruments, one becomes aware of the subtler forces of nature, and the modes of their action, all that is magnetic in it.... Nervous, electric, faint always with some inexplicable faintness, these people seem to be subject to exceptional conditions, to feel powers at work in the common air unfelt by others, to become...the receptacle of them, and pass them on to us in a chain of secret influences.[18]

Here the daughters lead to a macabre revelation:

> But now wind drops, dust settles; thereupon
> There lurches past, his great eyes without thought
> Under the shadow of stupid straw-pale locks,
> That insolent fiend Robert Artisson
> To whom the love-lorn Lady Kyteler brought
> Bronzed peacock feathers, red combs of her cocks.

The blind life-denying passion of the daughters in this poem finds full expression in the repulsive vacuity of Robert Artisson. It is proper for the revelation to include "something which is as unforeseen, as completely organised, even as unique" as this fourteenth-century minor devil and his slave of passion. But our initial shock of surprise gives way to a shock of recognition. Aside from his oblique Yeatsian ancestry (the boar without bristles in his malevolent aspect; the "shape" of the Second Coming, with "gaze blank and pitiless as the sun, ...moving its slow thighs"), Artisson was ready to take his place in this poem. Yeats himself had earlier suggested that he might be one of the Sidhe;[19] and Dame Alice Kyteler was virtually a human daughter of Herodias, for she was one of those witches who, according to popular belief, were called together at night by "a spirit named Herodias."[20] Her traffic with Artisson renders the human complicity in the barbaric dance of time, the abandonment of independence and dignity as man approaches the nadir of the historical cycle. Even the items of her sacrifice (according to Holinshed, "nine red cocks and nine peacocks eies")[21] were as though destined to take their place in the poem. The scream of a peacock or the crowing of a cock has often, in Yeats's work, heralded a new cycle or the entrance into eternity. But the speaker of this poem does not hear a living bird's annunciation. He sees the dismembered dead: mute testimony of time's outrage.

In "Dove or Swan" Yeats would define a civilization as "a struggle to keep self-control." It is "like some great tragic person, some Niobe who must display an almost superhuman will or the cry will not touch our sympathy. The loss of control over thought comes towards the end; first a sinking in upon the moral being, then the last surrender, the irrational cry, revelation—the scream of Juno's peacock."[22] The narrator of "Rosa Alchemica" similarly envisioned the end of his civilization and reflected that vision in his own soul. But because his will was weak, and because the dark forces of the abyss were correspondingly weak though decoratively elaborated, his cry barely touched our sympathy. After many more turns of Yeats's winding stair—after much controlled assimilation of those forces from beyond the ego—the speaker of "Nineteen Hundred and Nineteen" can have a stronger will and clearer perception of himself. Hence his own ethical dialectic, and no external Michael Robartes, can lead him on toward vision. Though far from "superhuman," he can gaze upon the complex image which the "troubled mirror" shows him and not sink unmanned into the half-deceit of any consolation.

ii.

A short step behind the details of "Nineteen Hundred and Nineteen" leads us to the archetypal opposites, the "old images ... awakened again to overwhelming life," which helped to shape the poem. Though not explicit, partly because Heine's gods cannot be named in this skeptical twentieth-century poem, they are present by clear association. What is that "ancient image made of olive wood," that "stump on the Acropolis"? As Yeats's version of Sophocles' ode "Colonus' Praise" suggests, it is

> The self-sown, self-begotten shape that gives
> Athenian intellect its mastery,
> Even the grey-leaved olive-tree
> Miracle-bred out of the living stone ...

Porphyry had called that image a symbol of the divine wisdom.[23] It had been given to Athens as a result of the ancient conflict over that city (depicted on the west pediment of the Parthenon) between Athene and Poseidon. The gods arbitrating the conflict determined to award the city to whichever produced the more useful gift for mortals—whereupon Athene created the olive and Poseidon the horse. The city was awarded to Athene, and the Sophoclean ode proclaims:

> Nor accident of peace nor war
> Shall wither that old marvel, for
> The great grey-eyed Athene stares thereon.

However, in "Nineteen Hundred and Nineteen" that "stump" has been burnt by sea raiders who are effectively agents of the newly rebellious Poseidon the Earth-shaker, himself associated with "the circle of the moon / That pitches common things about."

Indeed, out of Poseidon's sea arises a double attack: both Persian and British soldiers are sent by the multiform ruler of the waves— Asiatic or *primary* power (foreshadowed by the sinking into Asia of Athenian and Irish cultures) to overcome the unity and order of *antithetical* wisdom. Though "troubled" water appears no more than obliquely, that destructive power is the indefinite and passionate sea of history that was "claiming" the orderly world of "Rosa Alchemica." The "levelling wind" that here clamors of "approaching night" is that "roof-levelling wind, / Bred on the Atlantic" in "A Prayer for My Daughter," where, not with gong but with drum, the years come in a frenzied dance "Out of the murderous innocence of the sea" to drown the "ceremony of innocence" as it is drowned by the "tide" of "The Second Coming." And Poseidon's horses—which are the nation's pride when subject to Athene's intellect, as in "Colonus' Praise"—have broken loose: "Violence upon the roads: violence of horses." ("At the Abbey Theatre" had related sea, horses, and *primary* political power more explicitly.) As intellectual order is overturned but its dark psychic compensation, as "drowsy chargers" become dragon and nightmare, the ancient war between Athene and Poseidon is re-opened.

A similar understanding of the two gods had informed neo-Platonic readings of the *Odyssey* and also helped to shape Yeats's own accounts of journeys through salt blood or mackerel-crowded seas toward monuments of unageing intellect or Plotinian Isles of the Blessed. (In Joyce's *Ulysses,* Poseidon, the multiform ruler of the blinding, disintegrative, and generative whirlpools of life, pervades all; Athene is more difficult to find.) Moreover, Poseidon merges with Dionysus (hysteria, fertility, ecstasy, dispersal), and Athene with Apollo (mastery of unifying intellect in artistic and civic order). Plotinus had suggested, as another symbol of the fall into time, the myth of Dionysus, who contemplated his image in the mirror given him by the Titans and was thereupon rent asunder; and Thomas Taylor called Dionysus and Apollo the two-fold work of the demiurge, the division into species and the harmonization into a whole.[24] In consonance with such analogies, which have psychological bases, in "Rosa Alchemica" the sea is a Dionysian abyss, and in "Colonus' Praise" the "horses of the sea" (which Yeats, departing from Sophocles, assigns to Poseidon) are those of Manannan son of Lear (or the sea), who is not only a Protean shape-changer but also a Dionysian spirit of vitality. Cuchulain fights those horses (in the revised "Cuchulain's Fight with the Sea"), and his sea death is related also (in *The Only Jealousy of Emer* or *Fighting the Waves*) to the lure of Fand, who comes (like other Sidhe, dancers, bacchantes, or daughters of Herodias) from the country-under-wave.

But when that disorderly force which produces and destroys life may speak freely through the self, Manannan may enter Yeats's work as protagonist. Yeats's "rambling shambling travelling man" and his Jack the Journeyman, for example, recall the shape-changer in the tale of O'Donnell's Kern, who is a "poor rambling shambling flighty loon," a "frisky flighty strolling fellow."[25] In "Three Songs to the One Burden"—where also "ride the fierce horsemen"—Mannion, the Roaring Tinker, claims descent from Manannan. In "News for the Delphic Oracle" nymphs and satyrs copulate in that sea foam with which Manannan's horses are commonly identified. And in "High Talk," a poem uttered by just such a "frisky flighty strolling fellow," the metaphorical identity of Malachi Stilt-Jack and Manannan comes clear in the last line:

> I, through the terrible novelty of light, stalk on,
> stalk on!

> Those great sea-horses bare their teeth and laugh
> at the dawn.

That Yeats had long correlated those archetypal opposites which
may be named Athene and Poseidon with the cycles of time is evident from his association, in 1899, of the beginning of winter, the
victory of the Fomor (powers of death, dismay, cold, darkness) the
"horse-shaped Pucas, who are now mischievous spirits," the "horses
of Manannan, who reigned over the country of the dead," the sea
itself, and the neo-Platonic reading of the sea as "a symbol of the
drifting indefinite bitterness of life."[26] His still earlier remark that
"when Shakespeare compares the mind of the mad Lear to the 'vexed
sea,' we are told at once something more laden with meaning than
many pages of psychology,"[27] indicates the awareness of correspondences that could lead in "Nineteen Hundred and Nineteen" to the
use of sea, horse, nightmare, dragon, and bacchantes to render a contemporary losing battle with Lear's *hysterica passio,* that force whose
"element's below."

"The best wine is the oldest, the best water the newest." Yeats
understood Blake's aphorism to mean that the wine of old images
and emotions must be rediscovered in the water of new experience
and sensation.[28] He therefore chose (and, in part, was chosen) to
dramatize the immanence of the gods or moods no longer by a
mysterious fantasy in the manner of Heine's *Gods in Exile,* Pater's
Denys l'Auxerrois or *Apollo in Picardy,* or his own "Rosa Alchemica,"
but by a symbolic presentation of historical and psychological reality.
Contemplating his image in the troubled mirror of contemporary
history, the speaker of "Nineteen Hundred and Nineteen" re-enacts
an ancient "fall into division."

iii.

"The Statues" also opposes clarified form to limitless indefinite
life, but here not Dionysus but Apollo is the informing mood. Disillusionment is mastered by hope and determination; the speaker enacts a "resurrection into unity." Almost every phrase emerges from
a lifelong meditation upon the meaning of history.

Pythagoras planned it. Why did the speaker stare?
His numbers, though they moved or seemed to move
In marble or in bronze, lacked character.

Yeats had been early introduced by Balzac's Pythagorean novels to
the view that "Everything here below exists only by Motion and by
Number," and "motion and number are engendered by the Word."[29]
Now Pythagoras' semidivine Word—like that of Michael Angelo in
"Long-Legged Fly"—engenders a statue form that itself may engender
an entire cultural order possessing Unity of Being. Probably it was
Pater who first, for Yeats, related that Pythagorean plan to Greek
sculpture. The "perfect visible equivalent" of the Pythagorean rhythm,
he wrote, "is in those portrait-statues of the actual youth of Greece."
Created at a moment in history when man was "at unity with himself, with his physical nature, with the outward world," those statues
present what Pater called a "colourless, unclassified purity of life,"
a "blending and interpenetration of intellectual, spiritual, and physical
elements, still folded together, pregnant with the possibilities of a
whole world closed within it," yet "characterless, sofar as *character*
involves subjection to the accidental influences of life."[30] In 1909
Yeats had likewise contrasted modern art, which is interested in
"character, in the revolt from all that makes one man like another,"
and in which some "limiting environment or idiosyncrasy is displayed," with Greek sculpture, in which the presence of "that ancient
canon discovered in the Greek gymnasium" shows "a compact between the artist and society." Such art celebrates, he said, Blake's
"resurrection into unity."[31]

Probably Dürer's theory of measurement, which he also related
to that canon of beauty, had helped him so to praise in Blakean
terms what Blake had denigrated as mathematic form: "Grecian is
Mathematic Form: Gothic is Living Form, Mathematic Form is
Eternal in the Reasoning Memory: Living Form is Eternal Existence."[32] Yeats had read the compass with which Blake's Urizen
measures the fallen world as symbol of "the great wound" or the
"fall into division," and as late as 1906 he said that art "shrinks from
what Blake calls mathematic form."[33] But even then he was coming
to understand the value of the "measurer-out," both ethical and

aesthetic, and of those Western forces, power and body. Sturge Moore's book on Dürer, published in 1905, probably called to his fuller attention an artist, praised by Blake,[34] who carried aesthetic measurement into the realm of mathematic form in a way quite consonant with some positive Blakean symbolism. Dürer held that the ideally proportioned human body, belonging to the unfallen Adam, had been "parcelled out among his vast progeny in various amounts as a consequence of the fall." That beauty of form "Durer considered it part of an artist's business to recollect and reveal ... in his work." Such recollection, Moore said, "is very much what took place in the evolution of Greek statues,"[35] and Dürer's own studies in measurement resulted in prelapsarian figures of Adam and Eve. As Yeats said in 1909, such art, carried to its "logical conclusion," would result in the "creation of one single type of man, one single type of woman."[36] And as he knew, Blake had also described the process of "Collecting up the scatter'd portions" of the primal man's "immortal body."[37] Living Form could therefore be one with Mathematic Form.

Before writing the opening lines of "The Statues," however, Yeats had also read Spengler, whose discussion of the idea is yet closer to the implications of this stanza:

> The most valuable thing in the Classical mathematic is its proposition that number is the essence of all things *perceptible to the senses*. Defining number as measure, it contains the whole world-feeling of a soul passionately devoted to the "here" and the "now." ... In the free-standing statue of a naked man ... every essential and important element of Being, its whole rhythm, is exhaustively rendered by surfaces, dimensions and the sensuous relations of the parts. The Pythagorean notion of the harmony of numbers ... seems to be the very mould for a sculpture that has this ideal.[38]

The marble and bronze of "The Statues," therefore, are not "ornamental" as in "Nineteen Hundred and Nineteen" but have a complex social relevance, which is presented through startling but traditional symbolism. In 1909 Yeats had differed from Pater in seeing in the measured statues not repose and moderate passion but "that energy which seems measureless."[39] His Blakean modification brought him close (as he may have known) to Heine's dictum that "the truly heroic, which we recognize in the marble images of the Gods of Antiquity, ... does not consist as our aesthetic philosophers suppose

in eternal calm without passion, but in eternal passionate emotion
without unrest."[40] The staring people, blind to that fact, might prefer
a "prosaic art, celebrating the 'fall into division' " and hence stressing
"character"—[41]

> But boys and girls, pale from the imagined love
> Of solitary beds, knew what they were,
> That passion could bring character enough,
> And pressed at midnight in some public place
> Live lips upon a plummet-measured face.

Knowing the attraction of *antithetical* unity, they repeat the act of
Heine's Maximilian, who as a boy had fallen in love with a statue
and, one night, after impatiently tossing on his bed, stole out to it:

> my heart was beating wildly, and at last I kissed the lovely goddess
> with such passion and tenderness and despair as I have never in this
> life kissed with again. And I have never been able to forget the
> fearful and sweet sensation which flowed through my soul as the
> blissful cool of those marble lips touched my mouth.[42]

Though this hint of the abyss between yearning life and deathlike
ideal (which also appears in Gautier's elaboration of the Pygmalion
theme in "Ne touchez pas aux marbres" and Baudelaire's in "La
Beauté") enters *A Full Moon in March* and the final song of *The
Only Jealousy of Emer,* in "The Statues" the two components stand
in creative harmony. As in "Long-Legged Fly" girls at puberty may
find the first Adam in their thought, so here the Greek recollection
of that first Adam guides reproduction. The last two lines of the
stanza appropriately balance private passion and public order, body
and intellect, temporal and eternal, the many and the one. Such is
the Unity of Being planned by Pythagoras.

> No! Greater than Pythagoras, for the men
> That with a mallet or a chisel modelled these
> Calculations that look but casual flesh, put down
> All Asiatic vague immensities,
> And not the banks of oars that swam upon
> The many-headed foam at Salamis.
> Europe put off that foam when Phidias
> Gave women dreams and dreams their looking-glass.

That retort moves the Yeatsian dialogue still further from any celebration of abstract intellect and more clearly engages the historical process. The integral process of incarnation is the modelling of calculations, the thinking of the body. For such artists, as Spengler had said, "The chisel ... is the compass." Indeed, Spengler's own thought foreshadowed the sequence of these two stanzas: "Doubtless Pythagoras was the first in the Classical Culture to conceive number scientifically as the principle of a world order of comprehensible things ... but even before him it had found expression, as a noble arraying of sensuous-material units, in the strict canon of the statue..."[43] Moreover, that artistic creation was a heroic victory—and more immediately so than Pater had implied when he called Greek marbles "a revelation in the sphere of art, of the temper which made the victories of Marathon and Salamis possible."[44] The Greek liberation from Asia results not from the defeat of the Persians at Salamis but directly from that of the formless by form, of the chaotic sea by intellectual control. This is a subjective battle, of which the more famous battle in history is a mere projection or reflection. Yeats had learned also from Nietzsche, here, who had called his own task in studying Greek culture that of understanding

> why the Dionysian Greek needed to become Apollinian: that is, to break his will to the monstrous, manifold, uncertain, dreadful, on a will to measure, to simplicity, to orderly arrangement in rule and concept. The immoderate, disorderly, Asiatic lies at his base: the valor of the Greek consists in the struggle with his Asiaticism: beauty is not given him as a present, any more than logic, than naturalness of custom—it is conquered, willed, won by fighting—it is his victory.[45]

In "The Statues" that victory is the creation and discovery of man's true image. Europe puts off the foam; the mirror of history becomes clear. Man sees no shadow but an ideal dream—in effect a foam-born god or goddess, or as Gautier had said, "Un secret idéal par Phidias sculpté."[46]

Hegel had called a similar process the Greek liberation from Nature through man's self-realization. The ageing Yeats knew Hegel's account of the defeat of "Asiatic vague immensities" in *The Philosophy of History*;[47] but he had already been more deeply affected by Nietzsche, by Spengler (for whom number and the statue finally meant *"measure in contrast to the immeasurable"* and *"cosmos"* in contrast to *"chaos"*),[48] and by Pater, whose essay on Winckelmann uses the Hegelian phases of symbolic, classical, and romantic art. In the East, Pater wrote,

> from a vagueness, a want of definition, in thought, the matter pre-
> sented to art is unmanageable, and the forms of sense struggle vainly
> with it. The many-headed gods of the East ... are at best overcharged
> symbols ...

A Greek statue, however, suggests nothing "beyond its own victorious fairness"; the "mind begins and ends with the finite image, yet loses no part of the spiritual motive."[49] So in "The Statues" that "many-headed" Asiaticism is put down by those who create what seems "but casual flesh."

The third stanza, as it symbolizes a double lapse into Yeatsian Asia, continues to parallel Pater's Hegelian account. In Greek thought, Pater said, the lordship of the soul "gives authority and divinity to human hands and feet."

> But just there the Greek thought finds its happy limit; it has not
> yet become too inward.... It has indeed committed itself to a train
> of reflexion which must end in defiance of form, of all that is out-
> ward, in an exaggerated idealism. But that end is still distant: it has
> not yet plunged into the depths of religious mysticism.

When it does so, art will present "faces fixed immovably into blank types of placid reverie."[50] For Yeats too that *primary* monism de-velops from knowledge implicit in the Greek achievement, after the moment of equilibrium is past:

>   One image crossed the many-headed, sat
>   Under the tropic shade, grew round and slow,
>   No Hamlet thin from eating flies, a fat
>   Dreamer of the Middle Ages. Empty eyeballs knew
>   That knowledge increases unreality, that
>   Mirror on mirror mirrored is all the show.
>   When gong and conch declare the hour to bless
>   Grimalkin crawls to Buddha's emptiness.

The "Dreamer" whose "empty eyeballs" have this knowledge (which would be understood by the speaker of "Meru") develops from those statues with empty eyeballs which "Gave women dreams and dreams their looking-glass." (Those Greek eyes, Yeats said, were "gazing at nothing.")[51] As reflected in art, that historical "image" is a statue type which crosses the sea from Greece into Asia (penetrating north-western India with the conquests of Alexander the Great precisely when, according to *A Vision,* Greece "loses itself in Asia"),[52] grows "round and slow," and, assuming the aspect of a medieval dreamer, becomes the statue of the Buddha as developed by Gandhara sculptors. The fullest development of those statues, from A.D. 300 to 600, was contemporary with the rise of medieval mysticism; and the poem equates the two developments. As Greek statues led to the Indian Buddha, Greek thought led through Plato and Plotinus to medieval idealism. Hence, as the second stanza describes the emergence of an *antithetical* civilization from the foamy sea of *primary* Nature, the third must describe its subsidence into the void, the *primary* now conceived as God.[53]

Spengler, describing a similar spiritual movement, had said that the catharsis of the Apollonian soul leads toward a "statuesque steadiness and will-less ethos" much like the Buddhist Nirvana. "When one thinks of it, there is nothing preposterous in the idea of Socrates... sitting by the Ganges..." That kinship, he said, separates Greek and Indian from modern Faustian man, "whose ethic is manifested in the Shakespearean tragedy of dynamic evolution and catastrophe."[54] The speaker of "The Statues" makes a similar but not identical distinction: "No Hamlet thin from eating flies." The mystical return to the *primary,* a religious irony underlying all finite achievement, is different from the modern capitulation to the abstract. Hamlet perceives no divine emptiness but only a buzzing multiplicity. Undernourished by a diet of bloodless abstractions, he is one of those "flycatchers" mentioned in "The Crazed Moon," or what Yeats called

> the wavering lean image of hungry speculation, that cannot but because of certain famous Hamlets of our stage fill the mind's eye. Shakespeare himself foreshadowed a symbolic change, that is a change in the whole temperament of the world, for though he called his Hamlet "fat" and even "scant of breath," he thrust between his fingers agile rapier and dagger.[55]

As flycatcher—whether a Minnaloushe following the last phases of the moon or a Swiftian spider (for Yeats stressed in later years the negative implications which that image of introverted modernity had for Swift)[56]—Hamlet has been deprived of the world as Europe was deprived of it by Descartes, Newton, and Locke, who gave Europe "its excrement instead." In restoring that world, Berkeley had fought another Salamis; and yet another, Yeats thought, might be about him now.[57]

Hence the fourth stanza of "The Statues." Though not denying the Eastern knowledge that every era approaches the phases of saint and fool, the speaker is not yet ready to crawl, dehumanized, to the divine emptiness. That final consummation, when gong and conch (or the great clock tower) declare the hour to bless, may be for such as Ribh the hymen of the soul; but it is for this man of Western civilization (as for the Yeats of the 1909 diaries) a kind of death. Not ready to give that last kiss to the void, he would re-enact the passion of the Greek boys and girls. He clings to the vital illusions of incarnate and hence powerful knowledge, aware that "Western minds who follow the Eastern way become weak and vapoury, because unfit for the work forced upon them by Western life."[58] He turns then to the work forced upon him by the disintegration foreshadowed by Hamlet; he fastens upon one scene in the midst of modern chaos, and his questions are emphatic assertions:

> When Pearse summoned Cuchulain to his side,
> What stalked through the Post Office? What intellect,
> What calculation, number, measurement, replied?

That resurrected spirit which Pearse summoned to aid the Easter Rising was, according to George Russell, one of those "great imaginations" which bring about the unity of "the national being."[59] But as that triple series—"calculation, number, measurement"—may suggest by its echo of the *Book of Wisdom,* the speaker also has in mind that principle of incarnation to whom (Madame Blavatsky had said) *"are committed Weight and Measure and Number"*: that Satan or Samael who is "the shadow of the Lord" or "God in the manifested world."[60]

> We Irish, born into that ancient sect
> But thrown upon this filthy modern tide
> And by its formless spawning fury wrecked,

Climb to our proper dark, that we may trace
The lineaments of a plummet-measured face.

This final sentence reveals the previously indefinite speaker as an actor who is one with his race, and one with a "sect" which contains all those who, armed with measurement, have fought Poseidon. The dramatic perspective leads from the speaker back to Pearse (whose editor had called him "a second Cuchulainn, who battled with a divine frenzy to stem the waves of the invading tide"),[61] to Cuchulain himself, and on to those legendary first settlers of Ireland who were Greeks, and to Pythagoras himself who was held to be a teacher of the Druids.[62] Climbing, the Irish now repeat the Greek act of putting off the Asiatic foam. Greek culture, said Nietzsche, had been "a chaos of foreign forms and ideas," its religion "a battle of all the gods of the East." But the Greeks learned to "organise the chaos, by taking Apollo's advice and thinking back to themselves, to their own true necessities, and letting all the sham necessities go."[63] Because the Irish are re-enacting an ancient drama, for them as for Yeats the means of separating "accidental from vital things" and so organizing the chaos is a return to the past; and they are guided by that "sense of possession" which Yeats once called "the very centre of the matter."[64] They climb toward a midnight more complex than that of the first stanza: their "proper dark" (both possessive and normative), their dark fountain of rebirth. They do not simply press "Live lips"; they "trace"—perceive and re-create, in Vichian fashion —the "lineaments" of that ideal.

That word "lineaments" is used deliberately: "The Beauty proper for sublime art," said Blake, "is lineaments, or forms and features that are capable of being the receptacles of intellect." Accordingly Blake presented in his "Beautiful Man," for whom Apollo was the model, his "idea of intellectual Beauty";[65] Yeats presents in this Apollonian poem, which stresses the "bounding outline,"[66] his own comparable idea. Both artists were working with an understanding of the cosmic and psychological magnetism of statues that Plotinus had described in his own language: the presence of the "Soul of the All," he said, "will be secured all the more readily when an appropriate receptacle is elaborated, a place especially capable of receiving some portion or phase of it, something reproducing it, or representing it, and serving like a mirror to catch an image of it."[67]

Though "intellect" is dominant, the image caught in "The Statues" is that of a complex unity of being. Instead of succumbing to the Dionysian "passion for destruction growing out of a hatred for the destructibility of all things," the speaker knows Hector's Apollonian "will towards preservation growing out of a love for human achievements in their vulnerability."[68] For him as for Nietzsche's Greeks, the "measurement" of the statues is not given as a present; it is his victory. Just as Pearse assumed a heroic stance before he could summon Cuchulain, so the Irish must "climb" that they may "trace." As an actor in history, the speaker is neither Spengler's Greek who "lacks all idea of an inner development and therefore all real history" nor his Faustian who makes merely a "yearning effort towards the Apollinian ideal."[69] He has a fuller awareness of the perpetual transaction between Being and Becoming. The "clarified spirits" such as the summoned Cuchulain "own the truth, they have intellect," said Yeats; "but we receive as agents, never as owners, in reward for victory."[70] His drama of active "tracing" or creative perception can take place only in an experienced history, which implies human freedom. In the panorama of "Dove or Swan" freedom could not be imaginatively realized, and elsewhere Yeats vacillated between the determinism suggested by external contemplation and the freedom subjectively experienced:

> Civilisation rose to its high tide mark in Greece, fell, rose again in the Renaissance but not to the same level. But we may if we choose, not now or soon but at the next turn of the wheel, push ourselves up, being ourselves the tide, beyond that first mark. But no, these things are fated; we may be pushed up.[71]

But for the speaker of "The Statues" there is no such conflict. Whatever fated "hour" he may recognize in past or future, in the living present he is not pushed up; he climbs.

"Freedom of the spirit," Nicolas Berdyaev has said, "belongs only to him who no longer feels history as an exterior imposition, and who begins to apprehend it as an interior event of spiritual significance." That requires that he seek "an inner profound and mysterious tie with the historical object," that "the subject of historical knowledge should sense and discover what is essentially historical within himself."[72] The discovery of such a tie, binding the speaker of "The Statues" to his race and to European history, is thus a Yeatsian return to the sources of power, a "claim made upon the future." Yeats would understand Berdyaev's statement that only "a prophetic vision of the past can set history in motion; and only a prophetic vision of the future can bind the present and the past into a sort of interior and complete spiritual movement."[73] In Yeats's own words: "History is necessity until it takes fire in some one's head and becomes freedom or virtue. Berkeley's Salamis was such a conflagration, another is about us now?"[74]

But if the man who apprehends history as an interior event of spiritual significance is no longer passive, neither does he possess, in any restrictive sense, the power that flows through him. We "receive as agents, never as owners." Through the active speaker, Samael, the fallen angel battling within time, utters the heroic cry, calling the body to resurrection. In its rich historical implications that cry includes (as D. H. Lawrence said any "vital truth" must include) "the memory of all that for which it is not true."[75] Its final sentence earns Yeats's own tribute to that moment when Lucifer stands among his friends: "life herself has made one of her eternal gestures, has called up into our hearts her energy that is eternal delight."[76]

XI · BURIED MEN

An Cathaoirleach: Do you not think we might leave
the dead alone?
Dr. Yeats: I am passing on. I would hate to leave
the dead alone.
—Seanad Eirann, *Parliamentary Debates*[1]

"And if my dearest friend were dead
I'd dance a measure on his grave."
—"Tom O'Roughley"

---

i.

WE MAY READ in *Louis Lambert,* which increasingly came to be
one of Yeats's "sacred books," that the "angel borne upon the
wind does not say: 'Ye Dead, arise!' He says: 'Let the Living arise!' "[2]
It is quite in harmony with Balzac's meaning that, in Yeats's poetry,
the living who respond to the trumpeting voice of Michael or Samael
include not merely the old gods but also buried men. Their resurrection is frequently enacted in Yeats's memory-haunted elegies—

Discoverers of forgotten truth
Or mere companions of my youth,
All, all are in my thoughts to-night being dead[3]

—and in his celebrations of family and Anglo-Irish traditions. But
buried men entered his dialogue with history in yet other ways, their
presence gathering force as Yeats himself moved toward that con-

dition in which (to use Auden's bleak modulation of the theme) "he became his admirers."[4]

In "Parnell's Funeral" the theme of burial and subterranean or interior continuance relates to that sacrifice exacted by the lunar goddess of history which had entered "Two Songs from a Play." But here the perspective is that of dramatic experience. Beginning with history, not myth, the speaker looks back from 1933 to 1891— and sets the stage:

> Under the Great Comedian's tomb the crowd.
> A bundle of tempestuous cloud is blown
> About the sky; where that is clear of cloud
> Brightness remains; a brighter star shoots down ...

But the strange lights and the falling star (witnessed by many at the funeral)[5] suggest the myth:

> What shudders run through all that animal blood?
> What is this sacrifice? Can someone there
> Recall the Cretan barb that pierced a star?

In keeping with the dramatic focus, the specific memory is that of an artifact of a previous age, which merely implies the cycles of "Two Songs ..." or such an astrological comment on the beginning of our era as this: "a conjunction of the stars in the sign of the Virgin has marked the fatal hour on the dial of the sky as on the dial of history, shooting its black arrow into the solar heart of the Christ."[6]

> Rich foliage that the starlight glittered through,
> A frenzied crowd, and where the branches sprang
> A beautiful seated boy; a sacred bow;
> A woman, and an arrow on a string;
> A pierced boy, image of a star laid low.
> That woman, the Great Mother imaging,
> Cut out his heart. Some master of design
> Stamped boy and tree upon Sicilian coin.

That design brings into focus the previous hints of spiritual influx and sacrifice of spiritual to bestial—"a fallen flare" as in "The Mother of God," an engendering and destructive shudder as in "Leda and the Swan," the hysteria of blood as in "Two Songs from a Play"—and

suggests that Parnell may be one of those avatars whose lives punctu-
ate history. The next line then comes as no surprise: "An age is the
reversal of an age."

But in this poem the reversal is not envisioned from afar; it is
experienced:

> When strangers murdered Emmet, Fitzgerald, Tone,
> We lived like men that watch a painted stage.
> What matter for the scene, the scene once gone:
> It had not touched our lives. But popular rage,
> *Hysterica passio* dragged this quarry down.
> None shared our guilt; nor did we play a part
> Upon a painted stage when we devoured his heart.

It is not now "As though God's death were but a play." Indeed, the
very shift from detached contemplation to recognized complicity is
for this speaker the essence of the reversal of the age. It controls the
structure of the poem itself, which, though fundamentally from the
perspective of dramatic experience, moves from an envisioned past
event (or play, as the elliptical stage directions suggest) to the present
experience of its meaning, from third person and suggested ignorance
("Can someone there / Recall . . . ?") to first person plural and asserted knowledge. The fourth stanza, introducing the first person
singular, completes that movement. The speaker, recognizing himself as a microcosm of Irish history, stands in the center of his own
stage:

> Come, fix upon me that accusing eye.
> I thirst for accusation. All that was sung,
> All that was said in Ireland is a lie
> Bred out of the contagion of the throng,
> Saving the rhyme rats hear before they die.
> Leave nothing but the nothings that belong
> To this bare soul, let all men judge that can
> Whether it be an animal or a man.

That ethical movement, recalling "Nineteen Hundred and Nineteen,"
"Meditations in Time of Civil War," and other fruit of Yeats's long
dialogue with an interior Lucifer, is here the final meaning of the
ritual sacrifice itself. The speaker takes upon himself the collective

guilt and rage; one of the murderers of the scapegoat becomes a voluntary scapegoat.

It is a meaning appropriate not to the age of O'Connell, "the Great Comedian," but to the new age of Parnell. The popular and gregarious yield to the "solitary and proud..., buskin following hard upon sock"—just as, Yeats thought, the Greeks hurled "upon some age of comedy their tragic sense."[7] Hence the *hysterica passio,* at first the popular rage, the baying of the Irish hounds who are always, in Goethe's phrase, "dragging down some noble stag,"[8] becomes the noble hysteria of a figure strikingly reminiscent of Lear himself— sinned against and sinning, reducing himself to a state of nothingness or nakedness as he discovers the true meaning of "unaccommodated man." Recognizing his share in the collective guilt, he would attain his fully human stature. In doing so, he embodies that historical change which Yeats had observed after Parnell's death, when "the accumulated hatred of years was suddenly transferred from England to Ireland." The Irish began to have a "passion for reality" and a "satiric genius"; they were learning "that original virtue arises from the discovery of evil."[9] Indeed, unbalanced by the fullness of his tragic knowledge, somewhat like the mad Lear of Act IV, the speaker is both Irish satirist and Irish rat being rhymed to death.[10] He is both slayer and slain in the ritual sacrifice. As Yeats wrote of Ireland: "We had passed through an initiation like that of the Tibetan ascetic, who staggers half dead from a trance, where he has seen himself eaten alive and has not yet learnt that the eater was himself."[11]

But the speaker of this poem, awakened from the trance, has that knowledge. He now awakens more fully, questioning his own historical interpretation: "The rest I pass, one sentence I unsay." In the cold light of later reflection, the vision of a national transformation in that initiatory moment must fade.

> Had de Valera eaten Parnell's heart
> No loose-lipped demagogue had won the day,
> No civil rancour torn the land apart.

And so with Cosgrave, O'Duffy,

> —but I name no more—
> Their school a crowd, his master solitude;

> Through Jonathan Swift's dark grove he passed, and there
> Plucked bitter wisdom that enriched his blood.

The remarkable last two lines continue the eucharistic imagery but suggest also another food, a fruit bringing bitter knowledge of good and evil, in a dark grove that is both the sacred wood of initiation and the *selva oscura* of all our wanderings.

The poem celebrates, then, not merely the modern Irish "cult of sacrifice" which Yeats was meditating during the Easter season of 1933,[12] but the less popular though more universal cult of tragic victimage. Thinking of Swift, Yeats wrote later the same year: "Perhaps every historical phase may have its victims—its poisoned rat in a hole."[13] He had long believed that psychology and religion testified to the existence of such victimage; and his own dialogue with history convinced him of its reality. The artist who is victim (Yeats once mentioned Beardsley as an example) assumes even despite himself the illnesses of his age, knows them, measures and judges them, and renders them in an objective vision.[14]

That is why, in "Parnell's Funeral," the speaker's refusal to grant that Ireland's politicians have eaten Parnell's heart does not leave us simply with a tribute to a buried man who fails to live. The speaker himself, in dancing a *measure* on that grave, has eaten that heart. He now has the bitter wisdom of the heart in Swift's "blood-sodden breast": the knowledge of his own participation in that evil of which he is victim. Like the Tibetan ascetic who sees himself eaten alive, he knows with Schopenhauer that the will "buries its teeth in its own flesh," that the "inflicter of suffering and the sufferer are one."

> If the eyes of both were opened, the inflicter of suffering would see that he lives in all that suffers pain.... And the sufferer would see that all the wickedness which is or ever was committed in the world proceeds from that will which constitutes *his* own nature also, appears also in *him,* and that through this phenomenon and its assertion he has taken upon himself all the suffering which proceed from such a will and bears them as his due, so long as he is this will.[15]

In other words, the speaker knows the ethical implications of that transformation of which Yeats would speak in 1936, the alchemical version of Buddha's injunction, "Be ye lamps unto yourselves." The soul, he would say, "must become its own betrayer, its own deliverer, the one activity, the mirror turn lamp."[16]

ii.

Increasingly possessed by the dead who arise, judged and judging, measured and measuring, Yeats often recalled that "modest creed" of Shelley's "The Sensitive Plant":

> That garden sweet, that lady fair,
> And all sweet shapes and odours there,
> In truth have never passed away;
> 'Tis we, 'tis ours, are changed; not they.[17]

When the speaker of "Quarrel in Old Age" translates that creed into defiant assertion, willed belief, the result is not "rhetoric," or "the will trying to do the work of the imagination,"[18] because the element of will itself is implicitly declared and measured. The reiterated and tersely general assertions, the disturbingly dehumanizing phrase "lonely thing," and the final fixing upon a past sensation—all indicate that the poem is about the intense desire which may induce that sense of conviction:

> All lives that has lived;
> So much is certain;
> Old sages were not deceived:
> Somewhere beyond the curtain
> Of distorting days
> Lives that lonely thing
> That shone before these eyes
> Targeted, trod like spring.

A similar subsuming of philosophical doctrine to the speaker's present attitude or experience occurs whenever Yeats engages the continued life of the dead. "The Sensitive Plant" asserts that

> For love and beauty and delight
> There is no death, nor change; their might
> Exceeds our organs, which endure
> No light, being themselves obscure.

But Yeats's poetry focuses upon the psychological state of Ribh, whose eyes have become "open to that light," or of Tom the Lunatic, who complains of a momentary relapse into obscurity:

> Something made these eyeballs weary
> That blinked and saw them in a shroud.

In the last poems, Yeats often renders the state of speakers who move toward the condition of those solar visionaries, opening themselves to that timeless realm, while yet maintaining their place in the experienced drama of history.

Even in those poems where the speaker does not quite move beyond our ordinary experience, the preoccupations are symptomatic. "The Circus Animals' Desertion" speaks of a lifetime of enchantment:

> Character isolated by a deed
> To engross the present and dominate memory.

"Beautiful Lofty Things" enumerates such images, and in "The Municipal Gallery Revisited" the speaker does not simply look back upon such a past but says: "Around me the images of thirty years." Those present images body forth a life and a history, for contemplation and judgment:

> You that would judge me, do not judge alone
> This book or that, come to this hallowed place
> Where my friends' portraits hang and look thereon;
> Ireland's history in their lineaments trace...

But elsewhere the past does not require a gallery of portraits in order to make itself felt as a real presence. What Yeats asserted of recent history was true of his own last years: "Since Poincaré said 'space is the creation of our ancestors,' we have found it more and more difficult to separate ourselves from the dead when we commit them to the grave..."[19] As he put it in "Under Ben Bulben":

> Though grave-diggers' toil is long,
> Sharp their spades, their muscles strong,
> They but thrust their buried men
> Back in the human mind again.

It is a bolder and more inclusive statement of what "In Memory of Major Robert Gregory" hints in a metaphor disarmingly close to common speech: "All, all are in my thoughts to-night being dead." Where the intensely living images of the earlier poem insinuate themselves into the mind, those more schematic and yet more violent images of the later poems force themselves upon us—and the speakers correspondingly stress, with a harsh wit appropriate to their ballad rhythms, the bare bones of their ambiguously metaphorical doctrine. They speak in exultant mockery—

> *The ghost of Roger Casement*
> *Is beating on the door*

—or in dry consolation—

> Whether man die in his bed
> Or the rifle knock him dead,
> A brief parting from those dear
> Is the worst man has to fear[20]

—or in weary longing to escape the eternal complexities of human life—

> Because of those new dead
> That come into my soul and escape
> Confusion of the bed,
> Or those begotten or unbegotten
> Perning in a band,
> *I bend my body to the spade*
> *Or grope with a dirty hand.*

As this last poem, "The Spirit Medium," reminds us, Yeatsian speakers are haunted by the voices as well as the images of the dead. The metaphor of the medium, which had long rendered Yeats's sense of being a mouth through which the depths within or beyond might speak, is a useful key with which to approach the balladlike poems of his last years.

iii.

The voices of these poems form part of the final music of his dialogue with history. There is, in Hallam's phrase, "no foolish self-desertion," but Yeats is closer to Irish balladry than ever before. His desire for the "natural momentum" of common speech[21] and his admiration for "hereditary stamina and a great voice" (sensed in "As ye came from Walsinghame," as in Burns's "Elegy on Captain Matthew Henderson" and Higgins's "The Ballad of O'Bruadir")[22] had led him into what he now called "the main road, the road of naturalness & swiftness." Wanting "vast sentiments, generalizations supported by tradition"—"We alone," he said, "can think like a wise man, yet express ourselves like the common people"—he felt "the lilt of songs" in his blood.[23] He sought "a vivid speech that has no laws except that it must not exorcise the ghostly voice" of the folk song heard through modern utterance.[24]

Of course, he had long admired the "ballad that gradually lifts ... from circumstantial to purely lyrical writing." He had early lamented the passing in Spenser's England of the "poetry of the will," the "old marching rhythms, that once could give delight to more than expedient hearts."[25] And in *The Celtic Twilight* he had heard in the work of "the last gleeman," Michael Moran, the salty, self-parodying laughter that would later ring through his own poetry. His valedictory to Moran hides the seed of the later style in the lush vegetation of the earlier:

> Let us hope that some kindly middle region was found for him, where he can call dishevelled angels about him with some new and more rhythmical form of his old
>
> > Gather round me, boys, will yez
> > Gather round me?
> > And hear what I have to say
> > Before ould Salley brings me
> > My bread and jug of tay;
>
> and fling outrageous quips and cranks at cherubim and seraphim. Perhaps he may have found and gathered, ragamuffin though he be, the Lily of High Truth, the Rose of Far-Sought Beauty, for whose lack so many of the writers of Ireland ... have been futile as the blown froth upon the shore.[26]

A comparable middle region is now created in Yeats's own verse, in which an earthy yet ethereal gleeman sings "John Kinsella's Lament for Mrs. Mary Moore" or "A Drunken Man's Praise of Sobriety." A voice comes from that region (not simply "kindly") where life merges capriciously, ludicrously, terrifyingly with death—

> O mind your feet, O mind your feet,
> Keep dancing like a wave,
> And under every dancer
> A dead man in his grave

—where the only sobriety possible ("Down, hysterica passio!") is the intoxicated perception of the influx of voices from beyond, or the imminence of the speaker's own translation to the realm of voices:

> An old ghost's thoughts are lightning,
> To follow is to die.[27]

The long and fragmentary heroic poem of Yeats's career seems to end now with a funeral march that is also marching-song and scherzo, a sometimes raucous medley through which we hear the voice of that eighteenth-century ballad "The Night before Larry Was Stretched":

> —the rope gave a jerk there,
> No more sang he, for his throat was too small;
> But he kicked before he died,
> He did it out of pride.[28]

We also hear voices of the Jacobite ballad-poets of the early eighteenth century, most notably that Egan O'Rahilly who cries, Yeats had said, "in a translation from the Gaelic that is itself a masterpiece of concentrated passion—

> The periwinkle and the tough dog-fish
> Towards evening time have got into my dish."[29]

Thanks to the ironic reversal in Irish history, at evening time the Anglo-Irish Yeats could feel, contemplating the new Catholic bourgeois state, that bitter passion which the Jacobite poets had felt as they contemplated in Ireland "the house of the Poor, the lonely house, the accursed house of Cromwell."[30] In "The Curse of Cromwell" those Jacobite poets speak through him more richly and vigorously than they could have spoken in his early years of Irish nationalism:

> You ask what I have found, and far and wide I go:
> Nothing but Cromwell's house and Cromwell's murderous crew,
> The lovers and the dancers are beaten into the clay,

And the tall men and the swordsmen and the horsemen, where
                              are they?
And there is an old beggar wandering in his pride—
His fathers served their fathers before Christ was crucified.
          O what of that, O what of that,
          What is there left to say?

Echoes of "Kilcash" and of O'Rahilly's "Last Lines" (both in Frank
O'Connor's translation)[31] are capped by an ironic refrain that recalls
"Nineteen Hundred and Nineteen":

          Man is in love and loves what vanishes,
          What more is there to say?

The second stanza, indicting the new rulers of two different eras for
their crude avarice, may echo another voice of lifelong importance to
Yeats:

    He that's mounting up must on his neighbour mount,
    And we and all the Muses are things of no account.
    They have schooling of their own, but I pass their schooling by,
    What can they know that we know that know the time to die?

Speaking in *Unto this Last* of the "roots of honor," Ruskin had
declared that the soldier, pastor, physician, and lawyer all know "when
to die," and with that fact he challenged the nineteenth-century merchant: "For truly, the man who does not know when to die, does
not know how to live."[32]

    The poet of "Kilcash" ended his complaint with a prayer for the
resurrection of the buried past:

          I beseech of Mary and Jesus
          That the great come home again
          With long dances danced in the garden
          Fiddle music and mirth among men,
          That Kilcash the home of our fathers
          Be lifted on high again . . .

"The Curse of Cromwell" ends more ambiguously, with "another
knowledge that my heart destroys"

Because it proves that things both can and cannot be;
That the swordsmen and the ladies can still keep company,
Can pay the poet for a verse and hear the fiddle sound,
That I am still their servant though all are underground.

That knowledge—arising from the speaker's vision of the super-
naturally lighted house—may imply yet another turn of the gyres of
Irish and Western history, as Egan O'Rahilly and others in their
visionary poems had foretold the return of the Stuarts. But primarily
it is the destructive knowledge also possessed by the spirit medium
that the poet is, at his peril, serving forces that though "underground"
have never been for him more alive than now—forces that alienate
him from what others recognize as human life:

> And when I pay attention I must out and walk
> Among the dogs and horses that understand my talk.

Another speaker so alienated is Henry Middleton, in life Yeats's
recluse cousin, but now in "Three Songs to the One Burden" a voice
of scorned folk wisdom on the "storm-bitten green" of twentieth-century Ireland:

> When every Sunday afternoon
> On the Green Lands I walk
> And wear a coat in fashion,
> Memories of the talk
> Of henwives and of queer old men
> Brace me and make me strong;
> There's not a pilot on the perch
> Knows I have lived so long.

Speaking through the poet himself, Henry Middleton gains what
Yeats had said the Middletons lacked: "the pride and reserve, the sense
of decorum and order, the instinctive playing before themselves that
belongs to those who strike the popular imagination."[33] Here the
"playing" involves an ironic distance from the claims set forth with
eloquence, and arrogance, in "The Municipal Gallery Revisited":

> John Synge, I and Augusta Gregory, thought
> All that we did, all that we said or sang
> Must come from contact with the soil, from that

Contact everything Antaeus-like grew strong.
We three alone in modern times had brought
Everything down to that sole test again,
Dream of the noble and the beggar-man.

And in the first of the "Three Songs..." Mannion the Roaring Tinker similarly plays with a grotesque version of the eugenics of *On the Boiler*:

Could Crazy Jane put off old age
And ranting time renew,
Could that old god rise up again
We'd drink a can or two,
And out and lay our leadership
On country and on town,
Throw likely couples into bed
And knock the others down.

"Could that old god rise up again," he sings; but the "rambling, shambling" Manannan is at least comically resurrected in the singer himself, along with the "jovial tinkers" of seventeenth-century ballads.[34]

After such voices of semiparody comes the strangely contrasting hieratic refrain: *"From mountain to mountain ride the fierce horsemen."* It is not that Yeats is "anxious for his dignity," as one critic has suggested;[35] rather, the "burden" of each stanza points to the burden or theme of the three songs. Here as elsewhere in Yeats's late verse, these horsemen suggest the tragic heroism of Ireland and of all history:

All those tragic characters ride
The meet's upon the mountain-side.[36]
But turn from Rosses' crawling tide,

Mannion and Middleton, who spit comically into the face of time, present the Dionysian vitality and Antaean wisdom in Ireland's "heroic wantonness." But in the third song the voice is that of the ballad singer himself, one actor in the drama of Irish history addressing others:

Come gather round me, players all:
Come praise Nineteen-Sixteen,
Those from the pit and gallery
Or from the painted scene
That fought in the Post Office
Or round the City Hall,
Praise every man that came again,
Praise every man that fell.
From mountain to mountain ride the fierce horsemen.

The "playing" has shifted from the comic to the tragic mode; the mythical horsemen now loom more closely behind their human images. As the song closes with a glance at the future—

And yet who knows what's yet to come?
For Patrick Pearse had said
That in every generation
Must Ireland's blood be shed.
From mountain to mountain ride the fierce horsemen

—the burden merges firmly with the song, implying an endless historical drama, a tragic battle and its comic variations. The last line resounds with its increment of overtones—the voices of Mannion, Middleton, ballad singer and Pearse included in that complex voice which will soon, in "Under Ben Bulben," instruct us: "Swear by those horsemen..."

The dead shake in their shrouds most ambiguously in the last balladlike poem Yeats wrote, "The Black Tower." Addressing the reader as if he were an envoy demanding surrender, the poem pulls him into the re-enactment of a lifelong battle waged against the seemingly victorious forces of history. In 1889 the defender of Manannan's tower had hurled melodramatic defiance:

"Last of my race, three things I rule alone—
My soul, my prey, and this my heapèd pile.
I pace remembering. From my misty throne
I bellow to the winds when storms make moan,
        And trample my dark isle."[37]

In 1919 the speaker of "A Prayer for My Daughter," who also paced remembering and who heard the same "sea-wind scream upon the tower," gave both scene and symbolism less vague romanticism and more subdued yet intense personal and historical force. Now in 1939 that wind shakes the buried men upon the mountain. The verse itself is yet more circumstantial, more laconic; but its increasingly short, tense, weighted lines rhythmically prepare for the haunting refrain which contains all the eery romance excluded from the verse:

> Say that the men of the old black tower,
> Though they but feed as the goatherd feeds,
> Their money spent, their wine gone sour,
> Lack nothing that a soldier needs,
> That all are oath-bound men:
> Those banners come not in.
>
> *There in the tomb stand the dead upright,*
> *But winds come up from the shore:*
> *They shake when the winds roar,*
> *Old bones upon the mountain shake.*

We may say that the dead stand because of the vertical burial of Irish heroes,[38] but the poem's diction increases the effect of indomitable but suspended life: "stand ... upright" suggests not merely placement but also the act of rising again, and "shake" may be either passive or active, because of wind or rage. The poem renders again the destructive and sustaining knowledge that things both can and cannot be. The king seems dead—and not dead:

> If he died long ago
> Why do you dread us so?

No facile hope in the resurrection of the Irish heroes, however, disturbs the bleakness of the poem or detracts from the speaker's defiance. Perhaps the "dark grows blacker" just before dawn or before a new lunar cycle, but the speaker makes no prophecies. In *him* the legions of the past stand upright, shaken but undefeated:

> *They shake when the wind roars,*
> *Old bones upon the mountain shake.*

And that refrain carries the voice of another buried man, friend of Yeats's youth:

> The Saints in golden vesture shake before the gale,
> The glorious windows shake...

Though tradition and tone were quite different, Lionel Johnson himself exhibited a muted heroic defiance, as "In Memory of Major Robert Gregory" had suggested. Yeats had heard in Johnson's Greek and Latin learning "A long blast upon the horn that brought," if not aid for an embattled Roland, at least "A little nearer to his thought / A measureless consummation that he dreamed." It is appropriate that now, in the very dead of winter, celebrating the black tower at the nadir of the cycle, Yeats should transmute the saints of "The Church of a Dream" (the Johnson poem he recalled "most vividly")[39] into his heroic dead.

> There still, although the world autumnal be, and pale,
> Still in their golden vesture the old saints prevail...

Surely it was not the first such transmutation of that poem: rhythm and idea suggest it in "Mohini Chatterjee," also on the deathless dead:

> Over the blackened earth
> The old troops parade...

Johnson's next line, "Alone with Christ, desolate else, left by mankind," may lurk in the conclusion of "An Acre of Grass," that other poem where the dead are explicitly shaken:

> Forgotten else by mankind,
> An old man's eagle mind.

Johnson had sounded that note so congenial to Yeats in other poems, Christian and pagan: in "The Age of a Dream," "We hunger against hope for the lost heritage"; in "Julian at Eleusis," "Still am I faithful to the lonely faith." But unlike the mature Yeats, Johnson could also say (as in "Nihilism") of that living death: "the eternal tomb / Brings me the peace which life has never brought." "The Church of a Dream" therefore ends not with the vigor of the old saints but with the somnolence of a priest for whom suffice "Melancholy remembrances and vesperal." When Johnson asks, in "The Age of a Dream,"

> Now from the broken tower what solemn bell still tolls,
> Mourning what piteous death?

—we may hear Yeats's answering cry, "Saddle and ride, I heard a man say," to the accompaniment from the tower of *"A slow low note and an iron bell."*[40] Nevertheless, Yeats's poetic relation to that buried friend may be epitomized by two lines from a poem he had echoed in "Easter 1916"[41]—Johnson's "Parnell":

> But from the dead arise
> Voices, that bid us wake.

With the horsemen who ride on past the tolling bell, past the ending of natural cycles, Yeats closes his work. He had written in *The Celtic Twilight* of the "pagan powers": "northward in Ben Bulben, famous for hawks, the white square door swings open at sundown, and those wild unchristian riders rush forth upon the field . . ."[42] Their ride takes place "where Ben Bulben mixes with the sea wind,"[43] where the evil pig slew the sun-hero Diarmuid. But the twilight in which Yeats finally evokes that scene is not sunset but a "wintry dawn." "Under Ben Bulben" is his last modulation of what Blake called "eternity's sunrise."[44]

As is proper, Yeats prefaces his initiatory and valedictory utterance with an injunction:

> Swear by what the sages spoke
> Round the Mareotic Lake
> That the Witch of Atlas knew,
> Spoke and set the cocks a-crow.

> Swear by those horsemen, by those women
> Complexion and form prove superhuman,
> That pale, long-visaged company
> That air in immortality
> Completeness of their passions won;
> Now they ride the wintry dawn
> Where Ben Bulben sets the scene.

> Here's the gist of what they mean.

If the burden of our oath is uncertain, it nonetheless implies our preparation and allegiance. We are already to some degree knowledgeable men. We have heard of the solar transfiguration that took place

When that exultant Anthony
And twice a thousand more
Starved upon the shore
And withered to a bag of bones!
What had the Caesars but their thrones?[45]

We have heard of Shelley's Witch, a Naiad, image of the soul or swan exercising its full power to envision the shadows of life:

> she passes along the Nile "by Moeris and the Mareotid lakes," and sees all human life shadowed upon its waters in shadows that "never are erased but tremble ever"; . . . and because she can see the reality of things she is described as journeying "in the calm depths" of "the wide lake" we journey over unpiloted.[46]

And we have heard of the Sidhe, who, their haughtiness freed from the pre-Raphaelite languor of the early poetry, now "air in immortality / Completeness of their passions won." Images that Yeats might earlier have separated as solar and lunar, Christian and pagan, visionary and heroic, are grouped here as transcendent ideals: human passion, action, and vision wrought to their uttermost—yet also something other than flesh and blood.

The prefatory injunction already describes several tangents to the circle that is the heart of the poem's meaning. The following parts, setting forth with such offhand terseness the "gist" of the apocalyptic message that (as in the *Völuspa*) sets the cocks a-crow, describes yet other tangents. In Part II it is the traditional wisdom concerning man's collective and individual nature.

> Many times man lives and dies
> Between his two eternities,
> That of race and that of soul,
> And ancient Ireland knew it all.

The generic "man" renders that doctrine of transmigration more complex than popular belief. There is but one multiple transmigrant—"a universal self dwelling in all selves" or what Yeats called from the more humanistic perspective of this poem "man self-sufficing and eternal."[47] Were the generic "man" not clearly used at first, the omission of the indefinite article in the succeeding lines might seem to result from laconic speech alone. But the phrases "Whether man

die in his bed" and "the worst man has to fear" point not to cut-off
individuals but to the polar humanity defined in that first sentence.
The reference to "buried men" is the first that stresses plurality—and
those men are, in the act of death, being thrust "Back in the human
mind again." That mind is generic and individual at once. One
could gloss the lines by referring to *Anima Mundi,* the Collective
Unconscious, or Brahma, but such glosses would merely substitute
other metaphors for that which Yeats has finally chosen. His terms
implicitly lay claim, on behalf of humanity, to the mysterious reaches
of power and knowledge that lie beyond the full control or possession
of the individual. That very comprehensiveness of reference helps to
unify the supernaturalism of Part I and the humanism of Part II.
Those superhuman images are archetypes of the human, and their
locus too is "the human mind."

In Part III, as Yeats reminds us of a wisdom known by us as individuals rather than as a race, he does not omit individualizing terms:

> You that Mitchel's prayer have heard,
> "Send war in our time, O Lord!"
> Know that when all words are said
> And a man is fighting mad,
> Something drops from eyes long blind,
> He completes his partial mind,
> For an instant stands at ease,
> Laughs aloud, his heart at peace.
> Even the wisest man grows tense
> With some sort of violence
> Before he can accomplish fate,
> Know his work or choose his mate.

The example of John Mitchel, who so violently reversed the Christian
petition, is a reminder that any individual may attain proximately—
through that doubling of the intellect, that unification of conscious
and unconscious, which completes his partial mind—the state of vision
that is fully evident in those images by which he swears. As Yeats
said, "I find my peace by pitting my sole nature against something
and the greater the tension the greater my self-knowledge."[48] Offer-
ing the human counterpart of those images, this section marks another

step in the poem's progress from symbolic sources and sanctions to
their immediate implications. The next steps are the prescriptions
for Western artist and Irish poet.

That for the Western artist recalls Gautier's injunction (as
imitated by Austin Dobson)—

> Paint, chisel, then, or write;
> But, that the work surpass,
> With the hard fashion fight,—
> With the resisting mass[49]

—but Yeats directs such heroic activity toward Transfiguration and
Incarnation:

> Poet and sculptor, do the work,
> Nor let the modish painter shirk
> What his great forefathers did,
> Bring the soul of man to God,
> Make him fill the cradles right.

Both goals are sketched with a final audacity, the decorum only of
"heroic wantonness." First the creative process of "Long-Legged Fly"
and "The Statues"—"Measurement began our might."

> Michael Angelo left a proof
> On the Sistine Chapel roof,
> Where but half-awakened Adam
> Can disturb globe-trotting Madam
> Till her bowels are in heat,
> Proof that there's a purpose set
> Before the secret working mind:
> Profane perfection of mankind.

Such art brings to consciousness that process inherent in the "secret
working mind" which is more than individual:

> How many centuries spent
> The sedentary soul
> In toils of measurement
> Beyond eagle or mole,
> Beyond hearing or seeing,

> Or Archimedes' guess,
> To raise into being that loveliness?
>
> .   .   .   .
>
> What death? what discipline?
> What bonds no man could unbind,
> Being imagined within
> The labyrinth of the mind,
> What pursuing or fleeing,
> What wounds, what bloody press,
> Dragged into being
> This loveliness?

So, developing a passage from Edwin Arnold—

> Out of the dark it wrought the heart of man,
>   Out of dull shells the pheasant's pencilled neck;
> Ever at toil, it brings to loveliness
>   All ancient wrath and wreck[50]

—*The Only Jealousy of Emer* had described the transmigratory measurement of experience which is the foundation for the artistic process. For the artist of Incarnation even religious art is a means of realizing that "profane" goal, transcendent in source, fleshly in realization. For the artist of Transfiguration "backgrounds for a God" (the indefinite article emphatically present now) are but means of creating gardens for a human soul:

> Quattrocento put in paint
> On backgrounds for a God or Saint
> Gardens where a soul's at ease;
> Where everything that meets the eye,
> Flowers and grass and cloudless sky,
> Resemble forms that are or seem
> When sleepers wake and yet still dream,
> And when it's finished still declare,
> With only bed and bedstead there,
> That heavens had opened.

The transcendental dream, whose source can never be experienced, is rendered in an art which, like "News for the Delphic Oracle," depicts the Sabbath of Creation.

> Gyres run on;
> When that greater dream had gone
> Calvert and Wilson, Blake and Claude,
> Prepared a rest for the people of God,
> Palmer's phrase, but after that
> Confusion fell upon our thought.

"Palmer's phrase"? Not quite. Even the lesser dream has for this speaker heroic implications that Palmer did not see. Echoing the epistle to the Hebrews, Palmer had said that Blake's work shows us "the drawing aside of the fleshly curtain, and the glimpse which all the most holy, studious saints and sages have enjoyed, of that rest which remaineth to the people of God"[51] But here those artists drew aside no such curtain; they themselves prepared a primal garden.

The "divine" as the unknowable source of the human and the heroic goal of the human: such is the religious bearing of these four sections. Part V turns to the task before Irish poets, who are to scorn "unremembering hearts and heads"—to be aware of the buried men thrust into the human mind and of the purposes set before it—and to cast their minds on the past in order to create a heroic future. The final section, after that summary of the life which haunted the speaker of "The Curse of Cromwell," returns to the tone of the prefatory injunction, with its more coldly passionate images:

> Under bare Ben Bulben's head
> In Drumcliff churchyard Yeats is laid.
> An ancestor was rector there
> Long years ago, a church stands near,
> By the road an ancient cross.

Yeats had invoked that ancestor, John Yeats,

> He that in Sligo at Drumcliff
> Set up the old stone Cross,

in "Are You Content?" as a buried man who might judge his own accomplishment: "Eyes spiritualised by death can judge." In "The Old Stone Cross" another such had uttered his judgment of the modern world—doubtless the armored man buried in 871 under hazel crosses, whose ghost continued to keep watch at the Drumcliff churchyard.[52] Yeats had placed that sentinel, *"The man in the golden breast-plate,"* under the cross his great-grandfather had erected. Now Yeats himself, after long hovering on the storm-beaten threshold, has joined that rector and that soldier.

> No marble, no conventional phrase;
> On limestone quarried near the spot
> By his command these words are cut:
>> *Cast a cold eye*
>> *On life, on death.*
>> *Horseman, pass by!*

But who tells us this? Though gravediggers' spades are sharp, their muscles strong, we have been listening to the voice of the buried man thrust violently into our mind: "from the dead arise / Voices, that bid us wake." The strategy of the poem is to enact its creed.

In retrospect the opening injunction—"Swear...Swear..."—takes on some of the uncanny force of that uttered by Hamlet's old mole, who worked in the earth so fast. Thinking of that injunction, recalling those horsemen who "air in immortality / Completeness of their passions won," we may read the epitaph as addressed not merely to us but to all horsemen, including the speaker, now in "the human mind." Distinctions dissolve;

> Many times man lives and dies
> Between his two eternities...

—and who now rides the wintry dawn? Finally, "Under Ben Bulben" is heroic Man's self-exhortation, a "measure" danced on his own grave. Our eyes partly spiritualized by death, we have some intimation—in the phrase of that ancient Prospero, the man in the golden breast-plate—"what unearthly stuff / Rounds a mighty scene."

XII · THE ROCKY VOICE

The Ruins of Time builds Mansions in Eternity.
                    —Blake[1]

Follow, poet, follow right
To the bottom of the night,
With your unconstraining voice
Still persuade us to rejoice...
        —Auden, "In Memory of W. B. Yeats"

---

i.

I T WAS YEATS's determined search for the apocalypse in the midst of
the cycle of time—for tragic affirmations in which the very stones
might rejoice—that earned Auden's tribute. At the beginning, of
course, Yeats was very close to that Stephen Dedalus who also expounded Blake's aphorism:

> Know all men, he said, time's ruins build eternity's mansions. What
> means this? Desire's wind blasts the thorntree but after it becomes
> from a bramblebush to be a rose upon the rood of time. Mark me
> now. In woman's womb word is made flesh but in the spirit of the
> maker all flesh that passes becomes the word that shall not pass away.[2]

Stephen quite properly places the gospel of Louis Lambert in the
landscape of Yeats's early poetry. But the formula hardly suggests
the vigor and complexity of Yeats's long exploration of its meaning.
If at first he turned too hastily from the blasted tree, the cross of
duality and time—

The old brown thorn-trees break in two high over Cummen
  Strand,
Under a bitter black wind that blows from the left hand...[3]

—to seek a Rose that is a distant, impossible joy even when ostensibly
incarnate, increasingly he realized the arduousness of the Great Work.
The rose which "opens at the meeting of the two beams of the cross"
is found in "the mingling of contraries." The bramblebush itself must
"*break* in flower"; the poet must "build" the mansion or "artifice of
eternity" from time's ruins, from the crossed sticks of scarecrow age
or the opposites in the gyres of history.

> Like the clangour of a bell,
> Sweet and harsh, harsh and sweet,
> That is how he learnt so well
> To take the roses for his meat.[4]

Out of the strong, when the strong measure and declare their own
qualities without fear or self-deception, may come sweetness. "The
lion and the honeycomb, what has Scripture said?"[5] Seeking that
"strange interfusion of sweetness and strength" which he, like Pater,
had found in Michael Angelo and in Blake,[6] Yeats saw all time become a stormy landscape, with "Old ragged elms, old thorns innumerable," and the "sound / Of every wind that blows"—an "acre
of stony ground" or a vast desert which might rejoice and blossom
as the rose. "We begin to live when we have conceived life as
tragedy."[7]

Another important image for that tragic setting, where history may
be accepted and so transcended, where life may paradoxically "begin"
amidst its continual ending, is Yeats's Purgatory. Among the haunted
and haunting speakers of the last poems is the mock-Dante of "The
Pilgrim," who sets forth an unearthly scene as part of a balladeer's
landscape:

> All know that all the dead in the world about that place
>   are stuck,
> And that should mother seek her son she'd have but little
>   luck
> Because the fires of Purgatory have ate their shapes away...

That voice itself may come from another buried man, the ageing William Carleton whom Yeats had described—reduced to poverty, drinking "more than was desirable," his genius "gradually flickering out" but sending up many a "bright, heavenward spark"[8]—a Carleton who now recalls his youthful pilgrimage to St. Patrick's Purgatory at Lough Derg with as much relish as satire. The silent humorist whom Carleton had met there, becoming one with an old man out of *Mother Goose,* now breaks his silence most surprisingly:[9]

> And there I found an old man, and though I prayed all day
> And that old man beside me, nothing would he say
> *But fol de rol de rolly O.*

The old man is joined in the next stanza by the chorus of "all the dead in the world," and in the last stanza by the singer himself, who, leaning upon the public-house wall, thus assumes his place in the drunken, death-haunted Purgatory of time.

> A drunkard is a dead man,
> And all dead men are drunk.[10]

Such delirious transcendence of temporal experience is not attained, of course, by all those who are subject to that destiny of simplified action, heightened passion, and obvious repetition which is Purgatory. In the play *Purgatory* itself, the half-mad old man who is haunted by his mother's marriage with a groom knows no such release. Dimly seeing that marriage (which resulted in the "killing of a house," the destruction of a cultural tradition) as re-enacting a primal fall—a fall also projected on the screen of Irish history—and hoping to annihilate its consequences and so free his mother's soul from its repetition of her wedding night, he kills his own son. But, as a sign of his failure, he hears again his father's approach on that wedding night:

> Hoof-beats! Dear God,
> How quickly it returns—beat—beat—!

At galloping speed, that is a hallucinatory image of Nietzsche's eternal recurrence. The old man prays for release from a history that is (like that which Stephen Dedalus knew) a compulsively repetitive nightmare:

O God,
Release my mother's soul from its dream!
Mankind can do no more. Appease
The misery of the living and the remorse of the dead.[11]

But mankind can do more; the play does not fully endorse that final speech. Yeats could almost say with Nietzsche: "I perform the great experiment. Who can bear the idea of Eternal Recurrence? He who cannot endure the sentence, 'There is no redemption,' ought to die out."[12] In not enduring that sentence, in seeking by violence to annihilate history (and thus embodying Yeats's own moments of rage against Irish degradation, rage "to end all things"), the old man succeeds only in perpetuating it through another crime. It is "action: / The struggle of the fly in marmalade." Release from the circling necessity comes through acceptance and total understanding—not "action" but "art" or other contemplation which is "but a vision of reality."[13] The play itself—dramatizing in those hoofbeats the endless sequences which have power "because of all those things we do, not for their own sake but for an imagined good"—renders a solution which Yeats had earlier described: it holds the repetitive dream "in the intellectual light where time gallops." The dead themselves, to know release, must enact that solution: they must explore "their moral life,...its beneficiaries and its victims"; and after "so many rhythmic beats the soul must cease to desire its images, and can, as it were, close its eyes."[14] And so, analogically, with the living. All that one can do to help another suffering soul (as Dr. Trench of *The Words upon the Window-Pane* knows) is to give understanding: "The more patient we are, the more quickly will it pass out of its passion and its remorse."[15] The true perspective on the action of Yeats's other plays of "dreaming back" is not provided by the consciousness of Swift or Mrs. Henderson, Christ or Judas, the soldier or Diarmuid and Dervorgilla. There, as in *Purgatory,* the release is implicit in the consciousness which can accept in contemplation the terrible vision of the play.

Because such contemplation can lead through acceptance toward ecstasy, Yeats's poetic alchemy became increasingly paradoxical. He cried out against history, "All's changed!" and he sought another change: "We shall all be changed, in a moment, in the twinkling of an eye, at the last trump."[16] And the two changes were increasingly one. Increasingly new life appeared in the midst of death, the philosopher's stone in the midst of destruction. We may recall his view of Synge's Deirdre, moving in her paroxysm of "tragic ecstasy" beyond "time and persons to where passion, living through its thousand purgatorial years, as in the wink of an eye, becomes wisdom."[17] At such a moment the actress' foot should touch, Yeats said, "the unchanging rock, the secret place beyond life,"[18] that "flagstone under all" of *The Shadowy Waters,* that alchemical *lapis* which is source and goal of the manifest world. The *"fol de rol de rolly O"* that rings out across Lough Derg is a comic version of that ecstasy, an audible sign of the tragic stone. For those flame-eaten shapes, this life has become the element of fire; though stuck eternally in that place, they have their release.

The speakers of the early poetry do little more than yearn for such a moment. That of "He Remembers Forgotten Beauty" laments the loss of past loveliness and then sighs for a time when all will pass but Beauty's apocalypse, all

> But flame on flame, and deep on deep
> Throne over throne where in half sleep,
> Their swords upon their iron knees,
> Brood her high lonely mysteries.

For him the present is nonexistent except as a locus of reverie over the tapestries of past and future. But Yeats came to see that the trump of judgment must blow now, that the world must end in every poem. Like Nietzsche's suprahistorical man, the speaker must be one for whom "the world is complete and fulfils its aim in every single moment."[19] Such a man is most fully in time even as he most fully transcends it. Hence transience and transcendence begin to fuse:

> All changed, changed utterly:
> A terrible beauty is born.

But even in "Easter 1916" the incorruptible stone embodies death more than eternal life:

> Hearts with one purpose alone
> Through summer and winter seem

> Enchanted to a stone
> To trouble the living stream.

The vision must move from that terrible contrast—

> Minute by minute they live:
> The stone's in the midst of all

—to a *lapis* which is both life and death, both Incarnation and Transfiguration.

That is why the Plotinian journey of "Sailing to Byzantium" is completed only in aspiration. The poem hints at the alchemical goal, the quintessence or "bird born out of the fire,"[20] a stone—"hammered gold and gold enamelling"—placed so firmly in a living world that it contains the ironies of the "terrible beauty" of "Easter 1916." Significantly, however, that stone is not dumb, troubling the living with memories of a past moment; it sings of "what is past, or passing, or to come." It is no sleepy mystery; though unliving, it is more lively than its drowsy Byzantine setting. But it is not more alive than the richly passionate speaker, who endows with vitality both sensual music and purgation by fire. And that irony stresses the fact that finally the speaker is his own bird—a "living philosophical stone," in Robert Flood's phrase[21]—soul clapping its hands and singing in its own "artifice of eternity." He has changed, in a moment, but still sings of time.

Reworking Blake's doctrine of "self-annihilation," fusing in one instant what Schopenhauer called the "will, of which life is the mirror, and knowledge free from the will, which beholds it clearly in that mirror,"[22] Yeats could find history transcended in an eternal moment of striving and contemplation. So the subjective tragedians Dante and Villon had found it, he thought: and "we gaze at such men in awe, because we gaze not at a work of art, but at the re-creation of the man through that art, the birth of a new species of man . . ." Attempting like them to "live for contemplation" and yet keep his "intensity,"[23] Yeats discovered his tragic stone in such poems as "Sailing to Byzantium" and "Among School Children." In them is created a new species of man who—unbeknownst to himself, as it were—*is* his contrary, and so, though "mirrored in all the suffering of desire," would not change his luck.[24] Hence the piercing vigor, even exultation, in the conclusions of such poems, where expression of desire is at the same time ecstasy in the attainment of the true goal.

That is so even of the conclusion of "In Memory of Eva Gore-Booth and Con Markiewicz," where the speaker seems, like the old man of *Purgatory,* to have no recourse but violence:

> The innocent and the beautiful
> Have no enemy but time;
> Arise and bid me strike a match
> And strike another till time catch;
> Should the conflagration climb,
> Run till all the sages know.
> We the great gazebo built,
> They convicted us of guilt;
> Bid me strike a match and blow.

The plea harks back (through *Where There Is Nothing* and Tolstoy's *The Kingdom of God Is within You*) to the gospel utterance, "I came to cast fire on the earth; and would that it were already kindled!"[25] But the tone quite consciously mingles proud declaration, courtly fealty, sly conspiracy, Castiglione's "recklessness," and an absurdly childlike make-believe. The speaker is fully aware of the nature of that flame which he seeks. The actual conflagration or apocalypse with which the poem concludes is the "last judgment" of self-knowledge and self-revelation. Consequently his own yearning can include that other exhilarating moment when "the images from *Anima Mundi* . . . would, like a country drunkard who has thrown a wisp into his own thatch, burn up time."[26]

Throughout Yeats's middle years that emotion was usually not "joy" but "ecstasy." "Joy is of the will which labours," he said, "which overcomes obstacles, which knows triumph. The soul knows its changes of state alone. . . . Yet is not ecstasy some fulfilment of the soul in itself, some slow or sudden expansion of it like an overflowing well?"[27] But another turn of the gyre and that ecstasy meant even for the speakers of the poems a conscious and triumphant power. The "shaping joy" so transformed the sorrowful contemplation of irremediable evil that there was born a "tragic joy," an exultant bit of news for the Delphic Oracle, or even a nonsensical *"fol de rol de rolly O."*

The most comprehensive rendering of that *lapis* which climaxed Yeats's re-enactment of the Great Work is "Lapis Lazuli." It is an explicit defense of poetic gaiety against a criticism he had met in his youth[28] and now mockingly repeats.

> I have heard that hysterical women say
> They are sick of the palette and fiddle-bow,
> Of poets that are always gay ...

He might once have retorted with Dowson's "Villanelle of the Poet's Road,"

> Unto us they belong,
> 　Us the bitter and gay,
> Wine and women and song.

But his own full answer, given as another war approaches, claims far more and claims it more gaily and more seriously. All the world's a stage, and men and women are players that strut and fret their hour; but they ought not accept their roles with the melancholy of Jacques or the despair of Macbeth:

> All perform their tragic play,
> There struts Hamlet, there is Lear,
> That's Ophelia, that Cordelia;
> Yet they, should the last scene be there,
> The great stage curtain about to drop,
> If worthy their prominent part in the play,
> Do not break up their lines to weep.
> They know that Hamlet and Lear are gay;
> Gaiety transfiguring all that dread.
> All men have aimed at, found and lost;
> Black out; Heaven blazing into the head:
> Tragedy wrought to its uttermost.

All may know the Shakespearean tragic ecstasy which Yeats had described as "one half the self-surrender of sorrow, and one half the last playing and mockery of the victorious sword, before the defeated world."[29] Their souls like Deirdre's may experience that change in the twinkling of an eye—that "change upon the instant,...like the sudden 'blacking out' of the lights of the stage."[30] Blackout and blazing Heaven, ultimate loss and gain, are infinite in each subjective climax. Though all roles may now end amid a more general blackout as airplanes roar overhead, it "cannot grow," declares the gaily irascible poet, "by an inch or an ounce."

As the poem's focus widens further, that gaiety appears the creative force underlying all history:

> On their own feet they came, or on shipboard,
> Camel-back, horse-back, ass-back, mule-back,
> Old civilisations put to the sword.
> Then they and their wisdom went to rack:
> No handiwork of Callimachus,
> Who handled marble as if it were bronze,
> Made draperies that seemed to rise
> When sea-wind swept the corner, stands;
> His long lamp-chimney shaped like the stem
> Of a slender palm, stood but a day;
> All things fall and are built again,
> And those that build them again are gay.

Works of art here are no eternal objects set apart from the flux of time, like the bird of "Sailing to Byzantium"; nor is this panorama merely a fond reverie upon lost objects, as in "He Remembers Forgotten Beauty." Yet this speaker too now moves away from the flux of life toward the stasis of art:

> Two Chinamen, behind them a third,
> Are carved in lapis lazuli,
> Over them flies a long-legged bird,
> A symbol of longevity;
> The third, doubtless a serving-man,
> Carries a musical instrument.

But this speaker does not enter into the scene carved in lapis lazuli in order to turn his back on the tragic scene of the world process. This bird, though stone, symbolizes longevity rather than eternity; and the artifact itself experiences the ravages and renewals of time:

> Every discoloration of the stone,
> Every accidental crack or dent,

> Seems a water-course or an avalanche,
> Or a lofty slope where it still snows
> Though doubtless plum or cherry-branch
> Sweetens the little half-way house
> Those Chinamen climb towards...

Those Chinamen themselves neither brood in "half sleep" nor merely sing of time to a drowsy emperor. As the speaker contemplates the scene which is just beyond his ordinary vision, he finds them to be spectators of time and participators in it:

> ...and I
> Delight to imagine them seated there;
> There, on the mountain and the sky,
> On all the tragic scene they stare.
> One asks for mournful melodies;
> Accomplished fingers begin to play.
> Their eyes mid many wrinkles, their eyes,
> Their ancient, glittering eyes, are gay.

In those stony lineaments we can no longer distinguish time's ruins from eternity's mansions.

That living philosophical stone is the end of Yeats's Great Work, insofar as it had an end. At every moment all falls in ruin and all is re-created—and under all, the flagstone of a now possible joy. Yet a couplet from "What Was Lost" indicates how difficult, still, was that joy:

> Feet to the Rising and Setting may run,
> They always beat on the same small stone.

Indeed, Yeats could still call it an "impossible aim"[31]—impossible for the man himself. Not that the Chinamen are the antitheses of a yearning speaker; they are rather the absolute embodiments of his own resilient exaltation. But he himself is no biographical Yeats; he is the re-creation of the man through the art.

Though the opposites within the poem, Western tragic heroes and Chinese sages, imply the two movements of the soul (Incarnation and Transfiguration atop Mount Tabor) and the two perspectives upon history (dramatic experience and panoramic vision), each here reaches out to include the other. In 1930, thinking of the "sage," Yeats thought "of something Asiatic, and of something which belongs to modern Europe—the Pedlar in *The Excursion,* an old Hermit in *The Well at the World's End,* passages in Matthew Arnold." The image, he said, had collapsed today; it could not survive "without that despair which is a form of joy and has certainly no place in the modern psychological study of suffering." And he asked: "Does not that soldier become the sage ... when some Elizabethan tragedy makes him reply to a threat of hanging, 'what has that to do with me?' "[32] So in "Lapis Lazuli" the doomed Western heroes merge with the Asiatic sages; or, in Nietzschean terms, the Apollonian heroes, who oppose the destructive forces of the universe but go down in defeat, merge with the Dionysian satyr chorus, which rejoices in the fall of the hero and in that eternal life which gives birth to all things and destroys and reabsorbs all things. For both, the "delight in the tragic is a translation of the instinctively unconscious Dionysian wisdom into the language of the scene." Thus the poet, like Nietzsche's Greek, "who is so singularly qualified for the most delicate and severe suffering, consoles himself: he who has glanced with piercing eye into the very heart of the terrible destructive processes of so-called universal history, as also into the cruelty of nature, and is in danger of longing for a Buddhistic negation of the will. Art saves him, and through art life saves him—for herself."[33]

However, as I have suggested earlier, Yeats found his own half-dumb thought reflected and clarified not only in Nietzsche but elsewhere as well. In 1896 he had declared that William Morris "held nothing that gave joy unworthy, and might have said with Ruysbroeck, 'I must rejoice without ceasing, even though the world shudder at my joy.' "[34] Later, criticizing Synge's *Riders to the Sea* as "too passive in suffering," he had quoted from one of those "passages in Matthew Arnold" (who "showed himself a great critic by his reasons" for withdrawing *Empedocles on Etna*) to prove his point.[35] Arnold had cited Schiller's statement, "All Art is dedicated to joy," and had elaborated its implications:

> In presence of the most tragic circumstances, represented in a work of Art, the feeling of enjoyment ... may still subsist: the representation of the most utter calamity, of the liveliest anguish, is not sufficient

to destroy it: the more tragic the situation, the deeper becomes the enjoyment; and the situation is more tragic in proportion as it becomes more terrible.[36]

Yeats also found sanction for an active joy in Swift's "savage indignation." "Hate," he said in 1936, "is a kind of 'passive suffering' but indignation is a kind of joy.... We that are joyous need not be afraid to denounce." After quoting Ruysbroeck again, he concluded: "Joy is the salvation of the soul."[37]

Swift there joins Raftery, Lear, and Oedipus as a vehicle of that joyful wrath which was the emotion of Blake's prophetic reprobate Rintrah. As Yeats had said of Oedipus:

> He raged against his sons, and this rage was noble not from some general idea, some sense of public law upheld, but because it seemed to contain all life, and the daughter who served him as did Cordelia Lear—he too a man of Homer's kind—seemed less attendant upon an old railing rambler than upon genius itself. He knew nothing but his mind, and yet because he spoke that mind fate possessed it and kingdoms changed according to his blessing and cursing. Delphi, that rock at earth's navel, spoke through him.... I think he lacked compassion, seeing that it must be compassion for himself, and yet stood nearer to the poor than saint or apostle, and I mutter to myself stories of Cruachan, or of Crickmaa, or of the road-side bush withered by Raftery's curse.[38]

Recalling that the "delight in ... vehemence" in that curse had taken "out of anger half the bitterness with all the gloom,"[39] we can see that such wrath is not hatred, not "accusation of sin" born of fear or limitation. Those have been purged away, along with "passive suffering," and what is left is the primal vitality and exhilaration reborn through self-knowledge and self-acceptance.

Though compassion or pity may be absent, Yeats can then speak not merely of rage and joy but even of "love" as existing at the heart of this destructive universe—as in a passage which recapitulates these themes:

> The arts are all the bridal chambers of joy. No tragedy is legitimate unless it leads some great character to his final joy.... I can hear the dance music in "Absent thee from felicity awhile," or in Hamlet's speech over the dead Ophelia, and what of Cleopatra's last farewells, Lear's rage under the lightning, Oedipus sinking down at the story's end into an earth "riven" by love?

These themes then combine with Blake's apocalypse and Schopenhauer's sublime, as Yeats modified them and refound them in Dante and Villon:

> Some Frenchman has said that farce is the struggle against a ridiculous object, comedy against a movable object, tragedy against an immovable; and because the will, or energy is greatest in tragedy, tragedy is the more noble; but I add that "will or energy is eternal delight" and when its limit is reached it may become a pure, aimless joy, though the man, the shade, still mourns his lost object. It has, as it were, thrust up its arms towards those angels who have, as Villiers de L'Isle Adam quotes from St. Thomas Aquinas, returned into themselves in an eternal moment.[40]

Though Heracles the shade still mourns his lost object (like the speaker of "Sailing to Byzantium" and other poems), the released will has thrust up its arms toward the unfallen Heracles[41] and would not change its luck.

The narrator of "Rosa Alchemica" had himself glanced into the heart of the destructive processes of universal history and had sought salvation in that "eternal moment." What he had not found, his creator did find as he climbed that winding purgatorial stair toward those moments when, in the twinkling of an eye, in the glitter of lapis lazuli, all might be changed. Then, as in "The Gyres," the fire of the world process might be transmuted to light:

> Hector is dead and there's a light in Troy;
> We that look on but laugh in tragic joy.

Then even that cosmic philosophical stone, that "rock at earth's navel," might speak to him and through him:

> Out of cavern comes a voice,
> And all it knows is that one word "Rejoice."

ii.

The historical implications of that movement from cycles to immanent apocalypse, that discovery of the alchemical *lapis* in the midst of destruction, appear also in Yeats's lunar myth. After the yearning lunar images of the early poetry, the most negative phase of that myth is in "The Crazed Moon":

> Crazed through much child-bearing
> The moon is staggering in the sky;
> Moon-struck by the despairing
> Glances of her wandering eye
> We grope, and grope in vain,
> For children born of her pain.

Millennial groping for rebirth here leads only to the contrast of the stillborn children of the present and the living vigor of the past, a historical contrast which had been experienced microcosmically in "On a Political Prisoner" and "In Memory of Eva Gore-Booth and Con Markiewicz":

> Children dazed or dead!
> When she in all her virginal pride
> First trod on the mountain's head
> What stir ran through the countryside
> Where every foot obeyed her glance!
> What manhood led the dance!

That youthful beauty is resurrected in the imagination only momentarily. The envisioned dance yields to another image of the experienced dance of the living dead:

> Fly-catchers of the moon,
> Our hands are blenched, our fingers seem
> But slender needles of bone;
> Blenched by that malicious dream
> They are spread wide that each
> May rend what comes in reach.

These skeletal figures do not know that despair which is a form of joy; their malice itself seems to result from their desperate longing for past vitality.

As a "last judgment" of a soul who has experienced the self-destructiveness of one kind of romanticism, the poem attains its own sardonic apocalypse. It is a judgment that quite properly emerges from the matrix of romantic metaphor itself. Milton's

> wandring Moon,
> Riding neer her highest noon,

> Like one that had bin led astray
> Through the Heav'ns wide pathless way

was for Blake a "Moon terrified"[42]—as later for Ribh "the scared moon." Imaging for Shelley the hysteria of loneliness and transience, it rose from the murky east

> like a dying lady lean and pale,
> Who totters forth, wrapp'd in a gauzy veil,
> Out of her chamber, led by the insane
> And feeble wanderings of her fading brain...

In Wilde's *Salome* that crazed moon regained ancient millennial connotations: "The moon has a strange look tonight...," said Herod. "She is like a mad woman who is seeking everywhere for lovers.... She reels through the clouds like a drunken woman..." Symbolizing and governing the end of an era, such a moon was for Yeats a Blakean harlot weaving old England's winding sheet. The children born of such a harlot are, as he had said, "spectral desires to desolate the world."[43]

Hence, though the envisioned dance of the past recalls such reveries as those of Edward Carpenter—

> On the high tops once more gathering he will celebrate with naked dances the glory of the human form..., or greet the bright horn of the young moon which now after a hundred centuries comes back laden with... all the yearnings and the dreams and the wonderment of the generations of mankind—the worship of Astarte and of Diana, of Isis or the Virgin Mary...[44]

—the *Totentanz* of the present, caused by such yearning, must be a colder version of the dance of Dowson's witches:

> We the children of Astarte,
> Dear abortions of the moon,
> In a gay and silent party
> We are riding to you soon.

Those witches, "yearning, yearning, yearning," contemplate with delighted self-pity and self-horror their "lichened arms" that lean on the "ends of endless night."[45] But the abortion of Yeats's crazed moon recognizes in himself and others a more sharply dehumanized image:

fingers that "seem / But slender needles of bone."[46] *Fin-de-siècle* indulgence has yielded to an almost Dantesque vision.

But if that moon "seeking everywhere for lovers" attracts and is met by one who does not yearn but gaily yields his own vitality, a very different apocalypse occurs, as in *A Full Moon in March.* Here too the "old ritual of the year: the mother goddess and the slain god,"[47] suggests what Mario Praz has called the "romantic agony." In a manner recalling *Salammbô* as well as *Salome,* the Swineherd dies because of the frigid lunar Queen who is enamored of him; and in her lofty niche, she also recalls the marble statues of Heine, Gautier, or Baudelaire. But no more than such statues is she merely the goal of masochism or necrophilia. The matrix of history, she descends from her absolute realm to enter a slaying and fructifying union with the temporal—with the hero, poet, or other manifestation of the solar cycle, who must die to create. At full moon in March, when all cycles begin,[48] the new creation is born from the death of the old. The Stroller in *The King of the Great Clock Tower,* an earlier version of the play, learns that the ringers in the tower "have appointed for the hymen of the soul a passing bell."[49] Aengus tells him,

> "On stroke of midnight when the old year dies,
> Upon that stroke, the tolling of that bell,
> The queen shall kiss your mouth..."[50]

We recall that other line, "I celebrate the silent kiss that ends short life or long," sung by the chorus in *Oedipus at Colonus*[51] about the death of another solar hero, a "railing rambler" who had wed his mother and who sinks into an earth " 'riven' by love." For such, as for Ribh, the void is fruitful.

The fable dramatizes the Blakean view that "All things before they can create are compelled to die in Western twilight, for life exists merely through willing and joyous or unwilling and mournful sacrifice of life." Blake had described an abortive part of that sacrifice in *The Book of Thel,* where "a feeling...mourns its own inevitable death into fulfilment."[52] The descent there refused by Thel is now accepted by Yeats's Queen. For, just as the solar hero must die, the corruptible thus putting on incorruption, so the lunar heroine must descend, the incorruptible thus putting on corruption:

Why must those holy, haughty feet descend
From emblematic niches, and what hand
Ran that delicate raddle through their white?
My heart is broken, yet must understand.
What do they seek for? Why must they descend?

For desecration and the lover's night.[53]

However, some excised lines show most clearly how far Yeats's celebration of the fallen was from Blake:

I call to mind the iron of the bell
And get from that my harsher imagery,
All love is shackled to mortality,
Love's image is a man-at-arms in steel;
Love's image is a woman made of stone...[54]

Blake himself had sung:

'Twas the Greeks' love of war
Turn'd Love into a Boy,
And Woman into a Statue of Stone—
And away fled every Joy.[55]

The Yeatsian joy must emerge tragically amid the fallen world of
Incarnation, amid what, in his Blake study, Yeats had called the contest of "fierce fire" and "the external cold and feminine maternal
nature," of "the fallen spirit and the fallen 'mirror,' or of *scorpio* and
virgo."[56]

That contest and conjunction translate into extreme and reciprocal
terms the sexual dialectic between swan and shadow or self and
Daimon which runs through Yeats's work from *Mosada*, with its
Inquisitor and Moorish enchantress, to *On the Boiler*, where we read:
"When a man loves a girl it should be because her face and character
offer what he lacks, the more profound his nature the more should
he realise his lack and the greater be the difference. It is as though
he wanted to take his own death into his arms, and beget a stronger
life upon that death."[57] Accepting one's opposite, yielding one's
limited identity and redeeming one's Swineherd or Queen, one enables creation to emerge. Anything else is mere continuation. That
process inheres in every imaginative act, when conscious and un-

conscious are wed: "A writer must die every day he lives, be reborn, as it is said in the Burial Service, an incorruptible self, that self opposite of all that he has named 'himself.' "[58]

In the new creation, then, cycle merges with apocalypse. The severed head of the Stroller sings:

> What's prophesied? What marvel is
> Where the dead and living kiss?
> *What of the hands on the Great Clock face?*
> Sacred Virgil never sang
> All the marvel there begun,
> But there's a stone upon my tongue.
> *A moment more and it tolls midnight.*[59]

An alternative refrain—"*What says the Clock in the Great Clock Tower?*"—shows yet more clearly the song's derivation from Nietzsche's dithyramb on Eternity, which begins:

> O man! Take heed!
> What saith deep midnight's voice indeed?[60]

For Yeats as for Zarathustra, that is the moment when suprahistorical man may transcend the cycles while remaining within them, when his vision may cause all things to be eternalized. The prerequisite for that moment is his acceptance of all, his learning that "Pain is also a joy, curse is also a blessing, night is also a sun."[61]

Much else that Yeats had found in his early search for a pattern in history pointed toward this central fable of the imagination. Frazer had noted how the priests of the goddess sacrificed their fertility that they might give her a means of discharging her beneficent functions.[62] Re-enacting the death of the solar god, the human priest becomes the god. That translation of human to divine is what Madame Blavatsky had called "the oldest of permutations in theogony, the Son becoming his own father and the mother generated by the Son." In every religion, she said, the male combined "the human attributes as the 'Sun, the Giver of Life,' " and the female combined "all the other titles in the grand synthesis known as Maia, Maya, Maria, etc.,"[63] the natural matrix. Yeats himself completed such a synthesis when, rewriting *The King of the Great Clock Tower* as *A Full Moon in March,* he eliminated the King: "reduced to essentials, to Queen and Stroller, the fable should have greater intensity." Madame Blavatsky had said of the goddess, "She is the Queen and she is the King ...," and had added that for early Church fathers "the Moon was Jehovah's living symbol: the giver of Life and the giver of Death, the disposer of being—in *our* World."[64]

Yeats had summarized the moon's symbolic potential in his essay on Shelley, where he saw her as governing "the life of instinct and the generation of things," and also ("a cold and changeable fire set in the bare heavens") as governing "chastity and the joyless idle drifting ... of generated things." She "may come to men in their happy moments as she came to Endymion, or she may deny life and shoot her arrows; but because she only becomes beautiful in giving herself, and is no flying ideal, she is not loved by the children of desire."[65] Yeats's Queen "whose emblem is the moon" is loved not by one of the "children of desire" who hates incarnate life but by her own "child and darling," a Swineherd who recalls Shelley's Earth spirit. Yeats had said of that apocalyptic climax of *Prometheus Unbound,* which contains the love dialogue of Earth and Moon, that the pale frozen Moon "only becomes a thing of delight when Time is being borne to his tomb in eternity, for then the spirit of the Earth, man's procreant mind, fills it with his own joyousness." In that resurrection into unity, as in *A Full Moon in March,* the snow " 'is loosened' from the Moon's 'lifeless mountains.' "[66]

Yeats's deceptively casual introduction to the play must be read in the light of such symbolic potential. He said that, trying to put into a dance play his early story "The Binding of the Hair," based "on some old Gaelic legend," he found that he "had gone close to Salome's dance in Wilde's play."[67] But the process was not so fortuitous. He was working out the full implications of the cyclical myth which, as I have suggested earlier, he had glimpsed long ago in the tales of the miraculous heads of Donn-bo and Lomna. In the early story Aodh (or "fire") is loved by Dectira ("mother of the blazing sun," or the "light that overspreads the sky ... after he has just sunk below it"[68]), who appropriately finds his head at evening and then hears it sing its tribute to her hair. Yeats there followed the legend of Donn-bo, in having the singer killed in battle; whereas in the legend of

Lomna, the hero is beheaded at the order of his mistress. *A Full Moon in March,* now admitting such female cruelty and including in the Queen the destructive aspects of the world matrix, fuses Dectira and her dark complement, the sorceress Orchil—or tender Venus and murderous Astarte. Divested of Irish setting, the lyric and prophetic head approaches that of Mimir, Orpheus, or St. John—a collocation probably reinforced by Mallarmé's "Cantique de St. Jean," in which the head sings at the moment of decapitation. (Yeats also knew that the similarity between Leonardo's St. John and Dionysus meant for Patmore that St. John was Christ's complement, "natural love," and suggested to Gautier those pagan gods of Heine who took employment in the new religion.[69]) Whereas Aodh merely swore by the Red Swineherd, the later Stroller himself becomes Swineherd—recalling those Celtic and Greek swineherd priests in the service of the Death-goddess whose sacred beast was the pig.[70] Whereas the yearning speaker of "The Valley of the Black Pig" bows before the "master of the still stars," the Orc or boar who may end his cycles, this gay Swineherd is murdered, wed, mourned, and transmuted by the mistress of that realm, who plays both Venus and boar to his Adonis. Much, for Yeats, was implicit in what in *The Celtic Twilight* he called that "evil pig that slew Diarmuid where Ben Bulben mixes with the sea wind."[71]

Far from being an empty play, "as though a dramatist, ignorant of Christianity and history, were to make a play out of the communion service,"[72] *A Full Moon in March* thus condenses the myth of *The Resurrection* and reverses its perspective. No longer is the divine drama—Virgin and Star, beating heart of Dionysus—given at the end a basis in the flaming heart of man. Now the Swineherd's heart itself becomes the Star. Shelley's own version of the Adonis myth had likewise translated mortal to immortal:

> The soul of Adonais, like a star,
> Beacons from the abode where the eternal are.

But for Yeats that change in a moment, in the twinkling of an eye, must cause the myth to emerge from the humblest of ditties:

> I sing a song of Jack and Jill.
> Jill had murdered Jack;

The moon shone brightly;
Ran up the hill, and round the hill,
Round the hill and back.
A full moon in March.

Jack had a hollow heart, for Jill
Had hung his heart on high;
The moon shone brightly;
Had hung his heart beyond the hill,
A-twinkle in the sky.
A full moon in March.[73]

As the very dung of swine is transmuted, Yeats is dramatizing
with freedom but in much detail a process upon which the alchemists
had played endless variations. It is the "spiritualization of the soil,"
the marriage of heaven and earth, universal and particular, spirit and
body, Kether and Malkuth on the Sephirotic Tree, or *"Crown of
gold"* and *"dung of swine."* The equivalence of crown and dung,
asserted in the opening song, is important in the formulas: "Take the
foul deposit (*fecem*) that remains in the cooking-vessel and preserve
it, for it is the crown of the heart." Other writers allude to a precious
stone that was cast upon the dungheap or to metals "that are reputed
base, that stink and withal smell sweetly."[74] But the opening song
refers to the ambivalence of the Swineherd as much as to the royal
marriage. Queen and Swineherd are that Moon and Sun, Silver and
Gold, Virgin Mercury and Virgin Sulphur, whose warring marriage
is repeatedly described by the writers in *The Hermetic Museum,*
upon which Yeats had drawn for "Rosa Alchemica." The "fiery male
must be fed with a snowy swan, and then they must mutually slay
each other and restore each other to life."[75] That requires the Swineherd's resurrection and the Queen's descent: "the sages bid you to revive the dead (that is, the gold which appeared doomed to a living
death) and mortify the living (that is, the mercury which, imparting
life to the gold, is deprived of the vital principle)." The sages also say,
"Invert the elements, and you will find what you seek." Then "you
will find that the heavenly has assumed an earthly body, and that
the earthly body has been reduced to a heavenly substance."[76] Among
the many analogues in classical myth, some are close to Yeats's sym-

bolism for the wedding and double transmutation at the end of the play: "the blood of Adonis trickling upon the snowy breast of Venus..., the transfiguration of the soul of Julius Caesar into a Comet..., the Moon kindled by Phaethon's conflagration."[77]

The singing head itself renders another alchemical symbol, prelude to the marriage. The warring Sun and Moon coalesce into one body, called death, blackness, shadow, and similar names. "Hence it is said: 'Extract the shadow thereof from the splendour.'"[78] That blackness is the putrefaction of the first matter, the *caput mortuum* or dead head. If the *rota* is viewed as the travel of the sun-hero, it is "the head of Osiris in the *nigredo* state." But as a Golden Dawn document states, on the seventh day the *caput mortuum* shall become "either a precious stone or a glittering powder."[79] The Swineherd, having undergone his creative death, is translated into the heavens.

These are all metaphors for spiritual processes in the macrocosm and the microcosm. The Sun and Moon, wrote Thomas Vaughan, "are adequate to the whole world and coextended through the universe."[80] Their marriage is for Yeats no arcane chemical reaction but a psychic and aesthetic experience. On one level, the star that was the Swineherd's heart is the artifact itself, the total marriage of opposites into which the biographical swineherd of "The Circus Animals' Desertion," with his "mound of refuse" in "the foul rag-and-bone shop of the heart," may be transmuted. The historical fact becomes eternal constellation; the Phoenix flies. Vaughan described the process in terms as lucid as any used by the alchemists. After an initial separation and recombination of the opposites, after the Dragon has turned to a Swan (or the Queen revealed her beauty), the Phoenix may be fed "with the fire of his father and the ether of his mother." Then "he will move in his nest and rise like a star of the firmament. Do this and thou hast placed nature *in horizonte aeternitatis*."[81] In Yeats's art as in alchemy, that Paracelsian goal is the end of a long process, under a slow natural fire, of separating out the psychic opposites, simplifying them, and recombining them in more intense form. That conquest of the world is the practical result of Yeats's pursuit of his own mask, "simplification through intensity." As man and mask join, the eyes glitter, a star twinkles, heaven blazes into the head.

Of course, I have been expanding discursively the multivalent process which Yeats's play itself renders in a dramatic, choreographic, and musical form of the most direct kind—not "a philosophical idea" but "a spiritual experience." But if his assumptions concerning the form and content of the soul's drama are at all correct, a performance of his play should exert strange power even if but dimly understood. Jung's own analysis of the alchemical marriage as psychological projection lends considerable weight to that view. Yeats himself might well feel that his work "is not drama but the ritual of a lost faith"[82]— for he knew that ritual projects and objectifies a psychic reality known by the participants. In any case, he presented here the essence of his own tragic drama: the dialogue of the stroller with his opposite or the poet with the matrix of history which produces him, lures him onward, brings him suffering and delight, and offers him the chance of a lifelong creative death.

Remembering that Cuchulain too is solar hero, *persona* of the poet, fighter with the sea, and lover of lunar beauties, we can see why the dance with the severed head recurs in *The Death of Cuchulain*. The myth, with its new clarity, moves back into the Irish setting; Cuchulain's death at the hands of the Blind Man is the recurrent end of the heroic—another manifestation of the basic cycle. Here, in the absence of a clear apocalypse, the joy is that of Swiftian indignation and heroic acceptance, in Cuchulain, in the harlot (a satyr chorus that "beholds the god"[83]), and in the old man who scorns the dancers of Degas: "They might have looked timeless, Rameses the Great, but not the chambermaid, that old maid history. I spit! I spit! I spit!"[84] It is that joy which, while defying time, need not anxiously prolong its own temporal existence. It is the joy of "symbolic" art—as Yeats had once presented Blake's position—rather than the prudence of mimetic art, which teaches us (like the Blind Man) to preserve our physical body.

In another late play, tragedy takes the familiar step toward comedy. In accordance with his own theory, the myth itself dies in Western twilight, is dissolved by comic analysis, and we enter the ambiguous realm of "pure unified experience."[85] Comically central in *The Herne's Egg* is the uncertain status of the divine, the possible mistaking of symbol for fact. Like the Swineherd or Cuchulain, Congal

accepts his destiny and attains a subjective victory over the Nobodaddy
in the sky:

>   Are you up there?
>   Your chosen kitchen spit has killed me,
>   But killed me at my own will, not yours.

But his apocalypse is amid recurring cycles of folly. He is not reborn
as star or bird:

>   All that trouble and nothing to show for it,
>   Nothing but just another donkey.[86]

Attracta, the lunar viceregent of the Herne, comes off somewhat better
in her madness and practicality—as the Queen always dances around
the head of the hero. If she is deceived in her midnight marriage
with the Herne, the thunder is nonetheless with her and intimidates
the objective witnesses. Spiritual and sensual experience merge—and
who is to tell the Herne from his comic shadows?

Yeats's own sense of the limitation of his ritual drama is evident
as he combines it too with its opposite, and showers the embodied
passions with cold laughter. But the realism of his aesthetic alchemy
is also evident. No artistic apocalypse is final. Continued growth
demands that every image be consumed, that Zen "poverty"[87] be
accepted. As the seven Anglo-Irish sages knew, wisdom comes of
renewed beggary. The gyre turns once more, and the fol-de-rol of
The Herne's Egg itself brings release in the Purgatory of this world.

iii.

Perhaps one image above all epitomized for Yeats that descent
into the abyss where one meets one's opposite—that descent to the
"bottom of the night," in Auden's phrase, where burns the Blakean
tiger, the fruitful mystery of evil. Odin, the prophetic god-man who
sacrificed himself on the World-tree in order to learn the secret of
the Runes, also broke in flower on the blasted thorn:

>   I trow I hung   on that windy Tree
>   nine whole days and nights,
>   stabbed with a spear,   offered to Odin,
>   myself to my own self given,

high on that Tree   of which none hath heard
  from what roots it rises to heaven.

None refreshed me ever   with food or drink,
  I peered right down in the deep;
crying aloud   I lifted the Runes,
  then back I fell from thence.[88]

Odin implied for Yeats all the power of art and life, the individual soul become a lamp unto itself, "its own betrayer, its own deliverer, the one activity,"[89] in a tragic moment of full action, passion, and perception. Odin combines, Yeats said in 1909, "self-realisation and self-sacrifice," the classical and the Christian.[90] Creatively accepting his destiny, he is fixed and he fixes himself to the tree of antinomies known by the speaker of "Vacillation":

And he that Attis' image hangs between
That staring fury and the blind lush leaf
May know not what he knows, but knows not grief.

Great poetry and philosophy, Yeats said, come from "invisible warfare, the division of a mind within itself, a victory, the sacrifice of a man to himself."[91] He saw that sacrifice in Synge and in Strindberg, "that tortured self-torturing man who offered himself to his own soul as Buddha offered himself to the famished tiger."[92] Yeats too, becoming eater and eaten, engaged in his dialogue of passion, self-judgment, and prophecy, plucking the "bitter wisdom" from that abyss. It is that process (epitomized also in Boehme's cycle of descent, reascent, and consequent reconciliation of the contrary wills) which ultimately lies behind Yeats's statements to the effect that "the artist's joy...is of one substance with that of sanctity."[93] From that point of view, "the whole visible world is just the objectification, the mirror, of the will, conducting it to knowledge of itself, and...to the possibility of deliverance"[94]—but to a deliverance more paradoxical and more creative than that which Schopenhauer knew.

Clearly, Yeats's ideal of "man self-sufficing and eternal"[95] should not be mistaken—as many critics have mistaken it—for the *hubris* or narcissism of swan without shadow. Though it does contain such pride, Odin's eternal moment is also the continually renewed self-judgment of one for whom every day is a Last Day. Raftery "never dramatised anybody but himself"; Oedipus "knew nothing but his mind."[96] And though Yeats could reprove his own minstrel-self for singing "as if there were no tale but your own tale,"[97] he knew that the poet must live, through the only self he can fully know, a universal tragedy. That is why he would have endorsed Emerson's advice to "read history actively and not passively," to "esteem his own life the text, and books the commentary," that the Muse of history might "utter oracles."[98] He knew, too, that the poet must live the tragedy of his own day. And that is why, I think, he would have accepted as a partial explanation Jung's comment on Zarathustra's apostrophe to himself:

> And now
> Self-hunted,
> Thine own quarry,
> Thyself pierced through...
>
> Now
> Alone with thyself,
> Split in thine own knowledge,
> Amidst a hundred mirrors,
> To thine own self false,
> Amidst a hundred memories
> Uncertain...
>
> Why didst thou hang thyself
> With the noose of thy wisdom?
> Why hast thou enticed thyself
> Into the old serpent's Paradise?
> Why hast thou stolen
> Into thyself, thyself?

Such Odins, Jung said, engaged in self-murder and self-fertilization, may seem to be raging against themselves. But insofar as the symbolism thrown up by their suffering is archetypal and collective, it is a sign that they are not suffering merely from themselves but "from the spirit of the age."[99] In raging against themselves, Yeats's subjective heroes and birds have been declaring and measuring a more than personal evil. They are, as Yeats said of Swift, victims of their phase of history.[100].

The kind of victimage Yeats endured and his reaction to it ("a man of my time,... my poetical faculty living its history"[101]) were summarized in his comment on two other victims, Villon and Beardsley. He felt keenly "that suffering of Villon... in whom the human soul for the first time stands alone before a death ever present to imagination, without help from a Church that is fading away," but asked: "is it that I remember Aubrey Beardsley, a man of like phase though so different epoch, and so read into Villon's suffering our modern conscience which gathers intensity as we approach the close of an era? Intensity that has seemed to me pitiless self-judgment may have been but heroic gaiety."[102] One need add only that Yeats's own heroic gaiety usually results from, if it sometimes masks, a pitiless self-judgment. In his mature poetry he stands as he wished, "a man so many years old, fixed to some one place, known to friends and enemies, full of mortal frailty, expressing all things not made mysterious by nature with impatient clarity,"[103] but also a man reflecting an exploration and judgment of all in his own depths that might correspond to the impulses of his time.

If, unlike another who dramatized in his personal vision of history the lineaments of a Last Day, he failed to see "all things set in order" —if, from poem to poem, and even within poems, the reader must construct transitions, correlate symbols, adjust to new points of view— that limitation is also a strength. We "sing amid our uncertainty," he said;[104] and the terrifying freedom of that quarrel with himself was the condition of an exploratory poetry at one with his time:

> It was not that I do not love order, or that I lack capacity for it, but that—and not in the arts and in thought only—I outrun my strength. It is not so much that I choose too many elements, as that the possible unities themselves seem without number.... Perhaps fifty years ago I had been in less trouble, but what can one do when the age itself has come to *Hodos Chameliontos*?[105]

Moreover, his work has the harmony not of Dantesque vision but of vital growth, not of the alchemical stone but of the Great Work. As man if not as artist, Yeats would agree with another modern spiritual alchemist: "The goal is only important as an idea; the essential thing is the *opus* which leads to the goal: that is the goal of a life time."[106] So it is that, though his poetry so largely celebrates the ecstasy of tragic defeat, his career has the continual progress of heroic victory. All his final discoveries were momentary; all enriched the work. His tragedy itself increasingly modulates into the joy of comic or heroic affirmation. As he celebrates creation's very self, the immovable obstacle moves.

Underlying that *opus* was the interior dialogue that I have attempted to trace—a dialogue with a complex *doppelgänger* whose presence signifies both death and creative rebirth:

> I call to the mysterious one who yet
> Shall walk the wet sands by the edge of the stream
> And look most like me, being indeed my double...

Shelley too had said, in lines which have often puzzled commentators but which must have been plain enough to Yeats,

> The Magus Zoroaster
> Met his own image walking in the garden.[107]

Yeats knew that Shelley's "shadows" must have had "more than a metaphorical and picturesque being to one who had spoken in terror with an image of himself."[108] Not long before his own death, Shelley had met that image walking on the terrace, and it had demanded of him: "How long do you mean to be content?"[109] Understandably, that image seems to have been in Yeats's mind during his last years: he used the question as a title—"Are You Content?"—and paraphrased the image's taunt: *" 'What then?" sang Plato's ghost. 'What then?' "* But the most explicit facing of that shadow toward the end and perhaps the most poignant evocation of the depths underlying the final joy of Yeats's tragic stone is "The Man and the Echo."

From the oracular cavern of "The Gyres," from the stony recesses of history, had come the one word "Rejoice!" But here, as the dialogue is internalized, that rocky voice becomes Irish and personal. The entire subjective dialogue strangely recalls—even to the reference to stricken rabbit or dying hare—a passage in Amiel's journal:

> When a man can no longer look forward in imagination to five years,
> a year, a month, of free activity—when he is reduced to counting

the hours, and to seeing in the coming night the threat of an unknown fate—it is plain that he must give up art, science, and politics,
and that he must be content to hold converse with himself, the one
possibility which is his till the end. Inward soliloquy is the only re-
source of the condemned man whose execution is delayed. He with-
draws upon the fastnesses of conscience. His spiritual force no longer
radiates outwardly; it is consumed in self-study. Action is cut off—
only contemplation remains. . . . Like the hare, he comes back to die
in his form, and this form is his consciousness, his intellect—the
journal, too, which has been the companion of his inner life. As long
as . . . he has a moment of solitude, this echo of himself still claims
his meditation, still represents to him his converse with his god.[110]

The cleft of Alt is the abyss of the self where all things are called in
question; and now as always, that abyss includes for Yeats the "fastnesses of conscience":

> All that I have said and done,
> Now that I am old and ill,
> Turns into a question till
> I lie awake night after night
> And never get the answers right.
> Did that play of mine send out
> Certain men the English shot?
> Did words of mine put too great strain
> On that woman's reeling brain?
> Could my spoken words have checked
> That whereby a house lay wrecked?

And, overwhelmed by the problem of measuring his interaction with
contemporary history, overwhelmed by that task of exploring his
"moral life, . . . its beneficiaries and its victims,"[111] which he had seen
as that of the dead in Purgatory, the Man lapses into despair:

> And all seems evil until I
> Sleepless would lie down and die.

But the Echo's ironic reinforcement of that despair—"Lie down and
die"—can only stimulate him anew to strong acceptance of his task,
the "spiritual intellect's great work" of self-measurement and self-
judgment which ultimately dissolves all images. The Echo's next
answer—"Into the night"—carries the Man beyond any possible mono-

logue of mirrors, through honest skepticism toward renewed experience of those powerful and suffering images of this life which are
one with himself but not simply within himself:

> O Rocky Voice,
> Shall we in that great night rejoice?
> What do we know but that we face
> One another in this place?
> But hush, for I have lost the theme,
> Its joy or night seem but a dream;
> Up there some hawk or owl has struck,
> Dropping out of sky or rock,
> A stricken rabbit is crying out,
> And its cry distracts my thought.

That Man is on what Buber calls the "narrow ridge," being blessed
and perplexed as he wrestles with his Daimon. At such a moment
he is one of those who, in the words of "Ego Dominus Tuus," "Own
nothing but their blind, stupefied hearts."

Aside from the late poetry itself, there is no more striking indication of Yeats's "winding, gyring, spiring treadmill of a stair," with
its repeated calling of all things into question, than his letter to
Dorothy Wellesley of May 1937. There he sharply contrasted himself with Mallarmé: "He escapes from history; you and I are in history, the history of the mind." He continued: "I begin to see things
double—doubled in history, world history, personal history."[112] I begin! He had long ago "swallowed the formulas," as he put it—
though they were for him no mere "bundle of formulas, not faggots
but a fire." And he had all his life, despite a shrewd realism, been
intermittently "plunged into the madness of vision, into a sense of
the relation between separated things" that he could not explain. "As
above, so below." He had been able to find the Emerald Tablet
imaged on Wordsworth's "still St. Mary's lake," as on the lake at
Coole Park, where

> Under the October twilight the water
> Mirrors a still sky...

But he had seen the tragically fallen and divided reality also in that
"sunless pool" described by William Watson—the pool of *King Lear.*

with "depths that mirror thundering skies," where "Love the slain with Love the slayer lies."[113] At one moment of vision the wild swans "drift on the still water"; at another, "the swan drifts upon a darkening flood." As at Coole, so in the abyss of the self, and so in the "troubled mirror" of history.

Central to his visionary dialogue had been the repeated discovery, in and through all folly and pride, that only he who allows himself to end can experience the "Condition of Fire"[114]—the unnamable source of that "freedom" which he knew Swift served and that "love" which he called "a form of the eternal contemplation of what is"[115]— and so be renewed. Surely that is why he could now say, hovering on yet another threshold, "Perhaps there is a theme for poetry in this 'double swan and shadow.'"

NOTES

The following abbreviations are used in the notes:

Au   *The Autobiography of William Butler Yeats* (New York, 1953)
CP   *The Collected Poems of W. B. Yeats* (New York, 1956)
CPlays   *The Collected Plays of W. B. Yeats* (New York, 1953)
CW   *The Collected Works in Verse and Prose of William Butler Yeats*, 8 vols. (Stratford, 1908)
E&I   Yeats, *Essays and Introductions* (New York, 1961)
E&Y   *The Works of William Blake,* ed. E. J. Ellis and W. B. Yeats, 3 vols. (London, 1893)
P&C   Yeats, *Plays and Controversies* (London, 1923)
V-A   Yeats, *A Vision* (London, 1925)
V-B   Yeats, *A Vision* (London, 1937)
1930D   Yeats, *Pages from a Diary Written in Nineteen Hundred and Thirty* (Dublin, 1944)

NOTES TO CHAPTER I

1. *P&C*, pp. 99-100 (1904).
2. *The Letters of W. B. Yeats,* ed. Allan Wade (New York, 1955), p. 887 (1937).
3. "The Poetry of W. B. Yeats," in *The Permanence of Yeats,* ed. James Hall and Martin Steinmann (New York, 1950), p. 343.
4. Wade, *Letters,* p. 741 (1928).
5. *1930D*, p. 54.
6. *Between Man and Man,* tr. R. G. Smith (New York, 1948), p. 29.
7. Arthur Symons, *Poems* (New York, 1902), II, 205. Yeats quotes from this translation and comments upon it in *Au,* p. 193.
8. Stéphane Mallarmé, "Le vièrge, le vivace et le bel aujourd'hui."
9. *CPlays,* p. 294.
10. *E&Y,* I, 276.
11. *Wheels and Butterflies* (New York, 1935), p. 97.
12. See *E&Y,* I, 246-50, for Yeats's reading of Blake's doctrine of the creative imagination, in harmony with this metaphor; and see *E&Y,* I, 275, for an explanation of Blake's "states" and "spaces" that implies several aspects of Yeats's own "swan and shadow." For a theosophical account of the reflection of God, see Helena P. Blavatsky, *The Secret Doctrine* (London, 1888), II, 235.
13. Blavatsky, *Secret Doctrine,* II, 465.
14. "Ribh in Ecstasy," *CP,* p. 284; "Coole Park and Ballylee, 1931," *CP,* p. 240.
15. "The Two Trees," *CP,* p. 48.

16. *Au*, p. 283 (1909).

17. Letter to Florence Farr (1901), quoted in Richard Ellmann, *Yeats: The Man and the Masks* (New York, 1948), p. 95.

18. Ruland's *Lexicon alchemiae,* quoted in *The Collected Works of C. G. Jung* (New York, 1953-), XII, 262. Jung's discussion of alchemical dialogue as a means of coming to terms with the unconscious also applies to the Hermetic doctrine of reflection. For Jung, "correspondence" is the alchemist's rationalization of psychological projection (XII, 234).

19. *Between Man and Man,* p. 180.

20. "What Then?" *CP,* p. 300; *Sophist,* 263 (Yeats often associated such interior dialogue with daimonic possession of the type Plato discussed in *Ion* and *Phaedrus*); "The Man and the Echo," *CP,* p. 338; "The Gyres," *CP,* p. 300.

21. Wade, *Letters,* p. 583 (1913).

22. *Kierkegaard's Concluding Unscientific Postscript,* ed. Walter Lowrie (Princeton, 1941), p. 141.

23. *1930D,* pp. 1-2.

24. *The Complete Works of Ralph Waldo Emerson,* ed. E. W. Emerson (Boston and New York, 1903-4), II, 7-8. Like George Russell, the early Yeats may have read much Emerson as well as Thoreau and Whitman. Certainly he could allude without condescension to Emerson's thought—*E&I,* p. 368; *P&C,* p. 87—and his note of 1886, "Talent perceives differences, Genius Unity" (see Richard Ellmann, *The Identity of Yeats* [New York, 1954], p. 7), parallels an Emersonian distinction made in the essays on "Plato" and "History" (*Complete Works,* IV, 51; II, 13 ff.).

25. "On Being Asked for a War Poem," *CP,* p. 153.

26. Wade, *Letters,* p. 819 (1933).

NOTES TO CHAPTER II

1. *Letters of Matthew Arnold to Arthur Hugh Clough,* ed. M. F. Lowry (London, 1932), p. 97.

2. *The Letters of W. B. Yeats,* ed. Allan Wade (New York, 1955), p. 294 (1898).

3. *The Education of Henry Adams* (Boston and New York, 1918), p. 457.

4. *P&C,* p. 172.

5. *The Complete Works of Ralph Waldo Emerson,* ed. E. W. Emerson (Boston and New York, 1903-4), II, 9.

6. *The Complete Writings of William Blake,* ed. Geoffrey Keynes (London, 1957), p. 390.

7. *Au,* p. 182. Yeats quotes the sentence as reported to him by Lionel Johnson, but it is developed as the conclusion to the essay on Pico, in Walter Pater, *The Renaissance* (London, 1910), p. 49.

8. "Yeats's Romanticism: Notes and Suggestions," in *The Permanence of Yeats,* ed. James Hall and Martin Steinmann (New York, 1950), p. 109.

9. *V-B,* p. 72.

10. *E&Y,* II, 152; *The Complete Works of S. T. Coleridge,* ed. William G. T. Shedd (New York, 1853), I, 436-37.

11. Blake, *Complete Writings,* p. 528; *E&Y,* I, 289.

12. Helena P. Blavatsky, *The Secret Doctrine* (London, 1888), II, 235.

13. See Richard Ellmann, *Yeats: The Man and the Masks* (New York, 1948), p. 96, and Blavatsky, *Secret Doctrine,* I, 411-24; II, 235.

14. *P&C,* pp. 112, 91-93; *E&I,* p. 340; *V-B,* p. 25. The 1910 passage may recall Goethe on Winckelmann: "We learn nothing by reading him, but we *become* something" (*Conversations of Goethe with Eckermann and Soret,* tr. J. Oxenford, [London, 1879], p. 221).

15. Wade, *Letters,* 170; *Complete Works of Oscar Wilde,* ed. Robert Ross (Boston [192-]), IV, 45, 253, 114, 30; *V-B,* p. 279.

16. *Essays in Criticism, 2nd Series* (New York, 1924), pp. 1-2.

17. Quoted by Emery Neff, *The Poetry of History* (New York, 1947), p. 151. Karl Löwith, *Meaning in History* (Chicago, 1949), argues that the most important philosophies of history resulted from the application of a nontemporal theological pattern to temporal events.

18. Pater, *The Renaissance,* pp. 124-26, 160.

19. *Au,* pp. 71, 82.

20. Wilde, *Complete Works,* IV, 269-70.

21. *E&I,* p. 102 (1901); *E&Y,* I, 241 (cf. *Au,* p. 55).

22. *Au,* p. 164. In 1914 Yeats wrote of "what Maxwell calls 'the impersonal mind' that speaks through dreams" (quoted by Richard Ellmann, *The Identity of Yeats* [New York, 1954], p. 233). Henry W. Nevinson (*Visions and Memories* [London, 1944], p. 55) noted in his diary of 1916 that Yeats "talked of Freud and Jung and the Subconscious Self, applying the doctrine to art." *Per Amica Silentia Lunae,* written in 1917, relies heavily upon More.

23. *E&I,* p. 95 (1900).

24. *Mythologies* (New York, 1959), p. 346 (1917).

25. Coleridge, *Complete Works,* III, 363.

26. Johann von Goethe, *Maxims and Reflections,* as quoted by Erich Heller, *The Disinherited Mind* (Cambridge, Eng., 1952), p. 24; William Wordsworth, *The Prelude,* Bk. 13, lines 375-76; *The Writings of Henry David Thoreau,* eds. B. Torrey and F. B. Sanborn (Boston, 1906), XVI, 164-65, and IX, 99; Emerson, *Complete Works,* II, 8-9.

27. Quoted by Heller, *Disinherited Mind,* p. 24. Cf. Wade, *Letters,* p. 810, and *Conversations of Goethe,* pp. 68-70.

28. "The Song of the Happy Shepherd," *CP,* p. 7.

29. *Mosada* (Dublin, 1886), p. 7.

30. *Wheels and Butterflies* (New York, 1935), pp. 92, 122.

31. *Ibid.,* p. 92.

32. Honoré de Balzac, *The Edition Définitive of the Comédie Humaine,* tr. G. B. Ives and others (Philadelphia, c. 1896-1900), XLI, 69-70, 79, 77. In 1934 Yeats said merely that Balzac's thought probably derived "from classical sources" and "is more like Vico's than Hegel's" (*E&I,* p. 468). Balzac's knowledge of Vico is evident in *Comédie Humaine,* XLVII, 293, and XXVIII, 50.

33. *Comédie Humaine,* XLI, 49-50.

34. *The Wanderings of Oisin* (London, 1889), p. 32.

35. *Au,* p. 189.

36. See *Au,* pp. 29, 53, and *E&I,* p. 438.

37. *Comédie Humaine,* XLII, 330, 347; XLVI, 335-36.

38. A. P. Sinnett, *Esoteric Buddhism* (Boston, 1888), pp. 246-47, 126-27 (for Yeats's reading of this in 1885, see Ellmann, *Man and Masks,* p. 61); *Wheels and Butterflies,* p. 92; *V-A,* p. xi.

39. Edouard Schuré, *From Sphinx to Christ,* tr. Eva Martin (London, n.d.), 34-35.

40. *E&Y,* I, 242.

41. *E&Y,* I, 272, 270-71.

42. Blake, *Complete Writings,* p. 334.

43. *E&Y,* I, 374, 271, 272.

44. Blake, *Complete Writings,* p. 293; *Wanderings of Oisin,* p. 48.

45. "Thoughts on Lady Gregory's Translations," in *The Cutting of an Agate* (New York, 1912), pp. 26-27; see *V-B,* pp. 262-63, for a discussion of that alternation in Blakean terms.

46. *Wanderings of Oisin,* p. 33; *Poems* (London, 1895), p. 38. See *E&Y,* I, 290, 300-302, and Blavatsky, *Secret Doctrine,* I, 386 ff. Compare the statement about the

twenty-seven churches in *E&Y*, I, 308, with that about the twenty-eight incarnations in *V-B*, p. 81.

47. *Poems* (1895), p. 286, and note of 1912 retained in *CP*, p. 457. See "Teigue mac Cein's Adventure," in *Silva Gadelica*, ed. Standish Hayes O'Grady (London, 1892), II, 391-92, a passage noted by Russell K. Alspach, "Some Sources of Yeats's *The Wanderings of Oisin*," *PMLA*, LVIII (Sept., 1943), 855.

48. *E&Y*, II, 75-76.

49. *The Collected Works of C. G. Jung* (New York, 1953-), XII, 355; Michael Maier, "A Subtle Allegory concerning the Secrets of Alchemy," in *The Hermetic Museum*, ed. A. E. Waite (London, 1893), II, 199-233. Yeats drew upon *The Hermetic Museum* for "Rosa Alchemica," as Thomas Dume has suggested in his unpublished dissertation (Temple Univ., 1950), "W. B. Yeats: A Study of his Reading." The *rota* also enters "The Fama Fraternitatis of the Meritorious Order of the Rosy Cross," with which Yeats was familiar: A. E. Waite, *The Real History of the Rosicrucians* (London, 1887), p. 72.

50. "The Tables of the Law," *Savoy*, No. 7 (Nov., 1896), p. 84. Dume, "W. B. Yeats," has noted the source in *The Literary Works of Leonardo da Vinci*, ed. Jean P. Richter (London, 1883), II, 291:

> Now you see that the hope and the desire of returning to the first state of chaos is like the moth to the light, and that the man who with constant longing awaits with joy each new springtime, each new summer, each new month and new year— deeming that the things he longs for are ever too late in coming—does not perceive that he is longing for his own destruction. But this desire is the very quintessence, the spirit of the elements, which finding itself imprisoned with the soul is ever longing to return from the human body to its giver. And you must know that this same longing is that quintessence, inseparable from nature, and that man is the image of the world.

51. For the composition of "The Wheel" see A. N. Jeffares, "W. B. Yeats and His Methods of Writing Verse," in *Permanence of Yeats*, ed. Hall and Steinmann, pp. 301-2; Wade, *Letters*, p. 720; *W. B. Yeats and T. Sturge Moore: Their Correspondence 1901-1937*, ed. Ursula Bridge (London, 1953), p. 154.

52. *Au*, p. 116.

53. *Poems* (1895), p. 33; Heinrich Heine, *Pictures of Travel*, tr. Charles Leland (Philadelphia and London, 1863), p. 379. Yeats echoed Heine on various occasions; for specific references to him (from 1888 to 1935) see *Letters to the New Island*, ed. Horace Reynolds (Cambridge, Mass., 1934), p. 166; *E&I*, p. 352; *The King of the Great Clock Tower* (New York, 1935), p. 21.

54. Heine, *Pictures of Travel*, p. 312.

55. Pater, *The Renaissance*, pp. 56, 57; *The Secret Rose* (London, 1897), p. 215; "Mr. Lionel Johnson's Poems," *Bookman*, XIII (Feb., 1898), 155; *Au*, p. 189. Yeats explicitly accepted the historical vision of the "Grande Chartreuse" in 1890, *Letters to the New Island*, p. 213.

56. See *Au*, p. 167.

57. *E&I*, pp. 302, 186.

58. *The Collected Works of Henrik Ibsen*, ed. William Archer (New York, 1911), V, 114.

59. *Ibid.*, V, xvi. Ibsen's "empires" may derive from Joachim by way of Lessing: see Otto Heller, *Henrik Ibsen* (Boston & New York, 1912), pp. 100-101. Spengler mentions both Lessing and Ibsen as Joachists: *The Decline of the West*, tr. Charles F. Atkinson (London, 1926-28), I, 20.

60. Goethe, *Sämtliche Werke* (Stuttgart and Berlin, 1902-7), V, 247-48. In Saint-Simonian theory an "organic" and a "critical" epoch together form a complete period. Two such periods, that of pagan polytheism and that of Catholic Christianity, have already occurred; a third is about to begin. See Hill Shine, *Carlyle and the Saint-Simonians* (Baltimore, 1941), pp. 30-49.

61. *Sartor Resartus,* ed. C. F. Harrold (New York, 1937), p. 112; *Critical and Miscellaneous Essays* (New York, 1898), III, 15-16; *Lectures on the History of Literature,* ed. R. P. Karkaria (London, 1892), pp. 31-32; *The French Revolution* (London, 1898), I, 10; *Critical and Misc. Essays,* IV, 180-81, and III, 104-5; *Lectures on the History of Literature,* p. 185.

62. *Au,* p. 130. In *On the Boiler* (Dublin, 1939), p. 25, when allowing himself an angry rhetoric like that of Carlyle, Yeats alluded to our civilization's approaching "the phoenix nest."

63. John Eglinton, *Two Essays on the Remnant* (Dublin, 1894), p. 14; *Au,* pp. 121, 118. For discussion of the influence of those named in this paragraph, see Thomas R. Whitaker, "The Early Yeats and the Pattern of History," *PMLA,* LXXV (June, 1960), 326-27.

64. See Allan Wade, *A Bibliography of the Writings of W. B. Yeats* (London, 1951), p. 299; *E&I,* p. 347; "Mr. Lionel Johnson's Poems," *Bookman,* XIII, 155.

65. *The Writings of Arthur Hallam,* ed. T. H. Vail Motter (New York, 1943), pp. 189, 190 (cf. *E&I,* p. 110).

66. *Au,* p. 116; Hallam, *Writings,* p. 190 (cf. *Au,* pp. 187-89).

67. Hallam, *Writings,* p. 190; *The Secret Rose,* pp. 63-64.

68. *E&I,* pp. 372-73; Emerson, *Complete Works,* IV, 46-47.

69. Sinnett, *Esoteric Buddhism,* p. 120; Lucy M. Garnett, *Greek Folk Poesy,* with essays by J. S. Stuart-Glennie (Guildford, 1896), pp. xxvi, 433; for Yeats's review of this, see "Greek Folk Poetry," *Bookman,* XI (Oct., 1896), pp. 16-17.

70. Emerson, *Complete Works,* IV, 52 ff.; Pater, *Greek Studies* (London, 1910), pp. 35, 252-53; for Yeats, Sophocles and Aeschylus are both "Phidian men": *V-B,* p. 269; Pater, *Plato and Platonism* (London, 1910), p. 24 (cf. *V-B,* p. 270). As Ruth C. Child has noted—*The Aesthetic of Walter Pater* (New York, 1940), p. 89*n*—Pater drew upon Nietzsche (who later influenced Yeats directly); but Nietzsche learned much from Emerson: see H. Hummel, "Emerson and Nietzsche," *New England Quarterly,* XIX (Mar., 1946), 63-84.

71. *Mythologies,* p. 340; *Autobiography of John Stuart Mill,* ed. John J. Coss (New York, 1924), p. 115.

NOTES TO CHAPTER III

1. *The Elder or Poetic Edda,* ed. and tr. Olive Bray (London, 1908), pp. 291-95.
2. *E&I,* p. 44.
3. *E&I,* p. 471 (1934).
4. "The Song of the Happy Shepherd," *CP,* p. 7, originally "Song of the Last Arcadian," *The Wanderings of Oisin* (London, 1889), pp. 74-75.
5. Honoré de Balzac, *The Edition Définitive of the Comédie Humaine,* tr. G. B. Ives and others (Philadelphia, 1896-1900), XLVI, 334.
6. *E&Y,* I, 293, 273.
7. *E&Y,* I, 357.
8. *Mythologies* (New York, 1959), p. 174; *E&Y,* I, 301 and cf. II, 290-91.
9. Oswald Spengler, *The Decline of the West,* tr. Charles F. Atkinson (London, 1926-28), I, 191; *E&I,* pp. 201-2; *Wheels and Butterflies* (New York, 1935), p. 92.
10. See *The Collected Works of C. G. Jung* (New York, 1953-   ), XII, 159-60, where the technique is elaborated in terms consonant with Yeats's imaginative development.
11. *E&Y,* p. 193 (1898); *P&C,* p. 91 (1904).
12. As quoted in *P&C,* pp. 82-83 (1904); Yeats had frequently used a different version as epigraph, beginning with *The Countess Kathleen* (London, 1892).

13. Joyce, "The Day of the Rabblement," quoted by Herbert Gorman, *James Joyce* (New York, 1939), p. 72.

14. See Michael Fixler, "The Affinities between J.-K. Huysmans and the 'Rosicrucian' Stories of W. B. Yeats," *PMLA*, LXXIV (Sept., 1959), 466-67. But Fixler underestimates the relation to Pater.

15. "Rosa Alchemica," *Savoy*, No. 2 (Apr., 1896), p. 56 (cf. Walter Pater, *The Renaissance* [London, 1910], p. 49, and *Au*, p. 182); *Savoy*, No. 2, p. 57.

16. Nietzsche, *Beyond Good and Evil*, p. 141 (in *The Complete Works of Friedrich Nietzsche*, ed. Oscar Levy, 18 vols. [Edinburgh and London, 1909-24]).

17. *Au*, p. 289.

18. *Savoy*, No. 2, p. 56.

19. *Plays*, p. 205 (1902). Cf. *The Complete Writings of William Blake*, ed. Geoffrey Keynes (London, 1957), p. 578; Jung, *Collected Works*, XI, 164 ff., on "The Problem of the Fourth."

20. *Savoy*, No. 2, pp. 61-62, 58. Yeats speaks of the "ninth key" of Valentinus; but the closest parallel is found in the Fourth Key (*The Hermetic Museum*, ed. A. E. Waite [London, 1893], I, 331):

> At the end of the world, the world shall be judged by fire, and all those things that God has made of nothing shall by fire be reduced to ashes, from which ashes the Phoenix is to produce her young. For in the ashes slumbers a true and genuine tartaric substance, which, being dissolved, will enable us to open the strongest bolt of the royal chamber.
> After the conflagration, there shall be formed a new heaven and a new earth, and the new man will be more noble in his glorified state than he was before.

21. *Savoy*, No. 2, p. 62.

22. *Ibid.*, p. 63.

23. Herman Melville, *Moby Dick*, ed. Willard Thorp (New York, 1947), p. 261. In 1914, without being able to recall the author, Yeats paraphrased Ishmael's apostrophe to Pythagoras: see "Swedenborg, Mediums, and the Desolate Places," in Augusta Gregory, *Visions and Beliefs in the West of Ireland* (New York and London, 1920), II, 315, and *Moby Dick*, p. 402.

24. Jung, *Collected Works*, XII, 86. For parallels between immersion in the unconscious, the myth of the night sea journey, and alchemical dissolution, see *ibid.*, XVI, 244-45.

25. *Savoy*, No. 2, pp. 63, 69, 62.

26. *Ibid.*, p. 67.

27. *Ibid.*, p. 70; "To his Heart, Bidding It Have no Fear," *CP*, pp. 61-62.

28. *Savoy*, No. 2, p. 67.

29. *Ibid.*, p. 57; *Early Poems and Stories* (New York, 1925), p. 467. The alchemical peacock's tail is a symbol of wholeness but an intermediate stage between *nigredo* and *albedo* or Vaughan's Dragon and Swan. See Jung, *Collected Works*, XII, 213, 220-21, 399; and Milton O. Percival, *William Blake's Circle of Destiny* (New York, 1938), pp. 206-7.

30. *Savoy*, No. 2, p. 59.

31. *The Letters of W. B. Yeats*, ed. Allan Wade (New York, 1955), p. 402; *V-B*, p. 105.

32. Blake, *Complete Writings*, p. 530.

33. Jacob Boehme, *Six Theosophic Points* (Ann Arbor, 1958), pp. 148-49. Recalling the period of the early nineties, Yeats said (*Letters to the New Island*, ed. Horace Reynolds [Cambridge, Mass., 1934], pp. xi-xii): "I knew Blake thoroughly, I had read much Swedenborg, had only ceased my study of Boehme for fear I might do nothing else. . ."

34. Blake, *Complete Writings*, p. 631.

35. "The Tables of the Law," *Savoy*, No. 7 (Nov., 1896), pp. 81, 82.

36. Blake, *Complete Writings*, p. 198. This overcoming of the law has also, of course, a Pauline basis: Romans 10:4 and 13:10-12.

37. *Savoy*, No. 7, pp. 83-84.

38. *The Tables of the Law and The Adoration of the Magi* (London, 1904), pp. 32-33.

39. T. S. Eliot, *Selected Essays* (New York, 1950), p. 380.

40. *CPlays*, pp. 72-73.

41. *Savoy*, No. 7, p. 86; *CPlays*, pp. 288-89.

42. *Wheels and Butterflies*, p. 102.

43. *E&I*, p. 129; Blake, *Complete Writings*, p. 756.

44. *E&Y*, I, 277.

45. Blake, *Complete Writings*, p. 523; Jung, *Collected Works*, XI, 209.

46. Blake, *Complete Writings*, p. 199.

47. *The Tables of the Law. . . ,* p. 51.

48. Lynn Thorndike, *A History of Magic and Experimental Science* (New York, 1929), I, 363-65.

49. *Au*, p. 292.

50. Coventry Patmore, *The Rod, the Root and the Flower* (London, 1950), pp. 103, 117. Yeats alluded to Patmore frequently during the first decade of the century.

51. *Mythologies*, p. 336.

52. *E&I*, p. 318; *Au*, p. 196.

53. Karl Müllenhoff, cited by Bray, *The Elder or Poetic Edda*, p. lxxviii. Yeats's knowledge of Vala is evident in *E&Y*, I, 336.

54. *Au*, p. 282; *E&I*, p. 321: "a victory, the sacrifice of a man to himself."

55. Augusta Gregory, *Gods and Fighting Men*, intro. by Yeats (London, 1904), p. xviii.

56. Quoted by Stanislaus Joyce, *My Brother's Keeper* (New York, 1958), p. 209.

57. Martin Buber, *The Eclipse of God* (New York, 1957), p. 87.

58. Jung, *Collected Works*, XI, 49, 48.

59. *The Tables of the Law. . . ,* p. 38; Blake, *Complete Writings*, p. 346.

60. *E&I*, p. 41.

61. "The Death of Oenone," *Bookman*, III (Dec., 1892), 84.

62. *E&I*, p. 36.

63. *The Complete Works of Ralph Waldo Emerson*, ed. E. W. Emerson (Boston & New York, 1903-4), III, 26-27.

64. *E&I*, p. 44.

65. *Au*, p. 223; *P&C*, pp. v-vi.

66. Jung, *Collected Works*, V, 292.

67. *Ibid.*, XVII, 184-85.

68. *Ibid.*, XVII, 180.

69. Quoted in Richard Ellmann, *Yeats: The Man and the Masks* (New York, 1948), p. 6.

70. "Parnell's Funeral," *CP*, p. 276.

NOTES TO CHAPTER IV

1. *The Works of Thomas Vaughan*, ed. A. E. Waite (London, 1919), p. 322.

2. *Letters to the New Island*, ed. Horace Reynolds (Cambridge, Mass., 1934), pp. 190-92.

3. *The Letters of W. B. Yeats*, ed. Allan Wade (New York, 1955), p. 211.

4. "William Blake and His Illustrations to the Divine Comedy," Part II, *Savoy*, No. 4 (Aug., 1896), p. 26; "William Blake," *Bookman*, X (Apr., 1896), 21.

5. "Aglavaine and Selysette," *Bookman*, XII (Sept., 1897), 155; Maurice Maeterlinck, *The Treasure of the Humble*, tr. Alfred Sutro (London, 1907), p. 42. See Yeats's

laudatory review of an earlier edition, "The Treasure of the Humble," *Bookman*, XII (Jul., 1897), 94.

6. Helena P. Blavatsky, *The Secret Doctrine* (London, 1888), I, 646; Richard Ellmann, *Yeats: The Man and the Masks* (New York, 1948), p. 97; Florence Farr, *Bernard Shaw, W. B. Yeats, Letters*, ed. Clifford Bax (New York, 1941), p. 51.

7. *E&I*, p. 187 (1897), p. 197 (1895).

8. *Savoy*, No. 7 (Nov., 1896), p. 87.

9. *Au*, pp. 202-3.

10. *E&I*, p. 248.

11. Note to first publication, *Savoy*, No. 2 (Apr., 1896), p. 109.

12. "Mongan Laments the Change That Has Come upon Him and His Beloved," *The Wind Among the Reeds* (London, 1899), p. 22; for an allusion to Diarmuid's death see *CW*, V, 89.

13. *CPlays*, p. 245; *Secret Doctrine*, I, 70.

14. *The Complete Writings of William Blake*, ed. Geoffrey Keynes (London, 1957), pp. 241 ff. John V. Kelleher has suggested to me that Yeats knew the Irish meaning of "orc." There are earlier connections between "Orcus" and "Phorkys." Cf. Robert Graves's speculations on the porcine god of death, *The White Goddess* (New York, 1948), pp. 192, 346.

15. *The Wind Among the Reeds*, p. 101; for his use of Rhys and Frazer, see *ibid.*, pp. 95-99.

16. *The Wanderings of Oisin* (London, 1889), p. 45.

17. "The Death of Cuchulain" (1892), *CW*, I, 148. For Cuchulain as sun-hero see John Rhys, *Lectures on the Origin and Growth of Religion as Illustrated by Celtic Heathendom* (London, 1888), p. 90-91 *et passim*. The sea death, not cited by Rhys but harmonious with the cycle, was selected by Yeats despite the fact that it differs from the death given in the bardic tale. See *The Countess Kathleen* (London, 1892), p. 140, for his statement of reliance upon Jeremiah Curtin, *Myths and Folklore of Ireland* (Boston, 1890), pp. 324-26.

18. Orchil is identified in *Poems* (London, 1895), p. 285; "Rosa Alchemica," *Savoy*, No. 2 (Apr., 1896), p. 69; "The Binding of the Hair," *Savoy*, No. 1 (Jan., 1896), 137-38; Rhys, *Celtic Heathendom*, p. 497. Yeats had described that cyclical sea death in Blakean terms as Urizen's sinking westward like the sun sinking into the sea, *E&Y*, I, 277.

19. A line from the dawn scene of Blake's *Europe* is included (*Savoy*, No. 2, p. 64); the exiled gods are alluded to (p. 60); and the discovery of the devotees seems a violent reworking of Heine's tale, in *The Gods in Exile*, of the fisherman who comes upon a Bacchanalian rout (*The Prose Writings of Heinrich Heine*, ed. Havelock Ellis [London, 1887], pp. 270 ff.); for Poe and the symbolist tradition, see pp. 66-67; for the Irish resurgence and the Armageddon, see pp. 63-64.

20. *Savoy*, No. 2, p. 61.

21. "Into the Twilight," *CP*, p. 56.

22. *E&I*, p. 267; C. G. Jung comments on this mercurial progress in his *Collected Works* (New York, 1953-), XI, 314.

23. *Ideals in Ireland*, ed. Augusta Gregory (London, 1901), pp. 105, 106. Russell was still presenting essentially this position in *The National Being* (Dublin, 1916), p. 129.

24. "America and the Arts," *Metropolitan Magazine*, XXII (Apr., 1905), p. 53; see also Wade, *Letters*, pp. 418, 423, and *P&C*, pp. 76, 85-86.

25. *P&C*, p. 114; "Upon a House Shaken by the Land Agitation" (1909), *CP*, p. 93. His criticism of the middle classes rose to a bitter climax during the *Playboy* controversy of 1907 (*P&C*, pp. 192-98).

26. *P&C*, p. 15.

27. *E&I*, p. 250 (1907).

28. *Letters to the New Island*, p. 109; Wade, *Letters*, p. 434.

29. *Ideas of Good and Evil* (London, 1903), p. 201.

30. Wade, *Letters,* p. 379; *E&I,* p. 308 (1909).

31. Wade, *Letters,* p. 402.

32. *Ibid.,* pp. 403, 402. Because of such similarities, occultists have absorbed Nietzsche's thought with ease. See, e.g., Edouard Schuré, *From Sphinx to Christ,* tr. Eva Martin (London, n.d.), pp. 177-82. Noting Nietzsche's lack of frankness regarding his sources, P. D. Ouspensky, in *A New Model of the Universe* (London, 1931), p. 127*n,* has claimed that, despite the lack of explicit reference to contemporary occult literature, Nietzsche "obviously knew it well and made use of it." But acquaintance with neo-Platonism and with Schopenhauer would account for many similarities: e.g., Thomas Taylor, in his edition of *The Works of Plato* (London, 1804), II, 622-23, called the "Dionysiacal" and "Apolloniacal" the twofold work of the demiurgus.

33. See Yeats's annotation to Nietzsche quoted in Richard Ellmann, *The Identity of Yeats* (New York, 1954), p. 97.

34. Wade, *Letters,* p. 513. Most of this reading occurred from 1905 to 1909 (see *ibid.,* pp. 449, 536).

35. *If I Were Four and Twenty* (Dublin, 1940), pp. 8-9. First published in the *Irish Statesman* in 1919.

36. *Beltaine,* No. 1 (1899), pp. 21-22, and No. 2 (1900), pp. 22-23.

37. *P&C,* pp. 122-23, 156.

38. *E&Y,* I, 301; cf. the "symbolic garden of Eden" which follows the dawn (I, 272).

39. *Samhain* (1908), pp. 8-9.

40. *Au,* pp. 298, 292-93, 304-5.

41. *E&I,* p. 316.

42. *E&I,* p. 354.

43. *E&I,* p. 318 (1910); cf. *Au,* p. 297 (1909): "The soul of Ireland has become a vapour and her body a stone." As images of Transfiguration, the Magi also foreshadow the sages of "Sailing to Byzantium" and the ivory images "staring at miracle" in *V-B,* p. 280.

44. Blake, *Complete Writings,* p. 199.

45. *Mythologies* (New York, 1959), 333-34, 335-36, 337, 340.

46. Ellmann, *Man and Masks,* 222-23, 228.

47. *Mythologies,* p. 340.

48. *E&I,* pp. 287, 288.

49. Arthur Schopenhauer, *The World as Will and Idea,* tr. R. B. Haldane and J. Kemp (London, 1896; 4th ed.), I, 346. For Yeats's early reading of Schopenhauer, see *E&I,* p. 347. Similarities of phrasing are often striking; but Yeats may have absorbed many of the ideas from Blake, Boehme, and theosophical writers.

50. Schopenhauer, *World as Will and Idea,* I, 346.

51. *Au,* p. 318.

52. They are intellect and love, head and heart, or Jupiter-Saturn and Mars-Venus conjunctions (*V-B,* pp. 207-208).

53. The moment of the Lark: Blake, *Complete Writings,* p. 526; cf. *E&I,* p. 271.

54. *P&C,* pp. 217-18.

55. *World as Will and Idea,* I, 265.

56. *If I Were Four and Twenty,* pp. 4-5, 20-21. He seems to be prophesying something like the Phase 24 which he later said was anticipated in Péguy and Claudel (*V-A,* p. 212).

57. *If I Were Four and Twenty,* pp. 8, 9.

58. The outline, prepared about 1934, is printed in A. N. Jeffares, *W. B. Yeats: Man and Poet* (London, 1949), pp. 351-52; *E&I,* p. 447.

59. Blackmur, "The Later Poetry of W. B. Yeats," in *The Permanence of Yeats,* ed. James Hall and Martin Steinmann (New York, 1950), p. 50.

60. Plotinus, *The Enneads,* tr. Stephen MacKenna (London, 1917-30), I, 22. Yeats

read this translation of the Oracle in 1918: see T. R. Henn, *The Lonely Tower* (London, 1950), p. 133*n*. Long before discovering Toynbee's formula—schism in the state, schism in the soul—Yeats probably knew Pater's comparable assertion (*Plato and Platonism* [London, 1910], pp. 24-25): "The soul,... the inward polity of the individual, was the theatre of a similar dissolution."

61. As Harold Bloom has noted, *Shelley's Mythmaking* (New Haven, 1959), pp. 111-12.

62. The *primary* dispensation begins under Mars-Venus or Christ (Yeats later thought that Christ rather than Buddha should have appeared in "The Double Vision of Michael Robartes") and the *antithetical* dispensation under Jupiter-Saturn or the Sphinx (*V-B*, p. 208). Cf. "Conjunctions," *Cp*, p. 287.

63. Wade, *Letters*, p. 851.

64. *E&I*, p. 440.

NOTES TO CHAPTER V

1. *The Complete Writings of William Blake*, ed. Geoffrey Keynes (London, 1957), p. 629.

2. R. G. Collingwood, "The Theory of Historical Cycles" (II), *Antiquity*, I (1927), p. 446.

3. "Gratitude to the Unknown Instructors," *CP*, p. 249.

4. *Letters to the New Island*, ed. Horace Reynolds (Cambridge, Mass., 1934), p. 174; Augusta Gregory, *Visions and Beliefs in the West of Ireland* (New York and London, 1920), I, 287 (note 38).

5. *W. B. Yeats and T. Sturge Moore: Their Correspondence 1901-1937*, ed. Ursula Bridge (London, 1953), pp. 104-5.

6. *Ibid.*, p. 150 (1929); Oswald Spengler, *The Decline of the West*, tr. Charles F. Atkinson (London, 1926-28), I, 56, 46, 165.

7. William Wordsworth, *The Prelude*, Bk. 6, lines 151 ff.

8. "The Gift of Harun Al-Rashid," *CP*, pp. 443, 444.

9. Percy Bysshe Shelley, "The Revolt of Islam," VII, xxxi-xxxii. In 1900 Yeats alluded to the passage (*E&I*, p. 78). Blake, *Complete Writings*, p. 605.

10. Blake, *Complete Writings*, p. 528.

11. Arthur Schopenhauer, *The World as Will and Idea*, tr. R. B. Haldane and J. Kemp (London, 1896; 4th ed.), I, 318. Jacob Burckhardt had accepted that view of the rivalry between poet and historian: see *Force and Freedom*, ed. J. H. Nichols (New York, 1943), p. 153.

12. Benedetto Croce, *The Philosophy of Giambattista Vico*, tr. R. G. Collingwood (London, 1913), pp. 29, 230. Cf. *V-B*, p. 207. For Yeats's reading of Croce, see Joseph Hone, *W. B. Yeats, 1865-1939* (London, 1942), pp. 393-94.

13. *E&Y*, I, 289; Helena P. Blavatsky, *The Secret Doctrine* (London, 1888), II, 235. See also her description (II, 214) of Tiphereth, the divine manifestation that is "a circle formed of spirals": "Coiled within, so as to follow the spirals, lies the serpent...; the cycle representing...the divine mind..., and the serpent..., the *Shadow of the Light*..."

14. Collingwood: "The Theory of Historical Cycles," (II), *Antiquity*, I, 446; "Oswald Spengler and the Theory of Historical Cycles," *Antiquity*, I, 325.

15. For other instances of Yeats's long wrestling with these antinomies see: *E&Y*, I, 242; "Rosa Alchemica," *Savoy*, No. 2 (Apr. 1896), p. 58; *Yeats and Moore: Their Correspondence*, p. 131; *1930D*, pp. 18-19. He was delighted yet later to discover Ludwig Fischer, *The Structure of Thought*, tr. W. H. Johnston (London, 1931), which traces the antinomic structure of thought through the history of philosophy (see *The Letters of W. B. Yeats*, ed. Allan Wade [New York, 1955], pp. 783-84). He would probably have been yet more delighted to find the basis of his system now sup-

ported by G. R. Levy—*The Gate of Horn* (London, 1948), p. 303—who asserts that the gyres of Anaximander "made philosophy possible by taking over from religion a spatial and temporal rhythm in which thought could move." Anaximander held that the "separation of opposites" was "produced by the whirling motion of the one substance, *Diné.*" And that is "the spiral movement whose long history, as pathway of the earliest divinities and of their human votaries," Miss Levy follows from its source in early cave entrances, past the Cretan Labyrinth, the Druid temple, and the Ziggurat, to the Greek mysteries and Greek philosophy. Yeats would have recognized the "winding path" in which his thought is wound, the gyre in which the Byzantine sages perne as they descend, the whirlwind in which the *sidhe* dance, and Blake's "ever-varying spiral ascents to the heavens of heavens," which, bent down, become the Druid serpent temple or Yeats's coiling history.

16. *V-B*, p. 81; cf. the similar statement in *E&Y*, I, 308, and Howard Brinton, *The Mystic Will* (New York, 1930), p. 23: "In every completed act of the will the soul goes from earth through hell to highest heaven and back to earth again. This is the dialectic of all organic life."

17. *V-B*, p. 255. Croce (*Philosophy of Giambattista Vico*, p. 132) had noted that the lack of progressive enrichment in Vico's history caused men and events to lose their individual character.

18. *V-B*, p. 302.

19. *V-B*, p. 25.

20. W. M. Flinders Petrie, *The Revolutions of Civilisation* (London, 1911), pp. 4-5, 9-10; *V-B*, p. 268. Yeats apparently read Petrie in 1921: see *V-B*, p. 261.

21. Petrie, *Revolutions of Civilisation*, Fig. 57; *V-B*, p. 271.

22. Wade, *Letters*, p. 666; see Henry Adams, "The Rule of Phase Applied to History," in *The Degradation of the Democratic Dogma*, ed. Brooks Adams (New York, 1919), 287-308; and *The Education of Henry Adams* (Boston and New York, 1918), pp. 457, 482, 498.

23. *Degradation of the Democratic Dogma*, pp. 300-304, 309-10.

24. *V-B*, p. 257.

25. *V-A*, pp. 174-75; cf. the more tentative statement in *V-B*, pp. 257-58.

26. Cf. Strzygowski, *The Origin of Christian Church Art*, tr. O. M. Dalton and H. J. Braunholz (Oxford, 1923), p. 153: "the North, like the East, ... excluded the human figure."

27. *V-B*, p. 302; Strzygowski, *Christian Church Art*, p. 5; *V-B*, p. 271; Strzygowski, *Christian Church Art*, pp. 51-52 (cf. *V-B*, pp. 271-72).

28. *Christian Church Art*, pp. 14, 33, 35.

29. *Ibid.*, pp. 41, 48.

30. *E&I*, p. 159 (1900), *Mythologies* (New York, 1959), p. 357 (1917).

31. *The Complete Works of Ralph Waldo Emerson*, ed. E. W. Emerson (Boston and New York, 1903-4), II, 9; Henry David Thoreau, *A Week on the Concord and Merrimack Rivers*, p. 310 (in *Complete Works* [Boston and New York, 1929]).

32. *V-B*, pp. 270-71.

33. *Kierkegaard's Concluding Unscientific Postscript*, ed. Walter Lowrie (Princeton, 1941), p. 141.

34. *V-B*, p. 270.

35. Pater saw, on the one hand, "the centrifugal, the Ionian, the Asiatic tendency, ... working with little forethought straight before it, in the development of every thought and fancy; ... delighting in brightness and colour, in beautiful material, in changeful form everywhere," and, on the other, the centripetal, Doric, or "salutary European tendency, which ... enforces everywhere the impress of its sanity, its profound reflexions upon things as they really are, its sense of proportion." These "met and struggled and were harmonised in the supreme imagination, of Pheidias, in sculpture—of Aeschylus, in the drama." (Walter Pater, *Greek Studies* (London, 1910), pp. 252, 253, 35.) The antithesis of Doric and Ionic formed the basis of Yeats's description of

the "horizontal dance" at other full moons: he noted in Byzantium, with Strzygowski's help, the contrast of Greco-Roman figures and decoration of Persian origin (*V-B*, p. 281; *Christian Church Art*, pp. 150-51), and in the Renaissance the contrast of Donatello or Michael Angelo, who reflect "the hardness and astringency of Myron," and Jacopo della Quercia or Raphael, who "seem ... Ionic and Asiatic" (*V-B*, p. 291.)

36. *E&I*, pp. 92-93 (1900); *Prometheus Unbound*, IV, lines 402, 400, 357.

37. *V-B*, p. 271; cf. Pater, *Plato and Platonism* (London, 1910), pp. 24-25. When Yeats adds that, as Greek civilization loses itself in barbarism, Alexander is "but a part of the impulse that creates Hellenised Rome and Asia," he may be recalling H. G. Wells, *The Outline of History* (New York, 1921), p. 365. T. R. Henn, *The Lonely Tower* (London, 1950), p. 198, has suggested that Yeats used Wells.

38. *V-B*, p. 273; "The Madness of King Goll," *CP*, p. 17; *V-B*, pp. 244-45. Yeats may have been led to Mommsen by Croce's statement (*Philosophy of Vico*, p. 243) that he brought to maturity Vico's view of Roman history. Mommsen supported Yeats's vision of the decline of Rome into mechanism—Theodor Mommsen, *The History of Rome*, tr. W. P. Dickson (New York, 1903), V, 326—and probably supported the parallel of Christ and Caesar by calling Caesar "the entire and perfect man" and saying, "In his character as man as well as in his place in history, Caesar occupies a position where the great contrasts of existence meet and balance each other" (V, 313).

39. *V-B*, pp. 273-74.

40. *V-B*, p. 277; Orwell, *Dickens, Dali, and Others* (New York, 1946), p. 166.

41. *V-B*, p. 279.

42. *V-B*, pp. 279, 280-81. Blavatsky distinguished between the Serpent and the Devil of Christianity (*Secret Doctrine*, I, 198, 410; II, 528).

43. *V-B*, pp. 291-92; see Blavatsky, *Secret Doctrine*, I, 411 ff., 71-72, and II, 214. There are many affinities with the decadent visions of Byzantium. Yeats knew many of the works discussed by Mario Praz, *The Romantic Agony*, tr. Angus Davidson (London, 1951; 2nd ed.), pp. 383 ff., and his own work contains a similar split between inspiration and erudition. A. N. Jeffares has noted (*W. B. Yeats: Man and Poet* [London, 1949], pp. 260, 261, 334) Yeats's use of O. M. Dalton, *Byzantine Art and Archaeology* (Oxford, 1911) and W. G. Holmes, *The Age of Justinian and Theodora* (London, 1912). But the important fact is that Yeats drew from them only specific bits of description: Dalton has nothing to correspond with Yeats's general view, and Holmes engages in a comprehensive attack upon Byzantine culture.

44. *Au*, pp. 70, 337, 338; Blake, *Complete Writings*, pp. 776, 777. In fact, though ironically qualified, Yeats's Byzantium is close to the Platonic ideal as described by R. C. Lodge, *Plato's Theory of Art* (London, 1953), p. 252: the citizens are "living in a kind of dream-*aura*. They are all parts of one and the same dream," which has "a sense of guidance towards a final, ideal vision. This vision they are capable of apprehending (for the most part) only through art."

45. Blake, *Complete Writings*, p. 484.

46. *On the Boiler* (Dublin, 1939), p. 37.

47. *V-B*, p. 283; cf. Wells, *Outline of History*, p. 556.

48. *V-B*, p. 285. The Virgin of Dreux significantly stands, no longer "that majestic queen who was seated on a throne." Her portrayal is part of Pierre de Dreux's "masculine compliment." (Henry Adams, *Mont St. Michel and Chartres* [Boston and New York, 1913], p. 188.)

49. *V-B*, p. 287. Like Vico (Croce, *Philosophy of Vico*, p. 223) and Pater (*Greek Studies*, pp. 267-68), Yeats draws a parallel between Homer and chivalric romance.

50. *V-B*, p. 287.

51. *V-B*, pp. 288-89.

52. *V-B*, p. 291. Yeats thus resolved geometrically the conflicting claims in behalf of the Middle Ages and the Renaissance as the time of "ideal unity." Cf. *Au*, p. 174. In 1938 he would summarize the resultant ambivalence yet more flatly: "I

detest the Renaissance because it made the human mind inorganic; I adore the Renaissance because it clarified form and created freedom" (*On the Boiler*, p. 27).

53. *V-B*, pp. 291-92. Yeats apparently refers to Dante's discussion of beauty as harmony (*Convito*, I, v, 95; III, xv, 117; IV, xxv, 130).

54. *V-B*, pp. 292-93; Baldassare Castiglione, *The Book of the Courtier*, tr. Thomas Hoby (London, 1928), p. 311.

55. *E&I*, p. 472 (1934) (the last phrase is quoted from the poem "Old Tom Again"); Pater, *The Renaissance* (London, 1910), p. 125.

56. *V-B*, pp. 293, 299; in 1924 Yeats wrote with mingled audacity and irony: "We are Catholics but of the school of Pope Julius the Second and of the Medician Popes, who ordered Michael-angelo and Raphael to paint upon the walls of the Vatican, and upon the ceiling of the Sistine Chapel, the doctrine of the Platonic Academy of Florence, the reconciliation of Galilee and Parnassus." (*To-Morrow*, I [Aug., 1924], 4, quoted in Richard Ellmann, *Yeats: The Man and the Masks* [New York, 1948], p. 246.)

57. *V-A*, pp. 211-12, 213-15.

58. Croce analyzes (*Philosophy of Vico*, pp. 39-40) Vico's confusion of "eternal ideal history," or "the forms, categories or ideal moments of the mind in their necessary succession," with the empirical determination of the order in which forms of civilization have appeared. A similar confusion is evident in Yeats's conflicting statements of intention.

59. *CPlays*, p. 243; *V-B*, p. 299.

60. *V-B*, p. 300; Adams, *Degradation of Democratic Dogma*, p. 308.

61. Quoted by Erich Heller, *The Disinherited Mind* (Cambridge, Eng., 1952), p. 66. See Schopenhauer, *World as Will and Idea*, I, 265, 346.

62. *V-B*, p. 275.

63. Yeats, ed., *The Oxford Book of Modern Verse* (New York, 1937), p. xxvii; *Au*, p. 214 (1922). Cf. *Yeats and Moore: Their Correspondence*, p. 67 (1926). Coleridge's statement occurs in his *Complete Works*, ed. William G. T. Shedd (New York, 1853), III, 233.

64. *Oxford Book of Modern Verse*, p. xxxiii; *Au*, p. 165 (1922). In 1926 Whitehead reinforced Yeats's hope that the "mechanic philosophy" might be abandoned: "What Whitehead calls 'the three provincial centuries' are over. Wisdom and Poetry return" (*Yeats and Moore: Their Correspondence*, p. 93).

65. *Oxford Book of Modern Verse*, p. xxxv.

NOTES TO CHAPTER VI

1. Plotinus, *Enneads*, tr. Stephen MacKenna (London, 1917-30), I, 89.

2. *V-A*, p. 251.

3. *V-B*, pp. 140-44. For Yeats's placement of himself in Phase 17 see Richard Ellmann, *Yeats: The Man and the Masks* (New York, 1948), pp. 236-37.

4. *The Letters of W. B. Yeats*, ed. Allan Wade (New York, 1955), p. 741.

5. "Rosa Alchemica," *Savoy*, No. 2 (Apr., 1896), p. 61.

6. C. G. Jung, *Modern Man in Search of a Soul* (New York, 1933), p. 197.

7. *E&I*, p. 317.

8. Wade, *Letters*, p. 262 (1896).

9. *Ibid.*, p. 741.

10. *V-B*, p. 141; Wade, *Letters*, p. 741.

11. *V-B*, p. 84.

12. *E&I*, p. 448 (1934).

13. *V-B*, p. 179.

14. "Upon a House Shaken by the Land Agitation," *CP*, p. 93.

15. *V-B*, p. 94.

16. *V-B*, pp. 180-82.

17. *E&I*, pp. 215, 216 (1903).

18. *Mythologies* (New York, 1959), pp. 352-53, correlates Spenser's Garden and *Anima Mundi*, and quotes appropriate lines from *The Faerie Queene*, III, vi, 30.

19. *Wheels and Butterflies* (New York, 1935), p. 22.

20. *E&Y*, I, 277. Cf. *E&Y*, I, 396, for a description of the fall as a wound producing the sexes or "spectre" and "emanation."

21. A. N. Whitehead, *Science and the Modern World* (New York, 1925), p. 80 (Yeats's enthusiasm for what he took to be Whitehead's views is evident in *W. B. Yeats and T. Sturge Moore: Their Correspondence 1901-1937*, ed. Ursula Bridge (London, 1953), pp. 86-87, 89, 92, 99); *The Complete Writings of William Blake*, ed. Geoffrey Keynes (London, 1957), p. 636.

22. *E&Y*, I, 277, 398.

23. *The Collected Works of Henrik Ibsen*, ed. William Archer (New York, 1911), V, 439.

24. Yeats read Goblet d'Alviella by 1898 or 1899: see Wade, *Letters*, pp. 296-97, and *The Wind Among the Reeds* (London, 1899), p. 74. In *The Migration of Symbols*, intro. by Sir George Birdwood (Westminster, 1894), pp. 143 ff., he describes the Hebrew *ashêrîm*, and relates them to Trees of Life in other countries. In the Vedas sometimes "it is the tree of the starry firmament whose fruits are precious stones, at other times it is the tree of the cloudy sky whose roots or branches shoot out over the canopy of heaven, like those sheaves of long and fine-spun clouds which, in the popular meteorology of our country, have been named *Trees of Abraham*" (p. 161). Cf. Helena P. Blavatsky, *The Secret Doctrine* (London, 1888), II, 97-98. This is also the Sephirotic Tree, with which the adept may identify himself in meditation: cf. Israel Regardie, *The Golden Dawn* (Chicago, 1937-40), III, 271. According to a theory cited by Blavatsky (*Secret Doctrine*, II, 356), before the fall this tentpole of Eden had passed through the Equator.

25. Blake, *Complete Writings*, p. 516.

26. See Plotinus, *Enneads*, II, 154-59; cf. *Yeats and Moore: Their Correspondence*, p. 94, for a reference to this basis.

27. See "A Needle's Eye," *CP*, p. 287, and Joseph Campbell, *The Hero with a Thousand Faces* (New York, 1956), pp. 40 ff.

28. *Au*, p. 282 (1909).

29. *V-B*, pp. 258-61.

30. *E&I*, p. 87 (1900).

31. "The Immortality of the Soul," *The Complete Poems of Dr. Henry More*, ed. A. B. Grosart (Edinburgh, 1878), p. 80.

32. Cf. "He Gives His Beloved Certain Rhymes," and "An Image from a Past Life," and, given this complex, the conclusion of "When You Are Old."

33. Alexander Pope, *The Rape of the Lock*, V, 129-30.

34. For the first, cited in Richard Ellmann, *The Identity of Yeats* (New York, 1954), p. 260, see Sir James Frazer, *The Golden Bough* (London and New York, 1922; one-vol. ed.), p. 388; for the second, Walter Pater, *Greek Studies* (London, 1910), p. 52; for the third, Frazer, *Golden Bough*, p. 389.

35. Blake, *Complete Writings*, p. 425.

36. *Ibid.*, pp. 292-93; cf. *E&Y*, I, pp. 373-76.

37. *E&Y*, I, 352, 356-57; II, 76; I, 343; II, 174. Cf. *V-A*, p. 213.

38. Cf. "Vacillation" and the cover of *The Secret Rose* (reproduced in Ellmann, *Identity*, p. 65); for an analogous picture, see *The Collected Works of C. G. Jung* (New York, 1953-), XII, 245. Reuben Brower, *The Fields of Light* (New York, 1951), pp. 87-88, has noted the implication of the torches. Cf. the symbolic torches in *The Tables of the Law and The Adoration of the Magi* (London, 1904), pp. 35-38.

39. Ellmann, *Identity*, p. 262.

40. *CPlays*, pp. 371, 373.

41. Blake, *Complete Writings*, p. 516.

42. Heinrich Heine, *Pictures of Travel,* tr. Charles Leland (Philadelphia and London, 1863), p. 197.

43. Henn, *The Lonely Tower* (London, 1950), pp. 191, 244; plate opposite p. 240.

44. *V-B,* p. 285; Pater, *Greek Studies* (London, 1910), p. 228.

45. Blake, *Complete Writings,* p. 609; Yates alludes to the passage in *E&Y,* I, 304, and *E&I,* p. 117.

46. King Abundance, Wisdom, and Innocence suggest Crown, Wisdom, and Understanding (or Father, Son, and Holy Spirit) at the peak of the Sephirotic Tree. They are often portrayed as the woman clothed with the Sun, stars above her head and moon at her feet (see Regardie, *Golden Dawn,* I, 25; diagram opposite I, 147), an image related to the Goddess and Child high on the Tree of Life, to which Yeats often alludes. Or the moon itself may be considered the Ark, and Noah—like King Abundance—be identified with the creative spirit moving on the matrix of the waters, and his "consort, Titea," with such maternal or virginal figures as Rhea and Vesta; or again, in the Ark Noah may worship "before the 'body of Adam,' which body is the image of, and a *Creator* itself" (Blavatsky, *Secret Doctrine,* II, 145, 144, 468).

47. *The Upanishads,* tr. Swami Prabhavananda and Frederick Manchester (New York, 1957), pp. 46-47; *E&I,* p. 272.

48. Henry More had described the "whirl-pool-turnings of the lower spright" (*Complete Poems,* p. 134)—essentially Yeats's gyres—in his paraphrastical interpretation of the Delphic Oracle upon Plotinus, one model for Yeats's various descriptions of the journey through the sea of generation to the condition of fire. The speaker of "Sailing to Byzantium" petitions those standing in the "holy fire" to consume his heart away, much as More had said of the blessed, "the purity/ Of holy fire their heart doth then invade ..." (*ibid.,* p. 135). (Henn, *The Lonely Tower,* p. 133, has suggested Yeats's indebtedness to that poem for his own "The Delphic Oracle upon Plotinus.") But Yeats had long known of the myth and the correlated allegorizing of Ulysses' wanderings: in 1899 he had called the sea "the drifting indefinite bitterness of life" and associated it with voyages like that of Oisin (*The Wind Among the Reeds,* p. 90). Since he used Thomas Taylor's translation of Porphyry, he doubtless knew Taylor's appendix "On the Wanderings of Ulysses," *Select Works of Porphyry* (London, 1823), pp. 241 ff.

49. Blake, *Complete Writings,* p. 359.

50. *The King of the Great Clock Tower* (New York, 1935), p. 46.

51. *Yeats and Moore: Their Correspondence,* p. 154.

52. Blake, *Complete Writings,* p. 179.

53. Wade, *Letters,* p. 731. One such formula begins with "Ten parts of celestial slime." "Separate the male from the female, and then each from its earth ... Conjoin after separation in due, harmonic, vital proportion. The soul ... shall restore its dead and deserted body by a wonderful embrace. The conjoined substances shall be warmed by a natural fire in a perfect marriage of spirit and body ..." (*The Works of Thomas Vaughan,* ed. A. E. Waite [London, 1919], p. 30).

54. For Yeats's own symbolic and historical reading of this poem, see Wade, *Letters,* pp. 823-26.

55. *E&Y,* I, 270-71; *E&I,* pp. 467-68. Ribh focuses on a different aspect of the complete process charted in *A Vision:* see *V-B,* p. 102, on "Contests of the Antithetical within Itself," and *V-B,* p. 93, on each smaller phase sinking into its own *primary.*

56. *The Complete Works of Ralph Waldo Emerson,* ed. E. W. Emerson (Boston and New York, 1903-4), II, 292.

57. *Au,* p. 318; *Mythologies,* p. 332.

58. *E&Y,* I, 294.

59. Blake, *Complete Writings,* p. 509.

60. *E&I,* p. 469; Blavatsky, *Secret Doctrine,* II, 357, 403.

61. *CPlays*, p. 210; Henry David Thoreau, *Walden*, pp. 108-9 (in *Complete Works* [Boston and New York, 1919]); *Au*, p. 293.

62. *CP*, p. 223.

63. *The Works of Jacob Behmen*, with figures by William Law (London, 1764), II, 105; "All Souls' Night," *CP*, p. 225.

64. Plotinus, *Enneads*, I, 125; IV, 77; *Works of Behmen*, II, 105.

65. *E&I*, p. 288 (1906).

66. *E&I*, pp. 421-22 (1932).

67. J. Krishnamurti, *Commentaries on Living* (*Third Series*) (New York, 1960), p. 8; *E&Y*, I, 273.

68. *V-B*, pp. 132-33. The earlier and weaker lines—"Show much politeness, gentleness, / Ceremony in this place"—are closer to *A Vision*. See *Letters on Poetry from W. B. Yeats to Dorothy Wellesley* (New York, 1940), p. 178.

69. Pater, *The Renaissance* (London, 1910), p. 208. Wilde had given this idea more of the sexual force Yeats later insisted upon (*Complete Works of Oscar Wilde*, ed. Robert Ross [Boston, (192-)], IV, 34): "The Greeks ... set in the bride's chamber the statue of Hermes or of Apollo, that she might bear children as lovely as the works of art that she looked at in her rapture or her pain." *CPlays*, p. 73; *If I Were Four and Twenty* (Dublin, 1940), p. 14.

70. Pater, *The Renaissance*, p. 75.

71. *The Wind Among the Reeds*, p. 72.

72. *John Sherman and Dhoya* (London, 1891), p. 65. Yeats had included Empson's "Arachne" in *The Oxford Book of Modern Verse* (New York, 1937), p. 416.

73. Pater, *The Renaissance*, p. 75.

74. See, e.g., sonnets XXIII, XXVIII, XXIX, XXX, LIX, and Robert J. Clements, "Eye, Mind, and Hand in Michelangelo's Poetry" *PMLA*, LXIX (Mar., 1954), 324-36.

75. *E&I*, p. 316; "Michael Robartes and the Dancer," *CP*, p. 174.

76. More, *Complete Poems*, pp. 143, 91. For a brief survey of the medieval tradition see John M. Steadman, "Chaucer's Eagle: A Contemplative Symbol," *PMLA*, LXXV (Jun., 1960), 153-59. Yeats slightly misquotes a passage from Shelley's *The Triumph of Life* which has a related meaning (*E&I*, p. 94). A. N. Jeffares quotes several analogous passages from Blake (*W. B. Yeats: Man and Poet* [London, 1949], p. 317), though implying that the imagery is a Blakean creation and considerably over-simplifying Yeats's use of it.

77. *The Complete Works of S. T. Coleridge*, ed. William G. T. Shedd (New York, 1853), III, 231. For Yeats's preoccupation with this motif in Coleridge's poetry, see *E&I*, p. 463.

78. Nietzsche, *Thus Spake Zarathustra*, p. 139 (in *The Complete Works of Friedrich Nietzsche*, ed. Oscar Levy, 18 vols. [Edinburgh and London, 1909-24]).

79. "Upon a House Shaken by the Land Agitation," *CP*, p. 93; "To a Wealthy Man . . . ," *CP*, p. 106.

80. Regardie, *Golden Dawn*, II, 104.

81. *Ibid.*, II, 180.

82. Isaiah 40:31.

83. Vaughan, *Works*, pp. 417-18.

84. Augusta Gregory, *Gods and Fighting Men*, intro. by Yeats (London, 1904), pp. xx, xxi; *CPlays*, pp. 170, 174, 293; Wade, *Letters*, p. 425.

85. *V-B*, p. 191; *E&I*, p. 408n.

86. *The Ten Principal Upanishads*, tr. Shree Purohit Swami and W. B. Yeats (New York, 1937), p. 22.

87. *Complete Poetic and Dramatic Works of Robert Browning* (Boston and New York, 1895), p. 1009. Yeats alludes to the passage in 1896 (*E&I*, p. 112) and echoes it in 1902 (*E&I*, p. 61).

88. *E&I*, pp. 463, 462.

89. *E&I*, p. 291.

90. *Meister Eckhart,* tr. R. B. Blakney (New York, 1957), 206; Percy Bysshe Shelley, "Hymn of Apollo."

91. Yeats preferred to the limited Platonic Ideas the "archetypes of all possible existences whether of man or brute" (*Wheels and Butterflies,* pp. 32-33), drawn from Plotinus (*ibid.,* p. 95).

92. *John Sherman and Dhoya,* p. 116 (cf. Blake, *Complete Writings,* p. 130: "Why a little curtain of flesh on the bed of our desire?"); *Letters on Poetry to Dorothy Wellesley,* pp. 110, 112.

93. See Jung, *Collected Works,* XVI, 317-18.

94. Blake, *Complete Writings,* p. 758.

95. F. A. C. Wilson's reference to "a bitter moral"—*W. B. Yeats and Tradition* (New York, 1958), p. 223—exemplifies his frequent distortion of tone and meaning because of an overriding concern for allegorical substructure.

96. *Wheels and Butterflies,* p. 70.

97. *Works of Behmen,* II, 99.

NOTES TO CHAPTER VII

1. *The Complete Works of Ralph Waldo Emerson,* ed. E. W. Emerson (Boston and New York, 1903-4), II, 10. This aspect of the Vichian view of history Emerson may have found in Cousin: "Study humanity as a whole, first in yourself and in your consciousness, then in that consciousness of the human race which is called history." (Victor Cousin's *Introduction,* cited by Kenneth W. Cameron, *Emerson the Essayist* [Raleigh, N. C., 1945], I, 311.)

2. *The Works of Jacob Behmen,* with figures by William Law (London, 1764), II, 58.

3. *V-B,* pp. 301-2.

4. Plotinus, *The Enneads,* tr. Stephen MacKenna (London, 1917-30), III, 41-47, 49.

5. As Virginia Moore tends to do in *The Unicorn* (New York, 1954), p. 377.

6. Quoted in "Swedenborg, Mediums, and the Desolate Places," in Augusta Gregory, *Visions and Beliefs in the West of Ireland* (New York and London, 1920), II, 339. For an application of the image to the process of "dreaming back" and hence to the motif of purgatory (which I discuss in Chapter XII), see *V-B,* p. 226. Cf. also the description of the separation of individual consciousness, which returns to the spiritual sphere, and the volitional impulses, which remain with the astral shell in *Kama loca,* given by A. P. Sinnett, *Esoteric Buddhism* (Boston, 1888), pp. 152-53.

7. Helena P. Blavatsky, *The Secret Doctrine* (London, 1888), II, 122-23. Yeats used that motif of the mortal and immortal twins in a play of 1884, *Love and Death* (Richard Ellmann, *The Man and the Masks* [New York, 1948], p. 35).

8. *Secret Doctrine,* II, 235.

9. *Au,* p. 53; *1930D,* p. 54; *Au,* pp. 28, 29.

10. *E&I,* p. 448.

11. *Au,* p. 72; J. B. Yeats, *Early Memories* (Dublin, 1923), p. 7.

12. Tate, *On the Limits of Poetry* (New York, 1948), p. 321.

13. *Au,* pp. 286-87.

14. *Letters to the New Island,* ed. Horace Reynolds (Cambridge, Mass., 1934), p. 174.

15. *Ibid.,* pp. 168, 172-73.

16. *Ibid.,* p. 109.

17. *The Letters of W. B. Yeats,* ed. Allan Wade (New York, 1955), pp. 187-88.

18. *Letters to the New Island,* p. 174. He later used the metaphor in reverse to expound the conception of divine influx: "as though a hand were thrust within a hundred gloves, one glove outside another." ("Swedenborg, Mediums, and the Desolate Places," in Gregory, *Visions and Beliefs,* II, 304.)

19. *Letters to the New Island,* pp. 95, 163.

20. *1930D*, p. 7.

21. "The Life of Patrick Sarsfield," *Bookman*, IX (Nov., 1895), 59.

22. "Irish National Literature" (II), *Bookman*, VIII (Aug., 1895), 138. Nevertheless, Yeats could refer with qualified admiration to "Dr. Joyce's careful and impartial and colourless volumes" (Wade, *Letters*, p. 250) and to "Mr. Lecky's great history" ("Irish National Literature" [IV], *Bookman*, IX [Oct., 1895], 21). He had in mind P. W. Joyce, *Old Celtic Romances* and *A Short History of Ireland*, and W. H. Lecky, *A History of Ireland in the Eighteenth Century*.

23. *The Complete Writings of William Blake*, ed. Geoffrey Keynes (London, 1957), p. 600, which Yeats endorsed in "Mr. Standish O'Grady's *Flight of the Eagle*," *Bookman*, XII (Aug., 1897), 123; *Stories from Carleton*, intro. by Yeats (London, 1889), p. xvi.

24. Wade, *Letters*, p. 250 (1895).

25. "Mr. Standish O'Grady's *Flight of the Eagle*," *Bookman*, XII, 123; "Irish National Literature" (II), *Bookman*, VIII, 139.

26. "Mr. Standish O'Grady's *Flight of the Eagle*," *Bookman*, XII, 124; O'Grady, *The Flight of the Eagle* (Dublin, 1897), p. 287. O'Grady alludes to Mangan's version of the Elizabethan poem "Roisin Dubh."

27. "Mr. Standish O'Grady's *Flight of the Eagle*," *Bookman*, XII, 123; *Complete Works of Oscar Wilde*, ed. Robert Ross (Boston, [192-]), IV, 27. O'Grady acknowledges indebtedness to Carlyle and Scott: *The Flight of the Eagle*, v; *Red Hugh's Captivity* (London, 1889), pp. 8, 14. The introduction to the latter book is a fair defense of his method.

28. "Irish National Literature" (II), *Bookman*, VIII, 139. Yeats quotes from Mill, "Michelet's History of France," *Dissertations and Discussions* (London, 1859), II, 138.

29. "Mr. Standish O'Grady's *Flight of the Eagle*," *Bookman*, XII, 123.

30. For a brief account of Michelet's Vichian reliving of history, see Edmund Wilson, *To the Finland Station* (New York, 1940), p. 25.

31. "Mr. Standish O'Grady's *Flight of the Eagle*," *Bookman*, XII, 123.

32. See "Irish National Literature" (I), *Bookman*, VIII, 106; *E&I*, p. 248.

33. *Samhain* (1908), p. 8.

34. *Representative Irish Tales*, ed. Yeats (London, 1891), I, 2.

35. *Stories from Carleton*, p. xvi; "Irish National Literature" (I), *Bookman*, VIII, 107.

36. *Samhain* (1908), p. 8.

37. *E&Y*, I, 278.

38. *Au*, p. 63.

39. *Au*, p. 93.

40. *Au*, p. 280.

41. T. R. Henn, *The Lonely Tower* (London, 1950), p. 98.

42. *E&I*, p. 255.

43. *Au*, p. 279.

44. *Au*, pp. 132-33.

45. Wade, *Letters*, p. 583 (1913).

46. *Au*, p. 288.

47. *P&C*, p. 175.

48. *The Writings of Arthur Hallam*, ed. T. H. Vail Motter (New York, 1943), p. 194.

49. Wade, *Letters*, p. 98.

50. *Au*, p. 53.

51. Augusta Gregory, *Gods and Fighting Men*, intro. by Yeats (London, 1904), pp. xx, xxi.

52. *Au*, p. 304.

53. *P&C*, pp. 99, 115.

54. *E&Y*, I, 415, 357.

55. *E&Y*, I, 273; Arthur Schopenhauer, *The World as Will and Idea*, tr. R. B. Haldane and J. Kemp (London, 1896; 4th ed.), I, 265.

56. *Au*, pp. 164, 165.

57. *E&I*, pp. 254-55. The passage continues: "and he is known from other men by making all he handles like himself, and yet by the unlikeness to himself of all that comes before him in a pure contemplation. It may have been his enemy or his love or his cause that set him dreaming, and certainly the phoenix can but open her young wings in a flaming nest; but all hate and hope vanishes in the dream..." Cf. *World as Will and Idea*, I, 256: if "we give ourselves up to pure will-less knowing, we pass into a world from which everything is absent that influenced our will and moved us so violently through it. This freeing of knowledge lifts us as wholly and entirely away from all that, as do sleep and dreams; happiness and unhappiness have disappeared..."

58. *E&I*, pp. 321, 322.

59. *World as Will and Idea*, I, 328.

60. *E&I*, p. 255.

61. *P&C*, p. 123; *CPlays*, p. 75; Wade, *Letters*, p. 454.

62. See *1930D*, p. 21.

63. *E&I*, pp. 337, 338, 303, 339.

64. Thomas Parkinson, *W. B. Yeats: Self-Critic* (Berkeley, 1951), p. 108.

65. *Shelley's Prose*, ed. D. L. Clark (Albuquerque, 1954), p. 282.

66. *E&I*, pp. 12, 163, 112, 131, 140, 102.

67. *P&C*, p. 113.

68. *Au*, p. 314; *E&I*, pp. 319, 239.

69. *E&I*, p. 339.

70. Algernon Charles Swinburne, *William Blake, A Critical Essay* (London, 1906), p. 146*n*.

71. Blake, *Complete Writings*, p. 613; *E&I*, p. 310.

72. *E&Y*, I, 415; Jacob Boehme, *Six Theosophic Points* (Ann Arbor, 1958), pp. 149, 175.

73. *E&I*, p. 207 (attributed to Patmore in *P&C*, p. 161); *E&I*, p. 351; cf. Patmore, *Principle in Art* (London, 1898), pp. 32-33.

74. Patmore: *Principle in Art*, pp. 31-34, and *The Rod, the Root and the Flower* (London, 1950), p. 146.

75. *Au*, p. 317.

76. *Au*, p. 283; see also Wade, *Letters*, pp. 466, 477 (1906).

77. Patmore, *Principle in Art, and Religio Poetae* (one-vol. ed.; London, 1913), pp. 293-94: "to the eye which is not congenial, the fresh manifestation of genius in almost any kind has something in it alarming and revolting; and it is welcomed with an 'Ugh, ugh! the horrid thing! It's alive!' A man of genius who is also a man of sense will never complain of such a reception from his fellows." The attribution to Plutarch is in *W. B. Yeats and T. Sturge Moore: Their Correspondence 1901-1937*, ed. Ursula Bridge (London, 1953), p. 13 (1907).

78. Percy Bysshe Shelley, *Prometheus Unbound*, I, 627; *Au*, p. 303 (1909).

79. "Remorse for Intemperate Speech," *CP*, p. 249.

80. *E&I*, pp. 350-51.

81. *Mythologies* (New York, 1959), p. 333.

82. *Au*, p. 125.

83. "A Dialogue of Self and Soul," *CP*, p. 232.

84. "Stream and Sun at Glendalough," *CP*, p. 250.

NOTES TO CHAPTER VIII

1. *The Complete Writings of William Blake*, ed. Geoffrey Keynes (London, 1957), p. 516.

2. *Au*, pp. 158-59.

3. See the 1909 diary quoted by A. N. Jeffares, *W. B. Yeats: Man and Poet* (London, 1949), p. 180. Jeffares suggests (*ibid.*, pp. 178-82) that the interest was stimulated by George Moore's attack in *Ave* and by Lily Yeats's interest in the subject; Richard Ellmann suggests (*Yeats: The Man and the Masks* [New York, 1948], pp. 206 ff.) that the family was a refuge from uncertainty.

4. *If I Were Four and Twenty* (Dublin, 1940), pp. 9-10.

5. *On the Boiler* (Dublin, 1939), p. 22.

6. Cf. Louis L. Martz's perceptive discussion of Yeats's relation to more orthodox meditative techniques, *The Poetry of Meditation* (New Haven, 1954), pp. 326-29.

7. Paul Claudel, *L'Otage* (Paris, 1911), pp. 28-29. For Yeats's admiration, see *If I Were Four and Twenty*, p. 3, and Mary Colum, *Life and the Dream* (Garden City, 1947), p. 372.

8. *If I Were Four and Twenty*, p. 13.

9. Soloviev, *The Justification of the Good*, tr. N. A. Duddington (London, 1918), p. 349.

10. *E&I*, p. 210.

11. *E&I*, p. 79.

12. *E&I*, p. 297.

13. For example, the same idea works its way through Kabbalistic thought into Hasidism: see Martin Buber, *Hasidism and Modern Man*, ed. Maurice Friedman (New York, 1958), pp. 105, 187 ff.

14. "Old Gaelic Love Songs," *Bookman*, V (Oct., 1893), 19-20.

15. *If I Were Four and Twenty*, p. 12.

16. *Ibid.*, p. 11. Cf. the "Wine-press of Los," in Blake, *Complete Writings*, p. 513.

17. Claudel, *L'Otage*, p. 27. Yeats noted that in Claudel and Péguy the Eucharist merges with the wheat and vine of the French countryside (*If I Were Four and Twenty*, p. 3).

18. *Au*, p. 5.

19. *V-A*, p. 61.

20. Isaiah 35:1; Blake, *Complete Writings*, p. 148.

21. William Wordsworth, *The Prelude*, Bk. 2, lines 349 ff.; Samuel Taylor Coleridge, *Anima Poetae* (Boston, 1895), 115.

22. For an earlier description of Eastern traditionalism ("the painting of Japan, not having our European Moon to churn its wits...") see *E&I*, p. 225 (1916).

23. Cf. *V-B*, p. 268.

24. See *E&I*, pp. 103-9 (1901). There, as in this poem, Yeats has an eye for the tragic ironies in both porcelain and clay. A simpler use of the metaphor appeared in *The Countess Cathleen* (*CPlays*, p. 29).

25. Yeats's use of such a foil comes, of course, from literary tradition as well as from personal experience. He used it more simply for romantic pathos in *The Countess Cathleen*, as Cathleen says of the gardener (*Poems* [London, 1895], p. 98):

> Pruning time,
> And the slow ripening of his pears and apples,
> For him is a long, heart-moving history.

In *L'Otage* (p. 14), amidst the breaking of nations, occurs this dialogue:

> Coufontaine: Il était temps de nous mettre a l'abri.
> Je reconnais le vent de mon pays.
> Sygne: Quel dommage! Les pommiers étaient si beaux!
> Il ne restera pas un pépin sur l'arbre.

26. Quoted in *E&I*, p. 84 (1900); see *Selected Works of Porphyry*, tr. Thomas Taylor (London, 1823), p. 185.

27. *E&Y*, 61.

28. *Select Works of Porphyry*, p. 181.

29. Cf. *E&I*, p. 87 (1900).

30. Blake, *Complete Writings*, p. 154.

31. Claudel, *L'Otage*, p. 54.

32. For a more explicit image of the blindmen, see "A Dialogue of Self and Soul," *CP*, p. 232, or "On a Political Prisoner," *CP*, p. 181; for Yeats's possession of Moreau's "Women and Unicorns," see *The Letters of W. B. Yeats*, ed. Allan Wade (New York, 1955), p. 865.

33. "The Phases of the Moon," *CP*, p. 161.

34. "Ego Dominus Tuus," *CP*, p. 159.

35. *Au*, p. 200.

36. *Au*, p. 285.

37. *P&C*, p. 161.

38. Coventry Patmore, *Principle in Art, and Religio Poetae* (one-vol. ed.; London, 1913), pp. 244, 290.

39. As Richard Ellmann has suggested, *The Identity of Yeats* (New York, 1954), p. 223.

40. *Mythologies* (New York, 1959), p. 342.

NOTES TO CHAPTER IX

1. *1930D*, pp. 54-55.

2. *Wheels and Butterflies* (New York, 1935), p. 98.

3. *1930D*, p. 10.

4. *Wheels and Butterflies*, p. 7.

5. *E&I*, p. 428 (1932).

6. *Further Letters of John Butler Yeats*, selected by Lennox Robinson (Dundrum, 1930), pp. 57 ff.

7. *Ideals in Ireland*, ed. Augusta Gregory (London, 1901), pp. 105, 106.

8. *Letters to the New Island*, ed. Horace Reynolds (Cambridge, Mass., 1934), pp. 90-91.

9. See *The Letters of W. B. Yeats*, ed. Allan Wade (New York, 1955), pp. 154*n*., 156.

10. *Representative Irish Tales* (London, 1891), I, 2-3, 11.

11. *Ibid.*, I, 5-6, 7.

12. Inscribed in Quinn's copy of the collection, quoted by Allan Wade, *A Bibliography of the Writings of W. B. Yeats* (London, 1951), p. 214.

13. Gregory, *Gods and Fighting Men*, intro. by Yeats (London, 1904), pp. xxii-xxiii.

14. *The King of the Great Clock Tower* (New York, 1935), p. 27.

15. "Ireland 1921-1931," *Spectator*, CXLVIII (Jan., 1932), 137.

16. *Idem.*

17. Seanad Eirann, *Parliamentary Debates*, V, 434-43, contains Yeats's speech, and V, 443-80, the angry debate that followed.

18. *P&C*, pp. 192-93.

19. See Ezra Pound, *Guide to Kulchur* (London, 1938), p. 155.

20. Seanad Eirann, *Parliamentary Debates*, V, 443.

21. Wade, *Letters*, p. 295.

22. *W. B. Yeats and T. Sturge Moore: Their Correspondence 1901-1937*, ed. Ursula Bridge (London, 1953), p. 114.

23. *CW*, V, 27 ff.

24. See Wade, *A Bibliography of Yeats*, pp. 38-39, for some original titles. John V. Kelleher called my attention to the prototype.

25. *The Complete Writings of William Blake*, ed. Geoffrey Keynes (London, 1957), p. 342.

26. *CW*, V, 37-38.

27. *1930D*, p. 54.

28. *E&I*, p. 78 (1900).

29. *P&C*, p. 41.

30. Alfred Tennyson, "Merlin and the Gleam."

31. *1930D*, p. 8.

32. Cf. an early draft of "The Tower": "Why could no Rabbi say / That Eternal Man / Rested the seventh day" (Richard Ellmann, *The Identity of Yeats* [New York, 1954], p. 225*n*.).

33. *The Letters of John Keats*, ed. Maurice B. Forman (London, 1952; 4th ed.), pp. 334-35. The tone with which Yeats evokes the symbolic paradise in the last part of "The Tower" also suggests Keats (*Letters*, p. 102): "...almost any Man may like the spider spin from his own inwards his own airy Citadel—the points of leaves and twigs on which the spider begins his work are few, and she fills the air with a beautiful circuiting. Man should be content with as few points to tip with the fine Web of his Soul, and weave a tapestry empyrean full of symbols for his spiritual eye, of softness for his spiritual touch, of space for his wandering, of distinctness for his luxury." Cf. Yeats's use of the spider to describe subjective men, *Au*, p. 116.

34. *P&C*, p. 123; *Au*, p. 311.

35. *1930D*, pp. 5-6.

36. *1930D*, p. 4.

37. *1930D*, p. 28. Though here distorting Swift's thought to bring it closer to his own, he qualified these views for publication (see *Wheels and Butterflies*, pp. 16-20); and he was at least correct in finding in Swift, who partly followed Polybius, a strong suspicion that the irony of history might require the rise and fall of successive civilizations. See Jonathan Swift, *A Tale of a Tub, with Other Early Works*, ed. Herbert Davis (Oxford, 1939), pp. 217, 228 ff.

38. *1930D*, p. 28.

39. *1930D*, p. 55.

40. Collingwood, *An Autobiography* (London, 1939), pp. 113, 114, 115. Cf. Benedetto Croce, *History as the Story of Liberty*, tr. Sylvia Sprigge (New York, 1941), pp. 19-20: "the present state of my mind constitutes the material, and consequently the documentation for an historical judgment.... Man is a microcosm, not in the natural sense, but in the historical sense..." But Yeats would reject Croce's sharp distinction between the historical imagination and the "poetic fancy" (*ibid.*, p. 127).

41. *CPlays*, p. 383.

42. *1930D*, p. 6.

43. *Wheels and Butterflies*, pp. 7-8.

44. *P&C*, p. 95.

45. "The New Irish Library," *Bookman*, X (June, 1896), 83.

46. *1930D*, p. 6.

47. *1930D*, pp. 17, 41, 42.

48. *1930D*, pp. 17-18.

49. *V-B*, pp. 214-15. The passages occur in what Yeats called "an admirable and exciting book," D. T. Suzuki, *Essays in Zen Buddhism, First Series* (London, 1927), pp. 234, 241*n*.

50. Wade, *Letters*, p. 922. See Suzuki, *Essays in Zen Buddhism*, pp. 47, 51, 216, 260-61.

51. *V-B* p. 215.

52. *E&I*, pp. 397, 398 (1931).

53. *1930D*, p. 41.

54. Oliver St. John Gogarty, *Wild Apples*, intro. by Yeats (Dublin, 1930), sig. A-7.

55. *E&I*, p. 399.

56. *E&I*, pp. 401, 402.

57. Gogarty, *Wild Apples*, sig. A-6–A-6ᵛ.

58. *The King of the Great Clock Tower*, p. 26.

59. Wade, *Letters*, p. 773.

60. *Wheels and Butterflies*, pp. 21-22.

61. *V-B*, pp. 145 ff., 293 ff.

62. *Wheels and Butterflies*, p. 7.

63. *Wheels and Butterflies*, pp. 22-23.

64. *V-B*, pp. 270, 281, 291. With the Asiatic "flower-like intricacy" compare the Persian decorations (*V-B*, p. 281) which are *primary*, and which Yeats found in Strzygowski.

65. *1930D*, pp. 51, 54. Cf. *Wheels and Butterflies*, p. 11.

66. *Wheels and Butterflies*, p. 23.

67. *Ibid.*, p. 27.

68. Samuel Taylor Coleridge, *Biographia Literaria*, ed. John Shawcross (Oxford, 1907), I, 201; *1930D*, p. 40.

69. "Rosa Alchemica," *Savoy*, No. 2 (Apr., 1896), p. 59.

70. Blake, *Complete Writings*, p. 766; *John Sherman and Dhoya* (London, 1891), p. 141.

71. *E&I*, p. 339.

72. *On the Boiler*, p. 22.

73. *E&Y*, I, 244.

74. *The Complete Works of Ralph Waldo Emerson*, ed. E. W. Emerson (Boston and New York, 1903-4), III, 37; *Wheels and Butterflies*, pp. 16-17.

75. *On the Boiler*, p. 22.

76. *E&I*, pp. 80 ff. (1900), contains a lengthy discussion of such symbolism. Alastor, for example, "passed in his boat along a river in a cave; and when for the last time he felt the presence of the spirit he loved and followed, it was when he watched his image in a silent well; and when he died it was where a river fell into 'an abysmal chasm'..." (p. 80). Alastor's apostrophe to the stream (lines 502 ff.) makes explicit the kind of symbolism Yeats's first stanza leaves implicit:

> "O stream!
> Whose source is inaccessibly profound,
> Whither do thy mysterious waters tend?
> Thou imagest my life. Thy darksome stillness,
> Thy dazzling waves, thy loud and hollow gulfs,
> Thy searchless fountain, and invisible course
> Have each their type in me..."

77. *Yeats and Moore: Their Correspondence*, p. 69 (1926).

78. *The Celtic Twilight* (*CW*, V, 28) foreshadows this passage. Yeats talked to an old man about Mary Hynes, and "about a poem in Irish, Raftery...made about her, and how it said, 'there is a strong cellar in Ballylee.' He said the strong cellar was the great hole where the river sank underground, and he brought me to a deep pool, where an otter hurried away under a grey boulder, and told me that many fish came up out of the dark water at early morning 'to taste the fresh water coming down from the hills.'"

79. Quoted by Joseph Hone, *W. B. Yeats, 1865-1939* (London, 1942), p. 455.

80. *John Sherman and Dhoya*, p. 65.

81. For Raftery's phrase, see *P&C*, p. 180.

NOTES TO CHAPTER X

1. *The Complete Writings of William Blake*, ed. Geoffrey Keynes (London, 1957), p. 152.

2. *E&I*, pp. 352-53 (1913).

3. Walter Pater, *Greek Studies* (London, 1910), p. 193 (cf. also pp. 220, 225, 251); Thucydides, *History of the Peloponnesian War*, I, vi.

4. *P&C*, pp. v-vi.

5. See *The Collected Works of C. G. Jung* (New York, 1953-), V, 249 ff.

6. "Into the Twilight," *CP*, pp. 56-57.

7. *CPlays*, p. 99.

8. Bespaloff, *On the Iliad*, tr. Mary McCarthy (New York, 1947), p. 105.

9. Nietzsche, *The Birth of Tragedy*, p. 61 (in *The Complete Works of Friedrich Nietzsche*, ed. Oscar Levy, 18 vols. [Edinburgh and London, 1909-24]).

10. W. M. Flinders Petrie, *The Revolutions of Civilisation* (London, 1911), pp. 4-5.

11. *Au*, p. 200.

12. A. N. Jeffares, *W. B. Yeats: Man and Poet* (London, 1949), p. 225. Symons' poem dates from 1897; Yeats's "The Hosting of the Sidhe" was published in 1893 and "The Secret Rose" in 1896.

13. *The Wind Among the Reeds* (London, 1899), p. 65.

14. *The King of the Great Clock Tower* (New York, 1935), p. 21. Yeats misremembers Heine's description as being of Salome. See *Atta Troll*, XIX.

15. Jacob Grimm, *Deutsche Mythologie* (Berlin, 1876; 4th ed.), I, 234-37, 526; II, 735, 778, 882 ff.; III, 282, 420. Grimm is also cited by Thomas Wright in Richard de Ledrede, *A Contemporary Narrative of the Proceedings against Dame Alice Kyteler*, ed. Wright (London, 1843), p. iv. Grimm assimilates Herodias, Diana, and other goddesses; Charles Leland, in *Aradia, or the Gospel of Witches* (London, 1899), 102-3, speaks of the association but questions the derivation from the Herodias of the New Testament.

16. See a report of the dance in a magazine which Yeats read and to which he contributed: G(eorge) N(orman), " 'Electra' and 'Salome,' " *The Mask*, I (Apr., 1908), 24b. Cf. also Yeats's memory of "some Herodiade of our theatre, dancing seemingly alone in her narrow moving luminous circle" (*Au*, p. 193).

17. *V-B*, p. 273.

18. Pater, *The Renaissance* (London, 1910), pp. 115-16.

19. Augusta Gregory, *Visions and Beliefs in the West of Ireland* (New York and London, 1920), I, 272.

20. Richard de Ledrede, *A Contemporary Narrative*, p. iii. According to Jeffares (*W. B. Yeats*, p. 328), Yeats read of this case in Carrigan's *History of the Diocese of Ossory* and St. John D. Seymour's *Irish Witchcraft and Demonology* (Baltimore, 1913), and also (*W. B. Yeats*, p. 226) read the British Museum Ms. which gives an account of the case. It seems probable that he consulted Wright's edition of that Ms., which Seymour mentions (*Irish Witchcraft*, p. 25).

21. Raphael Holinshed's *Chronicle of Ireland* (London, 1587), p. 69, cited in de Ledrede, *A Contemporary Narrative*, p. 46, and also in Seymour, *Irish Witchcraft*, p. 29.

22. *V-B*, p. 268.

23. *Select Works of Porphyry*, tr. Thomas Taylor (London, 1823), p. 197.

24. Plotinus, *The Enneads*, tr. Stephen MacKenna (London, 1917-30), III, 23; *The Works of Plato*, ed. Thomas Taylor (London, 1804), II, 622-23.

25. *CPlays*, p. 403; *CP*, pp. 251 ff.; "O'Donnell's Kern," in *Silva Gadelica*, ed. Standish H. O'Grady (London, 1892), pp. 317, 318. John V. Kelleher suggests a further comparison with "Manannan at Play," in Gregory, *Gods and Fighting Men* (London, 1904), pp. 104 ff.

26. *The Wind Among the Reeds*, pp. 89-90.

27. *E&Y*, I, 238.

28. *E&I*, p. 284.

29. Honoré de Balzac, *The Edition Définitive of the Comédie Humaine*, tr. G.B. Ives and others (Philadelphia, c. 1896-1900), XLVI, 335; XLII, 288. For Yeats's interest in Séraphita's numerology and in Balzac's suspicion of the "unreality" of number and movement—from the perspective of stanza three of "The Statues," see *E&I*, p. 443.

30. Pater, *Plato and Platonism* (London, 1910), p. 72; *The Renaissance*, pp. 222, 218, 219.

31. *Au*, pp. 304-5.

32. Blake, *Complete Writings*, p. 778.

33. *E&Y*, I, 398-99; *E&I*, p. 292.

34. See Blake, *Complete Writings*, pp. 461, 562, 586, 592 ff.

35. T. Sturge Moore, *Albert Durer* (London, 1905), 289-90.

36. *Au*, p. 304.

37. Blake, *Complete Writings*, p. 355, quoted by Yeats, *E&I*, p. 139.

38. Oswald Spengler, *The Decline of the West*, tr. Charles F. Atkinson (London, 1926-28), I, 63.

39. Pater, *The Renaissance*, p. 216; *Au*, p. 305.

40. Heinrich Heine, *Pictures of Travel*, tr. Charles Leland (Philadelphia and London, 1863), p. 384.

41. *Au*, p. 305.

42. "Florentine Nights," in *The Prose Writings of Heinrich Heine*, ed. Havelock Ellis (London, 1887), p. 184.

43. Spengler, *The Decline of the West*, I, 85, 58.

44. Pater, *Greek Studies*, p. 260.

45. Nietzsche, *Will to Power*, as translated by George A. Morgan, *What Nietzsche Means* (Cambridge, Mass., 1941), 334-35. Yeats himself summarized much of "The Statues" in *On the Boiler* (Dublin, 1939), p. 37: "There are moments when I am certain that art must once again accept those Greek proportions which carry into plastic art the Pythagorean numbers, those faces which are divine because all there is empty and measured. Europe was not born when Greek galleys defeated the Persian hordes at Salamis, but when the Doric studios sent out those broad-backed marble statues against the multiform, vague, expressive Asiatic sea, they gave to the sexual instinct of Europe its goal, its fixed type."

46. Théophile Gautier, "Ne touchez pas aux marbres."

47. See *V-B*, pp. 202-3; *On the Boiler*, p. 22; *E&I*, p. 466.

48. Spengler, *The Decline of the West*, I, 65, 63.

49. Pater, *The Renaissance*, p. 205. On the relation to Hegel, see Ruth C. Child, *The Aesthetic of Walter Pater* (New York, 1940), pp. 61-66.

50. Pater, *The Renaissance*, pp. 205, 206, 216.

51. *V-B*, p. 277.

52. *V-B*, p. 271. See also *The Letters of W. B. Yeats*, ed. Allan Wade (New York, 1955), p. 911: "In reading the third stanza remember the influence on modern sculpture and on the great seated Buddha of the sculptors who followed Alexander." In tracing the development from Phidian to Gandhara sculpture as symbol of the shift from humanistic to transcendental culture which occurred simultaneously in Europe and the East, Yeats does elliptically what Andre Malraux does with greater explicitness in *The Psychology of Art*, tr. Stuart Gilbert (New York, 1949), II, 15-65.

53. Cf. *V-B*, p. 203. The analysis of the poem by F. A. C. Wilson—*Yeats's Iconography* (London, 1960), pp. 299-301—errs in contrasting Grimalkin (as symbol of modern objectivity) with Buddha (as symbol of subjective religion). Throughout both of his volumes, Wilson's insistence on Yeats's allegiance to a "subjective" tradition confuses matters by using "subjective" to refer not only to states that are *antithetical* (or "subjective" in Yeats's sense) but also to certain states that are *primary* (or "objective" in Yeats's sense). Buddha is for Yeats spiritual *primary*, hence "objective."

54. Spengler, *The Decline of the West*, I, 347. Yeats would have reread this passage in Wyndham Lewis, *Time and Western Man* (London, 1927), p. 288 (see *W. B. Yeats and T. Sturge Moore: Their Correspondence 1901-1937*, ed. Ursula Bridge [London, 1953], p. 122).

55. *Au*, p. 61. The immediately preceding lines foreshadow this stanza so closely that they have led explication astray. (Vivienne Koch, for example, in *W. B. Yeats, The Tragic Phase* [London, 1951], 61 ff., has seen the poem as a result of Yeats's starting to celebrate an essentially "thoughtless" wholeness and then surprisingly exalting abstract calculation.) Yeats contemplates a portrait of Morris: "Its grave wide-open

eyes, like the eyes of some dreaming beast, remind me of the open eyes of Titian's 'Ariosto,' while the broad vigorous body suggests a mind that has no need of the intellect to remain sane, though it give itself to every phantasy: the dreamer of the middle ages. It is 'the fool of fairy . . . wide and wild as a hill,' the resolute European image that yet half remembers Buddha's motionless meditation . . ." The passage looks back upon Buddha from a European perspective (via the *primary* "fool of fairy" discussed in "The Queen and the Fool," *CW*, V, 158); the third stanza of the poem adopts the perspective of Indian art and merely glances at parallel European developments.

56. T. R. Henn, *The Lonely Tower* (London, 1950), p. 178, suggests a feline image; despite Yeats's earlier celebration of the subjective spider, a statement of 1937 (Wade, *Letters*, p. 892) testifies to the extreme nature of his late reaction against this: "You say that poetry cannot be changed but all my life I have tried to change it. Goethe said that all our modern poetry is wrong because subjective; and in the part in *The Battle of the Books* connected with the fable of the bee and the spider Swift has said the same. All my life I have tried to get rid of modern subjectivity . . ."

57. *1930D*, pp. 42, 50-51, 54. John V. Kelleher has suggested that "the filthy modern tide" is dirtied by that "excrement" and that through Berkeley the Irish can lay claim to the only modern classical thought and so ascend above the tide.

58. *Au*, p. 293. Cf. *On the Boiler*, p. 36.

59. Reprinted in George Russell, *The Living Torch* (New York, 1938), pp. 134-35.

60. *Book of Wisdom*, 11:20: "Thou hast ordered all things by Measure and Number and Weight"; Helena P. Blavatsky, *The Secret Doctrine* (London, 1888), II, 234, 235. As Yeats may have known, the same passage is echoed in Dürer's manuscript book, in support of artistic measurement: see Sir Martin Conway, *The Literary Remains of Albrecht Dürer* (Cambridge, Eng., 1889), p. 174.

61. P. Browne, ed., *Collected Works of Padraic H. Pearse* (New York, 1917), p. xix.

62. See, e.g., *The Voyage of Bran*, ed. Kuno Meyer, with essays by Alfred Nutt (London, 1895-97), II, 107; P. W. Joyce, *A Short History of Ireland* (London, 1893), pp. 123-26.

63. Nietzsche, *Thoughts Out of Season* (in *The Complete Nietzsche*), II, 99.

64. *P&C*, p. 175; *Letters to the New Island*, ed. Horace Reynolds (Cambridge, Mass., 1934), p. 174.

65. Blake, *Complete Writings*, 579-80; see Yeats's quotation, *E&I*, p. 121.

66. *E&I*, p. 121.

67. Plotinus, *Enneads*, III, 22.

68. Bespaloff, *On the Iliad*, p. 105.

69. Spengler, *The Decline of the West*, I, 183, 78.

70. *1930D*, p. 15.

71. *On the Boiler*, p. 29.

72. Berdyaev, *The Meaning of History* (New York, 1936), pp. 38, 21, 22.

73. *Ibid.*, p. 41.

74. *1930D*, p. 54.

75. Quoted by Harry T. Moore, *The Intelligent Heart* (New York, 1954), p. 174.

76. *P&C*, p. 115.

NOTES TO CHAPTER XI

1. Seanad Eirann, *Parliamentary Debates*, V, 442.

2. *The Letters of W. B. Yeats*, ed. Allan Wade (New York, 1955), p. 805; Honoré de Balzac, *The Edition Définitive of the Comédie Humaine*, tr. G. B. Ives and others (Philadelphia, c. 1896-1900), XLVI, 334.

3. "In Memory of Major Robert Gregory," *CP*, p. 130.

4. W. H. Auden, "In Memory of W. B. Yeats."

5. See *The King of the Great Clock Tower* (New York, 1935), p. 29.

6. Edouard Schuré, *From Sphinx to Christ*, tr. Eve Martin (London, n.d.), p. 259. For Yeats's comments on the historical meaning of woman and arrow, see *Mythologies* (New York, 1959), p. 340; *Au*, pp. 223-25, 342-44; Wade, *Letters*, pp. 266-67; A. N. Jeffares, *W. B. Yeats: Man and Poet* (London, 1949), pp. 105-7. Cf. Goblet d'Alviella's comments on such images, *The Migration of Symbols* (Westminster, 1894), pp. 152-57.

7. *Au*, p. 120; *V-B*, p. 269.

8. Quoted by Yeats, *Au*, p. 190.

9. *The King of the Great Clock Tower*, p. 30; *Au*, p. 125.

10. For many literary uses of the idea of Irish satirists' rhyming rats to death, see *A New Variorum Edition of Shakespeare*, ed. H. H. Furness *et al.* (Philadelphia, 1871-1956), VIII, 155n.

11. *The King of the Great Clock Tower*, p. 30. The identity of slayer and slain is also in the myth upon which Yeats drew: "the Tree as Mother killing the Tree as Son" (*Au*, p. 344). For Jung's comment on this myth see his *Collected Works* (New York, 1953-   ), V, 423-24.

12. Wade, *Letters*, pp. 808-9.

13. *Ibid.*, p. 819.

14. *Au*, pp. 199-200. For a relation to Huysmans' doctrine of substitution, see Michael Fixler, "Yeats's 'Rosicrucian' Stories and Huysmans," *PMLA*, LXXIV (Sept., 1959), 468-69.

15. Arthur Schopenhauer, *The World as Will and Idea*, tr. R. B. Haldane and J. Kemp (London, 1896; 4th ed.), I, 457-58.

16. *Maha-Parinivvana Sutra;* Yeats, ed., *The Oxford Book of Modern Verse* (New York, 1937), p. xxxiii.

17. See Yeats's discussion of the poem in 1900, *E&I*, pp. 73-74. For later quota-tions see *E&I*, p. 420, and *1930D*, pp. 46-47.

18. *E&I*, p. 215 (1903).

19. *Oxford Book of Modern Verse*, pp. xx-xxi.

20. "The Ghost of Roger Casement," *CP*, p. 304; "Under Ben Bulben," *CP*, p. 341.

21. Wade, *Letters*, p. 710 (1926).

22. *1930D*, p. 7.

23. *Letters on Poetry from W. B. Yeats to Dorothy Wellesley* (New York, 1940), pp. 64-65 (1936).

24. *E&I*, p. 524 (1937).

25. Wade, *Letters*, p. 322 (1899); *E&I*, pp. 379, 378 (1902).

26. *CW*, V, 71-72.

27. "The Spirit Medium," *CP*, p. 315.

28. "Three Marching Songs," *CP*, p. 327. The line in "The Night before Larry Was Stretched": "He kicked, too, but that was all pride."

29. *Au*, p. 132 (1922). He later included the translation, by James Stephens, in *The Oxford Book of Modern Verse*, pp. 220-21.

30. Quoted in *E&I*, pp. 375-76 (1902); I have not traced the quotation.

31. Richard Ellmann has noted the indebtedness to Frank O'Connor in *The Identity of Yeats* (New York, 1954), p. 194. Yeats included "Kilcash" in *The Oxford Book of Modern Verse*, p. 406. In O'Connor's version "Last Lines" ends: "My fathers followed theirs before Christ was crucified" (*The Fountain of Magic* [London, 1939], p. 63). Yeats quoted the line, slightly altered, in *The King of the Great Clock Tower*, pp. 25-26, and kept it in the first person in the early stages of his own poem (*Letters on Poetry to Dorothy Wellesley*, p. 131).

32. *The Works of John Ruskin*, ed. E. T. Cook and A. Wedderburn (London, 1903-12), XVII, 40. Some months after writing this poem, Yeats recalled having once violently argued with his father over *Unto this Last*, but—despite this parallel—claimed that he did not "remember a word" of the essay (*On the Boiler* [Dublin, 1939], p. 14). However, Ruskin was running in his mind: he considered *Fors Clavigera* to be

comparable to *On the Boiler* (*Letters on Poetry to Dorothy Wellesley*, pp. 163, 164).

33. *Au*, p. 10.

34. See *The Pepys Ballads*, ed. Hyder Rollins (Cambridge, Mass., 1929), I, 102.

35. Louis MacNeice, *The Poetry of W. B. Yeats* (London, 1941), p. 172.

36. "Alternative Song for the Severed Head...," *CP*, p. 279.

37. *The Wanderings of Oisin* (London, 1889), p. 32.

38. See T. R. Henn, *The Lonely Tower* (London, 1950), pp. 1, 238.

39. *E&I*, p. 493 (1936).

40. "Alternative Song for the Severed Head...," *CP*, p. 279.

41. Though fresher and more controlled, Yeats's lines,

> That is Heaven's part, our part
> To murmur name upon name,
> As a mother names her child
> When sleep at last has come
> On limbs that had run wild.
> What is it but nightfall?
> No, no, not night but death...

contain the memory of Johnson's rhetoric:

> A mother, and forget?
> Nay! all her children's fate
> Ireland remembers yet,
> With love insatiate.
> She hears the heavy bells:
> Hears, and with passionate breath
> Eternally she tells
> A rosary of death.
>
> .   .   .   .   .   .
> Not his, to hail the dawn:
> His but the herald's part.
> Be ours to see withdrawn
> Night from our Mother's heart.

42. *CW*, V, 124.

43. *CW*, V, 89.

44. *The Complete Writings of William Blake*, ed. Geoffrey Keynes (London, 1957), p. 179.

45. "Demon and Beast," *CP*, p. 184.

46. *E&I*, p. 85 (1900); see *E&I*, p. 84, for correlation of the Witch with the Naiad and soul in Porphyry's treatise on the cave of the nymphs.

47. *V-B*, p. 191; Wade, *Letters*, p. 805.

48. Letter to Ethel Mannin, quoted by Ellmann, *Identity*, p. 297.

49. Yeats knew Dobson's "Ars Victrix," and also Alfred Noyes's "Art" (a much freer imitation of Gautier's "L'Art"), whatever his knowledge of the original (Wade, *Letters*, pp. 749, 412).

50. Edwin Arnold, *Poetical Works* (New York, 1883), p. 149.

51. Hebrews 4:9; A. H. Palmer, *Life and Letters of Samuel Palmer* (London, 1892), p. 16; Yeats quoted the passage in 1896 (*E&I*, p. 125).

52. See "Drumcliff and Rosses," *CW*, V, 127-28.

NOTES TO CHAPTER XII

1. *The Complete Writings of William Blake*, ed. Geoffrey Keynes (London, 1957), p. 797. For Yeats's early interpretation of this aphorism, see Augusta Gregory, *Cuchulain of Muirthemne* (London, 1902), p. xiii.

2. James Joyce, *Ulysses* (New York, 1934), p. 385.

3. "Red Hanrahan's Song about Ireland," *CP*, p. 79.

4. "Another Song of a Fool," *CP*, p. 167.

5. "Vacillation," *CP*, p. 247.

6. Walter Pater, *The Renaissance* (London, 1910), p. 97.

7. *Au*, p. 116.

8. *Stories from Carleton* (London, 1889), p. xvi. Yeats called Carleton's account of his pilgrimage "a most wonderful piece of work" (*ibid.*, p. xiv). He also knew Calderon's *St. Patrick's Purgatory*, which he considered for the Abbey Theatre (*Beltaine* [May, 1899], p. 7), and Renan's statement that visions seen by pilgrims to Lough Derg, "once visions of the pagan underworld," gave Europe "new symbols of a more abundant penitence" and provided the framework of the *Divine Comedy* (*E&I*, p. 185 [1897]).

9. Carleton, *Traits and Stories of the Irish Peasantry* (Dublin, 1852), p. 252: "His eye would roll about from one person to another while fingering his beads, with an expression of humour something like delight beaming from his fixed, steady countenance; and when anything that would have been particularly worthy of a joke met his glance, I could perceive a tremulous twinkle of the eye intimating his inward enjoyment."

10. "A Drunken Man's Praise of Sobriety," *CP*, p. 310.

11. *CPlays*, p. 436.

12. Quoted by Erich Heller, *The Disinherited Mind* (Cambridge, Eng., 1952), p. 130. Cf. *V-A*, p. xiii: "I murmured, as I have countless times, 'I have been part of it always and there is maybe no escape, forgetting and returning life after life like an insect in the roots of the grass.' But murmured it without terror, in exultation almost."

13. "Ego Dominus Tuus," *CP*, p. 159.

14. *Mythologies* (New York, 1959), pp. 354, 353, 356, 357 (1917).

15. *CPlays*, p. 380.

16. I Corinthians 15:51-52.

17. *E&I*, p. 239 (1910).

18. *Au*, p. 319.

19. Nietzsche, *Thoughts Out of Season*, II, 14 (in *The Complete Works of Friedrich Nietzsche*, ed. Oscar Levy, 18 vols. [Edinburgh and London, 1909-24]).

20. *Mythologies*, p. 347 (1917).

21. "*Transmutemini, transmutemini, de lapidibus mortuis in lapides vivos philosophicos.*" See *The Works of Thomas Vaughan*, ed. A. E. Waite (London, 1919), p. 98n. and Waite, *The Real History of the Rosicrucians* (London, 1887), pp. 402-3.

22. Arthur Schopenhauer, *The World as Will and Idea*, tr. R. B. Haldane and J. Kemp (London, 1896; 4th ed.), I, 359.

23. *Au*, p. 165 (1922).

24. *Idem*.

25. Luke 12:49. Cf. Leo Tolstoy, *Complete Works* (Boston, 1905), XX, 241. For Yeats's reading of this work and its major influence on *Where There Is Nothing* (the trial of the forces of Law by the gospel of Love, in Act II), see *Au*, p. 275.

26. *Mythologies*, p. 365 (1917).

27. *Au*, p. 286 (1909).

28. "One woman used to repeat as often as possible that to paint pictures or to write poetry in this age was to fiddle while Rome was burning" (*Samhain* [1908], p. 10). Cf. the later memory in *The Oxford Book of Modern Verse* (New York, 1937), p. xi.

29. *E&I*, p. 254 (1907).

30. *Au*, p. 196 (1922).

31. *Letters on Poetry from W. B. Yeats to Dorothy Wellesley* (New York, 1940), p. 13 (1935).

32. *1930D*, pp. 8, 9.

33. Nietzsche, *The Birth of Tragedy* (in *The Complete Nietzsche*), pp. 127, 60-61.

34. "The Well at the World's End," *Bookman*, XI (Nov., 1896), 37. Thomas

Dume ("W. B. Yeats: A Study of his Reading," unpub. diss. [Temple Univ., 1950]) has suggested as Yeats's source a sentence given in Maurice Maeterlinck, *Ruysbroeck and the Mystics*, tr. Jane T. Stoddart (London, 1894), p. 135: "Out of all sufferings and all renunciations the man will draw for himself an inward joy; he will resign himself into the hands of God, and will rejoice to suffer in promoting God's glory."

35. *E&I*, pp. 336 (1910), 354 (1913).

36. *The Poetical Works of Matthew Arnold*, ed. C. B. Tinker and H. F. Lowry (London, 1950), p. xviii.

37. *Letters on Poetry to Dorothy Wellesley*, p. 126.

38. *V-B*, p. 28.

39. *E&I*, p. 337.

40. *On the Boiler* (Dublin, 1939), p. 35. For "Energy is Eternal Delight" see Blake, *Complete Writings*, p. 149.

41. *V-B*, p. 302.

42. Blake's comment on "Il Penseroso," *Complete Writings*, p. 619.

43. Percy Bysshe Shelley, "The Moon," from which Yeats quoted in *E&I*, p. 92; *Complete Works of Oscar Wilde*, ed. Robert Ross (Boston, [192-]), V, 29-30 (appendix to vol.); *E&Y*, I, 277.

44. Carpenter, *Civilisation—Its Cause and Cure* (London, 1889), pp. 46-47. For Yeats's reading of this, see *Letters to the New Island*, ed. Horace Reynolds (Cambridge, Mass., 1934), p. 100.

45. "The Three Witches," *Savoy*, No. 6 (Oct., 1896), p. 75.

46. Cf. Eliot's "Rhapsody on a Windy Night," with its Laforguean bitter lunacy, its piercing images of crooked pin, twisted skeleton, and crab's claw. But as early as 1891 a character in "John Sherman" had played with his "hard, crystalline thoughts" as "with so many bone spilikens" (*John Sherman and Dhoya* [London, 1891], p. 117), and Yeats saw Florence Farr's contrasting mental states—passionate unity and heterogeneous, destructive curiosity—in lunar terms as Demeter's golden sheaf and a heap of spilikens (*Au*, p. 75). Cf. also *Oxford Book of Modern Verse*, pp. xix-xxi, on bone as a modern symbol.

47. *A Full Moon in March* (London, 1935), p. vi.

48. *V-B*, p. 245.

49. *Mythologies*, p. 332.

50. *CPlays*, p. 400.

51. *CPlays*, p. 353.

52. *E&Y*, I, 273.

53. *CPlays*, p. 396.

54. *The Letters of W. B. Yeats*, ed. Allan Wade (New York, 1955), p. 817 (1933).

55. Blake, *Complete Writings*, p. 552.

56. *E&Y*, I, 303.

57. *On the Boiler*, p. 22.

58. *Au*, p. 277.

59. *CPlays*, p. 402.

60. *CPlays*, p. 403; Nietzsche, *Thus Spake Zarathustra* (in *The Complete Nietzsche*), p. 398.

61. *Thus Spake Zarathustra*, p. 396.

62. Sir James Frazer, *The Golden Bough* (London and New York, 1922; one-vol. ed.), p. 349.

63. Helena P. Blavatsky, *The Secret Doctrine* (London, 1888), I, 398, 396.

64. *A Full Moon in March*, pp. v-vi; *Secret Doctrine*, I, 386, 387.

65. *E&I*, p. 91.

66. *E&I*, pp. 92-93.

67. *A Full Moon in March*, p. vi.

68. John Rhys, *Lectures on the Origin and Growth of Religion as Illustrated by Celtic Heathendom* (London, 1888), p. 497. Rhys discussed Lomna, Mim and other

Celtic heads, *ibid.*, pp. 96-99, 567-68. For a comparison of the stories of Lomna and Donn-bo, see Enid Welsford, *The Fool* (New York, 1936), pp. 108-9. Yeats alluded to Lomna in *The Wind Among the Reeds* (London, 1899), p. 68. For Greek and other analogues of the singing and oracular Orphic head, see Ivan M. Linforth, *The Arts of Orpheus* (Berkeley, 1941), pp. 128 ff.

69. *V-B*, p. 212; Pater, *The Renaissance*, p. 118.

70. Cf. Robert Graves, *The White Goddess* (New York, 1948), pp. 184, 192. Aodh's oath may indicate Yeats's early association of poet, solar hero, and swineherd. The reference is to that swineherd of Bodb the Red (king of the Munster fairies) who, after many transformations, is final victor in the battle of the Two Bulls. See "Rosa Alchemica," *Savoy*, No. 2 (Apr., 1896), p. 64, and Gregory, *Cuchulain of Muirthmne*, pp. 268-75, with Yeats's comment, p. xv. Rhys connects the Welsh Kulhwch, "Him of the Pig-sty," with Cuchulain as solar hero (*Celtic Heathendom*, p. 487).

71. *CW*, V, 89. Cf. the knight in the story "Out of the Rose," who dies, like boar-hunters Adonis and Diarmuid, in search of some pigs, and also the poem "Her Vision in the Wood."

72. Peter Ure, *Towards a Mythology: Studies in the Poetry of W. B. Yeats* (Liverpool, 1946), p. 90.

73. *CPlays*, p. 395.

74. Quoted by C. G. Jung in his *Collected Works* (New York, 1953-), XVI, 284; XII, 344. See also a writer quoted by Thomas Vaughan, *Works*, pp. 324-25, and Maier's paraphrase of Morienus, quoted by Jung, *Collected Works*, XII, 410.

75. *The Hermetic Museum*, ed. A. E. Waite (London, 1893), I, 336.

76. *Ibid.*, II, 177; I, 264; I, 342.

77. *Ibid.*, II, 277.

78. *Ibid.*, I, 263.

79. Jung, *Collected Works*, XII, 384n. (see also II, 366, and XVI, 297); Israel Regardie, *The Golden Dawn* (Chicago, 1937-40), III, 192.

80. Vaughan, *Works*, p. 94.

81. *Ibid.*, p. 282.

82. *W. B. Yeats and T. Sturge Moore: Their Correspondence 1901-1937*, ed. Ursula Bridge (London, 1937), p. 156 (1929).

83. Nietzsche had said that in the enchantment of the dithyramb, the Dionysian spectator "sees himself as a satyr, *and as a satyr he in turn beholds the god,* that is, in his transformation he sees a new vision outside him as the Apollonian consummation of his state" (*The Birth of Tragedy*, p. 68).

84. *CPlays*, p. 439.

85. In 1929 Yeats wrote that every myth must be consumed by intellectual analysis or "become a spectre," a Blakean rigid intellectual force which stifles imaginative life. After all myths are so consumed, there is "not even a drift of ashes on the pyre" (*Yeats and Moore: Their Correspondence*, p. 154). That dialectic of the imagination underlies the "private philosophy" which Yeats long tried to clarify, and which he partly expounded to Ethel Mannin in 1938. The repeated death in Western twilight is the consuming of myth or image at *"The Critical Moment."* When the image is dissolved, "we enter by free will pure unified experience" (Wade, *Letters*, p. 917).

86. *CPlays*, pp. 427, 428.

87. Wade, *Letters*, p. 917.

88. *The Elder or Poetic Edda*, ed. and tr. Olive Bray (London, 1908), I, 103. For Frazer's assimilation of Odin to Attis, see *The Golden Bough* (one-vol. ed.), pp. 354-55.

89. *Oxford Book of Modern Verse*, p. xxxiii.

90. *Au*, p. 282.

91. *E&I*, p. 321.

92. *Au*, p. 328 (1925).

93. *E&I*, p. 321.

94. Schopenhauer, *World as Will and Idea*, I, 345.

95. Wade, *Letters*, p. 805.

96. *P&C*, p. 180.

97. "The Old Age of Queen Maeve," *CP*, p. 386.

98. *The Complete Works of Ralph Waldo Emerson*, ed. E. W. Emerson (Boston and New York, 1903-4), II, 7-8.

99. Jung, *Collected Works*, V, 291-92.

100. Wade, *Letters*, p. 819.

101. *Oxford Book of Modern Verse*, p. xxxiv.

102. *V-B*, p. 290.

103. *Oxford Book of Modern Verse*, p. xxxvii.

104. *Mythologies*, p. 331.

105. *Au*, p. 226.

106. Jung, *Collected Works*, XVI, 200.

107. *Prometheus Unbound*, I, 192-93.

108. *E&I*, p. 77.

109. Newman I. White, *Shelley* (New York, 1940), II, 368.

110. Henri Frédéric Amiel, *Amiel's Journal*, tr. Mrs. Humphrey Ward (London and New York, 1885), p. 461.

111. *Mythologies*, p. 356.

112. *Letters on Poetry to Dorothy Wellesley*, p. 149.

113. Quoted in *Letters to the New Island*, p. 210; slightly misquoted years later, *V-A*, p. 116 (*V-B*, p. 182).

114. *Mythologies*, p. 364.

115. Wade, *Letters*, pp. 791, 876.

INDEX